Patterns of Entrepreneurship Management

PATTERNS OF ENTREPRENEURSHIP MANAGEMENT

FIFTH EDITION

Jack M. Kaplan
Columbia Business School

Anthony C. Warren
Penn State University

With Contributions from
Isabel Botero
Jerry Kagan
Jack McGourty
Marion Poetz

WILEY

VICE PRESIDENT & DIRECTOR	George Hoffman
EXECUTIVE EDITOR	Lise Johnson
DEVELOPMENT EDITOR	Jennifer Manias
ASSOCIATE DEVELOPMENT EDITOR	Kyla Buckingham
SENIOR PRODUCT DESIGNER	Allison Morris
MARKET SOLUTIONS ASSISTANT	Amanda Dallas
SENIOR DIRECTOR	Don Fowley
PROJECT MANAGER	Gladys Soto
PROJECT SPECIALIST	Nichole Urban
PROJECT ASSISTANT	Anna Melhorn
PROJECT ASSISTANT	Emily Meussner
EXECUTIVE MARKETING MANAGER	Christopher DeJohn
ASSISTANT MARKETING MANAGER	Puja Katariwala
ASSOCIATE DIRECTOR	Kevin Holm
SENIOR CONTENT SPECIALIST	Nicole Repasky
PRODUCTION EDITOR	Ezhilan Vikraman
COVER PHOTO CREDIT	© chungking/Shutterstock

This book was set in 10/12 Times LT Std by SPi Global and printed and bound by Lightning Source Inc.

Founded in 1807, John Wiley & Sons, Inc. has been a valued source of knowledge and understanding for more than 200 years, helping people around the world meet their needs and fulfill their aspirations. Our company is built on a foundation of principles that include responsibility to the communities we serve and where we live and work. In 2008, we launched a Corporate Citizenship Initiative, a global effort to address the environmental, social, economic, and ethical challenges we face in our business. Among the issues we are addressing are carbon impact, paper specifications and procurement, ethical conduct within our business and among our vendors, and community and charitable support. For more information, please visit our website: www.wiley.com/go/citizenship.

ISBN: 978-1-119-23905-5 (PBK)

ISBN: 978-1-119-18814-8 (EVALC)

Library of Congress Cataloging-in-Publication Data

Names: Kaplan, Jack M., author. | Warren, Anthony C., author.
Title: Patterns of entrepreneurship management / Jack M. Kaplan, Anthony C. Warren.
Description: 5th edition. | Hoboken, NJ : John Wiley & Sons, [2016] |
  Includes bibliographical references and index.
Identifiers: LCCN 2015038847 | ISBN 9781119239055 (pbk. : alk. paper)
Subjects: LCSH: Entrepreneurship.
Classification: LCC HB615 .K366 2016 | DDC 658.1/1–dc23 LC record available at http://lccn.loc.gov/2015038847

Printing identification and country of origin will either be included on this page and/or the end of the book. In addition, if the ISBN on this page and the back cover do not match, the ISBN on the back cover should be considered the correct ISBN.

Students past, present, and future who will learn
to change the world for the better

Preface

Working in a corporation, or even a smaller business, does not prepare you for the challenges, long hours, social sacrifices, and financial commitments involved in being an entrepreneur. If you know that your future goal is to become an entrepreneur, how can you truly understand the rewards and pitfalls of this choice? How do you acquire the information and skills needed to support you in realizing your goal? This book provides just that—the necessary information you need to get you started as a successful entrepreneur, even in today's ultracompetitive, hostile, turbulent, and global business environment.

We have had the privilege of teaching entrepreneurship courses for more than fourteen years—Kaplan at Columbia Business School in New York and Warren at Penn State. During this time, students, alumni, investors, small companies, and business colleagues have sought our advice regarding the topic of entrepreneurship. Both of us, being entrepreneurs ourselves, have also had the opportunity to gain extensive experience. Professor Kaplan served as the president of Datamark Technologies, a technology marketing company engaged in loyalty and electronic gift card programs, and Professor Warren was a founder of several companies and was a venture capitalist for a number of years. We also stay active as entrepreneurs, Kaplan having cofounded "Robotics Systems & Technologies, Inc.," a hospital automation company, and Warren, "Halare Inc.," a networked telemedicine company. Thus, not only are we both in touch with the most recent academic research findings and best practices regarding entrepreneurship, but also we have firsthand experience in starting and building companies. We hope to impart our practical knowledge and counsel directly to you through this book and its associated web resources.

Why This New Edition

Patterns of Entrepreneurship Management, Fifth Edition, supports a greatly enhanced interactive learning experience that addresses the challenges, issues, and rewards faced by entrepreneurs in starting and growing a venture. When we were asked to produce a fifth edition by our publisher, we believed that it would be a relatively easy task. As it turned out, the world of entrepreneurship is changing so rapidly that many of the topics in this new edition were not even on the horizon just three years ago. We have seen enormous changes in the investment climate, stunning new applications for social networks, and the evolution of new business models to fit this changing environment. Many of the chapters had to be completely rewritten. Also, in talking to our colleagues at a number of universities, we were asked to address three new special topics in entrepreneurship.

The first is *crowdsourcing*, which has grown enormously since the last edition. We invited Professor Marion Poetz from Copenhagen Business School, an expert in this field, to co-author a chapter on this topic.

Second, family-owned businesses play a major role in most economies. They have unique and challenging management issues. We devote a new chapter on this topic written by Dr. Isabel C. Botero from Stetson University. The Internet has revolutionized sales and marketing strategies for small businesses. Adjunct Professor .Jeremy Kagan from Columbia University has joined us to add content in Chapter 4 on the tools now available in digital marketing. Special thanks to Elizabeth Lott , Columbia EMBA 2014 and entrepreneur for the Tiny Updates, and canvas model example in Chapter 4.

Finally, Dr. Jack McGourty, also from Columbia Business School, has added to the discussions on the canvas model process and structure and the minimum viable product strategy.

In the last edition, we introduced the concept of "special topics in entrepreneurship" to enable teachers to design courses that address unique needs of students who may wish to focus on one type of venture. The first two topics were social and technology-based opportunities. To these we are adding the above-mentioned "family business" chapter. We have placed all three special topic chapters on the book website. The textbook, which covers all required core course materials, has two brand-new chapters—crowdsourcing and digital media marketing. All other chapters have significant revisions to bring them up to date. Still, this edition has kept the popular theme on *managing* a start-up. The authors have spent many years both as entrepreneurs and teachers and passionately believe that entrepreneurial skills can be acquired only by actually confronting the problems that challenge every entrepreneur. This text and accompanying website, therefore, differ from others in that they challenge students with real situations and examples on which they can practice the broad range of skills required to start and build a company in today's complex world. Throughout this book you will find tips on how to become a successful entrepreneur as well as issues to avoid.

The web projects and cases that accompany this book focus on the successes and failures of entrepreneurs and offer valuable business plan examples and assessment tools. Other outstanding features that the book offers are as follows:

1. *Focus on Real Entrepreneurs.* Throughout the text, we relate the material to real entrepreneurs, helping you understand how entrepreneurs position their companies to meet the various marketing, financial, and technological challenges. For example, each chapter starts with a short profile of an entrepreneur that illustrates the key issues that will be covered. These engage students as they immediately see the relevance of the chapter and are intrigued by an actual case chosen for its learning impact.

2. *Management Track.* This *learning track* is embedded in the book. The failure rate of new companies is 24 percent within the first two years and 80–90 percent within the first ten years. Most companies fail not because they are focusing on a bad idea or having insufficient funds, but because inexperienced founders are confronting complex management decisions without knowledge of the tools to make them. The *management track* is based on a real company, Neoforma, which constitutes a *master-case* for the entire book. Wayne McVicker, one of the founders, reported, in a diary form, the entire company history from concept to eventual sale, covering every conceivable management challenge that all entrepreneurs inevitably face. His book, *Starting Something,* became the basis of a new management course at Penn State. Students were so enthralled that we decided to enhance the materials. We took a film crew and interviewed many of the key characters—founders, investors, mentors, key hires, and even family members—who gave their personal views on many of the key management decisions that transpired. McVicker has agreed that we can embed elements of his book with the videos into this edition of *Patterns of Entrepreneurship Management* to provide a rich experience for students on the key management issues in entrepreneurship. We believe this is the first attempt to address important entrepreneurship management topics within a textbook. The materials have now been used with great success at many universities around the world, and we are pleased to incorporate them into this edition to greatly enhance the learning experience. Management topics are revisited in many of the remaining chapters with appropriate student exercises structured around the video materials on the book's website.

3. *Finance Track.* The book contains a complete set of materials covering entrepreneurial finance for non-finance majors. Every entrepreneur at some time needs to raise funds to grow the

company. Many make fatal mistakes early on because they haven't clearly thought through the personal implications imposed by the source of these funds. The issues of control, lifestyle, risk tolerance, and ambition all determine this choice. This book is the first to differentiate funding sources between closely held private businesses and high-growth equity-funded companies, and these are dealt with in two parts of Chapter 8 on financing. Understanding these two mutually exclusive routes for companies can save a lot of heartaches for entrepreneurs and their supporters. Additionally crowdfunding is covered in Chapter 5 and Chapter 9 describes how to manage funds carefully once they have been raised.

4. *Case Studies.* In addition to the master-case based on Neoforma, most chapters include a shorter case study that looks at a potential entrepreneurial opportunity. Answering the case study questions allows you to think critically about the various aspects of launching a business. Several case studies touch on important aspects of business such as setting up the management team, financing for early and growth ventures, and expanding ideas into viable business opportunities. Longer cases appear on the website, which provides additional interactive materials.

5. *From Idea to Opportunity. Patterns of Entrepreneurship Management* is not merely a concept-oriented textbook. Through powerful examples, cases, and exercises, students explore important "soft" issues such as how to continuously innovate, design sustainable business models, and create a culture in their companies that will increase their chances of success as they launch a new enterprise.

6. *Innovation and Technology Venture Framework. Patterns of Entrepreneurship Management* stresses the importance of innovation and technology. Throughout the book are sections devoted to creating a framework for screening ideas, thinking about strategy and business models, determining the capital and resources required, attracting management talent, and preparing the plan to ensure that practices are accepted and implemented effectively.

Organization Of the Book

The book has been designed to support seven different courses in entrepreneurship:

1. *Introduction to Entrepreneurship* teaches the student about the basics of the field, including the personal aspects of entrepreneurs, opportunity identification, and structuring. This course often includes teamwork in which students identify their own business opportunities and work them up into business plans and presentations to investors. For this course, some of the more detailed topics in management and finance can be omitted. Chapters 1–7 contain the core content.

2. *Entrepreneurial Finance* is a subject that is rather different from corporate finance, which is taught in most business schools. Chapters 8 and 9 provide a complete set of materials for such a course, with supporting readings taken from elsewhere in the book, especially Chapter 5's sections on crowdfunding.

3. *Entrepreneurial Management* is based on the master-case and the other management cases in the book. This is an experiential course and is best run in a seminar format.

4. *Business Planning* is covered extensively in Chapters 3, 5, and 6 with supplementary content in other chapters.

5. *Social Entrepreneurship* is supported by most of the chapters in the book but is enhanced greatly by the Special Topics in Chapter 12 on the book's website devoted entirely to this topic. This chapter covers the legal and taxation issues associated with social ventures as

well as the unique classes of business models and management skills that are required for such ventures.

6. *Technology Entrepreneurship* requires extra material to supplement that in the rest of the book. Chapter 13, on the book's website, has been developed from a highly successful course at Penn State designed specifically for scientists and engineers wishing to explore a career as an entrepreneur.

7. *Family Business Management* is covered in Chapter 14. This new addition to the content is found on the book's website.

The book covers three roadmap phases of entrepreneurship. Each chapter has been written to help students learn specific tasks needed to complete it with defined deliverables. A fourth section on the book website contains special topics in entrepreneurship.

Part One, "Getting Started as an Entrepreneur," includes six chapters that establish the foundation for starting a venture, from understanding the personal attributes of an entrepreneur, developing ideas, and recognizing business opportunities to exploring business models, preparing a winning business plan, and setting up the company. The master-case, Neoforma, is also outlined in the first chapter. Chapter 1 introduces the concept of entrepreneurship and emphasizes the entrepreneurial process and the steps to becoming an entrepreneur. Chapter 2 explores the role of innovation and its importance. Students learn techniques to become creative in developing new business ideas by building their own framework for analysis of situations. Chapter 3 is devoted entirely to the study of business models, providing students with frameworks for business model design with illustrative cases. Chapter 4 discusses how to analyze markets and potential customers and how to conduct a competitive analysis and create a marketing plan for the venture. Digital marketing methods are covered in detail. Chapter 5 covers the new field of crowdsourcing which has opened up entirely new ways for entrepreneurs to develop opportunities with limited resources. In Chapter 6, we cover business planning and in particular the new *lean plan* models. Chapter 7 describes the various forms that ventures may take as well as the processes of actually forming a company.

Part Two, "Funding the Venture," constitutes a complete module on entrepreneurial finance. It describes the many ways start-up companies can access the resources they need, including funding at different stages of growth. Chapter 8 has two parts: the first examines the methods entrepreneurs use to raise early-stage funding when their plan is to retain control of the company and make it a "lifestyle" business. These techniques, referred to as *bootstrapping*, are also important for entrepreneurs who later choose to grow a larger organization. Sources include friends, family, government grants, partners, and banks. The second part explains growth-funding sources from angel investors and venture capitalists whereby the entrepreneur sells shares in her company where ultimate wealth may be traded with loss of control. This extensive chapter is supplemented with the first part of Chapter 9, which teaches the fundamental financial management systems that should be installed early on in a company's development.

Part Three, "Building and Exiting," focuses on three functions that must be developed as the company begins to grow. Chapter 9 covers the management of two key resources: money and people. Here students learn the key skills in building and managing a team, including the establishment of a strong culture; finding, hiring, and even firing the right employees; and learning how to manage ambiguous conflicts of interest and ethical dilemmas. This chapter also describes key legal documents that a company will use. Chapter 10 will equip students with the skills needed to communicate an opportunity to different audiences, including customers, investors, bankers, and employees. No entrepreneur can be successful without the ability to communicate passion and drive to those who can help her reach her goals. Chapter 11 describes the exit strategies entrepreneurs may wish to consider, including selling the business, going public, being acquired, or transferring ownership to employees, family members, or a chosen management team.

Part Four consists of Chapters 12, 13, and 14 which can be found on the book's website, These cover three special topics for students with a particular interest in social-, technology-, or family business-oriented entrepreneurship. These topics are dealt with in considerable depth but may be valuable to all students through their enlightening examples for analysis. For example, Chapter 13 includes the complexities of intellectual property and its management.

Supplements

If instructors wish to incorporate all or part of the "management track" into coursework, then students can access the Neoforma casebook on the book's website. This is a shortened version of the full text of *Starting Something* by Wayne McVicker. Students may want to read the full version if they seek an even richer insight into the life of an entrepreneur. In addition, for instructors, the website provides access to a test bank, PowerPoint presentations, sample cases and business plans, answers to end-of-chapter questions, and financial and legal templates you will need to set up a business. The website can be accessed at www.wiley.com/college/kaplan.

The website gives students access to a variety of resources:

- Additional case studies that allow students to review key entrepreneurial concepts.

- Audiovisual presentations by entrepreneurs, venture capitalists, successful students, and the Neoforma characters.

- Sample business plans. These plans are divided according to market and stage of development. Downloadable plans are available for students.

- Case summary reviews.

- Downloadable legal documents. Students can download sample legal agreements, including stock and shareholder agreements, consulting contracts, and employee option plans, among others.

About the Authors

Jack M. Kaplan is an adjunct professor of entrepreneurial studies at Columbia Business School and of Smeal College of Business at Penn State University. He has taught the entrepreneurial courses for Launching New Ventures, The Business Plan, and The Entrepreneurial Manager. During his career, Kaplan started and managed three successful companies, concentrating on smart card technology, health-care information systems, and loyalty marketing programs. He was president of Datamark Technologies, Inc., an entrepreneurial business venture engaged in electronic gift card and loyalty marketing programs. Ceridian, a Fortune 500 company, acquired the company in November 2005.

Kaplan is the author of *Getting Started in Entrepreneurship*, published by John Wiley & Sons in January 2001. His previous book was *Smart Cards: The Global Information Passport*, and his articles have appeared in *Technology News* and *Crain's of New York Business*.

His professional seminar experience includes conducting courses on new product strategies for Fortune 500 companies, including MIT Enterprise Forum, Aetna Insurance Company, Panasonic Global Sales Group, and Johnson & Johnson. He was a judge for the Ernst & Young Entrepreneur of the Year award program in New York and has appeared on A&E Biography, CNN, and CNBC. He is a graduate of the University of Colorado and received his MBA from the City University of New York.

Dr. Anthony C. Warren was formerly the Farrell Professor of Entrepreneurship at the Smeal College of Business, Penn State University, named "the hottest school for entrepreneurship" by

Newsweek magazine and the recipient of the NASDAQ Center for Entrepreneurial Excellence Award in 2005. He led educational programs in entrepreneurship at the undergraduate, graduate, and executive levels. Under grants from the Kauffman Foundation, Dr. Warren created unique courses in entrepreneurship based on problem-based learning, which have been recognized by several national organizations as being at the forefront of teaching methods. These courses are being introduced into colleges and high schools across the country and overseas.

Prior to joining Penn State, Dr. Warren started and grew several companies and until recently was a venture partner in Adams Capital Management, a venture capital firm managing more than $720 million. He consults regularly with both small and large companies on subjects of innovation management. A regular speaker at national conferences, Dr. Warren is often quoted in the press regarding innovation and entrepreneurship. He has authored several patents and research papers on technical and business issues and has contributed to many books. He has a B.Sc. and Ph.D. from the University of Birmingham. He recently started a telehealth company for the treatment of chronic diseases.

Isabel C. Botero (Ph.D., Michigan State University) is an adjunct professor in the management department at Stetson University. She is also a principal at Fediuk Botero LLC. Her extensive published research interests include communication in and about family firms, influence processes in their organization, information sharing, and crisis management. She is the lead author of Chapter 14.

Jeremy Kagan is the founder and CEO of Pricing Engine, a web service that empowers users to benchmark, optimize, and expand their digital marketing campaigns. He is also an adjunct professor of marketing at Columbia Business School. He provided content on digital marketing methods in Chapter 4.

Jack McGourty (Ph.D.) is the director of Community and Global Entrepreneurship at the Columbia Business School and a faculty member teaching graduate courses in entrepreneurship, innovation, and technology management. He provided content on the canvas model techniques in Chapter 3.

Marion Poetz (Ph.D., Vienna University of Economics and Business) is an associate professor of innovation management in Copenhagen Business School's Department of Innovation and Organizational Economics. Her research revolves around innovation search and problem solving in a world of widely distributed knowledge. She has published in leading academic and practitioner journals. She is the lead author of Chapter 5.

Acknowledgments

It has been a privilege for us to work with many inspiring colleagues and entrepreneurs to collect material for this book. We relied on the contributions of many people in the preparation of this book to discuss trends and ideas in the exciting field of entrepreneurship.

Special thanks are due to Vince Ponzo, Director Entrepreneurship Programs of the Eugene Lang Center Murry Low Director of Columbia Business School; Michael Farrell and John and Bette Garber for their generous gifts and personal support for the Entrepreneurship programs at Penn State; and the Kauffman Foundation for its continuing interest in and funding of pedagogy research in entrepreneurship. Special thanks are also due to D Paul and Dr. Andrew Kaplan for their support . We are indebted to the staff at John Wiley & Sons for their support, including Lise Johnson, Project Editor, and Amanda Dallas, Market Solutions Assistant.

The chapter on social entrepreneurship had significant input from Dr. Robert Macy. He, in turn, was supported by research undertaken by Melany Cruz Rodriguez, a student in the Farrell Center for Corporate Innovation and Entrepreneurship at Penn State.

We would also like to thank the following entrepreneurs for helping to add a real-world perspective to this project:

Joel Adams	Brian Halligan	Donn Rappaport
Jennifer Andrews	Linda Holroyd	Brian Roughan
Chuey Anima	George Homan	Steve Sheetz
Craig Bandes	Scott Johnson	Nikolay Shkolnik
Matt Brezina	Dave Juszczyk	Paul Silvis
Wally Buch	Alvin Katz	Anil Singhal
Dennis Coleman	Jeff Kleck	Jack Russo
Neal DeAngelo	Elizabeth Lott	Parviz Tayebati
Dan Eckert	Ed Marflak	Ethan Wendle
Michael Farrell	Wayne McVicker	Anni Weston
William Frezza	Khanjan Mehta	Bob Zollars
Ted Graef	James Meiselman	
Ujjwal Gupta	Ankit Patel	

And the following professors for their insightful comments and guidance:

Tom Byers	Stanford University
Robert F. Chelle	University of Dayton
Alex DeNoble	San Diego State University
Sanford B. Ehrlich	San Diego State University
Raghu Garud	Penn State University
Nikolaus Franke	Vienna University of Economics and Business
Ralph Hanke	Missouri University of Science and Technology
Jeremy Kagan	Columbia University
Liz Kisenwether	Penn State University
Jack McGourty	Columbia University
Robert Macy	University of New Mexico
Paul Magelli	University of Illinois
Jonathan Michie	University of Oxford
Robert Myers	Fairfield Resources International
Ed Rogoff	Long Island University
Linda Treviño	Penn State University
Philippe Tuertscher	VU University Amsterdam

We also acknowledge the support and appreciation of our spouses, Dr. Eileen Kaplan and Kirsten Jepp. Our personal thanks also go to the diligent research and support of many of our students. Particular mention is due to Anupam Jaiswal and Supreet Saini at Penn State and to Anna Mary Loope, administrative assistant at the Farrell Center, PSU, who managed to keep us all on track.

LIST OF CASES, PROFILES, AND COMPANY EXAMPLES

Profiles are entrepreneurs' stories, mini-cases are short, illustrative examples, and cases are full case studies for student analyses.

Chapter No	Name	Type	Roadmap Topics
1	Wayne McVicker	Profile	A Typical Entrepreneur
1	Neoforma	Case	Master-Case in Management
2	Becky Minard and Paal Gisholt	Profile	Finding a Point of Pain
2	Greif Packaging	Mini-case	Building a Service
2	Blyth Candles	Mini-case	Incremental Innovation
2	Netflix	Mini-case	Disruptive Innovation
2	Pizza-on-a-truck	Mini-case	Thinking Big
3	Alexander Osterwalder	Profile	Building and Using Business Models
3	TinyUpdates	Mini-case	Using the Canvas
3	ChemStation	Mini-case	Franchising in a Business Model
3	BreatheSimple 1	Mini-case	Smoke-Screen Idea Testing
4	HubSpot	Profile	Digital Marketing
4	BreatheSimple 2	Mini-case	Web-Enabled Market Research
4	Glue Isobar	Mini-case	Viral Digital Marketing
5	FashionStake/David Gulati	Profile	Using Communities
5	Flitto	Mini-case	Using Volunteering Crowds
5	Goldcorp	Mini-case	Crowd-Based Problem Solving
5	Hello.com	Mini-case	Crowdfunding
5	Bragi	Mini-case	International Crowdfunding
?	Threadless	Mini-case	Using Customers for Product Design
6	Alex Shkolnik	Profile	Business Planning
6	Surf Parks	Case	Writing a Business Plan
7	Ethan Wendle	Profile	Setting Up the Company
8	James Dyson	Profile	Bootstrapping
8	BenchPrep	Mini-case	Funding Stages
8	Injection Research	Mini-case	Contingent Litigation
8	Xobni	Mini-case	Micro-equity
8	Best Lighting Products	Mini-case	Factoring
8	Jason Cong	Profile	Staged Investments
8	Coretek	Case	Use of Grants/Dilution Protection
9	Paul Silvis	Profile	Building a Great Culture
9	Teacher/Student Interaction	Mini-case	Conflicts of Interest

Chapter No	Name	Type	Roadmap Topics
10	Craig Bandes	Profile	Customizing Presentations
10	Leafbusters	Mini-case	Teaser
10	Railway Technology	Mini-case	Presentations
11	Alan Trefler	Profile	Private to Public Ownership
11	AEC	Mini-Case	Boutique Investment Banking
12	Khanjan Mehta	Profile	A Social Entrepreneur
12	Fairtrade	Mini-case	Pure Social Enterprise
12	HeartMath Institute	Mini-case	Hybrid Social Enterprise
12	Sea Tow Services	Mini-case	Hybrid Social Enterprise
12	Propeller Health	Mini-case	Dual Mission Enterprise
12	eno energy	Mini-case	Cooperative Green Energy
12	REI	Mini-case	Retailer's Cooperative
13	Ian Kibblewhite	Profile	Integrated IP Strategy
13	Ultrafast	Mini-case	Licensing
14	Richard Edelman	Profile	Family Business Entrepreneur
14	Motor Coils	Mini-case	Succession Planning
14	Sheetz	Mini-case	Professionalization
14	Wilkin & Sons	Mini-case	Reputational Asset

BRIEF CONTENTS

CONTENTS

PART III   BUILDING AND EXITING

9   MANAGING RESOURCES—MONEY AND PEOPLE   228

GETTING STARTED AS AN ENTREPRENEUR

"Getting Started as an Entrepreneur" includes seven chapters that establish the foundations of entrepreneurship from understanding the personal attributes and management challenges that entrepreneurs will confront to developing ideas, business opportunities, and setting up a company. Chapter 1 covers the personal attributes of entrepreneurs and the management skills needed within the context of a new business. This topic is right up front to assist you in understanding the makeup of a typical entrepreneur and how closely you fit the mold. It is important that you consider what you may be getting yourself into before starting on the road to identifying an opportunity. The latter part of this chapter describes the entrepreneurial process and the steps to becoming an entrepreneur. The scope of the business idea that you choose to follow should match your personal aspirations and lifestyle aims. Chapter 2 explains how ideas are developed into business opportunities in the early venture stage. Here, you will also learn why innovation is important and the techniques used to become creative in developing new business ideas. In today's complex world, it is no longer sufficient just to have an idea for a new product or service; to be successful, you have to wrap the idea inside a "way of doing business" that provides sustainable growth and profits. Chapter 3 is devoted entirely on showing you how to design such "business models." Your business, like every business, must have customers that choose to buy from you rather than a competitor. Chapter 4 shows how to apply digital marketing tools for research, analyze the market and potential customers, conduct a competitive analysis, create a marketing plan for the venture, and use the Internet to get to your customers. Chapter 5 introduces the broad and exciting concepts in crowd-sourcing resources, and in Chapter 6 how to structure a short business plan is learned. Finally, Chapter 7 explores the various forms that ventures may take and describes how to register your company officially.

1 The Entrepreneurial Process

"Good management is the art of making problems so interesting and their solutions so constructive that everyone wants to get to work and deal with them."

Paul Hawken, Environmentalist, Entrepreneur, Author

OBJECTIVES

- Place entrepreneurship in today's context.
- Understand what differentiates an entrepreneur from others.
- Classify different types of entrepreneurs.
- Explore what control means to you and the choices it affects.
- Learn the master-case story and context.
- Understand your strengths and limitations.
- Understand the spider-web model for small companies.
- Learn how to network and use mentors.
- Learn how to contain stress.
- Describe the five stages in the entrepreneurial process from opportunity analysis to scaling the venture.
- Learn the key growth issues for an entrepreneur.

CHAPTER OUTLINE

Introduction

Profile: Wayne McVicker—A Typical Entrepreneur

An Entrepreneurial Perspective

Commonly Shared Entrepreneurial Characteristics

Types of Entrepreneurs

The Need to Control

The Spider-web Model

Finding Early Mentors

Introduction

No sector of the economy is as vital, dynamic, and creative as entrepreneurship. For the past thirty years, the impact of entrepreneurs and small-business owners in the creation of new ventures has been felt in virtually all the world's mature as well as developing economies. The startling growth of entrepreneurial ventures forms the heart of our changing economic system as more employees work for these owners than for any other sector of the economy. In the United States today, the number of employees in small and entrepreneurial ventures is growing faster than in any other sector of the labor force, and there is no sign of a reversal in this trend. The Global Entrepreneurship Monitor states that as much as one-third of the differences in economic growth among nations may be due to differences in entrepreneurial activity. A key factor affecting the U.S. economy is the annual creation of 600,000 to 800,000 new companies, which produces many new jobs.[1] Entrepreneurship—the process of planning, organizing, operating, and assuming the risk of a business venture—is now a mainstream activity. Starting a business is never easy; it requires a special blend of courage, self-confidence, and skills—all of which determine the success or failure of an enterprise. The Internet has fundamentally changed the way entrepreneurs can flourish. It not only provides up-to-date market and technology information but also offers many useful support networks to entrepreneurs. Chapter 5 is devoted entirely to how you can access resources in many ways through "crowd-sourcing." Business schools everywhere *teach* the fundamentals of entrepreneurship, which were not even part of the curriculum until the 1990s.[2, 3]

Throughout this text, you'll read about entrepreneurs from many types of businesses. Their stories will help you explore possible paths for building your own successful career. You'll also have the opportunity to assess your present career profile and strategy and contrast them with the approaches these entrepreneurs have developed. The career choices and paths you take are deeply embedded not only in relationships but also in individual characteristics and valued outcomes. The path you follow will be based on a collected set of skills, knowledge, abilities, and experiences, as well as the recognition of unique opportunities. At the end of this chapter, we lay out the five-stage roadmap that every entrepreneurial start-up must navigate before success is achieved. Often, it is difficult to even see the road, let alone know where you are. But keeping the roadmap in mind will help you in your decision making along the way.

Profile: Wayne Mcvicker[4]—A Typical Entrepreneur

Wayne McVicker, originally trained as an architect, first had the idea of starting a company while working for Varian Corporation in California. The idea to create a new and transparent way to market complex medical equipment did not get much support within Varian, so together with another employee, Jeff Kleck, he started Neoforma. (Interestingly, more than 60 percent of ideas for start-ups come when working for someone else!) They did this with full knowledge of their employer. At first McVicker worked out of his home, while still full time at Varian, but eventually he untied the knot. Using loans from family members, his home equity, and retirement and college funds, he started building the company. He was fortunate to meet Jack Russo, a local attorney who took Wayne and his partner under his wing. Jack gave them a little money and introduced them to some local successful entrepreneurs who eventually invested in Neoforma. The company grew rapidly, continually putting Wayne and Jeff under stress to find money, people, and advisors. They made a number of common mistakes, including wrong hires, chasing fruitless initiatives, not delegating tasks, and gradually losing control of their company as venture capitalists and new managers entered the picture. Despite these trials and tribulations, the passion that Wayne and Jeff had to make health care better carried the company through to a public sale of stock and an eventual purchase by a group of large healthcare companies. After a short breather to get over the years of intense activity and stress, the founding partners started another company, Attainia, to do an even better job at opening up the healthcare market. Using the lessons learned from Neoforma, they were better equipped to avoid most of the start-up traps. Recently, Jeff and Wayne have handed over the management of Attainia to Jack McGovern and are exploring new start-up opportunities. (See the Appendix to this chapter for more on Wayne and Neoforma.) The Neoforma story is used as a master-case throughout this book. The case can be found on the book web site together with video clips of interviews with the key persons in the case.

An Entrepreneurial Perspective

The word *entrepreneur* came into English use in the seventeenth century from the French word *entreprendre*, which refers to individuals who "undertook" the risk of new enterprise. Early entrepreneurs were also "contractors" who bore the risks of profit or loss, and many were soldiers of fortune, adventurers, builders, and merchants.[5] Early references to the *entreprendeur* spoke of tax contractors—individuals who paid a fixed sum of money to a government for the license to collect taxes in their region. Tax entrepreneurs bore the risk of collecting individual taxes. If they collected more than the sum paid for their licenses, they made a profit; if not, they lost money.

Today the definition of *entrepreneurship* includes more than the mere creation of a business; it also includes the generation and implementation of an idea. Understanding this team concept is critical if you wish to be a successful entrepreneur. The idea of a sole individual being able to take on enormous risks, attempt innovations, leap without the appropriate background research, and succeed by working long hours and persevering at all costs is no longer relevant in today's global economy. Entrepreneurs also communicate effectively not only to their teams but also to external "stakeholders" such as investors, bankers, and corporate partners, who are necessary components of their growth path.

Commonly Shared Entrepreneurial Characteristics

Entrepreneurs share a number of characteristics.[6] Often these seem to be paradoxical or even mutually exclusive, which highlights their first key attribute:

- They have the ability to deal with ambiguity. They are comfortable with making decisions based on apparently conflicting and incomplete information. They do not need to nail down every detail, yet they can apply analytical skills when appropriate and necessary. They are also comfortable in complex situations; indeed, they can spot opportunities from what may seem to others a chaotic environment, often using an innate intuitiveness to extract patterns not obvious to competitors. Operating in fuzzy-edged gray areas is natural to them.

- They are self-starters, optimists, perseverant, energetic, and action-oriented.[7] What to others may seem a fatal blow is an opportunity for entrepreneurs to learn, pick themselves up, and see a new opportunity. Threats are turned into great new ideas.

- They are persuasive leaders, people-oriented, natural networkers, and communicators. Habitual entrepreneurs involve many people—both inside and outside the organization—in their pursuit of an opportunity. They create and sustain networks of relationships rather than going it alone, making the most of the intellectual and other resources people have to offer, all the while helping those people to achieve their goals as well. They lead by example rather than dictating.

- They are often creative and highly imaginative.

- They passionately seek new opportunities and are always looking for the chance to profit from change and disruption in the way business is done.

- They tolerate risk, but great entrepreneurs temper risk with reality.

- They work with urgency but balance this with a focus on long-term goals, too.

- They focus on execution—specifically, adaptive execution. People with an entrepreneurial mind-set *execute*; that is, they move forward instead of analyzing new ideas to death.

- They are open to change and do not hang on to old plans when they are not working. But they pursue only the very best opportunities and avoid exhausting themselves and their organizations by chasing every option. Even though many habitual entrepreneurs are wealthy, the most successful remain ruthlessly disciplined about limiting the number of projects they pursue.

These skills clearly conflict with the old idea of an entrepreneur being a loner coming up with new, out-of-context inventions in the basement without having the personal skills to create a valuable and exciting business.

> "As professors of entrepreneurship, we are often asked if it is possible to 'teach' someone to be an entrepreneur. My response is that you can't teach someone to acquire the drive, the hunger, the passion, and the tenacity to pursue an entrepreneurial path. However, give me someone who has such 'fire in their belly' and we can help them to develop critical entrepreneurial skills which will guide them along their journey."
>
> Alex Denoble
> *Professor of Management and Director of Academic Entrepreneurship Program, San Diego State University Entrepreneurial Management Center*

ROADMAP

IN ACTION | Entrepreneurs possess recognizable skills, many of which are embedded within us all. Understand these to uncover hidden traits, and develop them sufficiently to become a successful entrepreneur.

Many entrepreneurial skills do not apply only to starting a company, but have broader applications to other career paths and, indeed, to the way one deals with many of the personal challenges in one's life. As the world becomes more complex and job security in large organizations is no longer the norm, the ability to create and successfully build your own opportunities is vital. Therefore, even if you do not decide to start your own company (at least not yet), the lessons learned throughout this book will help you in whatever you do.

Types of Entrepreneurs

Until recently, people tended to think of the world of work in distinct categories. Most people worked either in someone else's business or in their own. The distinction between being an employee and being an entrepreneur was clear.

The rapid changes in the economy over the past two decades have blurred the lines between traditional employment and entrepreneurship. What counts now are portable skills and knowledge, meaningful work, on-the-job learning, and the ability to build effective networks and contacts, whether through teams or through the Internet. Many people now follow less predictable and even zigzagging career paths.

The distinction between managing your own operations and working for others has become blurred. Owning your own business may be a lifetime pursuit or just one part of your career.[8] Some people, called *serial entrepreneurs*, start, grow, and sell several businesses over the course of their careers. In any case, to be successful, you must develop the appropriate skill sets, strategic plans, and management team to enhance your possibilities of survival.

There are several different approaches to identifying entrepreneurial types. Ray Smilor, in his book *Daring Visionaries*, recognizes three kinds of entrepreneurs: aspiring, lifestyle, and growth entrepreneurs.

1. *Aspiring entrepreneurs* dream of starting a business; they hope for the chance to be their own bosses, but they have not yet made the leap from their current employment into the uncertainty of a start-up.

2. *Lifestyle entrepreneurs* have developed an enterprise that fits their individual circumstances and style of life. Their basic intention is to earn an income for themselves and their families.

3. *Growth entrepreneurs* have both the desire and the ability to grow as fast and as large as possible. These firms are the most dynamic job generators in the economy.

Within these categories, there are three subtypes that have grown in importance over the last few years. So important, in fact, that we include three "special topic" chapters on the book web site for students who wish to specialize in these areas;—Chapter 12, Social Entrepreneurship; Chapter 13, Technology Entrepreneurship; and Chapter 14, Family Businesses—Important and Different.

Social entrepreneurs are individuals with innovative solutions to society's most social problems. They are ambitious and persistent, tackling major social issues and offering new ideas for wide-scale change. Rather than leaving societal needs to the government or business sectors, social entrepreneurs find what is not working and solve the problem by changing the system, spreading the solution, and persuading entire societies to take new leaps. They often seem to be possessed by their ideas, committing their lives to changing the direction of their field. They are both visionaries and ultimate realists, concerned with the practical implementation of their vision. Social entrepreneurs present ideas that engage communities that have aligned aspirations.

Technology entrepreneurs have ideas triggered by developments in science and engineering. They usually have a strong education in those fields, an advantage that opens up opportunities for them that others might not see. Building ventures around new technology requires specialist knowledge in economics, markets, and social science, in addition to the purely business skills that other entrepreneurs master. Technology entrepreneurs must understand where their ideas fit into a complex environment, and learn that the best technical solutions do not always end up as the leader in the marketplace. The reorientation from "technology push" to "market-pull" is hard to make; more on this in Chapter 13.

Family-owned businesses comprise nearly 90 percent of U.S.-based companies and employ over 60 percent of the workforce. Such companies have unique management and governance issues and these are explored fully in Chapter 14.

One of the major mistakes entrepreneurs make when starting out is *not* to closely question what they want to be "when they grow up." Choosing the path of a lifestyle company creates certain advantages and disadvantages that must be carefully considered. If the goal is to employ maybe twenty or thirty people, to create a comfortable lifestyle for yourself and family members, and to retain control of the company, then the lifestyle path is for you. However, this imposes certain limitations on how you can fund the company. This path eliminates the possibility of selling part of the company for cash to pay for growth. A lifestyle company will not provide a way for investors to get a return on their investments through the sale of their ownership positions in the company. Not being honest with yourself at an early stage about control and lifestyle issues will lead to serious and unpleasant conflicts with investors if you take money from them and do not provide them a way to "exit" their investment.

ROADMAP

IN ACTION	The ambitions of entrepreneurs vary widely in scope. Understand your personal aims before embarking on an entrepreneurial journey.

Growth entrepreneurs, on the other hand, are much less driven by control or lifestyle. They recognize that to grow quickly, they will have to sell parts of their companies to raise cash. These investors will apply various levels of control. The aspirations of the founder and the investors are aligned; they both want to build a valuable company and sell it either to an established company or to the public via an IPO (initial public offering). The entrepreneur is willing to trade control for growth and wealth creation.

There is a third route, however—a lifestyle company that manages to grow fairly rapidly without taking in outside investors. These companies are a hybrid between the lifestyle company and the high-growth equity-financed company. We call these "growth bootstrapped" companies. In most cases, entrepreneurs do not plan it this way. They may start off as a lifestyle company and find that they can generate enough interest for their products or services that they can grow using the cash that they generate from sales. Or they may be in a place where there is little or no access to equity funds or their business does not match the industry knowledge and interests of investors.

It is important for you to think carefully as you decide if control and lifestyle are what drive you or if it is growth, visibility, wealth, or perhaps fame that fuels your ambition. Moving between these two different paths is difficult for reasons explored further in Chapter 8.

The Need to Control

The first decision that an entrepreneur should make is whether personal lifestyle and control are more important than growth and eventual wealth creation. If you believe that the idea for a new business is your baby, identify with it, believe you are the best person to grow the opportunity, and cannot conceive of handing the reins over to someone else, then a lifestyle choice is best. On the other hand, if you wish to grow the opportunity into something that is going to change the world and share the responsibility rather than control the venture, then a different set of options are open. Understanding how important control is will affect your willingness to share the management responsibilities and fundamentally impact your financial options.

ROADMAP

IN ACTION	Many problems that occur in entrepreneurial companies can be traced to conflicts over who controls what. Be completely honest with yourself on this issue *before* involving others.

Partners: Many well-known and highly successful companies were started by two or more partners: for example, Jobs/Wozniak at Apple, Hewlett/Packard at HP, Brin/Page at Google, and Allen/Gates at Microsoft. Studying successful companies shows that there is a lower chance of failure when there is more than one founding partner. This is not surprising, as one person is unlikely to have all the experience or personal attributes that are required to meet all the challenges. As we will see in the Neoforma master-case, Wayne and Jeff complement each other in ways that enable them to weather some heavy storms. On the other hand, having a partner who turns out to be incompatible can be fatal to the company.

Additionally, right from the beginning, any value that is created is immediately halved if there are two founders. There is a balance between increased likelihood of success and dividing the eventual wealth or cash flow. You should carefully consider on which side of this divide you feel more comfortable. Exercises at the end of this chapter and Chapter 8 will help you think through this process. If you feel that sharing the opportunity with a partner is best, you must carefully consider what personal values and ambitions are needed in a partner. Once an outline profile is prepared, the chances of meeting the right partner increase.

Hired Managers: Unfortunately, many companies fail because the founders do not confront their management limitations. It is one thing to have an idea, a passion, and the ability to get to the first sale of a product; it is another to build a strong organization with all the trappings of a larger company—human resources policies, structured training, international cash management, distribution channel development, and so on. The personal attributes of those who create the original idea and have the risk profile and passion to get a company off the ground are usually very different from the skills that are required as the company matures. It is rare indeed to find a first-time entrepreneur who can take it all the way. It is so rare, in fact, that most venture capitalists refuse to invest in companies in which the founder is not open to the idea of stepping aside at the appropriate time. You need to be brutally honest about your own limitations. First-time entrepreneurs have little or no experience and are often too optimistic about their own capabilities. In many cases, they can provide the vision and passion for a new opportunity but soon become overwhelmed as the company begins to take control of them, rather than the other way around. Bringing in new managers with more experience can often be a painful but necessary step; learn when to hand over to others before it is too late.

In the master-case, Wayne and Jeff accept from the very start that they are not the ones to take it all the way and, in fact, work hard to find their replacement. Even so, they have a really hard time handing their baby over to a stranger. There are two issues here: (1) Can you personally accept that it is time to step aside? (2) Can you do this without undermining your replacement? We have seen many companies fail from the inability of the entrepreneur to confront these issues. They take the company down with them still in the captain's cabin.[9] Certainly, if you are someone wanting to retain control, you should pay careful attention to your abilities to manage growth and seek guidance when the time calls for it.

Financing Options: If control is more important to you than wealth creation through sharing, you will have to limit your financing options to the so-called bootstrapping methods, bank loans, and the emergence of crowd-funding and forgo using true investors to provide funding for your company. This limitation may well restrict the growth rate of your business but can retain your ability to make all the key decisions, both good and bad. These two fundamentally different financing options are so important that we break Chapter 8 into two distinct parts to deal with them.

Opportunity Selection: If control of your own company is important to you and you are somewhat risk averse, you would be better off starting with a smaller opportunity. If, on the other hand, you are someone who is comfortable with sharing decisions and ownership, you may follow a more ambitious plan in which you intend to grow your company quickly with the help of one or more partners, outside investors, and advisers.

The Spider-web Model

The skills needed to run a small company with few resources are completely different from those required in a larger firm. In the early stages, the organization is more like a fragile spider's web, as shown in Figure 1-1; an attack that breaks one or two of the supporting threads could be fatal. An established company is more as a fortress with many specialized and organized troops ready to defend the enterprise, but a start-up has no legal department to deal with lawsuits, no head office to write checks, no cleaning service to clear the drains, and so on. The entrepreneur has to do it all, particularly in the first attempt, with no experience of being a multitasking, always-on-duty spider!

FIGURE 1-1
A Fragile Spider's Web

Finding Early Mentors

If the entrepreneur has limited experience and limited internal resources, then help from outside is necessary. Entrepreneurs must learn to be good listeners and find good advisers who can help make difficult decisions. Entrepreneurs need to develop networking skills and uncover and penetrate networks of possible partners, mentors, customers, investors, and others. Of course, the Internet has become a great place to immerse yourself into social networks through such web sites as MySpace, Facebook, and LinkedIn. Chapter 5 expands on this theme. However, the interactions that such virtual media elicit can be rather superficial and lack some important factors required to establish personal business networks. Networks function largely on trust, which takes time to develop and often requires lengthy, face-to-face discourse in a variety of situations. This trust becomes one of your personal assets and can be used to navigate networks through recommendations.

ROADMAP

IN ACTION   Entrepreneurs require good mentors, who are best found through networking. Identify highly connected people, and build trust with them.

There has been a lot of interest over the past few years in trying to understand the dynamics of network growth. Much of this work has been triggered by the Internet, which has fundamentally changed the way interconnectivity operates. The concept of "scale-free networks" has evolved.[10,11] In order to understand the implications of this concept, consider the following pair of easily recognized maps.

The U.S. interstate roadmap is typical of a network in which connectivity is made only to nearest neighbors. As shown in Figure 1-2, the network can grow incrementally because each link is a link between more or less equal intersections. The airline map is fundamentally different. Although having a similar number of nodes, some, the hubs, have a much higher connectivity than others. If I wanted to meet someone by chance, then standing at any of the interstate intersections would have a nearly equal probability. However, the chances are very different between, say, the airport concourses in Atlanta, Georgia, and College Station, Texas. Networks that are characterized by a

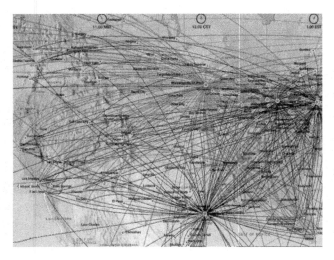

FIGURE 1-2

Comparison of US Road and Airline Networks

few nodes with very high interactivity and many that are not often visited are referred to as scale-free. The Internet is one such network. Certain web addresses, such as Yahoo!, MSN, Google, and Amazon, are hubs; nearly everywhere else is "remote." Scale-free networks can be very powerful tools for developing new ideas and markets, a topic we will return to in Chapters 3 and 5.

Entrepreneurs who wish to access know-how and help can apply these valuable concepts. As you will see in the master-case, Wayne and Jeff used networking extensively when they were getting started. They learned that there are certain people who are "hub-like," whose business life depends critically on personal connectivity. Professionals such as attorneys, accountants, bankers, salespersons, and venture capitalists all depend on their network to find opportunities. Farmers, teachers, and shop owners do not. Therefore, you should identify the "connectors" in your field and locality and arrange to meet and talk to them about your plans. Start very early because you need time to build trust and respect before they are likely to devote much time to helping you directly or recommending you to their own network. You will be surprised how often people are willing to help you if you are open and honest with them. You should not seek mentors who always agree with you. Make sure you have one or two who challenge your decisions constructively.

Managing Stress

Being a 24/7 entrepreneur running from one broken spider thread to another can easily distract you from making rational decisions. You become emotional rather than practical when choosing your actions. This is not helped by the fact that starting a company is not just a job; it is a passion, a dedication, even a life. The company can easily become all consuming, the only thing you think about, day and night. The swings from ecstasy to despair shown in Figure 1-3 come all too often and unexpectedly. Not surprisingly, therefore, every entrepreneur—without exception—has experienced conflicts between his or her personal life and the company. It is too easy to become so completely engrossed in the venture that you neglect your friends and family, and your own physical and mental health. This is dangerous as you lose balance in your judgments, forget to

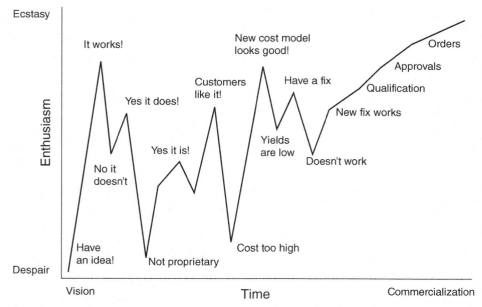

FIGURE 1-3

The ups and Downs of a Start-Up

seek ideas and mental stimulation except within the confines of the company, and allow emotion rather than logic to guide decisions. In the worst case, you bury yourself in an isolated cocoon away from the social comforts that could actually help you through the periods of stress. You need some tools to help you avoid this common trap:

- Before taking action, ask yourself, "How can I work smarter, not harder?"

- Get advice on time-management techniques.

- Plan some personal time with friends and family and stick to them.

- Try to have your workplace at least twenty minutes from home. This seems to be the right time span for you to mentally unlatch yourself from the company.

- Find someone you trust outside the company with whom you can discuss stressful situations to help you tone down emotional content.

- If you have a business partner, work on ways you can help each other through the tough times. Take time to talk before the relationship breaks down.

- Think about your own behavioral patterns and build in some slack time just to think.

- Force yourself to listen to friends and family about their lives; don't talk about just the company all the time. They may have interesting things to talk about, too.

- Delegate whenever possible, even if you think you are the only person in the world able to do the work.

- Try to see the funny side when things look really bad.

Contact your local chapter of SCORE (www.score.org) to find a retired, experienced executive who will help you on many of these issues for free and plug you into a valuable network. Balancing your personal and business lives is similar to walking a tightrope, and it is very easy to fall off.

ROADMAP

IN ACTION   An entrepreneurial life is inevitably stressful. Manage the different sources of stress effectively.

The Five-Stage Entrepreneurial Process

Entrepreneurs can increase their chances of success if they understand, follow, and implement the basic five-stage entrepreneurial process described in this section. These five stages, summarized in Figure 1-4, form the backbone of the entrepreneurial process. Each of the key stages includes a main focus activity, discusses tactics for completing tasks, and identifies the estimated amount of time required for each stage. Costs are provided for each activity, which can be used to plan budgets. We will also analyze the risks inherent in each stage and make suggestions for reducing potential problems.

Stage 1: Conducting Opportunity Analysis

The basic objective of this stage is to define the criteria that would make a business opportunity worthwhile. In this stage, the founder identifies the opportunity and creates a *vision for the company*. If there is no vision for the venture, the new idea is just a dream. Chapter 2 discusses the role of innovation in the economy and how entrepreneurs can learn to innovate new business

Stage 1 Conducting Opportunity Analysis (Chapters 2, 3, and 4)	• Innovate and create the vision • Develop a business model to maximize value retention • Conduct market analysis and research • Evaluate the competition • Research pricing and sales strategies
Stage 2 Developing the Plan and Setting up the Company (Chapters 6 and 7)	• Set goals and objectives • Start writing the plan • Determine pricing, market, and distribution channels • Prepare a concise business plan
Stage 3 Acquiring Financial Partners/Sources of Funding (Chapters 5 and 8)	• "Bootstrap" the company • Secure early-stage funding • Secure growth funding
Stage 4 Determining the Resources Required and Implementing the Plan (Chapters 9 and 13)	• Manage the finances • Determine value of licenses, patents, and copyrights • Prepare the organization for growth
Stage 5 Scaling and Harvesting the Venture (Chapters 10, 11, and 14)	• Communicate the opportunity • Discuss options and alternatives • Sell or merge • Transfer ownership to your family • Go public • Form a strategic alliance

FIGURE 1-4
The Five-Stage Entrepreneurial Process

concepts, as well as how you screen these business ideas and opportunities. The opportunity has to be embedded in a sustainable business model. All entrepreneurs must create a business model or framework that enables the new company to retain the value of its efforts. Otherwise, they can be quickly eroded by competition such that profits decline. Using a number of stimulating examples, Chapters 3 and 5 illustrate how it is possible to apply innovation to the overall business, not just to new products or services, and how to create a sustainable, highly profitable business that will retain its value and be an attractive opportunity for investors and, eventually, purchasers. In these chapters, we show how the Internet can be used to build value and how information on customers' behaviors can be mined to build barriers to competitors.

We'll also discuss various techniques that are used to evaluate the different categories of opportunities. Specifically, we'll look at the following:

• Evaluating business ideas (determining the idea's value and relevant factors, as discussed in Chapter 2)

• Protecting the idea (screening questions for patent protection and using an appropriate legal contract, as shown in Chapter 13)

• Building the vision, conducting market analysis to sustain a competitive advantage, and learning how to think big (as discussed in Chapters 3 and 4)

• Preparing a competitive analysis is covered in Chapter 4. Here, we describe how to undertake competitive analyses, determine marketing strategies, develop a pricing scheme for your products or services, and use the Internet to identify and engage with customers.

This stage usually takes at least a year because it details the pricing and sales strategies required. For example, Bill Gates and Paul Allen were in college when they saw a computer on the cover of *Popular Mechanics* magazine, which set their plan in motion. It took them more than two years to complete the business planning process that led to the creation of Microsoft, an undeniably successful venture.

Stage 2: Developing the Plan and Setting up the Company

In this stage, some ideas are discarded, and strategies are documented and converted to an outlined business plan. The focus at this stage is not on producing a fully fledged business plan but on documenting the main concepts for the company and the route planned for its growth. Increasingly tools such as the Business Model Canvas in Chapter 3 are being used to convey the key elements of a business plan. A fuller business plan is a vital yet dynamic document for the company; however, rarely does a newly formed company precisely follow its original plan. In addition, any plan must be tailored to the audience for which it is intended. For example, when raising money from investors or banks, one version might be required; when selling the company either to another corporation or to the public, other versions are needed; and, of course, a plan is needed to guide your management team as the company grows. There is a trend toward shorter, more concise business plans that helps when producing versions for specific audiences. Because the business plan is such a vital tool for the entrepreneur, we have devoted a full chapter to just this topic (Chapter 6). Chapter 7 describes how many entrepreneurs dedicate thought and planning to starting their businesses and determining the structures of the companies. Others establish their companies without much regard to how the business should be structured. Regardless of the amount of forethought, one of the most important decisions to make is how to legally structure a business. The legal form of the business proprietorship—C-Corporation, S-Corporation, partnership, or limited liability company (LLC)—should be determined in light of the business's short-term and long-term needs. We'll examine the pros and cons of each of these business structures as well as how to prepare a checklist to start a business.

Stage 3: Acquiring Financial Partners/Sources of Funding

Armed with a well-conceived plan, the next challenge is to focus on acquiring funding either through bootstrapping, finding financial investors and partners, or using crowd-funding. In most cases, entrepreneurs may not be aware of the many financing options available that would best meet the needs of the business. Therefore, it is important to know the expectations and requirements of various sources of funds.

Crowd-funding is one option that entrepreneurs should examine and this topic is covered in detail in Chapter 5. Chapter 8 has two parts: each addressing one of the two fundamentally different types of companies. Part A focuses entirely on funding a closely held company in which the founder(s) wish to remain fully in control of the company. Control restricts the company from certain sources of money, and the entrepreneur must creatively bootstrap the company to keep ownership positions from outsiders. Bootstrapping is a vital skill for all entrepreneurs; therefore, this part is also valuable even if the intention is to seek outside owners by selling equity, or shares, in the company at a later stage. This second form of financing is discussed in detail in Part B. Early-stage funding sources include self-funding, family and friends, angels, banks, and government sources. We'll discuss these and other options used to raise capital in both parts. Each potential source has certain criteria for providing financing, and these criteria are the focus of this stage. To increase the chances of success, we'll specify what sources are available for early-stage funding and discuss the requirements of financial partners. Part B also discusses sources for growth funding. We'll look at using private placements, attracting venture capital, and securing sources of debt financing. The chapter ends with different valuation methods and how much of the company to sell, at what price, and for what percentage of the deal. We'll also explain the risks involved in financing in terms of timing and the emotional stress and patience required.

Stage 4: Determining the Resources Required and Implementing the Plan

For those companies that have a unique technology, or business model, it is important to understand how these can be protected. Chapter 13 is a special-topic chapter on technology entrepreneurship. It explores the value of intellectual property and how to file patents, trademarks, and copyrights to gain a competitive advantage in the marketplace. The chapter provides an explanation of these forms of intellectual property (IP) and guides you toward effectively developing, protecting, and promoting your own IP.

> Don't give up.
> Don't ever give up.
> And when things look worst, just don't give up.
>
> Richard Foreman
> *former president and CEO of Register.com*

Entrepreneurs are asked to plan operations and evaluate decisions using financial accounting information. An understanding of managing financial operations will contribute to the success of the entrepreneurial business. Chapter 9 discusses financial statements; how to analyze these statements; and how to prepare budgets, ratios, and cash flow forecasts.

This chapter also covers the important issues regarding people management. Finding, interviewing, training, incentivizing and managing, and, yes, even firing, are important skills you need to build a culture for success.

Stage 5: Scaling and Harvesting the Venture

Chapter 10 provides you with a vital skill that all entrepreneurs need, namely, how to communicate an opportunity concisely and compellingly to new employees, investors, partners, and customers. An idea has no value unless others understand its potential, become excited about being involved, and are willing to participate enthusiastically in the venture. Here, you will learn about the different forms of communications, including video methods as well as how to prepare for a presentation, and what is expected at each stage of relationship development.

Finally, Chapter 11 highlights the methodology, procedures, and options available for entrepreneurs to scale the venture or consider an exit strategy. We'll discuss how to sell an equity stake to a partner, sell the business, transfer ownership to family members or employees, merge with another company, and implement a leveraged buyout. We'll also discuss planning for a public offering that offers an option to sell a portion of the venture and scale the business for growth. The objective of this chapter is to help entrepreneurs identify the best exit plan and be in a strong position to manage the process. Also, in Chapter 11, we tie together each of the issues covered in the book to show how they interact holistically in an actual company with tools and examples for you to learn true CEO skills.

The Growth of Entrepreneurial Companies

Despite the growing prominence of entrepreneurship, understanding of its key features and development stages lags. Mainstream media coverage frequently emphasizes the most unusual successes, creating misconceptions about the nature and evolution of most successful entrepreneurial firms. In theory, entrepreneurship includes several sub-disciplines, including small businesses, businesses owned by women, high-technology start-ups (refer to Chapter 13), home-based businesses, family-owned businesses (refer to Chapter 14), and those focused on a social mission (refer to Chapter 12). Businesses in these groupings have received the most intensive study.

Relatively little research has been done, however, on the distinctive features of growth companies. This is an important point because in many aspects entrepreneurial companies are indistinguishable from small businesses until they enter a "growth" phase, during which they are transformed into an almost entirely different entity. An entrepreneurial firm is one that grows large enough to influence the environment and, thus, become a pacesetter. Yet we cannot use growth alone to evaluate the real pacesetters, as 86.7 percent of all U.S. businesses employ twenty or fewer people.[12] The past fifteen years have been years of tremendous growth for entrepreneurial companies and for the individuals who make them thrive. During this time, entrepreneurs such as Bill Gates, Andy Grove, Steve Jobs, Meg Whitman, and Jeff Bezos have captured the public imagination and dominated the business news.

The reasons for this trend in entrepreneurship are clear. Each year at least 700,000 new businesses are started in the United States, and of these, a small portion turn out to be the fast-growth companies that propel the economy forward. Each year, this small set of businesses creates a disproportionate share of the new jobs and fuels the economy in numerous ways.

The Growth Period

Most businesses "start small and stay small." On the one hand, the business may not offer any productivity improvement and, therefore, may have no significant potential for entrepreneurial growth. On the other hand, even if a business does have growth potential, the business owner may prefer to grow it to only a certain point. As we mentioned earlier, not all entrepreneurs want to grow their businesses. Many entrepreneurs work toward the goal of growing the business to a certain level to provide a relatively steady stream of income and employment. The true challenges for these entrepreneurs and small-business owners are to avoid burnout from the daily operations and keep the entrepreneurial spirit that drove them into business in the first place.[13]

What distinguishes an entrepreneurial company from a small business is the ability of the venture owner to maneuver successfully through the transition stages necessary to handle distinctive periods of growth. In many cases, the growth period comes right from the start and is part of the initial vision for the company. In other cases, the growth period comes later or appears to arrive out of the blue. Each year, a certain number of small businesses make the transition to become entrepreneurial growth companies. One thing these growth companies usually have in common is an entrepreneurial mindset.[14]

Entrepreneurship Roller Coaster

Of course, life is not so predictable that you can follow each step in this book without being confronted with surprises, challenges, and disappointments. Indeed, one of the most important attributes of a successful entrepreneur is the ability to keep going under duress. Figure 1-3, adapted from *Commercializing New Technologies* by K. Jolly from an original chart from R. J. Skaldic, shows the ups and downs of a typical start-up from the original vision or idea through to commercial success. The challenge for the entrepreneur is to manage the periods of despair as well as celebrate the ecstatic events. As you follow the Neoforma story, you will be able to clearly identify many "ups and downs."

ROADMAP

| IN ACTION | The entrepreneurial life is unpredictable, challenging, and often stressful. Practice how to handle uncertainty effectively. |

So Why Become An Entrepreneur?

With such a roller coaster life, you might ask, "Why undertake such an uncertain journey?" People become entrepreneurs for many reasons. Some people are attracted to the perceived independence and freedom from the politics and restrictions of corporations. Being able to do your own thing, make your own decisions, and exert greater control over your working environment are attractive alternatives to the conformity—real or imagined—associated with life in a big company. Some may hit a plateau, see that they are blocked from further promotions, or recognize that they are not progressing as rapidly as they would like, and these conditions become motivating factors. We even tell our students that they should view being fired not as a negative, but as the trigger to start something exciting. Other people believe that building a company can provide them with opportunities for sustained growth and mobility. For others, starting their own company provides them with the flexibility they seek in their lives. And of course, for many, entrepreneurship offers a vehicle for creating huge financial rewards.

Use the Master-Case To Develop Management Skills

The failure rate of start-ups is very high. According to Timmons and others,[15] the failure rate of new companies is 24 percent within the first two years and 80–90 percent within the first ten years. However, most companies fail not from focusing on a bad idea or even having insufficient funds; they fail because the founders are confronting complex management decisions without experience or knowledge of the tools to make them. Throughout the book, we include sections on management issues that are aimed at providing you with an understanding of the unique personal challenges that an entrepreneur faces, especially in their first company adventure. You will examine your own strengths and, yes, weaknesses, and learn management skills to deal with the major decisions you will have to make.

Starting a company can be very stressful, with tremendous demands on your time and energy. This can take a toll on your personal life and affect friends and family in ways that are painful. You need to be honest with yourself and those near you so that the appropriate balance between your personal lifestyle and your new company can be struck.

In order to give you a real-life feel for the management ups and downs within a typical entrepreneurial start-up, we partnered with Wayne McVicker, who, with his cofounder, Jeff Kleck, started and grew a company called Neoforma until it was eventually sold. The two founders agreed to have us create a set of video interviews that we have arranged to illustrate different stress points of managing a start-up. The videos as well as brief synopsis of this master-case can be found at the book web site. (The synopsis is found under the Chapter 1 content section.) Throughout the book, you will be asked to revisit Neoforma to help you acquire key management skills by studying the master-case, viewing interviews, and working on exercises.

SUMMARY

The definition of an entrepreneur has evolved over time as the surrounding economic structures have become more complex. Today, *entrepreneurship* is defined as the process of creating something different by devoting the necessary time and effort; assuming the accompanying financial, psychic, and social risks; and receiving the resulting monetary rewards and personal satisfaction. Before embarking on an entrepreneurial journey, you should take some time to reflect on your own attributes, particularly your need to be in control. This will help you identify an opportunity and create a plan of action that is suited to you and increase the likelihood of success. The entrepreneurial process

consists of five stages: (1) conducting opportunity analysis, (2) developing the plan and setting up the company, (3) acquiring financial partners and sources of funding, (4) determining the resources required and implementing the plan, and (5) scaling and harvesting the venture.

The study of entrepreneurship has relevance today not just because it helps entrepreneurs better fulfill their personal needs, but because of the economic function of new ventures. More than increasing national income by creating new jobs, entrepreneurship acts as a positive force in economic growth and social benefits by serving as the bridge between innovation and application.

STUDY QUESTIONS

Q.1 What are the three types of entrepreneurs? With which do you most identify?

Q.2 What is the difference between technology and social entrepreneurs?

Q.3 Describe five common entrepreneurial personal attributes.

Q.4 If you start a company, will you expect to always be in control, or will you be willing to share control with others if that will help the company grow and make all

the participants wealthier? Describe your reasons for your choices.

Q.5 What is the spider-web model? How does it apply to start-up companies?

Q.6 What are the five stages of the entrepreneurial process?

Q.7 What are the growth issues entrepreneurial companies face?

EXERCISES

1.1 Some argue that entrepreneurship is largely based on chance and many people do not become entrepreneurs because they are never lucky enough to be in the right place at the right time. Alternatively, entrepreneurs are believed to *create* their opportunities by engineering situations that heighten the chance they find an opportunity. What is your view? Give examples to illustrate your answer.

1.2 Entrepreneurs often use networks to extend their "opportunity space." You never know when and how a network will be valuable or what sort of network you might need. Indeed, valuable networks can be created only when you are not looking for immediate benefit. How can you develop your own network *before* it may be useful?

1.3 Incompatible partners can destroy a company, yet good partners are invaluable. Taking a partner as an equal when you start a company immediately halves your potential upside. Is this worth it? You are considering starting a company. How would you find the ideal partner, and what would be his or her experience, personality, ambitions, and values?

Master-Case Exercises: If you have not yet read the master-case on the web site, do so. Then read the diary entries Months 14, 15, 18, 23, 24, 26, 30, 33, and 39.

Either as a team or as an individual produce a presentation on each of the following questions for class discussion. Only one or two slides for each are required to state the key points, which will then be expanded in the class.

Master-case Q 1: Map the networks that Wayne and Jeff had, starting from how they met, found investors, grew the company, and started again. How does your personal network link to them? Could you use this network?

Master-case Q 2: Despite the Internet, networks seem to require proximity and an entrepreneurial infrastructure. Why do you think this is so? Why are places such as Buck is found in entrepreneurial infrastructures? Do you know places such as this? How would you uncover them? On the book's web site read diary entries Prequel and Months 0, 21, 23, 24, 33, 45, and 46 and view the video selection, "Balance: Your Business or Your Life?"

Master-case Q 3: This was an extremely stressful and risky period for Wayne and Jeff as well as for the other key members of Neoforma. Why would they go through this again? Would you classify Wayne, Jeff, and Denis as "serial entrepreneurs?" Why do you think such persons repeatedly subject themselves to the uncertainties and the stress of starting companies? (Hint: See W. Baumol's views on entrepreneurs at https://www.sba.gov/sites/default/files/files/sb_econ2005.pdf.)

Master-case Q 4: Anni and Wayne started out with a dream that nearly became a nightmare for their family. Chart the key events in the story of Neoforma that threatened their personal relationship. What lessons can be learned from these events regarding how to balance work passion and personal lives?

On the book web site, read the diary entries Prequel and Months 0, 2, 19, 29, 57 and view the video selection, "The Mindset, the Passion: Do You Have What It Takes?"

Master-case Q 5: Entrepreneurship is sometimes discussed as the ability to deal with these apparent conflicts:

- **Ambiguity—Planning.** Start-up companies are usually exploring new opportunities where data, details, and the environment may be largely unknown. Yet without a plan, managers do not have a basis on which to make decisions. Yet the discipline of a business plan that is required is rarely followed.

- **Creativity—Discipline.** Many, though not all, start-up companies are based on a new idea or an innovative solution to an existing need. However, if everyone is creating new things all the time, then nothing will actually get done.

- **Urgency—Patience.** Entrepreneurs are driven people. Yet real advances take longer than planned—always.

- **Flexibility—Organization.** The need to respond rapidly to changing circumstances, new ideas, opportunities, and threats with limited resources requires a great deal of flexibility and the ability to change direction quickly. But as the start-up grows, it is impossible for the founders to control everything and make all the decisions. An organizational structure must be put in place, which inevitably begins to prevent just the flexibility that is needed for success.

- **Risk Taking—Risk Management.** Entrepreneurs are usually risk takers, yet too much risk does not create a successful organization and certainly may turn away investors.

- **Short Term—Long Term.** Every day presents a new challenge and possible change of direction, yet you must not lose sight of the ultimate goal.

How did the managers at Neoforma resolve these paradoxes?

Master-case Q 6: Managing a start-up requires a broad range of personal attributes, different from and more diverse than in a larger, more structured company. An entrepreneur must balance these often conflicting skills and traits. Pick eight from the list and show, with examples, how they were exhibited by Wayne and Jeff.

- Creative
- Analytical Ability
- Imaginative
- Comfortable in Networking
- Risk Taking
- Motivated to Achieve
- Highly Autonomous
- Leadership
- Persuasiveness
- Initiative Taking

- Commitment and Tenacity
- Tolerance for Ambiguity
- Unconventional
- Optimistic
- Intuitive
- Passionate in Enjoyment of Life
- Highly Energetic

INTERACTIVE LEARNING ON THE WEB

Test your knowledge of the chapter using the book's interactive web site.

ADDITIONAL RESOURCES

Kauffman Center for Entrepreneurial Leadership at the Ewing Marion Kauffman Foundation

Ewing Marion Kauffman established the Ewing Marion Kauffman Foundation to pursue a vision of self-sufficient people in healthy communities. The foundation, with an endowment of more than $2 billion, is based in Kansas City, Missouri. It directs and supports innovative programs and initiatives that merge the social and economic dimensions of philanthropy locally and nationally.

For more information, visit the center's web site at www.entrepreneurship.org.

National Dialogue on Entrepreneurship

In the summer of 2003, the Public Forum Institute began work under a grant from the Ewing Marion Kauffman Foundation to develop a National Dialogue on Entrepreneurship (NDE) to improve awareness of the value of entrepreneurship. The project is building on the forum's extensive background in national dialogues on economic issues and, in particular, a series of events and activities since 2000 focusing on women and entrepreneurship.

For more information and to sign up for the newsletter, visit the web site at www.publicforuminstitute.org.

American Women's Economic Development Corporation

(AWED), New York. AWED, a premier national not-for-profit organization is committed to helping entrepreneurial women start and grow their own businesses. Based in New York City, AWED also has offices in southern California, Connecticut, and Washington, D.C. It has served more than 150,000 women entrepreneurs through courses, conferences, seminars, and one-on-one counseling provided by a faculty of expert executives and entrepreneurs.

Catalyst, New York. This national nonprofit research and advisory organization founded in 1962 has a dual mission: (1) to help women in business and the professions achieve their maximum potential and (2) to help employers capitalize on the talents of women. Under the leadership of Sheila W. Wellington, president, the Catalyst library at 120 Wall Street offers resources on women for background research.

The National Association of Women Business Owners

(NAWBO), Washington, D.C. NAWBO propels women entrepreneurs into economic, social, and political spheres of power worldwide. NAWBO offers assistance in securing access to financial opportunities to meet, exchange ideas, and establish business ventures; educational programs, seminars, and leadership training; chapter programs, regional meetings, and national conferences; discounts on products and services; an international network of business contacts; visibility and clout in political arenas; and procurement opportunities.

Global Consortium of Entrepreneurship Centers (GCEC)

The Global Consortium of Entrepreneurship Centers (GCEC), formerly the National Consortium of Entrepreneurship Centers (NCEC), was founded in 1996. The intent of the organization is to provide a coordinated vehicle through which participating members can collaborate and communicate on the specific issues and challenges confronting university-based entrepreneurship centers. The GCEC current membership totals 200 university-based entrepreneurship centers ranging in age from well established and nationally ranked to new and emerging centers. Most of these centers have an outreach program to help budding entrepreneurs and are an excellent starting point to learn about support systems in their regions as well as being a place for resources and guidance materials. More information can be found at http://www.national-consortium.org/.

ADDITIONAL CASES FOR READING

There are several magazines that provide cases and tips for entrepreneurs. Stories are an excellent way of transferring knowledge, and these sources will provide you with many practical ideas to

The Small Business Administration
This Federal Agency has a number of planning tools and links to resources at its web site www.sba.org.

help you on your way: Entrepreneur Magazine at www.entrepreneur.com; Inc Magazine at www.inc.com; and Minority Business Entrepreneur Magazine at www.mbemag.com.

ENDNOTES

1. Findings by the Entrepreneurial Research Consortium, a publicly and privately sponsored research effort directed by Dr. Paul Reynolds at Babson College, indicate that 7 million adults are trying to start businesses in the United States at any given time. The Global Entrepreneurship Monitor, a joint research initiative by Babson College and the London Business School and sponsored by the Kauffman Center for Entrepreneurial Leadership, was launched in September 1997 to analyze entrepreneurial activity, its impact on national growth, and those factors that affect levels of entrepreneurial activity.

2. See Dale Meyer, plenary address at USASHE on February 15, 2001, "Changes in Entrepreneurship Curriculum." Courses in entrepreneurship are now taught at nearly one thousand colleges and universities. Entrepreneurship education programs for youngsters in the K-12 age range now exist in more than thirty states. The YESS!/Mini-Society entrepreneurship curriculum has been accepted by the U.S. Department of Education's National Diffusion Network as being effective in both acquiring knowledge and improving attitudes toward school and learning. In addition, according to the Global Consortium of Entrepreneurship Centers, the number of U.S. universities having such centers has grown from 50 to more than 250 in less than ten years.

3. See Marilyn Kourilsky, "Entrepreneurship Education: Opportunity in Search of Curriculum," Kauffman Center for Entrepreneurial Leadership, 1995.

4. See Wayne McVicker, *Starting Something* (Palo Alto, CA: Ravel Media, 2005), available in paperback and in digital format.

5. For a more complete discussion of the evolution of the term *entrepreneur* and theories of entrepreneurship, see "Theories of Entrepreneurship Historical Development and Critical Assessment" in *The Oxford Handbook of Entrepreneurship*, ed. Mark Casson, Bernard Yeung, Anuradha Basu, and Nigel Wadeson (Oxford: Oxford University Press, 2006), 33–56.

6. See Alex F. DeNoble, Doug I. Jung, Sanford B. Ehrlich, and Mark Butler, "A Paper on Entrepreneurial Self-Efficacy: The Development of a Set of Measures and a Preliminary Test of Their Properties," Entrepreneurship Management Center, College of Business Administration, San Diego State University, 1999. Paper submitted on September 23, 2001, at Babson Research Conference.

7. See Ray Smilor, *Daring Visionaries* (Holbrook, MA: Adams Media Corporation, 2001), xxiv–xv. Smilor is the president of the Foundation for Enterprise Development and former vice president of the Kauffman Center for Entrepreneurial Leadership.

8. A breakdown of types of lifestyle entrepreneurs can be found at the U.S. Department of Commerce, "Statistical Abstract of the United States," Bureau of the Census, Washington, DC, 2008. This report also provides a wealth of data on the state of entrepreneurship in the United States.

9. For a discussion of the problems that arise when founders are unable to give up control and hand over the reins to more experienced managers, see Noam Wasserman, "The Founder's Dilemma," *Harvard Business Review* (Feb. 2008): 103–109.

10. Two introductory books on how social networks can enhance businesses are David Silver, *Smart Start-Ups: How Entrepreneurs and Corporations Can Profit by Starting Online Communities* (Hoboken, NJ: John Wiley & Sons, 2007); and Larry Weber, *Marketing to the Social Web: How Digital Customer Communities Build Your Business* (Hoboken, NJ: John Wiley & Sons, 2007).

11. An excellent introduction to the changing world of networks can be found in Albert-Laszio Barabasi, *Linked: How Everything Is Connected to Everything Else and What It Means* (New York: Plume Press, 2003).

12. See U.S. Department of Commerce, "Statistical Abstract of the United States," Bureau of the Census, Washington, DC, 2008, for a wealth of data on small firms.

13. See William B. Gartner, Barbara J. Bird, and Jennifer A. Starr, "Acting As If: Differentiating Entrepreneurial from Organizational Behavior," *Entrepreneurship Theory and Practice* (Spring 1992): 13–27.

14. See Rita McGrath and Ian MacMillan, *The Entrepreneurial Mindset* (Boston: Harvard Business School Press, 2000), 2–3.

15. *It is extreme*ly difficult to obtain reliable data on the failure rate of startups www.businessweek.com/smallbiz/ news/coladvice/ask/sa990930.htm. However, a good summary can be found in Jeffrey A. Timmons and Steve Spinelli, *New Venture Creation*, 7th ed. (Princeton, NJ: McGrawHill/Irwin, 2006). For a more theoretical discourse on small firm failure. see: Robert Cressy, "Determinants of Small Firm Survival and Growth" in *The Oxford Handbook of Entrepreneurship*, ed. Mark Casson, Bernard Yeung, Anuradha Basu, and Nigel Wadeson (Oxford: Oxford University Press, 2006), 162–193.

2 The Art of Innovation

"I think all great innovations are built on rejections."

Louis-Ferdinand Céline, French Author

OBJECTIVES

- Understand the changing role of innovation.
- Create frameworks for innovating.
- Source and filter ideas and build them into opportunities.
- Analyze opportunities using a five-step process.
- Use a framework to evaluate a business opportunity.

CHAPTER OUTLINE

Introduction

Profile: Becky Minard and Paal Gisholt—Finding a Point of Pain

Why Innovation Is Important

Definition and Types of Innovation

Frameworks for Learning Innovation Skills

Finding and Assessing Ideas

Converting an Idea into an Opportunity

Summary

Study Questions

Exercises

Interactive Learning on the Web

Additional Resources

Appendix: The Bayh–Dole Act (Online)

Endnotes

Introduction

Entrepreneurs are often considered highly innovative, always coming up with unique ideas for new businesses. In fact, entrepreneurs do not have to be innovative to be successful, but they do have to understand and manage the innovation process within their companies. They may use innovations found elsewhere or use those continually developed within their own companies, even when they themselves are not the source of innovation. Therefore, it is important that an entrepreneur have a grasp of the nature of innovation and how it is generated and managed.

Innovation can have many facets. For example, Michael Dell is rightly considered an extremely successful entrepreneur. Yet for many years, Dell has built products similar to its major competitors, Hewlett-Packard (HP), Toshiba, Lenovo, and so on. What is unique about Dell is the *way* that these products are sold, manufactured, and delivered to its customers. The business methods employed religiously by Dell are what make the company successful, not innovation of new products. In contrast, Steve Jobs of Apple fame was the driving innovator behind Apple's ability to continually come out with unique-looking and uniquely functioning products and software architectures.[1] Therefore, we cannot understand entrepreneurship without exploring the entrepreneur's relationship with innovative processes. Michael Dell was innovative when he conceived the direct sale, made-to-order way of doing business that drove the initial success of his company. His competitors, after all, failed to see this model; having been caught unawares and locked into their old ways of doing things, they were unable to compete directly for a long while. Now every PC company has copied Dell's model putting pressure on the original innovator.

The frameworks in which a sustainable, high-profit company is constructed are called *business models*. This chapter focuses the innovation of initial ideas and determining whether they are a true opportunity. The next chapter builds on these concepts and explores new ways of thinking about how companies are designed using innovations not just in the products and services they sell but also in the *ways* they are offered.

Before delving into the complexities of business models, however, this chapter deals with the changing role of innovation in business, including definitions and types of innovation. We then show how you can learn to be innovative, how to seek out and screen ideas, and how to build them into creative new business opportunities.

A new company will usually start with an initial concept of how it will be structured to serve its customers, work with suppliers, and evolve. As the company grows, the entrepreneur will uncover knowledge about the company's environment that may not have been obvious at the outset. This new information must be fed into the company's plans to stimulate innovation, not only in products and services but also in the very fabric of how the company will operate within a unique business model.

The environment in which a new company finds itself is increasingly competitive, with pressures not only from local firms but from overseas competitors as well. Moreover, technological advances are accelerating, customers are becoming more informed, and new products and services are being generated at a breathtaking pace. Increasingly, the uniqueness of a product or service is not sufficient for success; the *way* they are embedded into a complete system of marketing, selling, production, delivery, and support can be more important. Certainly, without a winning business model, product and service innovations alone will remain interesting examples for the history books.

Profile: Becky Minard and Paal Gisholt—Finding a Point of Pain[2]

Becky Minard and Paal Gisholt met when they were students in the Harvard MBA program. In 1999, they formed SmartPak™ on Cape Cod. According to Becky, a horse lover, the company was born of necessity. "Feeding supplements was a disaster at our boarding barn. I have a horse that needs daily vitamin E, joint supplement, and a dose of daily wormer. I assumed he was generally getting his supplements. Then I noticed that the vitamin E lasted months longer than it should have. It's a white powder, so I checked his feed tub to see if it was in there. No trace of white powder. He did have a hefty dose of his daily wormer in there; maybe that would explain why I was going through it twice as fast as I should. Now it's hard to blame the barn staff since they have to feed thirty-five horses with an average of three supplements per horse. That works out to 105 supplements to be opened, measured, fed, and resealed. What a headache for them." Becky had just recognized the "point of pain" for both the horse owners and their minders.

Becky continued: "We wondered if others had the same problem, so Paal and I went out and talked to boarders, owners, and managers at other barns. All had many of the same problems. In a few cases, we found some moldy supplements or contaminated supplements (mouse droppings). We found many outdated supplements. The most consistent thing we found was that most of the feed rooms we visited had containers that had not been resealed after each use. Since then we have learned from manufacturers that oxygen, moisture, and sunlight are devastating to the potency of many supplements. Money down the drain."

These "points of pain" were solved by creating SmartPak. A horse owner can go to a web site and order custom-packaged daily supplies for individual horses. All the minder has to do is tear off the seal—similar to those used for six packs of yogurt—and empty the different food supplements into the horse's feed. Each patented pack comes clearly labeled with the horse's name and list of additives. The owner can now rest assured that his horse is well taken care of, and the barn helper's tasks are greatly simplified. SmartPak has now branched out into other pet supplies, allowing the company to grow to more than $100 million in sales in 2013. And in 2014, Becky and Paal could reap some of the financial benefits from their efforts when they sold a majority stake in the company to Henry Schein Animal Health and Oakhill Capital while remaining to run the company.

Why Innovation Is Important

We often hear such broad statements as "competition is becoming brutal," "markets are global," "the Internet has changed the rules of business," and so on. Let's look at some of the facts and see how they influence an entrepreneur.[3]

The Growth of the Internet and Access to Knowledge and Ideas

Relatively recently, computers (and other digital devices) have become connected in networks, and companies such as Google have developed automated search techniques. This is resulting in a cataclysmic shift from an emphasis on local products and productivity to global knowledge sharing. We are only just beginning to understand the implications and effects of this connectivity. Although it is notoriously difficult to accurately size the Internet, any estimate provides staggering statistics. According to research from the Miniwatts Marketing Group[4] in September 2014, more than 2.8 billion people worldwide had Internet access, which equates to a 39 percent penetration rate, North America having the highest at 85 percent and Africa the lowest at 21.3 percent. These numbers represent an average growth of 670 percent over the period between 2000 and 2014. At the same time, the information available to these Internet users is exploding, with more than 7 million new web pages being added *daily* to the more than 50 billion that, according to an estimate by Maurice de Kunder,[5] existed in August 2011. Over 1 billion independent web sites existed in October 2014, up from 270 million in 2011.[6] Now, it is just as easy to find an expert at a university in Melbourne, Australia, as it is to find one in Melbourne, Florida, or a corporate partner in Cambridge, Massachusetts, as it is in Cambridge, England. Social networks have grown alongside the Web. In 2015 Facebook could boast of 1.5 billion members, with two-thirds of these active daily.

To remain competitive today, it is no longer sufficient to rely on local know-how; indeed, it is vital to access the best ideas, technologies, research resources, and experts, wherever they are. For example, the networked world can support a biotech company with headquarters in Seattle; basic research undertaken at universities in San Diego, Edinburgh, and Auckland; scale-up of production in Singapore; and clinical trials in the newest members of the European Union. Its advisory board will undoubtedly be international in makeup. A management challenge—yes—but by assembling appropriate resources to compete quickly and efficiently, more certain success is in the offing. These knowledge-centered structures are variously referred to as "virtual knowledge networks" or "virtual clusters." (We discuss building "virtual companies" in Chapter 5.) They are fluid and may form and dissolve in short shrift when they are no longer valuable, whereas geographical-based clusters may take years to evolve with the danger of being outmoded and redundant. We can envision a world not long in the future where nearly everyone will be able to search the world's knowledge, locate experts on demand, and do this more or less for free. For an entrepreneur, this means access to more ideas, more stimulation, and more expertise when conceiving and growing a business opportunity. The Internet should be one of the entrepreneur's major tools.

The Internet and Customer Expectations

The Internet is also changing the way customers view suppliers. It enables us to find and compare products, even sometimes having the product made to order instantly; to choose when and how to have it delivered; and to decide how to pay for or finance the purchase. This is true in both business-to-business (B2B) and business-to-consumer (B2C) sales. We are being subtly educated to expect customized service and instant gratification as part of our buying experience. Products are being surrounded by service. We want *our* problems to be solved, not a standard product to buy. This shift, of course, is at the center of entrepreneurial companies such as Dell, eBay, Amazon, Netflix, and Google. The lesson is this: think service, not product; personalized solution, not third-party handoff. As you will see in the many cases in this book, these ideas can be applied to the most mundane product areas. (Business models built around service are discussed more deeply in the next chapter.)

The Internet's Impact on Business Models and Funding

The Internet is radically changing the way that entrepreneurs design new business models, access resources, market products, and fund their companies. These topics are dealt with later in Chapters 3, 4, and 5.

Mini-Case: Greif Packaging (www.greif.com)—Product to Service

A supplier of metal drums for shipping bulk chemicals, many of which are toxic, realized that it had no real competitive position and that profit margins were thin. An internal entrepreneur decided to listen carefully to customers. He saw there were unmet needs and new sources of value to be accessed. Customers did not want to buy and own steel drums; they just wanted to move toxic chemicals efficiently and safely. They did not want to deal with all of the details, such as finding a licensed trucker; filling in the government forms; and washing, cleaning, and refurbishing the drums. To meet its customers' actual needs, Greif converted its business model into a "trip leasing" company for specialty chemicals—the FedEx®of problem chemicals. Now, it solves the total trip problem for its customers—drum supply, cleaning, refurbishing, regulatory compliance, transportation, and tracking. Greif built a new web application and became an "Internet company." Although it subcontracts most support functions, it captures the value in the supply chain and builds long-lasting client relationships. The business model also builds barriers against competitors.

Barriers to Trade

Historical trade barriers for goods and services are rapidly being dismantled, opening up all markets to global suppliers. According to the World Trade Organization,[7] the number of international agreements signed annually to open up trade has ballooned from less than ten in 1950 to close to two hundred in 2000 and close to four hundred in 2014. Any new product can be copied within days and then manufactured and shipped into most markets within a few weeks. The entrepreneur's defenses against this happening are having a sound intellectual property strategy (see in the following and Chapter 13) and an innovative business model that supplies more than just a product (Chapters 3 and 5).

Access to Capital

Simultaneously with the elimination of trade barriers for goods and services, restrictions on currency trading have also been almost entirely removed. Now, daily cross-border trading in currency dwarfs the value of imports and exports. Although most currency trading is on a short-term basis, the lack of restrictions in the majority of economies to inward or outward foreign investment means that funds may now seek opportunities on a global basis and firms must *compete internationally* for finance. Fully 20 percent of mutual funds managed in the United States and a mainstay of U.S. personally managed pensions are now invested overseas.[8] Geographical location no longer provides any significant advantage for access to major sources of capital. Venture capital (VC) remains one source of funding that prefers proximity, but overall, VC funds are a very small part of total growth capital. Even VC is trending internationally. As reported recently,[9] leading "Sand Hill Road" VC firms are looking to target a significant part of new funds for investment in early-stage companies in Asia, hoping to bring their start-up management skills into markets where U.S.-style VC is little known. For the entrepreneur, this means that the competition for growth capital is becoming tougher, making the "bootstrapping" skills described in Chapter 8 important.

Technological Obsolescence

A product life cycle is the time that a product is able to command a high-profit margin in the market before it becomes obsolete or develops intense competition. Life cycles are continually declining. This is much more likely to be true for fast-moving consumer products such as food and detergents and for products in which the underpinning technology is driven by Moore's law[10] or is impacted by major technological shifts. According to an internal study conducted in the mid-1990s by HP,[11] the average period that HP's products remained major contributors to sales had fallen from four years in 1980 to well less than two years in 1995. More recent studies[12] measure product development times that have declined from an average of 225 days three years ago to less than 200 days now. In the portable communication business sector populated by such companies as Samsung, Apple, Google, Nokia, and Huawei, market life cycles are now shorter than product development cycles; that is, it takes longer to develop a product than the time it will be successful in the market. This is a challenge to even the most efficient engineering departments, which are shifting to around-the-clock global teams. Managing such complex projects across corporate, national, and cultural boundaries requires new skills that ensure the ability to get it right the first time.

ROADMAP

| IN ACTION | No matter in which market you are operating, standing still is not an option. Adapt and take advantage of new technologies, new customers, and new partners. |

Of course, in slower-moving sectors such as machine tools and locomotives, the evidence for rapidly declining product life cycles is not so obvious. However, even here, the impact of low-cost electronic computing power and the ubiquity of the Internet are accelerating the upgrades that customers expect. They want more than just a product; they anticipate nothing less than a total solution to their requirements throughout their ownership. These additional service components may cover not only financing and operator training but also remote condition monitoring for 24/7 online support and maintenance, performance guarantees with financial penalties, and even returns of the product for recycling at the end of its life cycle. For example, Dell has recently started a recycling service for used computers. The acceleration of product life cycles changes the way that intellectual property must be managed. In the past, the seventeen to twenty years of protection afforded by a patent was often valuable over its full life. But when technology evolves rapidly, twenty years of protection loses its value. Research by one of the authors[13] shows that companies are reevaluating the ways that they protect their intellectual property and are carefully selecting areas for long-term patent coverage, usually on fundamental inventions, and are forgoing patents for trade secrets elsewhere. Patent law requires inventors to "teach" what they have done within the patent document; this inevitably exposes concepts and know-how that may be better kept secret rather than giving competitors a jump start to catch up. An agile company[14] has moved on by the time patents are issued, so the patents may be of more value to competitors than to the owner. In the new innovation model, churning out patents is replaced by including the protection of intellectual property within the overall business strategy rather than a way of protecting an invention. And when patents are filed, they are written to protect both the "hard" invention and the unique business model surrounding it.

In some sectors, of course, patents will continue to be the principal method to retain protection from competition. For example, the long and expensive development cycles and regulatory hurdles governing pharmaceutical products encourage the use of patent protection. Even here, however, careful selection of what to patent and when to retain maximum advantage after perhaps a ten-year development cycle is a challenging task. We return to the strategy of intellectual property management in special topics, Chapter 13, "Technology Entrepreneurship."

The budding entrepreneur can learn several lessons here:

- It is becoming more and more difficult to build a company around a *single* product idea without strong patent protection. This is particularly true for consumer products that have a very short life cycle.

- Protective barriers must become part of any business model, whether via patents, trade secrets, uniqueness in the business model, or fast movement to market to stay ahead of competitors.

- Innovation is not a single event; one should never stop innovating.

- You should always imagine that there is someone, somewhere, having the same idea.

- The entrepreneur needs to solve customers' problems: think service, not product.

Summarizing the above, we are in a world in which access to knowledge and expertise, labor, and capital is truly global and transparently accessible, and in which technology relentlessly advances. Technical breakthroughs are no longer confined to just a few centers of excellence such as Bell Labs or MIT; the next breakthrough can just as easily occur in Bangalore, Beijing, or Brisbane as in Birmingham, Boston, or Boca Raton. Shorter product life cycles and rapid technological obsolescence make patents lose their power in monopoly preservation. In addition, companies can no longer rely on the earlier protections of trade and monetary restrictions, local labor preeminence, and cozy knowledge clusters to provide competitive advantages. The only way that sustainable advantages can be earned is through continuous innovation—innovation not only in product development, but in all aspects of business activity and at an ever-increasing rate. Of course, there has always been innovation in corporations. Indeed, William Baumol[15] argues that the unprecedented wealth generated in the major economies in the twentieth century would not have been possible without innovation. However, until relatively recently, many firms could survive and prosper without innovating: they competed in a protected environment.

ROADMAP

IN ACTION	Innovation is no longer a luxury; it is a necessity.

Definition and Types of Innovation

Definition of Innovation

In this book, we will use the following definition:

Successful innovation is the use of new technological knowledge, and/or new market knowledge, employed within a business model that can deliver a new product and/or service to customers who will purchase at a price that will provide profits.

This definition is built on the generally accepted work of Alan Afuah.[16] In order to focus the discussion and to emphasize the new innovation, we have added the following:

"Successful. . ."—to emphasize that we are not interested in innovation that fails to deliver and maintain value for the innovating enterprise or, in the case of social entrepreneurs (see Chapter 12), stakeholders and society in general.

". . .employed within a business model. . ."—to stress that innovation in the business model is at least as important as purely product or process technology. (This theme is developed in Chapter 3.)

". . .who will purchase at a price that will provide profits"—to stress that success requires that the innovator be able to extract benefit from the value created and not allow it to migrate to partners, customers, or offshore manufacturers.

Types of Innovation

There are two major classes of innovation: incremental and disruptive (sometimes referred to as radical). Incremental innovations are continual improvements on an existing product or service or in the ways that products are manufactured and delivered. Disruptive innovations are the result of major changes in the ground rules of competition, culminating in either a customer satisfying her needs in an entirely new way or in a totally new need being created through innovation.

The S-curve is often used to illustrate the difference in which the performance achieved by a new innovation is plotted against time (see Figure 2.1). When the innovation is first made, a period of experimentation ensues in which little performance improvement is made while the innovator tries different ways of reaching goals. As learning improves with experimentation, the advances in improvements accelerate quickly until a plateau is reached, at which time major efforts are required to make minor improvements—the region of limited returns. Usually, improvements can be made with *incremental* innovations, pushing the original curve higher. Then along comes a new innovation—usually from another place—which goes through the same cycle until it ends up giving a higher performance than the first idea and takes a major part of the market away from the first innovation. This is the radical change.

Example: The Evolution of Lighting

When Thomas Edison invented the incandescent lamp, it took many years before lamps were mainstream. First, he encountered difficulties in encapsulating the filament to prevent burnout, and houses had to be wired to receive electric power. But after twenty years or so, electric lighting became the preferred method. Electric lighting, a disruptive innovation, replaced candles. Since then, the electric lamp has undergone many incremental improvements, yet it remains fundamentally the same as Edison's original innovation. There are now only a few suppliers of lamps, and none of them makes good profits. Electric lamps are a commodity and are ripe to be replaced by two disruptive innovations—compact fluorescence bulbs and solid-state diodes. We can only

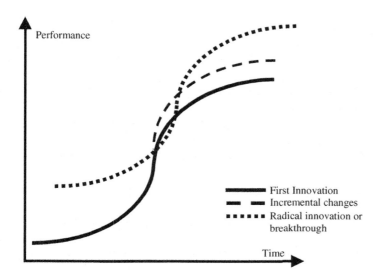

FIGURE 2.1
The S-Curves of Innovation

guess where the future may lie. For example, the firefly's tail is a very efficient converter of electrical energy to light using the unique properties of the enzyme, luciferase. With fuel costs rising rapidly, there is a big incentive to reduce energy consumption. Is the biolamp far away? The only assurance is that it *will not* be developed by one of the existing lamp manufacturers, for they are focused on incrementally improving the old ideas.

Edison's lamps nearly destroyed the candle industry—though not quite. There's money to be made in candles, too!

Mini-Case: Blyth Candles

In 1977, Robert Goergen, an entrepreneur, bought a small, barely surviving candle company in Brooklyn, New York. At that time, the company had annual sales of about $3 million. He changed the name to Blyth Candles,[17] and since then, he has built the company to the point where it is the largest candle supplier in the United States, with annual sales greater than $1 billion in 2010 despite a tough economic climate. Goergen and his family members still own 29 percent of the company, which is now publicly traded, making his personal wealth in the company's stock worth $130 million—not bad for a candlemaker. This has been achieved entirely via incremental innovations—perfumed candles for certain occasions and seasons, candles for outdoors, ornamental candleholders, and so on—and by buying smaller candle manufacturers that were not innovating at all.

Entrepreneurs, therefore, do not need a disruptive or radical innovation to create a new, successful, and profitable company. Continuous incremental innovation can also be sufficient.

Disruptive Innovation

The term *disruptive innovation* is often used to describe innovations that *disrupt* the status quo. As companies grow, they develop cultures and procedures that create internal barriers to change. The greater the mismatch of the innovation to the current know-how and the more it threatens to destroy existing product sales, the tougher it is for a large company to respond. The change can arise from a new technology. Kodak struggled with changing from being the leading supplier of photographic film and moving to an entirely new business based on digital imaging. All of the company's chemical know-how provides no advantage in the new world, and the more digital products that Kodak sells, the faster its film business will decline. Dell entered the PC market with a new direct-to-customer business model causing major problems for IBM who finally got out of the business altogether. Google came from nowhere to threaten behemoth Microsoft. It was start-up Intel that destroyed RCA's vacuum tube business, Amazon that challenges established retail chains, and Netflix together with Dish Networks that eventually forced Blockbuster Video into bankruptcy in September 2010.[18] Again and again, it is entrepreneurial start-ups that can take advantage of the larger company's inability to respond to disruption.

ROADMAP

IN ACTION   A small company, with no legacy to protect and account for, has an inherent advantage over larger enterprises, which are slow to change and adopt new ideas. Learn to swim among sharks.

To learn more about how large companies struggle with disruptive innovation, see Clayton Christensen.[19] And to learn how small entrepreneurial companies can partner with large companies, see Baumol's article.[20] As evidence that entrepreneurs and small companies are the source of the most important innovations, see Table 2.1.

Table 2.1   Some Important Innovations by U.S. Small Firms in the Last Century[21]

Air passenger service	Heat sensor	Prefabricated housing
Airplane	Helicopter	Pressure-sensitive tape
Articulated tractor	High-resolution CAT scanner	Programmable computer
Assembly line	High-resolution digital X-ray	Quick-frozen food
Audiotape recorder	High-resolution X-ray microscope	Reading machine
Bakelite	Human growth hormone	Rotary oil drilling bit
Biomagnetic imaging	Hydraulic brake	Safety razor
Biosynthetic insulin	Integrated circuit	Six-axis robot arm
Catalytic petroleum cracking	Kidney stone laser	Soft contact lens
Cellophane artificial skin	Large computer	Solid-fuel rocket engine
Computerized blood pressure controller	Link trainer	Stereoscopic map scanner
Continuous casting	Microprocessor	Strain gauge
Cotton picker	Nuclear magnetic resonance scanner	Strobe lights
Defibrillator	Optical scanner	Supercomputer
DNA fingerprinting	Oral contraceptives	Two-armed mobile robot
Double-knit fabric	Outboard engine	Vacuum tube
Electronic spreadsheet	Overnight national delivery	Variable output transformer
Free-wing aircraft	Pacemaker	Vascular lesion laser
FM radio	Personal computer	Xerography
Front-end loader	Photo typesetting	X-ray telescope
Geodesic dome	Polaroid camera	Zipper
Gyrocompass	Portable computer	

So don't be scared of those dinosaurs out there. Take advantage of their inability to respond to disruptive innovations, whether in products, services, or business models. Throughout this book, you will find many examples of entrepreneurial ventures. Think about whether they are based on a disruptive innovation and how this will affect the existing larger firms. Can they respond?

Frameworks for Learning Innovation Skills

Debate continues as to whether innovators must be born or such skills can be learned. The authors' research shows that, indeed, if someone has the desire to be an entrepreneur, then innovation skills can be effectively learned. The best way to achieve this expertise is by using examples and practicing the learned skills. In this section, we will outline some "innovation frameworks" that will help you in this regard. These frameworks are examples, not a complete list. In fact, you may be able to develop your own frameworks that you find more suited to your own personality and style.

ROADMAP

IN ACTION	Design your own personal antenna to continually scan the world around you, analyzing situations and looking for opportunities.

Analogies

Why innovate from nothing when many ideas have already worked well? The idea of this framework is to help transfer innovations from one field to another. Chapter 10 describes LeafBusters, a company that "outsources" the leaf collection and disposal services provided by municipalities to residents annually. LeafBusters claims that it can do this more efficiently because it can use the required expensive equipment for a longer season each year by "following the weather." Where did the founders of this company get this "obvious" idea? They read an article about crews that harvest crops under contract to farmers in the Corn Belt moving southward each year. The underlying drivers for the two businesses are the same: more effective use of expensive capital equipment through "following the seasons." The trick here is to analyze existing successful businesses and to get behind the immediate product or service to examine the underpinning principles. Then ask, "Where else can these be applied?"

Let us work through another analogy example. Dell is now supplying printers that connect to the Internet, and the printers have built-in "ink management software." The software analyzes usage, recommending when to print in black-and-white only, when in color, and so on. When it is time to replace the ink cartridge, the printer has already forecasted the need, contacted Dell via the Internet, and had ink drop-shipped on time. This is a valuable service to the consumer. It also locks in the purchasing to Dell supplies, preempting competition from low-cost refill stores. The consumer is happy, and Dell grows its revenue and profits. What other products/services could be analogous to this example?

Consider that household appliances that connect to the Internet are now also being offered.[22, 23] Initially aimed at monitoring performance so service calls can be scheduled before the appliances break down, this feature could be used as follows. The washing machine monitors usage and injects into the wash the appropriate detergent, softener, bleach, and so on, depending on the needs for the load. Like the printer, detergent usage forecast enables a supplier to drop-ship the product and place it into holders built in to the machines just in time to fulfill the consumer's needs. Currently, detergent manufacturers are not making any profits because they have to pay to have their products put on retailers' shelves and they compete in a commodity market with expensive advertising. There is little consumer loyalty; products on special are purchased more often. Consumers do not like carrying the heavy containers of detergent. Perhaps there is an opportunity for a new detergent manufacturer to join with an appliance manufacturer such as GE, Whirlpool, or Maytag to provide the "total washing solution." This would benefit the consumer both in service and cost, for it would no longer be necessary to advertise detergents separately or to use the inconvenient and expensive retail distribution chain.

Actually, Becky Minard and Paal Gisholt might have come up with the SmartPak idea by looking for an analogy. Cardinal Health (www.cardinal.com) does the same for hospital patients by taking over the internal pharmacy role. Patients' daily medicines are delivered, clearly labeled, to the bedside, reducing potentially dangerous errors and costs by eliminating the large inventories at hospitals and consolidating suppliers at central locations rather than at individual dispensaries. Both SmartPak and Cardinal provide services around their products and solve their customers' problems. Entrepreneurs learn to think like this: always analyzing intriguing innovations and thinking about where else the *principles of the concept*, not necessarily the details, can be applied. Get into the habit of questioning situations in this way. And don't look at only successes; often analyzing a failure can shine light on another situation where the reasons for failure may not apply.

Intersection of Technology Trends

We live in a world where technology is changing quickly. Watching cost and performance trends, particularly where they begin to intersect, can give rise to whole new innovative business opportunities. Let's consider digital photography, high-bandwidth communications, and ubiquitous wireless communications and think about some new business ideas. For example, imagine a digital camera with a wireless Internet connection. You could have your own personal web site to which your latest pictures are uploaded as soon as you take them. E-mails can be sent to friends and relatives immediately so they can participate with you in real time. Of course, this sounds a little like 3G phone cameras coupled to your Facebook page. But where is the business opportunity? What an interesting upgrade of services for a professional event photographer. Now, at your wedding, bar mitzvah, or the like, a photographer can post pictures as they are taken, and those friends and relatives who are unable to be there in person can enjoy the event as it happens. The photographer can also sell more pictures and albums to a wider audience because they are more likely to buy when they are closely involved in the event. Check out the Garmin Corporation, which started life as a manufacturer of electronic navigation systems for cars. This core business is threatened by Internet-compatible phones. So it has bundled together different sensor technologies around its GPS skills to enter new markets in sports, sailing, hiking, flying, and so on.

Solving Points of Pain

Entrepreneurs are quick to notice inefficiencies, inconveniences, and other points of pain and to use these to build new business opportunities.

Mini-Case: Netflix (www.Netflix.com)

Netflix provides rental DVDs through the mail rather than via the bricks-and-mortar rental outlets favored by Blockbuster. The founders of Netflix realized that Blockbuster's customers had points of pain; they had to drive to the store, search through rows of movies, often not find the one they were seeking as it was already rented out, and pay late charges if they forgot to return it on time. Netflix solved these points of pain by mailing the movies (made possible by the DVD format taking over from tapes—a technology discontinuity) directly to the customer. Movies can be kept as long as a consumer wishes with no late charges. When John Antioco, CEO of Blockbuster, first encountered Netflix, he did not see it as a threat, stating, "No one will want to wait three days for a movie." In fact, having a wish list and allowing a subscriber to hold several DVDs simultaneously avoids this supposed disadvantage. And because inventory is stored centrally, a greater selection is possible. The Netflix business model innovation is "disruptive" to Blockbuster, which has invested much in stores and local inventories. Netflix saw the impact of a disruptive technology on its own business through the evolution of broadband networks that can deliver on-demand streamed content and smoothly switched to this new delivery model. Netflix uses its extensive customer behavior database to continually provide a superior service.[24] It is interesting that Blockbuster did not see Amazon as an analogy to Netflix, just as Borders never saw Amazon as a threat until Amazon had taken a major share of the book market.

Entrepreneurs are continually noticing and analyzing points of pain. Practice this in your daily life and challenge yourself to find the business opportunity.

Analyzing Existing Businesses

Understanding how existing businesses work, their cost structure, and customer points of pain can lead to ideas about how they can be effectively attacked. In our classes, students usually start with thinking of business ideas related to things near and dear to their everyday experience. This is often pizza. Their business idea is to open yet another pizza parlor, with the innovation centered around new product ideas—Thai–French or Indonesian curry pizzas, for example.

Mini-Case: Pizza-on-a-Truck

After some simple research, the students expose a number of areas where the current pizza delivery services are unsatisfactory:

Customer points of pain	Owner's points of pain
Pizza arrives late.	Location is bad.
Pizza arrives cold.	Rent is high.
Phone takes forever to be answered.	Labor is expensive and unreliable.
Order taker is incomprehensible.	It is difficult to schedule
Pizza tastes of the packaging.	baking with deliveries.

Digging further, an analysis of the cost of making and delivering a pizza shows that the storefront and labor overhead far outweigh the cost of food ingredients. And the customers are unhappy.

So let's think outside the pizza box, and let's think really BIG. Let's ask ourselves how we can totally restructure the pizza business on a national basis and grab the lion's share of the pizza market. Are there any technical advances that might impact the pizza business? Here, you can get pretty creative. The following are some ideas culled from searching the patent database, surfing the web, and talking to experts in a number of different fields (remember: use the vast sources of information now available at your fingertips):

- Package delivery companies such as UPS and FedEx have invested heavily in software to optimize the most efficient routes for their vehicles depending on today's delivery addresses. How can this be applied to pizza delivery?

- Cars are commonly fitted with global positioning systems (GPSs) that determine where the car is and display a map and instructions on how to get to a desired location.

- Customers are increasingly becoming accustomed to using the Internet for ordering. Can this be applied to pizza ordering?

- Because labor reliability and costs are major issues for pizza outlets, Pizza Hut has developed working prototype robots for assembling pizzas automatically based on an order input. The robots make the pizza and feed it into an oven. The time in the oven depends on the size and ingredients so a perfect pizza comes out every time.

How can all these apparently unconnected developments be combined to create an entirely new pizza business?

Think about putting the robot and oven on a truck. Pizzas are made not in the sequence of the orders as they come in directly to the truck over the wireless Internet but in the order that optimizes delivery time based on knowledge of the location of the vehicle, the optimum routing, and the oven scheduling. Labor is reduced to one person, the driver, and there is no storefront at all. Customers are informed by e-mail or phone exactly when their pizza will be delivered, and it will always be fresh, having just popped out of the oven as the driver pulls up. And there is no need for flavor-destroying packaging to keep the pizza hot for twenty minutes while the driver goes to other locations or gets lost.

The results are better service, better pizzas, for a lower cost of doing business. Think about starting out in one or two locations first and either raising capital to expand into other markets or using a franchising model to cover the country. (See the next chapter for a discussion on franchising.) Look out Domino's and Pizza Hut! This example illustrates several ways in which entrepreneurs innovate. You may be surprised that it is a largely analytical process. The situation is deconstructed, ideas for stimulation are sought on the Internet, and a synthetic process is initiated whereby the different inputs are rearranged until a possible solution emerges. Entrepreneurs are very good at synthesizing new opportunities from a collection of apparently disparate concepts. They recognize patterns that others may not find obvious. Get accustomed to looking for such patterns through analogies, technology confluences, points of pain, and the like. You will find that you will quickly get better at this, and you may even develop your own personal frameworks for innovating. And do *not* be frightened to think big; usually bigger is easier than smaller.

Finding and Assessing Ideas

The previous sections show how to create new ideas for a business within innovation frameworks. For entrepreneurs just starting out, however, it may be necessary to seek some stimulation from idea sources. The world is full of ideas, but ideas are not opportunities, and opportunities are not ready-made to build a business around. Figure 2.2 shows how many ideas are required to start one business. Let us now look at how ideas can be built up and analyzed as real business opportunities.

ROADMAP

IN ACTION | The world is full of wonderful and freely available ideas. Ideas, however, are not businesses. Seek ideas and turn them into opportunities to build into valuable enterprises.

During your life, you will probably generate many ideas for potential businesses. With proper training and skill development, your creativity can flourish. The value of entrepreneurship education is that you will learn how to critically evaluate your ideas to locate the best opportunities for commercial success.

Maybe you have some starting concepts but question how original they are. You may be surprised to hear that not all entrepreneurs come up with unique ideas. You can be innovative without that initial generative impulse. Here are five ways to build upon already existing material and still provide a profit-driven concept:

1. Develop ideas as an extension or redesign an existing service (Marriott Senior Living Services; Sam's Club—an extension of Wal-Mart).

2. Resegment and create an improved service (overnight delivery, such as FedEx, or buying cheaper airline tickets from Priceline.com).

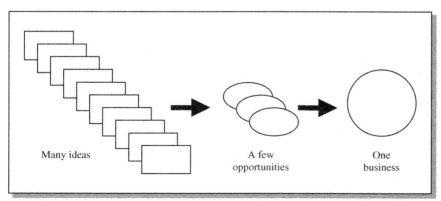

FIGURE 2.2
Many Ideas Are Filtered Down to One Business

3. Redifferentiate and market the product at a lower price (Internet shopping, Sam's Club).

4. Add value to an existing product or service (linked brands, such as PCs just for the Internet).

5. Develop or redesign a new version of an existing product (Snapple Iced Tea, fresh-baked chocolate chip cookies, and Krispy Kreme doughnuts).

Idea Assessment

The first step for any entrepreneur is to generate an idea for a new business. The entrepreneur must then assess the opportunities available for putting the idea into practice. Is this something that has been overdone? Has it been executed poorly in the past? Has anyone else thought of it? In short, is the idea a potential dead end, a niche on an existing opportunity, or an entirely unexplored chance to create a business?

There are many sources for ideas. The Internet has made idea searching much faster and broader, and it also makes it easy to check whether an idea has already been discovered and put into a business. Entrepreneurs source ideas from many places.

To get you started, we have assembled a "starter kit" of twenty-seven general idea sourcing web sites. The full list can be found on the book's web site at www.wiley.com/college/kaplan. The sites range from a pure list of ideas to franchising opportunities, patent auction sites, and sites committed to global scanning of new ideas. Take a look at some of the sites and use a search engine such as Google to start searching on your own. You will be amazed at the wealth and breadth of idea triggers that will get you thinking.

Probably the most underutilized sources for ideas are the U.S. and foreign patent databases. Chapter 13 deals with protecting your own ideas using patents. Here, we discuss patents as *sources* of ideas. There are more than 8 million patents issued in the United States. These can be searched by key words, owners, dates, and so on at the U.S. patent web site, www.uspto.gov. Many patents, of course, are filed to protect deep technology know-how. However, often forgotten are the simpler product ideas that their inventors may not have exploited for a number of reasons; perhaps they did not have the money or did not know how to develop a market, or perhaps the idea was before its time, either because the market was not ready or the means of making it practical were not yet available. Also, every patent has to describe why the invention is important, including prior ideas, and why the idea is useful. What a great place to pick others' brains! In fact, only about 10 percent of existing patents have actually been commercialized; the remainder are still potential opportunities.

Converting an Idea into an Opportunity

Many new companies are built around a disruptive or breakthrough technology. As we explained earlier, major corporations are surprisingly bad at exploiting "disruptive" innovations. Indeed, as Table 2.1 shows, many of the major breakthroughs are discovered and taken to market by small firms. Of course, many of these breakthroughs are good enough that the small company grows into a large firm. Remember that all large firms started small. The important point to grasp is that breakthroughs are more likely to be conceived and developed in small companies. An entrepreneur need not be the developer of the technology. In fact, small companies can access a wealth of new technologies from a variety of sources such as universities, government-funded research laboratories, and the companies that the government funds to carry out research and development (R&D). In fact, these sources are mandated by law to make the results of their research available to companies. (See the Bayh–Dole Act on the book's web site.)

ROADMAP

IN ACTION   Seek and use motivation, passion, and encouragement to convert an idea into a viable business opportunity and overcome many obstacles and roadblocks.

We have created two long lists of web sites that you can visit to browse the technological inventions that are available, one for universities and the other from U.S. government sources. These lists can be found at the book's web site, www.wiley.com/college/kaplan.

The Evaluation Process for the Idea

The entrepreneur will unquestionably need plenty of encouragement and support while developing a business idea. But in turning this idea into a concrete business, the entrepreneur will be faced with hard facts and cold reality. Armed with information gleaned from research, the entrepreneur is positioned to legitimately decide whether to proceed with the idea and work to sustain the venture.

Opportunity: Five Phases to Success

Identifying which business ideas have real commercial potential is one of the most difficult challenges that an entrepreneur will face. This section describes a systematic approach to reducing the uncertainties. The five-step model outlined in Figure 2.3 will help entrepreneurs to know a winning business area when they see one.[25]

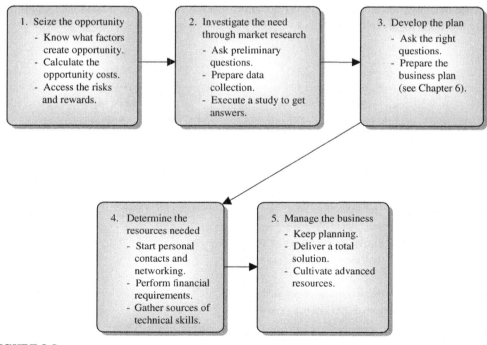

FIGURE 2.3
The Five Phases to Success

Phase 1: Seize the Opportunity

The basic objective is to define the criteria that would make a business opportunity worthwhile to pursue. To start the process, think about how much value an opportunity can add to a business. Rita McGrath's *The Entrepreneurial Mindset* describes the techniques that can be used to create an opportunity register. The register is like an inventory of opportunities. It is a list of your ideas for improving, or even completely reinventing, the current business model or going into entirely new opportunity spaces. The entrepreneur wants to store good ideas so they can be revisited to see how new ideas might fit in, determine whether the timing is right to implement older ones, or figure out what to eliminate as the direction becomes more defined. Record and revisit ideas that are generated.[26]

To evaluate the business opportunity, review the sequence of events in Figure 2.3 and answer the following questions from the perspective of both a personal and professional experience:

- What are the indicators that lead to this idea and opportunity?

- What are the conditions that permit the opportunity to occur?

- How will the future of this new product or service change the idea?

- How long time is the window of opportunity?

Time Horizon

A window of opportunity is a time horizon during which opportunities exist before something else happens to eliminate them. A unique opportunity, once shown to produce wealth, will attract competitors, and if the business is easy to enter, the industry will quickly become saturated. In this situation, the entrepreneur must get in quickly and be able to get out before revenues become dispersed in an overdeveloped market.[27] The factors that help the entrepreneur create opportunity for the business are given in Figure 2.4.

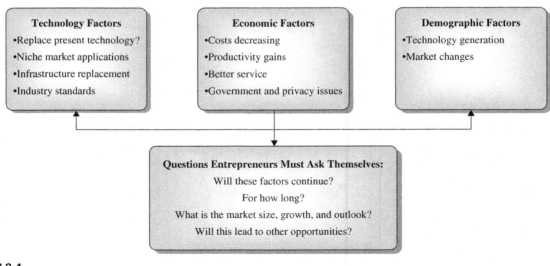

FIGURE 2.4
Factors That Create Opportunity

Evaluate Opportunity Costs

Opportunity costs are the value of benefits lost when one decision or idea alternative is selected over another. For example, suppose a software company refuses to deliver a software program because writing the software code will require the company to miss a major deadline for another company. The order for the software program would generate revenue of $25,000 and additional costs of $14,000. Then the opportunity cost and the net benefit lost associated with the software deadline is $11,000 (i.e., $25,000 minus $14,000).

Phase 2: Investigate the Need through Market Research

The first step is to identify, measure, and document the need for the product or service. This means making a specific financial forecast of the actual potential and anticipated return for this proposed product or service. This process is not the end; it's only the beginning. The topic of marketing will be explored more fully in Chapter 4, but for now, it will be considered as it fits into the opportunity analysis.

Marketing research need not be extensive, sophisticated, or expensive, but it must determine what customer satisfaction means for the target market. It should also provide other critical information about the target market used to develop marketing strategies. In some cases, the entrepreneur can survey the market to obtain information specifically tailored to the business's needs. However, judgment must be used to protect future marketing plans. The emergence of social networks and the associated tools may enable initial market research to be accomplished much quicker and at lower cost than in the past. An example used by Halare Inc. is provided in Chapter 4.

The questions later will assist in evaluating the actual climate surrounding the new company and preparing for the early stages of a new venture. Larger companies often outsource research to a marketing company, but this process will identify the steps and questions needed to custom-design the research and conduct it productively whether using interview methods or accessing social networks.

Preliminary Questions

At this point, the entrepreneur needs to solidify the purpose and object of the research. Those who are developing a particular product will want to focus on questions that can tell them about product features and distribution. A more service-oriented entrepreneur will consider other inquiries, directed at identifying the sources and beneficiaries of that service. Consider the goal now; it will save time and money later on. These areas and questions are meant to guide the direction of the research.[28]

Need. Will this product/service be serving customers' real needs? What is the overall market for the business? Are there special niches that can be exploited?

Niche/competition. What is different about the product or service that will cause the customer to choose it over the competition's product or service?

Proprietary questions. Can the product/service be patented or copyrighted? Is it unique enough to get a significant head start on the competition? Can the process be easily copied? Will the business concept be developed and licensed to others or developed and sold?

Cost and manufacture. How much will the customer be willing to spend for the product/service? How much will materials and labor time cost? How much will be needed in the future? Now?

Advertisement and packaging. What type of advertising and promotional plans will be used to market the product/service? Will the promotional methods be traditional or more innovative?

> "Find a need of the consumer that is currently not getting met, or inadequately met, and fill that need in a way that is appealing to the consumer and profitable for you."
>
> Pamela Pommerenke
> *Assistant professor,*
> *Department of*
> *Management,*
> *Michigan State*
> *University*

Sales. What distributions and sales methods will be used? Will the reliance be on independent sales representatives, company sales force, direct mail, door-to-door sales, supermarkets, service stations, or company-owned stores? Or will you rely almost entirely on Internet and social media marketing and sales?

Transport. How will the product/service be transported—via company-owned trucks, common carriers, postal service, airfreight, or over the Internet using an existing portal and system such as Amazon?

Employees. Can the company attract employees with the necessary skills to operate the business venture? Who are the workers? Are they dependable, competent, and readily available?

Start with Data Collection

The entrepreneur needs to find answers to the key questions, identified above, about the potential business. Data collection can come from a variety of sources. The sources to provide data collection are given in Figure 2.5. The more sources that are consulted, the more valid the results will be. However, it is not advisable to go overboard; the amount of available data can become overwhelming. Basically, the questions should be as specific as possible, the sources as relevant as possible, and the data collection as extensive as needed for the initial investment and planning to run smoothly.

Design and Execute a Study to Get the Answers

Once secondary sources of data have been exhausted, the entrepreneur must identify secondary resources to support the preliminary research. This is the stage when the entrepreneur should consult directly with existing business owners and experts in the field and ask pertinent, key questions.

The entrepreneur should target a small number of representative businesses. First, the entrepreneur must identify companies with similar products or services and inquire as to who may be willing to

Experts in the field	Contact well-known entrepreneurs to get advice.
Internet searches	Visit web sites on companies and new products or technologies.
Library research	Use college libraries to access references and specialized biographies.
Questionnaires/surveys	Use the mail, phone, Internet, or professional interviews. Write and prepare questions to make sure you collect appropriate data.
Existing research	Use investment banking firms, advisory searches, or consulting firms to gather data on existing research.
Trade associations	Visit trade shows and read trade publications.
Market research firms	Hire a firm to prepare a report or market survey for the proposed idea.

FIGURE 2.5
Sources for Finding Information

give advice or provide the names of other contacts without wasting a lot of time and money. Remember that the purpose of this exercise is to start a business, not to become a research expert.

Once the participants have been identified, solicit information from them to answer the key questions, which should be based on the most unbiased model available. To eliminate receiving questionable data, certain pitfalls must be avoided:

- Ensure that all of the participants are asked the same questions in the same manner.

- Get detailed—make certain that the answers are accurate by maintaining a precise, objective method of questioning.

- Train and monitor survey recorders and telephone interviewers to ensure consistent results.

Analyze the Data

What do the data reveal? How can they be interpreted? Examine the secondary sources that have been queried. How did the survey participants interpret their results? Write a final report modeled on the most thorough sources. This ensures that a record exists for the future and that others in the organization can refer to the study as necessary.

This may all sound too extensive—and expensive. Many entrepreneurs must do their market research with limited funds. Employ these cost-cutting recommendations:

- Use search engines, web pages, and online databases.

- Use social media methods to access potential customers.

- Use the telephone instead of mail surveys and door-to-door interviewing.

- Avoid research in high-cost cities.

- Test more than one product or service at a time.

- Avoid collecting unnecessary data.

One example of an inexpensive source is a local university. Professors and students are often involved in projects to help small companies develop marketing plans and undertake market research. Other examples include friends and relatives who own their own businesses, published interviews with successful entrepreneurs, and library resources. More detailed discussions on digital market research methods can be found in Chapter 4.

Phase 3: Develop the Plan

Once an opportunity has been identified, decisions must be made regarding performance and staffing. Who is going to do what? How will decisions be made? The result of the business plan should fully capitalize on all of the company's assets while maintaining flexibility. It also should be sufficiently broad to incorporate unexpected changes in the aim for success and profitability.

A business plan charts the current and future components of the business in about thirty to forty pages. Similar to a map, it should answer some basic questions. How far will the business have to go? What is the exact destination or goal? How will the destination be reached? What is the anticipated arrival time at each of the various stops or milestones? A good plan will do the following:

- Determine the viability of the business and application in selected markets.

- Provide guidance in planning and organizing the activities and goals.

- Serve as a vehicle to obtain financing and personnel for the business.

The business plan is the backbone of the business. This single document guides the entrepreneur at three critical junctures:

1. It simplifies decision making during *times of crisis*.

2. It is the roadmap at *points of indecision*.

3. It is a motivational guide during *setbacks or downturns*.

An extremely valuable outcome of preparing and writing an outline plan at this stage is identifying flaws and creating contingencies. The business plan compels the entrepreneur to carefully examine the prospective venture at its initial planning stage before significant capital has been invested.

If the plan reveals insurmountable flaws, the entrepreneur may need to abandon that particular opportunity. Although it is discouraging to return to the idea stage, consider two facts:

1. The groundwork has been laid, and the initial learning curve has been completed.

2. Only a relatively small amount of time and capital have been invested.

The entrepreneur should not ignore serious misgivings. Walking away at this stage and beginning again with a new idea and a strong attitude will impress investors and others already involved with the project.

A more detailed version of a full business plan is found in Chapter 6, but the entrepreneur can greatly benefit from considering these basic elements now.

Phase 4: Determine the Resources Needed

All businesses must address resource capabilities to foster venture development. However, for a start-up venture that uses new technology for its service or as its product, it is crucial. The new business must have the skills to match—and triumph over—the competition. Much like Darwin's survival of the fittest, in the business world, only the highly skilled will survive.

This section examines three aspects of assessing resource capabilities:

1. Personal contacts and networking
   Resources are needed to identify, contact, and establish a network with appropriate clients and vendors. Who will devote time to meeting people by traveling? Phone work? E-mail correspondence? Use of social networks? Time for networking may be a daily task, high on a priority list. (Do the management exercise Q.1 at the end of Chapter 1 if you have not already done so for more on networking.)

2. Financing requirements
   Sufficient capital is required to sustain the company for a specific length of time, possibly a one- or two-year period. The entrepreneur must carefully consider the financial elements required for implementing the plan. Begin by answering the following questions:

   • How much initial capital is needed?

   • What resources are available for financial support?

   • How long can the new business be self-financed, if necessary, and still withstand initial losses?

   • How long will it take to make the business profitable?

- What kind of profit margin will eventually result from the product or service? How can the revenue and financial model be presented to investors for their involvement in the business?

- After initial financing, new investors may be approached at a later date for further infusions of capital.

You will study the details of financing in Chapter 8.

3. Sources of technical skills
   The entrepreneur may have an idea but not possess the creative process and innovative technical skills to implement it. In that case, external skilled labor is needed. This may be someone the entrepreneur already knows, such as a coworker, or he or she might need to hire someone through want ads or an employment agency. Training costs need to be calculated into start-up costs. Furthermore, someone may be needed who can translate technical jargon to simplified terms for investors.

Phase 5: Manage the Business

So far, in this chapter, we've evaluated the opportunity, begun developing the plan, and assessed resource needs. Phase 5 entails running the business, applying a specific management structure and style to any questions, and handling difficulties and roadblocks to successes that may arise. The emphasis here is on the act of investing. Substantial time, money, experience, and energy have been invested in setting up. Now, the entrepreneur needs to break off from the path blazed by the most successful businesses and invest in people, operating procedures, and information technology. This involves the following two events:

1. Deliver a total solution
   Traditionally, small companies have assumed unchallenged territory and special distribution channels for their products. Today, however, all companies are playing in the same markets and providing the entire range of services for their customers. Investors and customers want to buy a total solution product or service.

2. Cultivate advanced resources
   The large-scale layoffs of highly skilled workers from major corporations create an important opportunity for a start-up company. These trained and effective personnel are looking to apply their business skills and experiences to start-ups. The results to the business include access to small companies and major corporations, capital, and productive market knowledge.

   Consider an example of a new technology that effectively transformed day-to-day services and how a business plan was crucial in making that opportunity a business reality.

Use the Framework to Evaluate and Test the Five-Phase Opportunity Concept

Now that we have completed the five phases of the opportunity analysis, use this framework to evaluate the issues that are stronger or weaker for the market, competition, management team, and financial requirements for the new business concept.[29]

Figures 2.6 to 2.9 list in greater detail the factors to be considered in each of these four categories.

Criterion	Stronger Opportunity	Weaker Opportunity
Need	Identified	Unclear
Customers	Reachable; receptive	Unreachable or loyalties established
Payback to user/customer	Less than one year	Three years or more
Product life cycle	Long, easier to recover investment	Short, difficult to recover investment
Industry structure	Weak or emerging competition	Aggressively competitive
Total available market	$100 million	Less than $10 million
Market growth rate	30 to 50 percent	Contracting or less than 10 percent
Gross margins	30 to 60+ percent	Less than 20 percent; volatile
Market share attainable (year 5)	20 percent or more	Less than 5 percent

FIGURE 2.6
Framework for Evaluating an Opportunity: Market Issues

Criterion	Stronger Opportunity	Weaker Opportunity
Profits after tax	10 to 15 percent or more; durable	Less than 5 percent; fragile
Time to: 　　Break even 　　Positive cash flow ROI potential	Less than 2 years Less than 2 years 25 percent or more per year	More than 3 years More than 3 years Less than 15 to 20 percent per year
Value Capital requirements	High strategic value Low to moderate; fundable	Low strategic value Very high; unfundable
Exit mechanism	Present or envisioned harvest options	Undefined; illiquid investment

FIGURE 2.7
Framework for Evaluating an Opportunity: Financial and Harvest Issues

Criterion	Stronger Opportunity	Weaker Opportunity
Fixed and variable costs Production, marketing distribution	Lowest	Highest
Degree of control Prices, channels of resources/distribution	Moderate to strong	Weak
Barriers to entry Proprietary protection Response/lead time	Yes 6 months to 1 year	None None
Legal contractual advantage	Proprietary or exclusivity	None
Sources of differentiation	Numerous	Few or none
Competitors' mindset and strategies	Live and let live; not self-destructive	Defensive and strongly reactive

FIGURE 2.8
Framework for Evaluating an Opportunity: Competitive Advantage Issues

Criterion	Stronger Opportunity	Weaker Opportunity
Management team	Existing, strong, proven performance	Weak, inexperienced, lacking key skills
Contacts and networks	Well developed, highquality, acceptable	Crude, limited, inaccessible
Risk	Low	High
Fatal blows	None	One or more

FIGURE 2.9
Framework for Evaluating an Opportunity: Management Team and Risk Issues

The most successful entrepreneurs know where they fit in the market and where they want to be. The framework plan should account for and accommodate changes in designing, testing, and marketing to prepare for the business opportunity. The issues that need to be described in more detail should include determining the improvement needed and anticipating the necessary time frames and how to remain competitive at all times.

Know How to Protect the Idea or Product

One question that might be encountered while conducting research and formulating a business plan is whether or not the idea/opportunity/product/service needs to be protected. The following evaluation screening identifies those conditions under which an idea may qualify for patent protection. See Chapter 13 for more details on patent protection.

Evaluation Screening for Patent Protection

1. Is the service, product, or idea unique to get a head start on the competition?

2. Does the service or product represent a breakthrough (either high tech or different from others)?

3. Is the field changing so slowly that the innovation will be valuable for at least ten years?

4. Have other, less expensive but adequate protective measures been explored?

5. Has an attorney discussed the options and recommended that a patent be pursued?

6. Is the fee for a patent search and application affordable?

If the answer to two or more of these questions was "yes," patent protection for the idea and opportunity should be seriously considered. However, if a disclosure document, which essentially protects the idea for the first year, will suffice, then that option should be considered first. What about marketing this idea to a large company as a customer? Most companies have their own internal R&D organization dedicated to monitoring and meeting the needs of their product or service lines. The best method for submitting an idea is to contact the company and ask for its disclosure conditions to review an idea.

Some companies, however, will sign a nondisclosure form, whereas others will not. Most will have their own protection form, which essentially states that, while they may agree to review or discuss an idea, their research department may have already thought of the idea long before. Let an attorney have the last word. Get a second (or even a third) legal opinion before committing to any legal expenditure. See Chapter 13 for more on these legal issues.

SUMMARY

Entrepreneurs must be comfortable with continuous innovation. They must understand the different categories and create their own personal frameworks for identifying new ideas and building on them. Innovation applies not only to a new product but to the business methods necessary to turn an idea into a sustainable, profitable business. Every business starts from an embryonic idea that is first analyzed to test whether it offers a real opportunity. If so, it is then built up until a complete business model to commercialize the idea has been designed.

Ideas can come from many sources. They can be a result of an entrepreneur's own innovation, which is best accomplished using some simple analytical frameworks, or they can be found in searching the Internet or in observing points of pain. Some good opportunities are the result of assembling what might at first seem to be unrelated ideas.

Generally, a great deal of useful information is readily available. Often, market research objectives must be modified to use available information. In some cases, the entrepreneur may choose to survey the market to acquire data designed specifically to fit the project's needs. In every case, the entrepreneur must apply some judgment to the data while trying to project future prospects.

Once this step is completed, the planning and developing process starts. All ideas must be further screened and evaluated to determine the feasibility of the opportunity. The best ideas are evaluated through test marketing and defining the resources to successfully launch the business.

STUDY QUESTIONS

Q.1 Why is innovation important, and how is it changing?

Q.2 What are the main two types of innovation? Give two examples of each type.

Q.3 What is meant by a "disruptive innovation?" Name two.

Q.4 What are the various ways to generate business ideas?

Q.5 Briefly describe the various methods of researching a business opportunity.

Q.6 List the five phases to complete an opportunity analysis.

Q.7 When does an idea need to be protected?

Q.8 Describe the evaluation screening process.

Q.9 Why do you think Dell was successful when other companies trying the same model failed?

EXERCISES

2.1 Finding an Idea and Turning It into an Opportunity

Go to the book's web site, www.wiley.com/college/kaplan, and browse a number of idea source web sites from the three lists. Use these as starters and browse until you find an idea that you think has merit for creating a business opportunity. Write a one-page synopsis of the idea, explaining why you think it is a good idea and how you would use it to build a business opportunity argument.

2.2 Preparing an Opportunity Cost Analysis

RJL Technologies provides custom services to its loyalty customers from Monday through Friday. David Lee, the coowner, believes it is important for the employees to have Saturday and Sunday off to spend with their families. However, he also recognizes that this policy has implications for profitability, and he is considering staying open on Saturday.

David estimates that if the company stays open on Saturday, it can generate revenue of $2,500 each day for fifty-two days per year. The incremental daily costs will be $500 for labor, $50 for transportation, and $150 for an office manager. The costs do not include a portion of monthly rent.

David would like to know the opportunity cost of not working on Saturday. Provide an estimate of the opportunity cost and explain why you do not have to consider rent in your estimate.

Management Exercise: Evolution of an Idea If you have not read the appendix in Chapter 1, do so then go to the book's web site and read diary entries Prequel and Months 2, 15, 18, 27, 31, 40, 41, 47, and 57 and view the video entitled "Seven Degrees of Separation." Either as a team or individually, produce a presentation on the following questions for class discussion. Only one or two slides are required to state the key points, which will then be expanded in class.

Master-Case Exercise Q1: Trace the evolution of Neoforma's products from the earliest idea to a commercial product or service. Include the false turns and abandoned ideas. What type of innovation was employed by Neoforma? Who outside the company had a major influence on the product developments? What lessons can you learn from the Neoforma case concerning the evolution of an idea from conception to a business opportunity?

INTERACTIVE LEARNING ON THE WEB

Test your knowledge of the chapter using the book's interactive web site.

ADDITIONAL RESOURCES

- **Office.com (www.office.com):** "This new way we work."
- **Digitalwork.com (www.digitalwork.com):** "Your business workshop."
- **Onvia.com (www.onvia.com):** "The premiere e-marketplace for small businesses."
- **Ideacafe.com:** "A fun approach to serious business."
- **Smartonline.com (www.smartonline.com):** "Small-business answers from small-business owners."
- **Workzsites.com (www.workzsites.com):** "Helping small businesses grow and prosper online."
- **Entrepreneurship (www.entrepreneurship.org):** "A world of resources for entrepreneurs."
- **Small Business Administration (www.sba.gov):** "Helping small businesses to succeed."

APPENDIX THE BAYH–DOLE ACT (ONLINE)

ENDNOTES

1. See Walter Isaacson, *Steve Jobs: A Biography* (New York: Simon and Schuster, 2011).

2. This profile was constructed from the company's web site and articles about the founders. Learn more about how SmartPak started and grew at www.smartpakequine.com and the analogous human services at www.cardinal.com/us/en/pharmacysolutions/.

3. For a number of examples and insights illustrating how global trends are impacting the business world, see Thomas L. Friedman, *The World is Flat* (New York: Farrar, Strauss and Giroux, 2005).

4. See www.miniwatts.com for the most recent data.

5. See www.worldwidewebsize.com/.

6. See http://royal.pingdom.com/.

7. Information on international trade can be found at www.wto.org.

8. See *Wall Street Journal*, August 4, 2004, "A Look At Market-Moving Numbers—Literally." Since then, cross-border currency trading has grown significantly.

9. See Phil Muncaster, "China and India scoop 17% of venture capital cash," Posted in "*Business*," May 14, 2012, www.theregister.co.uk/2012/05/14/vcindiachinasiliconvalley/.

10. The observation was made in 1965 by Gordon Moore, cofounder of Intel, that the number of transistors per square inch on an integrated circuit doubled every year since invention. Currently, data density is still doubling about every 18 months.

11. Conversation with Hans-Günther Hohmann, General Manager HP, Germany, August, 2000.

12. See John Teresko, "The PLM Revolution," *Industry Week* (January 2004).

13. "Innovation Models in the 21st Century," a project funded by the National Institute of Science and Technology, by G. Susman, and A.C. Warren, published in 2005. It can be found at www.smeal.psu.edu/fcfe.

14. See Nirmal Pal and Daniel Panteleo, *The Agile Corporation* (New York: Springer Press, 2005).

15. See William J. Baumol, *The Free Market Innovation Machine* (Princeton, NJ: Princeton University Press, 2002). There is an excellent short white paper on Baumol's ideas entitled "Entrepreneurship, Innovation and Growth: The David-Goliath Symbiosis," *Journal of Entrepreneurial Finance and Business Ventures* 7, no. 2 (Fall 2002): 1–10.

16. See Alan Afuah, *Innovation Management: Strategies, Implementation, and Profits* (New York: Oxford University Press, 1998).

17. The Blyth web site, www.blyth.com, is a good place to learn how the humble candle can be "innovated" into a global business.

18. See "What Happened to Blockbuster?" www.huffingtonpost.com/news/blockbuster-bankruptcy/.

19. Clayton Christensen has written extensively about "disruptive innovations" and the difficulty that large companies have in dealing with them. See *The Innovator's Dilemma* (Cambridge: Harvard University

Press, 1997) and *The Innovator's Solution* (Boston: Harvard Business School Publishing Corporation, 2003).

20. See William J. Baumol, *The Free Market Innovation Machine* (Princeton, NJ: Princeton University Press, 2002).

21. From the U.S. Small Business Administration Report, *The State of Small Business: A Report of the President* (Washington, DC: U.S. Government Printing Office, 1995), 114.

22. In 2000, Korea's LG Electronics, Inc., launched an Internet-enabled refrigerator, followed by an Internet-ready washing machine in what it expects will eventually be a family of Net-ready home appliances. The Internet LG Turbo Drum washing machine can connect to the Internet to download new programs to match new fabrics. In addition, according to Merloni, another appliance maker, "in the case of [our] washing machines, smart RFID tags on clothes will enable the appliances to select the washing program appropriate to the items in the load. If any incompatible fabrics end up in the drum, such as whites with colored items being washed for the first time, the display will tell the consumer which items to take out."

23. Whirlpool's Global Director of Energy and Sustainability, Warrick Sterling, stated in February 2011, "Consumers [sic] expectations have changed, where they expect things around them to be connected." Whirlpool is developing a range of Internet-connected home appliances.

24. "How Netflix Reversed Engineered Hollywood." Alexis C. Madrigal, Atlantic Magazine, Jan 2014.

25. See Jack M. Kaplan, *Getting Started in Entrepreneurship*, 2nd ed. (New York: John Wiley & Sons, 2001), 20–23.

26. See Rita McGrath and Ian Macmillan, *The Entrepreneurial Mindset* (Boston: Harvard Business School Press, 2000), 17–18.

27. See James Jiambalvo, *Managerial Accounting* (New York: John Wiley & Sons, 2001), 9.

28. See Jack M. Kaplan, *Smart Cards: The Global Information Passport* (Boston: International Thomson Computer Press, 1996), 15–17.

29. See Jeffry A. Timmons and S. Spinelli, *New Venture Creation* (Boston: Irwin McGraw Hill, 2006), 119–121.

Ideas into Business Models

3

"Architecture is one part science, one part craft, and two parts art."

David Rutten, Software Designer

OBJECTIVES

- Learn the importance of business models.
- Understand the key components of the Business Model Canvas.
- Learn how to apply the canvas to improve the venture.
- Use the Minimum Viable Product model to engage customers.
- Uncover value in supply chains.
- Use databases to engage and lock in customers.
- Compare licensing and franchising.
- Understand network models.
- Explore corporate partnering.

CHAPTER OUTLINE

Introduction

Profile: Alexander Osterwalder—Inventor of Canvas Model

Definition of Business Models

The Business Model Canvas

Testing Assumptions and Value Proposition

Mini-Case: "tinyUpdates"—Testing Your Idea with Customers

Minimum Viable Product Concept

Mini-Case: BreatheSimple "Smokescreen" Product Launch

Examples of Innovative Business Models

Mini-Case Business Model Example: DBI Using Data Collection

Mini-case: General Fasteners, Locking in Customers

Introduction

In the previous chapter, you learned about innovation—categories and frameworks for creating new ideas. The ideas were converted into possible business opportunities by using screening tools and then undertaking an initial opportunity analysis for feasibility. The focus was on product or service *ideas*. This chapter goes further into how these opportunities are packaged into novel business models. Designing a powerful business model requires blending all the aspects of the business into an integrated system where manufacturing, marketing, information, suppliers and customers, product development, and so on become one. This is not easy and requires the entrepreneur to build a way of thinking into the company—its culture—so continuous innovation becomes a daily routine. (How to build such a culture is dealt with in Chapter 9.)

This chapter covers business model design and implementation. After introducing a useful framework for thinking about business models, we rely heavily on examples to help you understand what is meant by an innovative model. We will examine how the Business Model Canvas can work as a blueprint for your business and help you create value for our business. Not only will the Canvas' nine sections provide you with tools to analyze your current idea, but it will help you recognize when you may need to "pivot" or adjust the idea or innovate further. Because there are almost as many novel business models as there are companies, rather than try to catalog them, we will present examples that will stimulate you as you plan your own company for growth. We will introduce different ideas that can be incorporated into a business model, learning how to capture value from suppliers and deciding when to use licensing or franchising. We also introduce the concept of the Minimum Viable Product (MVP) which is a method that can be used to test customers' likes and dislikes about your product before you devote too many resources to develop the "all singing and dancing" version which may not match market needs. Using the canvas model and the MVP in tandem helps to ensure that your first product is more likely to be successful and you won't have wasted time and money on the wrong idea in a poor business model.

"Someday, on the corporate balance sheet, there will be an entry which reads, 'Information'; for in most cases, the information is more valuable than the hardware which processes it."

Grace Murray
Hoppe*r*

ROADMAP

| IN ACTION | So now that you have examined your idea feasibility, it is time to embed it into a unique business model that will enable you to build a sustainable competitive position. |

Profile: Alexander Osterwalder—Inventor of Canvas Model

Alexander Osterwalder born in 1974 is an entrepreneur, speaker, and business model innovator. Together with Professor Yves Pigneur, he invented the Business Model Canvas, a practical tool to visualize, challenge, and (re)invent business models. The Canvas is used by leading organizations around the world, like GE, Procter & Gamble (P&G), Ericsson, and 3M. Alexander is a frequent keynote speaker and has held guest lectures in top universities around the world, including Stanford, Berkeley, MIT, IESE, and IMD. The Business Model Foundry, his current start-up, is building strategic tools for innovators. Strategyzer.com and the Business Model Toolbox for iPad are the Foundry's first applications. Alexander holds a PhD from HEC Lausanne, Switzerland, and is a founding member of The Constellation, a global not-for-profit organization aiming to make HIV/AIDS and malaria history.

Definition of Business Models

A business model provides a framework in which entrepreneurs can examine their business plans and explore alternative ways for their companies to function and grow profitably while building barriers to ward off competitors. It is more than a business strategy, for it describes how the different functions within a company work harmoniously together to build "more than the sum of the parts." The following definition captures the meaning: "A business model is a description of how your company intends to create value in the marketplace. It includes that unique combination of products, services, image, and distribution that your company carries forward. It also includes the underlying organization of people, and the operational infrastructure that they use to accomplish their work."[1]

A more concise summary definition can be stated as follows: "A business model is the way a company applies knowledge to capture value."[2] Note the emphasis on *capturing value*. Establishing value for your customers, and suppliers too, and building a company that can hold on to this value are key to optimizing your business model. The greatest inventions may not be able to retain the value that they can provide. For example, imagine that you have invented a simple instrument, costing less than a thousand dollars, to detect the early stages of Alzheimer's disease long before symptoms are detectable. Your test can enable preventive medication to be used to delay major patient needs for care and support for up to ten years. The value of this is clearly enormous, not only in financial terms but also in social benefits too. Ten years of *not* requiring full support could easily add up to hundreds of thousands of dollars. Yet who will pay you for your invention at a price that will reflect a major part of the value you are promising: patients, doctors, pharmaceutical companies, family members, health insurers, or the government? None of these potential customers has a way of paying you for the value you can provide, and it requires a really novel business model to do so. Perhaps you have some ideas on how to do this. When you review the examples in this chapter, think about how the companies have designed their businesses to both capture value and protect themselves against competitive attacks.

ROADMAP

| IN ACTION | Learn to question why some businesses are much more successful than others. Ask whether they have a unique business model that prevents competitors from taking away their customers. What is unique about what they do? Why do other companies have a problem competing? Try to see how their ideas might translate into your business. |

The Business Model Canvas

This technique is based on research work done by Alexander Osterwalder.[3] The framework (see Figure 3.1) has nine key topics to consider when exploring different business models. It is recommended that this be used in team sessions.

Often, the idea of writing an in-depth business plan and the time it takes are enough to deter you from actually sitting down and doing it. Questions like is my idea good enough, feasible, or profitable, how will it be structured, and so on need to be answered. These seem to be insurmountable obstacles and unanswerable questions leading to the question of "where do I start?" This may demotivate you from actually commencing.

The Business Model Canvas is a tool you can use to flush out your idea and get over the paralysis. It is a methodology to follow to create and think through the business model for your idea. Not only will the Canvas provide you with tools to analyze your current idea, but it will help you recognize when you may need to "pivot," or adjust, your business idea or innovate further. As Alexander Osterwalder and Yves Pigneur describe it in their book *Business Model Generation*, "this model can become a shared language that allows you to easily describe and manipulate business models to create new strategic alternatives. Without such a shared language it is difficult to systematically challenge assumptions about one's business model and innovate successfully." Indeed, more and more entrepreneurs are shifting from using a full business plan to using the canvas to communicate with potential investors, bankers, and other stakeholders.

Let's see how the Business Model Canvas can work as a blueprint for your business. As an analogy, when you start to build a house, you need a blueprint to plan how it should look, guide contractors on where everything should go, and the order in which it should be built. It would be unthinkable to start building without such a blueprint to get everyone on the same page. The same is true for your business. The Business Model Canvas is the first step in structuring a full business plan.

The Canvas uses nine basic building blocks as you can see in Figure 3.1. We will discuss each of the nine building blocks in more depth.

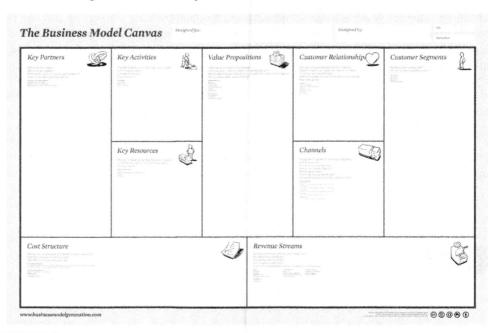

FIGURE 3.1
The Business Model Canvas

Start by filling out each of the nine areas. This helps to visually see and record your ideas. Don't worry if you don't know exactly what to write down in each box, which is the point of the exercise; it helps you understand what you think you know and also what questions which need to be answered. Just write everything down so that you can remember to address it. You will then work on each area in more detail to polish the blueprint once you see how everything fits together.

The Nine Areas

Customer segments are different groups of people or organizations your business is trying to reach. If you are going to build a profitable business, you need customers who are willing to pay for your goods or services. Start by identifying the customers you are targeting. You will need to have a clear understanding of their needs in order to fulfill them adequately. You may have only one group of customers or several groups of customers. Initially, you may be unsure of exactly who your customers are, but as you refine your Canvas, you will be able to hone in who your customers are more specifically and develop a more precise understanding of their needs.

Value propositions are the reasons the customer segment(s) will use your products or services instead of those from a competitor. Describe what you are offering to your specific customer segment(s). What customer problem are you solving? What value are you providing? Some value propositions may be innovative and represent a new or disruptive offer. Others may be similar to existing market offers, but with added features and attributes or at significant cost savings. This area is extremely important. Really hone in and understand what value you are creating and offering to your customers; this is the heart of why customers will use your product or service over your competitors.

Channels are the means you communicate with your customer segment(s) to deliver your value proposition. Through specific channels, you are able to not only raise awareness about your products or services but also offer ways in which your customer segments can interact with your organization. This could be from purchasing your products or services, providing customer support, or even providing a mechanism to collect customer feedback. Figure 3.2 shows the different channel phases and each of the questions you can begin to think about and answer. The Internet will most likely be one of your channels, and more discussion on this topic can be found in Chapter 4.

Channel Types			Channel Phases				
Own	Direct	Sales force					
		Web sales	**1. Awareness**	**2. Evaluation**	**3. Purchase**	**4. Delivery**	**5. After sales**
		Own stores	How do we raise awareness about our company's products and services?	How do we help customers evaluate our organization's Value Proposition?	How do we allow customers to purchase specific products and services?	How do we deliver a Value Proposition to customers?	How do we provide post-purchase customer support?
Partner	Indirect	Partner stores					
		Wholesaler					

FIGURE 3.2
Channel Phases
Source: http://www.businessmodelgeneration.com/

Customer relationships describe how you interact with and are perceived by your customer segments. Understand if your customers' expectations are personal and hands-on or a more automated relationship or even at a self-service level with very little interaction.

Revenue streams are the sources of income that you generate from customer segments. Incomes derive from delivering a value proposition at prices that customers are willing to pay. Multiple customer segments can deliver several revenue streams. Some of the questions that you can ask to better understand your revenue streams are as follows: "For what do they currently pay and how? How would they prefer to pay? How much does each revenue stream contribute to overall revenues? Is a sale a one-time event or are there ongoing revenues from a single customer? How long is the sales cycle?"

Key resources are the assets needed to deliver your value proposition(s). They can be physical, financial, intellectual, or human. They can be owned or leased or acquired from partners. If you are a product manufacturing company, physical assets to actually produce that product are going to be critical key resources, whereas if you are a service-based organization, personnel may be your key resource. Think about the resources for delivering your value proposition but also those required for other Canvas areas to function adequately. For example, your business model may rely heavily on brand recognition or new technology, which would need to be protected by patents and/or trademarks. (See Chapter 13 for more on this topic.)

Key activities are the critical actions needed to execute your business model successfully. Like key resources, they are required to create and offer a value proposition, reach markets, maintain customer relationships, and earn revenues. Key activities differ depending on business model type; Microsoft's key activities include software development, Dell must include supply chain management, and for McKinsey, they include problem solving.

Key partnerships are those noncustomer relationships necessary to execute the business model. Often, it is more cost-effective or efficient to forge partnerships to cut down on costs, take advantage of economies of scale, or even mitigate competitive risks. These partnerships can be, for example, a supplier which provides raw materials you need or other organizations that to which you outsource in order to reduce fixed costs. For example, insurers rely on independent brokers to sell policies rather than investing in an in-house sales force.

Cost structure is the main costs incurred in order to execute your business model. It is important to understand the main cost drivers within your business model because once you subtract these costs from your revenues, there needs to be a profit left! Your business may be competing on a low-cost structure, which would mean that your costs must be kept extremely low in order to pass that value on to your customers.[4]

Testing Assumptions and Value Proposition

You have now created your "first-cut" Canvas Model, but your work is not done. This is a working document that will be continually refined as you conduct customer interviews, undertake market research, and refine your idea. The next step in the development and evolution toward a refined Business Model Canvas is to start testing your assumptions and hypotheses. You need to talk to potential customers, suppliers, distributors, competitors, and so on and ask some of the questions outlined in the nine areas to better understand where you need to adjust your business model.

The most critical first step is to define who exactly are your customers.

Questions to ask yourself are the following:

1. Who are our customers, and how do we contribute to the value proposition that they are seeking?

2. How do we relate to these selected customers?

3. How do we segment these customers, and which are the most valuable to us?

4. How do we get to these customers?

5. Where are the major costs in reaching these customers? For our resources? For our activities?

Once you have defined your target customer segment(s), it is important to now talk to a few of these potential customers. Here, you will learn if the value proposition that you plan to offer is something your customers want, need, and are willing to pay for. It is at this juncture that you may learn that your value proposition is addressing something that is lacking in the market or alternatively you may find that you are offering something that your customers don't really want or aren't willing to pay for. You most likely will have to reconsider both what you plan to offer while redefining your first target customers and business model. This actual illustration demonstrates the processes involved.

Mini-Case: "tinyUpdates"—Testing Your Idea with Customers[5]

After graduating from Columbia University's Executive MBA program, Elizabeth Lott wanted to start her own company. With partner Tara Leininger, they had the idea to develop a "universal online registry for gifts." She engaged with potential customers in stages, learning from them and revising her business model along the way.

First Stage

Elizabeth started out believing she had a million-dollar idea for a consolidated online gift registry web site. The notion was that the current online gift registry environment is fragmented with every gift registry web site (and there are many) offering something just a little bit different. There was no single site making it easy to register for gifts from any retailer for any occasion and to easily share that registry with others. Elizabeth believed that aggregating the online gift registry process into a "one-stop shop" would become the preferred landing site not only for weddings and baby showers but also for bar mitzvahs, graduations, or any occasion!

Figure 3.3 shows the first Canvas attempt for the universal registry concept.

Second Stage

After filling out the Business Model Canvas, she started interviewing people about the online registries they used and their experiences with them. She quickly learned two critical things about her targeted customers. First, a large part of the market felt it was inappropriate and would feel awkward about sharing a registry for anything other than a wedding. Second, while some people acknowledged that most online registries available were cumbersome and generally didn't fulfill all of their needs, those needs were not very strong, urgent, or critical. It soon became clear that she was trying to create a business around something the potential customer base wouldn't consider using or really didn't feel they needed.

ROADMAP

IN ACTION	Don't commit the time and effort to write a full and detailed business plan until you have identified a strong value proposition that appeals to a defined customer group.

Key partners	Key activities	Value proposition	Customer relationships	Customer segment

• Large Department Stores
• Small Boutique Stores
• PayPal/Google Checkout
• Social Media Sites
• Party and Wedding planners/websites
• Search engines and existing ecommerce sites:
  - Google
  - Amazon
  - Yahoo
 	
• Specific women's publications like style.com to form partnership for customer base/leverage contacts
	• Website Development
	• Marketing, Customer acquistion and Increase partner network
	• Establish Ecommerce capabilities
	
	Key resources
	• Social Networking sites
	• Web Developer
	• On-line marketing consultant/team
		• Free & seamless personal organizational tool for registry system
		• Ability to maintain personal list of items you want.
		• Ability to categorize list and share with on-line social network.
		• Ability to add items to list that aren't online
		• Increased customer base for online retailers and small boutique stores without a web presence
		• Using PriceGrabber type softwar: Ability to find cheapest option for the things you want
			• GET - Search Ads, Social Media, word-of-mouth, partner relationships
			
			• KEEP – continually add new functionality to enhance user experience and maintain relevance in the space
			
			• GROW – promoting the referral network of current users (incentives); propaganda encouraging existing users to add to wish lists
			
			Channels
			• Customer's Social Media Networks: Facebook, Twitter, Pinterest
			• Retail Stores/Ecomm site
				• Mass market social media networks and users
				
				• Initial Market: target weddings and new births

Cost structure	Revenue streams
• Website and mobile app development/maintenance • Marketing costs to gain large user base	• Asset Sales - % of sales originating through website • Selling user data to retailers • Advertising on website • Free for users • Fees from vendors without registry capabilities in form of transaction fee

FIGURE 3.3
Universal Registry Idea Initial Business Model Canvas
Source: Elizabeth Lott.

However, Elizabeth, through the interviews, uncovered a need in another area. Many of the mothers interviewed stated that they were concerned about putting any information online about their child and wished, instead of a better online registry, that there was a better, more secure, and private online site to share pictures of their children. This led to a major "pivot" in the business idea and model.

Third Stage

Elizabeth and Tara reviewed the interview data and decided that it would be worthwhile to move from the original idea of an online universal gift registry to an online private photo sharing site geared toward parents. They went back to the Business Model Canvas and modified it to reflect the dramatic shift in direction.

ROADMAP

IN ACTION

Entrepreneurs need to listen to the feedback from the customer interviews and decide if the business idea is something to pursue or if the idea needs to pivot either by changing something subtle or dramatically. If the entrepreneur receives negative feedback from customers and after fully examining customer reactions to the product or service, a refinement of the idea will be needed.

Fourth Stage[6]

A basic web site was quickly launched with an option to submit an e-mail address to receive more information about the service. Through this basic web site, Elizabeth was able to gather more information on the idea and willingness to pay. A new name, "tinyUpdates," was conceived, and based on the input from the interviews and the "smokescreen" web site, the Canvas was modified as shown in Figure 3.4.

Minimum Viable Product Concept[7]

Elizabeth and Tara's basic web site enabled them to test their new concept and business model with an actual working system, which they could refine as they learned more about their customers' needs. This is an example of an MVP.

The MVP is considered a good approach to test a product's alignment with customer needs and expectations. The definition of this approach comes from Eric Ries, namely, "A Minimum Viable Product is that version of a new product which allows a team to collect the maximum amount of validated learning about customers with the least effort."[8]

The method of building quick inexpensive models and to learn about the desirability and viability of the product or service is through the MVP. The MVP allows the entrepreneur to build a minimum set of features for the product or service that brings the value proposition to life and allows testing with customers and partners. Using an MVP reduces risk and provides the best return on investment when launching a new product.

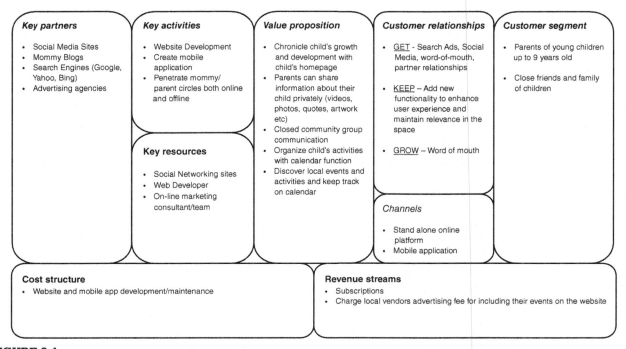

FIGURE 3.4
tinyUpdates Business Model Canvas—Final Version
Source: Elizabeth Lott

Entrepreneurs continually refine their products and business models through customer interviews, market research, and discussions with competitors, suppliers, and distributors. It is important to have many customer and marketplace discussions as to craft the "first cut" of the business model. Once achieved, the entrepreneur has early validation that a solution to a customer problem is of great value. Now begin to think about the best way to design and build the product.

Involving the customer early in the design process is consistent with the current lean start-up philosophy. Early product iterations allow a quick test of key business model assumptions and expected value. More importantly, it establishes an environment where the customer is actually co-creating the product, ensuring that the finished offering meets or exceeds marketplace expectations.

There is little debate that engaging the customer early in the design process is beneficial to the overall product development and launch process. However, entrepreneurs face many challenges in creating the product including, but not limited to, lack of technical expertise or domain knowledge, time pressures, and funding constraints. With this in mind, it is important to plan product design steps carefully and execute in small, focused increments. Let's break down the process into well-defined steps.

The Three-Step Process to Build a Minimum Viable Product[9]

Once you have conducted enough customer interviews to confidently define the problem and solution, you can begin early-stage product design and MVP development:

Step 1: Define the essential customer experience that the product needs to create in order to assess if the offering solves the problem in the way the customer values. From initial customer engagement, a shared understanding of the problem, solution, and value can be explored. Armed with this shared understanding, identify the minimum product features required to measure and validate.

Step 2: Next, decide on the best approach to illustrate the product's ability to solve the customer's problem. The initial MVP versions can take many forms such as sketches, graphic depictions or diagrams for physical products, web launch pages, screen mock-ups, and click-throughs for digital or software solutions. Later, MVP iterations take more functional forms such as scaled models, simple handmade or even 3D printed constructions, or working prototypes.

Step 3: As a final step, what measurements or metrics will be needed to validate the learning in this first MVP version? Asking customers to complete a short survey after they have reviewed and/or used the MVP is a perfectly good start.

After making these important design decisions, begin to build the first version of the product. Depending on the approach to illustrate the product, it is important to keep in mind that each iteration has a specific purpose. You must work hard to pare down your first version to the essential features required to test the problem and solution for the customer. This first version must focus on the primary problem and show that the product can solve that core issue. For this first version, you must eliminate any "nice-to-have" or nonessential features. As you receive customer feedback, you can add additional features to future product iterations. This focus is critical in the early product design stage. It reduces product development cycle time, eliminates distractions that might confound your testing results, and enables you to validate whether you have the right problem–solution for your customer prior to moving to the next iteration.

Customer Cocreation

Once the first MVP version is ready, it is time to engage the customer in what is sometimes referred to as "the customer cocreation process." Hopefully, this is not the first time you are interacting with potential customers. In fact, you should be building a network of early customers that are following you step by step. All the customers that you spoke with early while developing the first cut of your business model are perfect candidates for this phase of product engagement. In fact, customers that are following your progress and willing to engage you at each step are manifesting a strong interest in your product, an early validation itself.

In preparation to share your MVP and product information, there are ways that can make the customer cocreation process optimally effective. Start with a description of the problem you are trying to solve based on early customer engagement process. Even with customers that you have interviewed in the past, it is worth restating again, as your understanding of the problem has probably changed as you continually engage customers and the marketplace. Ask about the customer's experience when solving the problem, exposure to competitors' products, and what they continue to find challenging. Then, you can shift to the solution. Ask the customer to recommend how they would approach the solution. What would be valuable to them? Remember, stay open to customer ideas and do not bias the discussion with any preconceived notions.

Once you have solicited the customer's experience with the problem and solutions, show your early product version or MVP, describe core features, and ask for feedback. Remember, your MVP should provide visual stimulus or enable the customer to participate with actions whenever possible. Consider offering the customer a small selection of optional solutions, if feasible (Figure 3.5).

One method to test a potential product is to create a "smokescreen" product launch by drawing potential customers to a web site that outlines the product and seeks customer input

Mini-Case: BreatheSimple[10] "Smokescreen" Product Launch

As an early-stage company, Halare had limited funds to undertake extensive product development and market research but wished to determine whether the company could attract customers to its web site; whether, once there, they were likely to buy the product; and even what price they were willing to pay. With the advent of social networks coupled with search engine technology, such

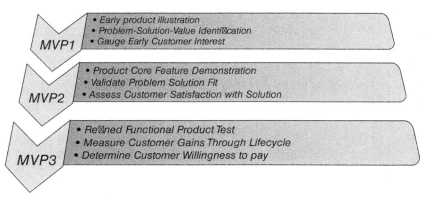

FIGURE 3.5
Minimum Viable Product Iterations
Source: Professor Jack McGourty

research can be automated and performed at minimal cost. The project goals were to cost-effectively gain web site traffic by creating a social networking presence and use this to gather customer information and preferences. The resources deployed by Halare were daily monitoring of the social networks, which took about fifteen minutes a day and $1,000 for "Google AdWords" campaign[11] to draw traffic to a simple web site, which the company called BreatheSimple.

The first task was to establish a Twitter account.[12] Twitter.com is a free, simple way to get in contact with customers. Users tweets to communicate to other users about a variety of experiences; tweets act much like online diary entries because they chronicle events as inconsequential as making a trip to the grocery story to others more significant, such as an asthma attack and the ensuing trip to the emergency room.[13] Furthermore, tweets are broadcast via e-mail or Twitter subscription to any other user that has chosen to *follow* or track the tweeter. From a marketing vantage, it is difficult to segment Twitter users based upon traditional demographics such as age, ethnic background, or financial status, as these are not always willingly provided or readily available. However, it is possible to identify potential customers based on behaviors and preferences. Tweets are searchable; a user can track any other Twitter user that has shown certain interests or demonstrated particular behavior patterns simply by entering keywords relevant to a desired search. For asthma, Halare identified "asthma," "nebulizer," and "inhaler" as keywords that will return a search that includes those users that fall within its target group. For depression treatment, the keywords will likely be much different. Take a look at the tracking page for BreatheSimple:

Breathe Simple
View my profile page

101   1,211   412
TWEETS   FOLLOWING   FOLLOWERS

Here are some sample "tweets" using the keywords:

 <3 #PSA: only way i can breathe while i sleep is if i use my **nebulizer** all night otherwise i cant breathe
about 8 hours ago from TwitterRide

 BountyHunter having a semi-asthma attack.,...breathing **nebulizer** isnt working...scared...cant breathe..
about 12 hours ago from web

 DenisNYCCouncil **Asthma attack** this morning is not how I wanted to start my day!
about 1 hour ago from UberTwitter

 ethegammer Took dogs out for a morning walk. Nice crisp day, which means of course that now I'm having trouble breathing. Thanks, **asthma**!
25 minutes ago from TweetDeck

 Ms_Gonzales http://twitpic.com/kd2k - Staying hm w/a sick baby 2day, she even had 2 get a **nebulizer** treatment frm the doc... :(
22 minutes ago from TwitPic

The second task was to drive traffic to the "Smoke-Screen" web site. This was done in two ways: first by attracting followers on the tweet network and sending tweets discussing the web site and its content and second by using a small Google AdWords campaign. You can do this by setting a maximum budget and varying keywords to see which are most effective in driving traffic to the web site that is shown here. Note the link to a survey and a place to provide e-mail contact addresses.

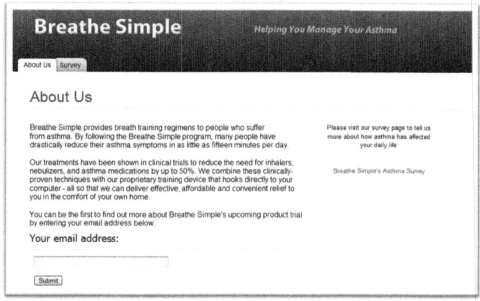

Source: Halare Inc.

Google also offers free software tools to monitor web site effectiveness called Google Analytics. These enabled Halare to monitor which keywords and tweets were the most efficient in driving traffic to the SmokeScreen site. Here is an example of typical results:

Once Halare had attracted potential customers to the web site, they were asked to fill out a short survey. The goal is to gather as much information as possible without asking too much of the visitor. Comparing the number of visitors to the site with the number that complete the survey *and* provide an e-mail contact address is a good indication of an expected *conversion rate* when the product is finally launched. Conversion rate is the percentage of site visitors that actually complete a purchase.

Here is the survey that Halare used in its first SmokeScreen campaign.

Tell us your name (only if you want to provide it)

[   ] [   ]

First   Last

How old are you?

- ⦿ Under 13
- ○ 20 - 29
- ○ 40 - 49
- ○ 60+

- ○ 13 - 19
- ○ 30 - 39
- ○ 50 - 59

Where are you from?

[United States ▼]

What's the worst part about having asthma? *

- ⦿ Inability to take part n the activities you enjoy
- ○ Anxiety or stress about having asthma attacks
- ○ Suffering an asthma attack
- ○ Relying on medication to feel better
- ○ Visits to the hospital because of persistant symptoms
- ○ Other

How frequently do you have an asthma attack? *

- ⦿ Very rarely, if at all
- ○ Once per month
- ○ Once per week
- ○ Multiple times per week
- ○ Daily

If you could purchase a product that promises to reduce the number of asthma attacks you have by half, how much would you be willing to pay for it, in USD? *

- ⦿ $0
- ○ $100
- ○ $200

- ○ $300
- ○ $400
- ○ $500+

[Submit]

Source: Halare Inc.

There are a number of Internet-based survey instruments such as SurveyMonkey, and by using one of these tools, the survey data can be analyzed automatically giving useful graphical outputs. Here is one example from the Halare campaign.

In this example, we can see how using social media, and so-called Web 2.0 tools, can provide an entrepreneur with a low-cost way of finding potential customers and questioning them about a new product or service. In addition, pricing options can be tested, and at least some idea can be estimated of the conversion rate that can be expected once you have a potential customer get to the web site. This method enables you to determine the *capture rate* of a new customer. Of course, this method does not answer the more complex issues about customer demographics and broader marketing tactics, but it does provide some quantifiable data about early adopters. For more on this subject, see Chapter 13. Already the customer is linked to the new company through an information exchange, and the entrepreneur has the first data to identify and define the marketing opportunities and issues. The embedded survey is the first step in determining what the MVP might look like and also act as a basis for formulating a marketing plan. In the next chapter, we learn how Halare took its market research to a more detailed level, again using web-based tools.

Customer Survey Report
This shows the details of the MVP survey.

Export Data

How old are you?

Choices	Percentage	Count
30 - 39	100%	1
	Total	1
	Unanswered	*1*

Where are you from?

Choices	Percentage	Count
30 - 39	100%	1
	Total	1
	Unanswered	*1*

What's the worst part about having asthma?

Choices	Percentage	Count
Having an asthma attack	50%	1
Anxiety or stress about having asthma attacks	50%	1
	Total	2
	Unanswered	*0*

Source: Halare Inc.

Advancing the Minimum Viable Product

It may be necessary to advance the version of the product or service through multiple iterations. For each iteration, you should ask whether the refined version will improve the customer experience, is the improvement measurable, and does it add to product superiority as compared to existing product solutions.

Ensure that these advanced versions create customer value and, if possible, provide an opportunity to collect some payment. Once functionality reaches the state where the customer can use it to solve the problem or some core aspect of the problem, it is a good time to test your assumptions about their willingness to pay for your solution. Whether you establish payment similar to the envisioned revenue model or pricing will depend on level of functionality and how close you are to launching your venture. You can justify charging a lower price to these early customer advocates in appreciation for their participation in the customer feedback process.

Once you have a functional MVP, you may consider launching a crowdfunding campaign for your product. This is an excellent way to solicit feedback from potential customers by asking for prepayment in the form of a funding request. By contributing to such a funding campaign, the customer is demonstrating their willingness to pay for the solution. This approach works particularly well if the customer's contribution matches the envisioned price of the final product. Then, you have validated both strong interest and willingness to pay your price. As your product goes through multiple MVP iterations, you may expand beyond early customers to include product designers, manufacturers, suppliers, and early investors. (For more about crowdfunding, see Chapter 5.)

Examples of Innovative Business Models

Mini-Case Business Model Example: DBI Using Data Collection

When Neal DeAngelo and his brother Paul left school in 1978, they decided to start their own company. Using a truck bought for them by their father and some standard mowing equipment, the two brothers provided services in "vegetation management" to businesses rather than homeowners. This choice of customer segment turned out to be the right one; businesses were more stable, and as the company, DBI Services, soon learned by listening carefully to them, businesses have greater and more complex needs than do homeowners. For example, "Class I" railroads are regulated by the federal government on the amount of vegetation that may grow on their rights of way. This, for example, mitigates against fire hazards and ensures a clear line of sight at crossings for safety. DBI realized that the value proposition for these customers was focused not on low cost but on the reliability and speed with which a service provider could treat the vegetation growing along the tracks. If any equipment breaks down on the railroad, the loss of income from trains not being able to run will greatly surpass any small cost savings for the service.

Understanding the customers' true needs has enabled DBI to build a dominant position in this sector by designing and building its own vegetation treatment road/rail vehicles. These vehicles rapidly mount the track and detect the location and type of vegetation along the line, mix optimized herbicides in real time, and spot-spray using robot arms on the truck. This minimizes the amount of chemical carried and used, limiting any environmental damage and coincidentally reducing the time needed to refill the containers with herbicides. By mapping the exact location of every plant using onboard GPS technology, the company ensures that its next service run can be accomplished in minimum time, with highly efficient use of chemicals and equipment. The proprietary data that the company collects on its clients' unique situations are a major competitive advantage, making it exceedingly difficult for a competitor to bid accurately on a contract and to compete in service. DBI has no patents but protects its know-how and data through trade secrets and works with universities to augment its own science and technology. Neal and Paul have now bootstrapped their business to more than $80 million in sales, using only bank loans to finance the growth. Their business model is based on the principles of providing business customers with reliable and customized services supported by proprietary information systems. Many students earn summer money by cutting grass; few grow a large and successful company from such a humble start.

Capturing Value in the Supply Chain

Any company finds itself in a supply chain. No company undertakes all of the functions required to deliver an end product from soup to nuts. Intel, for example, does not mine and refine the sand for making the silicon wafers for microprocessors. Rather, it purchases raw materials and manufacturing equipment from other firms. Neither does it sell computers or other electronic products. It focuses on what it does best: developing new silicon integrated circuits for use in the products of other companies such as Dell. Intel relies on other companies in the supply chain and focuses on extracting value from microprocessors, leaving the computer value to others. Intel's business model is structured to maximize its retention of value in what it offers in this supply chain. If you are opening a restaurant, you will require fresh ingredients from the markets, tableware, kitchen equipment, and staff. All these are components of your supply chain. You will also have to advertise, create promotional programs, and the like, all of which are your bought-in services. Every business is continually trying to maximize the value it can command and retain in its own supply chain or network. Sometimes, the business model to achieve this goal is not obvious. Return to the Greif example in the previous chapter and think about the move from being a commodity supplier of metal drums to a value-added service provider of "trip leasing."

Using Databases to Create Value

Selling snowblowers is a tough business. The majority of blowers are bought on impulse a day or two before a major snowstorm lands. And these storms are difficult to forecast. Competing for a last-minute sale of a snowblower requires that a potential customer has your product in mind when he/she goes to the store just before the snow hits. Toro greatly improved its efficiency in this regard by building an analytical software program that took into account several independent weather forecasts, had local advertisements ready to go into local print and radio media, and tied its own supply network and dealers together so they could get products into appropriate local outlets. This innovative combination of externally and internally created data helped the company capture greater market share from its competitors and reduce its cost of inventory that sat in stores where the sun was shining. Or consider Wal-Mart's vaunted supply chain software system, which detected a sudden upsurge in the sale of flags on September 12, 2001. Its purchasing department immediately contacted its suppliers and tied up nearly all of the short-term supply of U.S. flags worldwide, enabling Wal-Mart to be the sole source of flags for the next few weeks and bringing more customers into its stores.

ROADMAP

IN ACTION

We live in the information age. Data are being collected daily about nearly everything. Much of these data are freely available. Think how you can use data combinations creatively to generate greater value for your customers and sustain your competitive position. How many of these data must you generate yourself, and how many are free?

The fall in price of computers and data storage devices, coupled with the Internet, has made the use of digital information as a competitive weapon no longer the domain of just larger companies. Start-up companies can now harvest information technology to provide their customers with greater value and to create subtle barriers to competition. Indeed, this new low-cost digital freedom may even give smaller companies advantages over larger firms, which are encumbered by legacy data systems and cultures, freezing them in outdated business models. It was, after all, Amazon and eBay that pioneered online bookstores and auctions rather than Borders and Sotheby's. Amazon has expanded from selling just books to general on-line retailing with sales now challenging Wal-mart.

Capturing data on customer requirements and using it to create unique services or products can be a powerful way of adding value and keeping out competitors. Recall the discussion of Netflix earlier; that company changed the way consumers rent movies. The power of the Netflix business model derives not only from the convenience but also the ability to mine the data obtained by combining information from *all* customers nationwide. This enables the company to make suggestions on what you might like to rent based on not only your past rentals but also on matching your behavior with that of others with similar tastes. This ability is termed *collaborative filtering*. In addition, by getting instant feedback from their database (customers provide long lists of future wants), Netflix can balance its inventory centrally to meet both current and anticipated customer requirements, something that cannot be done on a local basis. Using this novel database structure, Netflix is able to provide its customers with a convenient, personalized service as it continually optimizes its own supply chain.

Amazon, Netflix, and the iTunes store are just three examples of what Chris Anderson refers to as "mining the long tail." (There is more about the long tail in Chapter 13.) The long tail consists of those products that appeal to only a few customers, are specialized, and are uneconomic to be placed in local stores or warehouses. Combining powerful search tools with collaborative filtering enables customers to find and access little-known books, movies, or music hidden in the long tails yet fit their personal taste. Because of both physical and financial constraints, retail stores are unable to store such large inventories or provide a customer an easy way to find what he/she wants. What other fragmented and specialist markets can be attacked using these concepts? Gathering data on your customers can give you a large advantage over competitors, especially if

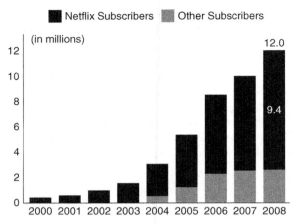

FIGURE 3.6
Netflix Gains First-Mover Advantage Using Data Mining
Source: Netflix, published data.

you use the data to continually improve customer satisfaction. If you can enter the market and build your database before anyone else, you achieve *first-mover advantage* in which it becomes harder and harder for competitors to get into the market and convince your customers to switch. Figure 3.6 shows how the first-mover advantage has worked for Netflix.

Locking-In Customers

Netflix and the DeAngelo brothers use customer data to provide superior services, making them tough competitors. This strategy can be taken a step further. Information can be shared between customers and suppliers, so that the one is closely locked into the other as business partners. A business model based on information sharing can provide high barriers against competitors because the costs involved in integrating incompatible data and computer systems can be prohibitive. On the other hand, the entrepreneur must be aware of becoming too dependent on one supplier or customer when the lock-in can become disadvantageous. A sound business model using data lock-in will have multiple partners so that the dependence on one partner is reduced.

Data lock-ins inhibiting a move to a competitor can be found in e-mail services, banking, insurance, health-care services, and social networks. Such lock-ins can also occur between businesses.

Mini-Case: General Fasteners, Locking in Customers

For years, suppliers of components to the major automotive companies have been squeezed more and more on price as the global competition in this sector has become increasingly tough. Even if a supplier has some proprietary technology, the large buyers such as GM and Ford are so powerful that they insist that their suppliers share their unique know-how so that they can play multiple competing suppliers against each other. Life is particularly tough when the component is simple to make, the product is not proprietary, and there is an oversupply. Faced with these daunting pressures on profits, General Fasteners (GF),[14] a manufacturer of bolts and other metal fasteners for the automotive industry, looked for an innovative business model to change its competitive status. It started by undertaking the engineering design for new car "platforms," taking responsibility for how the car would be reliably assembled. This requires special, hard-to-come-by engineering skills. GF then contracted to supply the car company with just-in-time components directly to the production lines, with 100 percent quality inspection and guarantees. GF either uses fasteners that are made in its own plants or purchases them from other suppliers. It manages an integrated supply chain from design to final assembly. This requires GF's computer systems to seamlessly integrate with car plants exchanging data in real time. They are "locked in" to their customers in both design and operations, making it difficult for competitors to displace them. They provide both products and services. In addition, by taking over the front-end skilled design work, their customers have no need to retain these expensive skills in-house for occasional use and, therefore, become more dependent on their supplier when they are ready to design a new family of cars.

ROADMAP

| IN ACTION | Gaining customers costs five times as much as retaining them. What information can you share with your customers that would provide benefit to both of you? Will this bind you together such that it would be difficult for your customers to change suppliers? In so doing, can you perform higher-value services that would make it even more difficult for a split? |

Licensing and Franchising

Licensing and franchising can be valuable components of a business model. They are often confused. This section describes their similarities and differences and explores when they are best employed as the basis or as a part of a business model.

Licensing and franchising refer to types of contracts between an *issuing* entity (the licensor or franchisor) and a *receiving* entity (the licensee or franchisee). These contracts grant the receivers certain rights to access certain intellectual properties, such as patents, trademarks, trade secrets, and copyrights, as discussed in Chapter 13.

The License Agreement and How to Use It[15]

A license agreement allows a licensee to use intellectual property (IP) under certain conditions as spelled out in the agreement. A license agreement usually includes the following key topics[16]:

- The licensor and licensee are identified together on the basis of their reasons for entering into the agreement. This helps ensure that there are no misunderstandings between the two parties.

- The licensed IP is precisely defined. This may give patent numbers, trademarks, and lists of trade secrets, together with a description of the products, services, and processes covered by the IP. The agreement also clearly states whether the licensor and licensee have any rights to improvements that either of them make in the future. It is usual for the licensor to have rights to any improvements made by the licensee; if not, then the licensor could find itself blocked by new inventions made by the licensee.

- The granted rights to the IP are carefully defined. Licensees may have a great deal of freedom, or they may be limited to selling products, making and not selling, and so on. Any limitations to rights are also stated here. For example, if the licensee is not allowed to further license the IP (referred to as sublicensing), this requirement is clearly stated. On the other hand, if sublicensing is allowed, then the terms of this stipulation must be clearly defined.

- The "territory" allowed for practice of the rights is defined. For example, if a licensee has a marketing presence in only one country, then the territories can be divided among several licensees. The Dyson case presented in Chapter 8 illustrates how breaking IP into territories can be used to bootstrap financing creatively. The company sold rights to regions where it had no presence in order to finance the home markets. Only later did Dyson repurchase these rights. If the IP covers several different applications, then an entrepreneur can license rights in market sectors where it does *not* intend to operate, using the proceeds to fund its core business.

- The level of exclusivity is defined. An exclusive license provides just one licensee the rights stated in the agreement. Of course, if there are licensees for different products, territories, or markets, each of these may or may not be exclusive. A nonexclusive license means that the licensor can enter into as many licenses as it wishes even if the rights are identical. For example, when you use Microsoft software, you are actually doing so under a license agreement. You do not expect this right to be exclusive, and Microsoft issues unlimited licenses to its products. It is also possible to offer limited exclusivity. For a small company, it is important to examine the advantages of these different strategies. Giving one large company exclusive rights to an important piece of IP may give too much control to a powerful outsider. On the other hand, granting unlimited licenses provides little competitive advantage to any one licensee. This should be considered only if the license is to the ultimate "end user," as is the case for the Microsoft Office suite of software. We usually recommend that a small company restrict the number of licenses it issues to two or three competitors. In this way, each has some advantages, yet not too much control is taken away from the entrepreneur.

- In exchange for gaining certain rights, the licensee pays fees to the licensor. These fees can be of several types. An *up-front* fee may be paid to initiate the contract. This fee can be very helpful to an early-stage company as a form of bootstrap funding. *Running royalties* are paid as a percentage of net sales of products or services. The percentage rate can range from 1 percent in the case of a simple product to 10 percent for a pharmaceutical formula once it has been approved for sale. *Advances* or *minimums* may be paid periodically to maintain the rights before royalty income is received. Minimums may prevent a licensee from just sitting on the rights and not trying to generate sales.

- Other terms include such items as terms of the agreement; treatment of confidentiality; payment scheduling and licensor's ability to audit sales; treatment of breaches of contract; any warranties, liabilities, and indemnifications offered by either party; and other general legal requirements.

- Licenses can be a key component of a business model. For example, an entrepreneur could license the rights to *market and sell* its products in certain markets while restricting any manufacturing. This strategy provides several benefits: the company needs less cash to develop its sales organization; partnering with a larger company can provide reputation and customer confidence, which is invaluable to an unknown company; and the income from the license can be used to fund other development activity. The Ultrafast case on the web site associated with this book describes how a small company supplying the car industry used licensing of noncore products to develop foreign markets, gain reputation, and provide early-stage, nonequity financing.

At the other end of the spectrum, some companies base their business models entirely on licensing and have no intention of producing or selling any product. For example, Intertrust Inc. in California[17] owns thirty-seven patents with another one hundred filed worldwide in the field of digital rights management (DRM). DRM is software that protects the copyrights of composers, writers, filmmakers, and software producers when the results of their efforts are transmitted electronically over the Internet. Intertrust recognized early on that this would be an important area for creating patents, which was borne out by the developments of such companies as Napster and the emergence of a number of high-profile lawsuits between copyright producers and users of their output. Intertrust's business model is to stake out the field by acquiring or developing a large portfolio of patents and then requiring purveyors of digital media to license these if they wish to continue to operate using technology and processes covered by the patents. License fees in this area can top $1 million up front, with continuing royalties based on sales.

The Franchise Agreement and How to Use It

A franchise[18] is defined as a "legal and commercial relationship between the owner (franchisor) of a trademark, service mark, trade name, or advertising symbol and an individual or group (franchisee) wishing to use that identification in a business." In this case, the franchisor is viewed as providing a "starting kit" for a new business, which enables the franchisee to create a new business with lower risk and costs than developing a business from scratch. Franchisors can grow their businesses into many locations without needing to raise the cash to do so, giving up total ownership of all the opportunity, while gaining some revenue in the form of fees to compensate giving up this upside. In exchange for lowering risk, the franchisee pays some profits to the franchisor but gains from national advertising, centralized product/service development, and reputation derived from a national or even an international reputation and image.

Probably the best-known franchise organization is McDonald's. Each location is owned by a franchisee committed to funding the facility and start-up costs but benefiting from a large and powerful central resource and strong brand. The franchisor has strict requirements regarding menus, quality, training, hygiene, facility design, and the like because any single bad franchise can seriously damage the value of all other local franchise holders. Such items as opening hours may also be required but may be left to the local owner. However, there are many other franchised organizations, and you can see the enormous variety at such web sites as www.franchiseworks.com, where many new franchise opportunities are offered.

An entrepreneur should not seek to be a franchisee or build a business as a franchisor without seeking competent legal advice. The field is littered with embittered partners, which can lead to expensive legal cases for resolution. These cases often arise because local conditions are highly diverse, whereas the franchise is based on creating uniformity across markets. Thus, a hairdressing franchisor may spend a lot on advertising the latest chic, short-haired styles from Europe, which may play well in New York or San Francisco but perhaps not so well in the Midwest. Sales may fall in one location and rise in another, leading to obvious concerns on fair use of fees. In contrast to licensing agreements, the federal government has issued regulations that require franchisors to prepare an extensive disclosure document called the Uniform Franchise Offering Circular (UFOC).[19] A copy of this document must be given to any prospective franchise purchaser before he or she buys a franchise. This law arose partly because of the concern that many potential franchisees did not understand the complexities and dangers of a franchise agreement, which ultimately led to legal wrangling and personal bankruptcies.

The franchise agreement allows a franchisee to participate in building a business together with other franchisees, under the rules stipulated by the franchisor and under certain conditions spelled out in the agreement. The agreement usually includes the following key topics:

- The franchisor and franchisee are defined together for the reason that they are entering into the agreement.
- The business of the franchise is stated, and the deliverables that the franchisor must provide to the franchisee are specified. These deliverables may vary considerably depending on the business type. They may include use of IP, trademarks and names, recipes, formulas, training and training manuals, design rules for facilities, promotional materials, operation manuals, forms of

advertising, products, or ingredients that must or may be bought from the franchisee, identification of a suitable site, and so on. It is important that these specifications be as complete as possible to avoid future disagreements. The limitations of the franchisee's business are defined. Usually, this entails a location or region of activities. There may be "area development rights," which are optional rights to develop multiple individual franchises in a specific geographic area.

The limitations may also spell out precisely what the franchisee may offer to its customers. Significant problems may arise in this area. For example, a restaurant franchisor based in California may stipulate that only organic health products be used in the foods sold; a franchisee in West Texas may find little market for this locally and wish to add barbecued meat products to the menu. The franchisor will argue that this devalues the franchise for everyone else by diluting the brand message, whereas the franchisee will claim that she cannot prosper when there is little market for organic health foods locally:

- The franchisor may offer to fund part or all of the start-up costs. This may be an option or mandatory. Usually, the franchisee must show that it has access to a sufficient amount of cash to fund the start-up.

- The commitments of the franchisee are defined. Again, these may be very broad and include such items as the minimum investment in the business, local advertising expenditures, meeting quality requirements, purchasing from approved suppliers, sharing new ideas with the franchisor, and using common software systems.

- In exchange for entering into the agreement and receiving support from the franchisor, the franchisee pays fees to the franchisor. These fees can be of several types. An *up-front* fee may be paid to initiate the contract. There is usually an advertising fee of up to 3 percent of net sales due to the franchisor and a royalty on net sales of several percent. The franchisee may also be obligated to purchase certain supplies from the franchisor or from "designated suppliers."

- There may also be items stating under what terms a franchisee can sell its business, including an option for the franchisor to purchase the business and make it a franchise-owned property. In this way, an entrepreneur can view franchising as an alternative route to building a large, wholly owned company using franchisees' funds for the growth phase. Franchisees may welcome this built-in exit strategy, giving them a fair return on their own investment and efforts.

- Other terms include such items as length of the agreement and conditions for renewal (the initial period agreed upon is typically around seven years), treatment of confidentiality, payment scheduling, and franchisor's ability to audit sales, treatment of breaches of contract, any warranties, liabilities and indemnifications offered by either party, and other general legal requirements, including a noncompete stipulation.

Unlike licensing, which is often only a small, if important, part of a business model, franchising is usually the core of a business model. However, even within the confines of a standard franchise agreement, entrepreneurs have managed to innovate powerful new business models.

Mini-Case: ChemStation

George Homan founded ChemStation in 1983, after he had spent some years as a distributor of industrial cleaning chemicals.[20] His close contact to customers led him to recognize that businesses do not want to handle bulky containers of cleaning chemicals. George saw an opportunity to provide a better service by offering custom-formulated, environmentally friendly industrial cleaning and process chemicals delivered to proprietary refillable containers, which are placed free of charge at customer facilities. ChemStation has used a franchise business model to expand rapidly nationally without the need for the founding entrepreneur to raise any external capital. ChemStation has used its franchisee network very effectively to get tremendous reach within the U.S. market. The first franchise was given in 1985, and since then, forty-eight franchises have been awarded. Today, there are fifty units operating in the United States, of which only two are company owned. George's elegant business model is depicted in Figure 3.7.

The franchisor's headquarters are based in Ohio, which also serves some local customers and uses its buying power to purchase cleaning chemicals at a price lower than small competitors can get. The headquarters also holds the secure and coded database of proprietary cleaning formulas for specific customer needs, whether to clean egg-packing equipment or the floors of a car assembly plant. A franchisee is granted a region to service and funds the local marketing, sales, and delivery services after paying an entry fee of about $1 million to ChemStation. In exchange, the franchisee gets access to the database on demand when a customer need is defined. This provides the formula for the optimum cleaner components and the usage instructions. In this way, the franchisee can provide customers with an immediate, proven solution to their cleaning problems.

In addition, if a major national company, for example, a rental car firm, would like every car to be cleaned the same way and have a distinctive, brand-building aroma, ChemStation can provide the formula to every franchisee for delivery to local offices. A small local firm is unable to guarantee this service. In the event that no solution for a customer's new problem can be found in the database and the franchisee develops the answer, then the franchise agreement commits them to submit the answer to the central database, where it becomes available to all franchisees and adds to ChemStation's intellectual assets. In this way, the franchise model is enhanced by the continual building of a proprietary database of customer solutions, adding greater value to both the franchisor and franchisees.

Whatever problems are solved at a franchisee's location are fed into the software package that has been devised by ChemStation, and the new solution becomes an integral part of the ChemStation database. The sharing of such information by the franchisees with headquarters is mandated by a written agreement between ChemStation and its franchisees. The database is a key asset for ChemStation, and it has the necessary software and framework in place to interpret the results and distribute the data. The database also builds barriers against competition. For example, ChemStation solved a cleaning problem at a Harley-Davidson plant within its shock absorber manufacturing division, which resulted in using one cleaning solution on one line and another

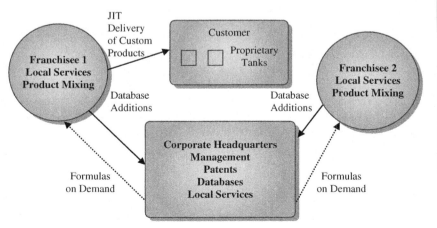

FIGURE 3.7
ChemStation's Franchise Business Model

solution for the adjacent sister line. This subtle know-how becomes part of ChemStation's data bank. Such captured knowledge helps to lock in customers and prevents competitors from gaining the account. Since its founding, ChemStation captured, in less than ten years, around 25 percent of the $300 million U.S. industrial cleaner market from local mom "n" pop suppliers. It has done so by providing customized cleaning solutions in an innovative business model, which includes elements of franchising, data mining of customer information, and customer lock-in. For another interesting use to build a business, see the Sea Tow example in Chapter 12, which employs franchising to build a social venture.

Models Built around Social Networks

The Internet has evolved to offer more than a static connection between a user and a web site. So-called Web 2.0[21] technologies have emerged that enable more complex and dynamic interactions. We have seen such companies as LinkedIn, Facebook, Twitter, and Instagram grow rapidly as social networking portals that enable individuals to create and manage their own social networks. While these businesses are intriguing in themselves as an entirely new form of business, it is interesting to consider how such social networking concepts can be applied to entirely new businesses that do more than just manage personal networks. Here are some examples to stimulate your thoughts.

Threadless.com sells T-shirts that are designed by customers. The best design each month is chosen by the customers. Threadless does not produce products unless they are highly rated by customers. Thus, the company gets free designs, free market research, and distribution via its popular web site. Designers are willing to enter the competition as winning a Threadless competition comes with personal fame and peer recognition.[22] Threadless makes money by selling award-winning clothes.

Syndicom.com, in contrast, builds extremely focused professional communities in the healthcare industry. These communities consist of people who wish to help each other in their daily practice and to contribute to important innovations. The company's first community was for spine surgeons, and more than 70 percent of the U.S.-based surgeons have freely joined this online community. Syndicom makes money by providing major companies access to these highly specialized communities for tasks such as market research, clinical trials, and product innovations.

Other interesting examples emerge daily. For example, specialist social networks can be created to get input from your most important customers on new products and ideas. P&G created Vocalpoint, a network of mothers with young children who are themselves actively involved in talking to other mothers. By spreading the word about new products, providing reviews of planned products, and making suggestions, this community of "opted-in" mothers receives free samples and notices of new products in the pipeline. They can also share ideas and tips with other mothers. P&G realizes that engaging highly motivated and active mothers can increase the rate that new product sales grow by establishing a buzz around the product and spreading the news by word of mouth, so-called viral marketing. Think how you can build social networks into your business as a way of getting sales leads and new ideas for products or services from your customers.

Corporate Partnering

We deal with corporations as a source of financing in Chapter 8. However, there are many other forms of relationships that can exist between small and large companies that can be mutually beneficial.[23] As we saw in Chapter 1, we live in a global economy where changes occur rapidly, even in the most stable of industries. Often, a small company may not have the resources or time to gain a share of a new market before its products, services, or even business models have become obsolete. Partnering with large companies may accelerate your growth. There are many different forms of corporate partnering. Here are some examples that illustrate the range of involvements that may occur:

- The large firm may make an investment in a smaller firm for reasons that are described in Chapter 8. For example, News Corp made an investment in NewsStand/LibreDigital,[24] which had developed novel ways of processing books and articles for publishing on the Internet. News Corp saw ways of both protecting the copyright of materials that it owns and creating new revenue streams by slicing and dicing content to provide greater value to customers. LibreDigital was eventually sold to RR Donnelley.

- A large firm has both reputation and networks that it can employ to help a small company. In the NewsStand case, News Corp wanted the company to be successful, so it is used its contacts to promote the company and its services. This is not a conflict as everyone benefits from the development of digital delivery of content.

- A large corporation can license rights to a small company's IP. When the license aids rather than competes with the smaller company, multiple benefits accrue. The Ultrafast case on the book's web site provides an excellent example to explore. A large licensee may also be effective in bringing in other licensees to expand the market further.

- Large companies have extensive sales networks that can be used by a smaller company, perhaps in regions where it would be too expensive to establish a sales force. Chapter 9 returns to this topic with an example of a marketing agreement to penetrate the Canadian market in this way.

- Large companies may have a complementary product or service that can be sold alongside a small company's product for mutual benefit. For example, a company that is interested in selling industrial gases can benefit from selling an entrepreneur's proprietary equipment that would use its gases. This builds on existing customer relationships and reputation and deals with such issues as stability, safety, and quality control methods that are usually not developed in a small firm.

- Despite the obvious benefits from partnerships between small innovative companies and larger corporations that have resources, contacts, reputation, and other things, often the relationships can become tense as cultural issues become dominant.[25] The master case has several examples of difficult relationships between Neoforma and the large health-care suppliers that saw the upstart initially as a threat before eventually buying the company at a much later stage.

SUMMARY

However good an opportunity seems, no longer is it sufficient to build a company around a single product or service; equal attention must be given to innovation of a business model that can capture and retain value against current and future competitors. We defined a business model and introduced the Business Model Canvas as a useful tool for questioning the assumptions as you build your business model. A second tool, the MVP method, works hand in hand with the Canvas as you stepwise explore your business options often working closely with your first customers. We also provided some illustrated frameworks to stimulate business model innovations including capturing more value in the supply chain, using proprietary data, finding ways to lock in customers, and embodying licensing, and franchising as components when constructing a model. The Internet has created new ways of using virtual social networks as business models in their own right or, perhaps more sustainable in the longer term, embedding these networks within a more traditional framework. Corporate networks can also play a significant role in business model development in a wide range of ways.

STUDY QUESTIONS

Q.1 What definition of *business model* do you find most useful, and why?

Q.2 Why does the canvas model help to better understand a business?

Q.3 How do the nine sections lead to a better understanding of the business model?

Q.4 Describe the MVP process and how is it best used with customers.

Q.5 Why was Greif Packaging, described in Chapter 2, able to capture more of the value in the supply chain? Where did the extra value come from, and were there others who lost the value they were selling?

Q.6 What is digital collaborative filtering? Name three companies that are successfully using this technique in their business models. Can you think of other businesses that might employ this technique in their business models? (Hint: Think of media companies, retail stores, and health care.)

Q.7 What do you find most innovative about the DBI business model? Can you think of similar examples where these concepts might be used?

Q.8 Name three similarities and three differences between a franchise and a license.

Q.9 List four types of corporate partnering with the advantages and potential disadvantages to both large and small companies.

EXERCISES

3.1 Think of a possible idea for a franchise business model. You can search the Internet for ideas if you wish. In this case, would you rather be the franchisee or the franchisor? Why?

3.2 Think of an example where Internet social networking has enhanced an existing business. Propose a new business idea based on the concept of social networking by thinking of a unique network of people with a common interest that could be accessed and motivated somehow using the Internet. What would be the sources of revenue?

Management Exercise: Corporate Partnering

Master-Case Exercises: If you have not yet read the appendix for the master case in Chapter 1 at the book's web site, do so. Then go to the book's web site and read the diary entries Prequel; Months 11, 12, 25, 40, 42, 47, 49, and 57; and Four Years Later and view the video selection, "David vs. Goliath: Dealing with Big Corporations."

Either as a team or individually, produce a short presentation on each of these questions for discussion. Only one or two slides for each are required to state the key points.

Master-Case Q 1: Why is it difficult for large companies to embrace change? Relate this to the reaction by the major companies to Neoforma's rise and the increasing power of the GPOs threat before eventually buying the company at a much later stage.

Master-Case Q 2: If you were the founder of a small company, what procedures would you use to develop and manage partnerships with larger companies?

Management Case Study: DBI

Go back and read the profile of Neal DeAngelo, and then watch the four video sequences of Neal DeAngelo on the book's web site. Also visit the company's web site. Consider the following questions:

1. Do you feel that Neal has a passion for what he and his brother are building? Are you willing to work as hard in the early years and take the personal risks?

2. DBI serves both private and government clients. In some cases, customers are mandated by law to take the lowest bid. How does DBI manage this situation? What sort of relationships does DBI have with its customers? How do these relationships shape the company's business model?

3. DBI has grown rapidly and has several locations. Does Neal think about forming a unique culture for the company, and if so, how can this be accomplished? Do you think the company has a clear plan?

4. Why does DBI outsource some research tasks to universities? What are the dangers in doing so?

Management Case Study: Ultrafast

We have created a case study for this chapter on the book's web site. It concerns a company started and grown by an entrepreneur after recognizing a point of pain when working for a larger company. The founder used licensing and government grants to bootstrap the company, retaining control before the company actually went bankrupt—however not before building a complete manufacturing plant to supply the car industry. We chose this case because failures often provide insights that are not seen in stories of success. Go to the book's web site at www.wiley.com/college/kaplan and watch the video sequence on the Ultrafast case related by one of the authors.

1. Describe how the company used licensing to accelerate its development. What advantages and disadvantages did this strategy have for the company in the short and long terms and for the tool licensees, Bosch and Atlas Copco?

2. Draw a diagram of all different types of companies in the supply chain that Ultrafast found itself, including bolt manufacturers, suppliers of automatic assembly equipment, hand tools used in repair workshops, companies that chemically treat car components, and the car manufacturers themselves. How do these relate to each other? What value did each of these supply to their customers *before* Ultrafast came on the scene? How is the value distribution changed when the Ultrafast method is proven and enters the market? Which companies can gain most from Ultrafast, and which can suffer? Is the business model followed by the company the best one for capturing the value from the invention?

3. Using licenses and government grants to bootstrap the company, the founding entrepreneur managed to retain full control of the company right to the end. Was this ultimately the best thing for him or the company? Why or why not? What lessons on ownership and personal ambitions can you gain from this example?

4. Imagine that you had started this company. What would you have done differently?

INTERACTIVE LEARNING ON THE WEB

Test your knowledge of the chapter using the book's interactive web site.

ADDITIONAL RESOURCES

The Licensing Executives Society is a professional organization for those practicing licensing and technology transfer. Their web site (www.lesusacanada.org/) provides information about licensing and has many links to other sites of interest on this topic.

For access to articles and advice on franchising, visit www.franchise.org/, where you can find excellent references and links to a number of valuable articles and learning tools.

For a summary of how to build a corporate culture that is open to innovation, see Chapter 9.

ENDNOTES

1. For an interesting discussion on business models, see Susan Lambert, *Making Sense of Business Models,* 2004 at www.flinders.edu.au.

2. IBM uses this definition for conveying the concept of business model innovation to its executives.

3. See *Business Model Generation*, A. Osterwalder, Yves Pigneur, Alan Smith, and 470 practitioners from 45 countries, self-published in 2010. This book describes the canvas and its use. Many examples are provided.

4. Interviewed and prepared by Elizabeth Allina, entrepreneur and Columbia EMBA graduate, November 10, 2014.

5. Prepared by Elizabeth Allina, November 15, 2014.

6. Ibid.

7. Prepared by Jack McGourthy PhD, Director, Community and Global Entrepreneurship Founder, Venture For All®, Columbia Business School.

8. Eric Reis, *The Lean Startup: How Today's Entrepreneurs Use Continuous Innovation to Create Radically Successful Businesses* (New York, NY: Crown Business, 2011).

9. Ibid.

10. The content for this section was provided by Matt Michaux, COO of Halare Inc., in July 2011.

11. For considerable detail on this topic, see Sebastian Tonkin, Caleb Whitmore and Justin Cutroni, *Performance Marketing with Google Analytics: Strategies and Techniques for Maximizing Online RO* (Indianapolis: Wiley Publishing, 2010).

12. See Hollis Thomases, *Twitter Marketing: An Hour a Day* (Indianapolis: Wiley Publishing, 2010).

13. For a broad overview of the use of social media in marketing, see Shama Kabani and Chris Brogan, *The Zen of Social Media Marketing: An Easier Way to Build Credibility, Generate Buzz, and Increase Revenue* (Dallas: BenBella Books, 2010).

14. General Fasteners is part of the MNP group of companies. More can be learned by visiting www.mnp.com.

15. For a detailed licensing how-to, see Richard Stim, *License Your Invention* (Berkeley, CA: Nolo Press, 1998). This book comes with a useful disc of all the necessary documents and forms needed for licensing. Also, the Licensing Executive Society provides useful contacts and further information on licensing at www.lesusacanada.org/.

16. Ibid.

17. See www.intertrust.com for a detailed description of the company's business. This site also links directly to the U.S. Patent and Trademark Office to see the thirty-seven patents owned by Intertrust in the field of digital rights management.

18. See the International Franchise Association and Horwath International, *Franchising in the Economy of 1990* (Evans City, PA: IFA Publications, 1991), 22–23. Also visit www.franchise.org for information on franchising and to review more than one thousand franchise opportunities.

19. A number of useful articles on franchising have appeared in *Entrepreneur* magazine, including discussions on the UFOC.

20. Based on an interview with George Homan in June 2004. You can learn more about the services ChemStation provides at www.chemstation.com.

21. The term *Web 2.0* is difficult to define precisely. Broadly speaking, it describes a range of applications that use dynamic, two-way interactions on the Internet rather than static, one-way information exchange. The field is changing rapidly.

22. Visit www.vocalpoint.com to learn more. An independent review can be found at www.viewpoints.com/Vocalpoint-review-9a920.

23. See Navin Chaddha, "Established 80 Alliances," *Forbes*, May 21, 2001, 76.

24. NewsStand is now called LibreDigital. For the rationale behind this Investment, see http://bookseller-association.blogspot.com/2007/01/news-news-corp-and-newstand.html. LibreDigital was purchased by Dun and Bradstreet in 2011.

25. See Michel Roberts, "The Do's and Don'ts of Strategic Alliances," *Journal of Business Strategy* (March–April 1992): 50–53.

Customers, Markets, Competitors in a Digital World*

4

"The digital revolution is far more significant than the invention of writing or even of printing."

Douglas Engelbart, American Engineer and Inventor

OBJECTIVES

- Conducting marketing research using digital marketing channels, preparing advertising campaigns, and search and pay per click.
- Applying and using digital tools, including Google.
- Using keyword lists to test the plan.
- Using digital channels to create demand.
- Understand viral marketing.
- Define a successful marketing plan and its relevance to new ventures.
- Learn how entrepreneurs prepare a marketing analysis plan.
- Learn how to define market segmentation.
- Describe the methods of a competitive analysis.
- Learn the process to position a product or service.
- Describe the methods for a price and sales strategy.

CHAPTER OUTLINE

Introduction

Profile: Brian Halligan, CEO and Founder, HubSpot

Conducting Marketing Research Using Digital Tools to Start the Venture

Mini-Case: BreatheSimple[1] Web-Based Market Research

Using Digital Channels to Create Demand

Formulating a Successful Marketing Plan

---

*The coauthor for this chapter is Jeremy Kagan, founder and CEO of Pricing Engine Inc., and professor of Digital Marketing at Columbia Business School.

Introduction

In order to prepare the marketing section of the business plan, the entrepreneur must understand the customers' needs and desires, their profiles, markets, and pricing, as well as be able to plan for the company's future strategies in each of these areas. This chapter provides the information and tools needed to do just that. Throughout, the two important elements to understanding the entrepreneur's role in marketing—and the key to understanding and dominating the competition—will be explained. A number of techniques and strategies can assist the entrepreneur in effectively analyzing a potential market. By using them, the entrepreneur can gain in-depth knowledge about the specific market and translate this knowledge into a well-formulated business plan.

This chapter addresses key issues in the marketplace and examines the major factors in marketing that entrepreneurs need to know. It also offers guidelines on attracting new marketing opportunities through digital marketing techniques and e-commerce solutions.

The business begins and ends with customers. Therefore, it is imperative to obtain and keep customers to sustain the business. By far the best assets for a business are its customers from which market analysis begins. Using digital tools makes it easier than ever before to determine the viability of a business, the most effective messaging and value propositions, and even to refine the offering itself. It has also created new models like software as a service (SaaS) and freemium pricing that allow new entrants to attack entrenched market leaders.

Profile: Brian Halligan, CEO and Founder, HubSpot

Brian Halligan is cofounder and CEO of HubSpot. In 2006, Brian Halligan and fellow MIT Sloan grad Dharmesh Shah launched HubSpot based on a bet that they could revolutionize marketing. Brian had two options after he graduated—he could have been a VP of sales at a really great company or a CEO at a not-so-great company. He chose to forego both those options and instead to start his own thing with Dharmesh. It's by far the best decision he ever made. Traditional, outbound-focused methods were outdated, and they realized that inbound marketing had begun showing major promise as a way to drive traffic and interest for companies.

Nine years later, HubSpot has become the pillar of the inbound marketing community, and its software platform now serves more than 10,000 companies in fifty-six countries. In October, HubSpot went public in a successful IPO and cemented itself as a thought leader in the marketing industry.

Prior to HubSpot, Brian was a venture partner at Longworth Ventures and a VP of sales at Groove Networks, which was later acquired by Microsoft. He has authored two books, *Marketing Lessons from the Grateful Dead* and *Inbound Marketing: Get Found Using Google, Social Media, and Blogs* which he cowrote with Dharmesh Shah. Brian serves on the boards of directors of Fleetmatics Group (FLTX), a global provider of fleet management solutions, and the Massachusetts Innovation and Technology Exchange (MITX). Brian was named Ernst and Young's Entrepreneur of the Year in 2011 and one of Glassdoor's 25 Highest Rated CEOs in 2014. In his spare time, he follows his beloved Red Sox and goes to the gym.

Conducting Marketing Research Using Digital Tools to Start The Venture

Entrepreneurs usually engage in marketing research for two reasons: (1) to identify the need and opportunity for the venture and (2) to understand marketing and customer issues that relate to the product or service.

The entrepreneur usually starts market research to identify issues and problems that are not apparent at first. Market research can be a very costly exercise, and start-up companies are usually short of money. One way to get some initial market data is to use Internet tools and social networks.

Using Digital Marketing Channels for Research, Testing, and Expanding the Business Idea

Thanks to the growth of digital media and e-commerce, the basic tasks of researching the market and testing concepts for a new business start-up have an array of new tools to draw upon. Free and low-cost tools abound to get a sense of the size of potential markets, identify key influencers and industry notables, and determine the potential customer base for a new product or service. More actively, a start-up can spend relatively little and get real-world data on things like value propositions and messaging and pricing models and even generate a list of potential customers to contact upon launch. Finally, all of these tools can similarly be used to assess the competition. This example shows how BreatheSimple, a company introduced in the previous chapter, used one web-based tool to refine its knowledge in just one niche market sector.

Mini-Case: BreatheSimple[1] Web-Based Market Research

The use of smoke-screen methods for testing the potential for a new product or service was illustrated in Chapter 3 using the Halare/BreatheSimple example. Such methods together with the "minimal viable product" concepts described in that chapter help refine the business model, explore value propositions, and uncover unmet needs of potential customers.

We continue here with the BreatheSimple case to show how using web-based market research tools can further focus the marketing strategy, understand key triggers for purchasing your product, and establish a pricing model. Specifically, further product research and development and customer testing determined that the BreatheSimple techniques can be applied to another vertical market sector to asthma relief, namely, the alleviation of snoring. To test this sector, Halare, the developer of the BreatheSimple techniques, used a web-based market research tool called "ask your target market" or aytm.com.

AYTM has an interesting business model. It has established a database of over 20 million respondents worldwide willing to answer market research questionnaires for a small fee. Halare wished to question 75 respondents concerned about snoring and its effect on their lives. AYTM samples its respondent database by first sending out a screening pair of questions that are totally unrelated. For example, in this case, "Do you or your partner snore?" and "Have you recently purchased a pair of Italian fashion shoes?" Based on proprietary sampling algorithms, AYTM sends these questions out to, say, about 1000 respondents in their database in order to assure reaching at least 75 snorers. Halare had specified the U.S. market only, an age range greater than 18 and no restrictions on gender or ethnicity. Other filters such as career, education level, parental status, and so on can be applied if deemed appropriate.

In this case, Halare wished to learn about the impact that snoring has on personal lifestyles and whether any remedies had been tried with any satisfaction. Additionally, how willing would someone be to use the BreatheSimple method, and how much they would pay for it? The total cost for this study was $388 and took less than four hours from start to finish! Here is a summary of some of the most important outcomes: more details regarding age, ethnicity, location, and so on were also determined:

Q.1: Do you ever wake up feeling groggy or tired because of your snoring or because of your partner's snoring? 69 percent answered yes. This shows that there is a direct impact on lifestyle for over two-third of the snoring population. In fact, snoring may have a major impact on the sleep partner of a snorer.

Q.2: Have you tried to solve your snoring problem with any of these solutions? These answers also show that snorers and their partners are concerned enough that they are proactive in finding methods to alleviate the symptoms. Respondents were asked to indicate which methods they used, which could then be analyzed further by Halare to determine pricing and reported efficacy of each method.

Q.3: How satisfied have you been with the snoring solutions you have tried? To explore this theme further, respondents were asked to classify their level of satisfaction with the methods that they have tried. Only about 25 percent report a high level of satisfaction, indicating that there is a substantial opportunity for a new method that can alleviate snoring. Figures 4.1 and 4.2 show the results from Q 2 and Q 3.

Halare's testing of an MVP has shown that for chronic snorers, symptoms could be reduced by 90 percent. But would customers actually put in the effort required to get these benefits? Hence, the next question:

Q.4: Would you consider trying a breathing exercise for twenty minutes a day for a few weeks if it reduced your snoring by 90 percent? 77 percent replied yes.

Finally, what is the perceived VALUE to the customer—how much will they pay?

Q.5: What is the most you would pay for a personalized training course that coaches you through these breathing exercises and gives you daily feedback? Figure 4.3 summarizes the rather more detailed data elicited by this question.

These data indicate that, despite a declared need and willingness, a significant percentage of snorers or their partners would not pay for alleviation. Yet there is a high proportion that would pay a significant price. Based on this skewed data, which is not unusual in such cases, Halare

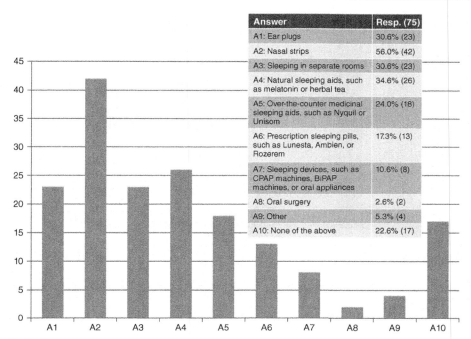

FIGURE 4.1
Use of Competitive Products

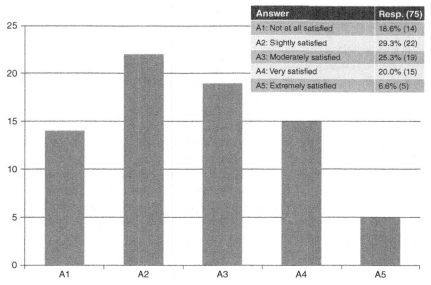

FIGURE 4.2
Level of Satisfaction with Current Solutions

decided to offer a tiered product offering to capture this market. The less than $0.99 category is based largely on a skeptical group of potential customers that think that "this is too good to be true and is probably a 'snake-oil' product." These customers need to be accessed and shown that there is real value here. Because there is an equal number of high-paying customers, Halare did not want to underprice the service either. Here is the "freemium" pricing strategy that Halare is adopting based on this research:

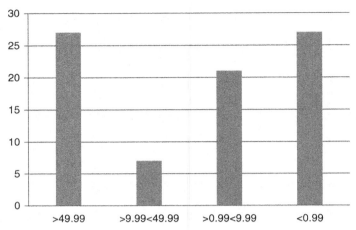

FIGURE 4.3
Acceptable Price Points for the Halare Solution

Level	Function	Price
1	Analyzes breathing health of the customer and compares the measurements with the larger peer population thereby establishing baseline data	Free
2	Trains customer to breathe more efficiently and establishes a relaxation program for general health improvement	$9.99
3	Trains customer to establish breathing patterns to alleviate snoring both in intensity and duration over a period of a few weeks	$29.99

The research also indicated that snorers' sleep partners can also be a target purchaser. This is supported by clinical research which shows that partners of snorers lose as much sleep and suffer from as much dangerous daytime drowsiness as if they snored too.

The BreatheSimple mini-case illustrates a low-cost, fast means of undertaking *primary market research—obtaining information directly from customers*. However, it is also vital to learn the size of the potential market. This is referred to as *secondary* research. Sizing the market and demand can be done in the digital universe by turning to the best source of information out there—the biggest search engine on the planet, Google. Google provides free tools to do research on search volumes, keywords, and traffic estimates as a by-product of its advertising-based revenue model. It took Halare just two hours to learn that 37 percent of U.S. adults over the age of thirty suffer from chronic snoring—60 million in total. This number is growing at the same rate as the obesity level. And 54 percent of the partners of snorers complain about sleep disturbance, supporting the company's targeted marketing campaign.

Applying and Using Digital Tools

One of the first places to start is a simple tool to determine relative demand based on searches. Google Trends (http://www.google.com/trends/) uses Google's search data to provide detailed information on the relative volumes of different search terms and phrases. This can be used in a variety of ways. First, one can identify the best keywords to use in messaging for a product based on where and how people are searching. Let's take a simple made up example of how one might want to launch a new store selling flowers. Should the name be "Acme Florist" or "Acme Flower Shop?" By comparing the relative volume of these search terms in our target location, we can actually let the way potential customers actually think of the retail shop determine our messaging and focus. A business can also test whether different variations of product and attributes show up more or less in search to determine the relative importance. Are there more searches for "cheap flowers" or "high-quality flowers?" This can indicate the most important market differentiators.

Using Keywords List to Test the Plan

Digging deeper into Google's toolkit provides even more useful tools. The keyword tool and traffic estimator are part of the free tools Google provides all potential advertisers through its AdWords program. A simple sign up is all that is required to access these tools. Once registered, the tools can be used to suggest relevant keywords around a product or category. These keywords can then be used to estimate the traffic volume the search engine sees per month on the relevant terms. The total amount of available searches is a terrific proxy for the number of people actively seeking a product or solution that can be serviced by a start-up.

Another use is to identify potential demand for a new product. If we are proposing a new, environmentally friendly carpet cleaner as a new product, an examination of the complementary searches for the problem the product is intended to solve can be used to estimate demand. In this case, searches like "environmentally safe carpet cleaner" or "green carpet cleaner" might indicate potential demand the product would be able to satisfy.

These keyword lists and associated traffic volumes can be taken even further into the development of a basic marketing budget. Google's tools will provide an estimate of the cost-per-click bid necessary for an ad to be shown next to the search terms selected. (Google's main source of revenue is the auction-based display of clickable ads next to its search results.) Even without launching an ad, Google will provide its estimate of the amount of clicks—visitors to a web site—that a bid and budget combination will provide. With a little experimentation and an estimate of how many visitors will buy your product or service, Google's estimates provide the best real-world estimate of the potential pool of customers per month and how much it will cost to reach and sell to them.

Similarly, social tools also exist to allow a new business to research the discussion around products and services. For example, the free tool Social Mention (socialmention.com) allows one to enter keywords and phrases into its search engine and return a snapshot of the conversations happening across various social media about those topics. One can identify associated keywords and phrases, key influencers, and top names and even get a rough sense of positive or negative sentiment. One use of this can be to see in what context a target customer group might be discussing a product area. For example, with a new skin care product, are the social media conversations focused on preventing sun damage or its moisturizing properties? Social media monitoring can provide information and insight on real behaviors rather than an expensive focus group.

Preparing the Market Approach to Test the Plan

A logical next step after using the Google tools to determine some potential market approaches and messaging is to actually deploy a small budget to test these in the real world. Creating a simple ad campaign in Google AdWords takes nothing more than writing a few text ads and placing a credit card. With the target keywords of potential customer searchers already identified, a new business can test value propositions and messaging to see what truly attracts potential customers. Let's use the previous flower shop example. Are people interested in a wide selection? Low prices? Same day delivery? Messaging on all of these can be tested and judged objectively based on the actual click-throughs indicating interest. A similar approach can be used to test different pricing models and options, or offers and specials to attract new customers. Many businesses will actually direct this traffic to a web site that is not yet ready to accept orders but simply advertises the product as "coming soon" and perhaps collects e-mail addresses for future notification. In this way, a product concept and messaging can be tested without even so much as investing in a real prototype!

Finally, all of these tools can be used to check out the competition. What kind of search volume is there on their brand name? What do social media conversations focus on? Insights generated here can inform product positioning and identify weaknesses in competitor's product line that can be exploited by your new offering.

A good example of this is the Halare entrepreneurial venture that used a dummy web site to gauge customer interest in its breathing training techniques for alleviating the symptoms of asthma described in the previous chapter.

Formulating a Successful Marketing Plan

How can marketing techniques be used to the entrepreneur's advantage? Consider the following areas and how each question can be answered to anticipate concerns from a marketing perspective:

> Marketing is important, but there is nothing more important to the success of most entrepreneurs than personal selling. As the expression goes, "Nothing happens until there's a sale!"
>
> Gerald E. Hills
> *Coleman Foundation Chair of Entrepreneurship, University of Illinois at Chicago*

1. **Set Marketing Objectives.** Marketing objectives are likely to be based on sales revenues and market share. They may also include related objectives such as sales presentations, seminars, ad placements, and proposals submitted to prospective customers.

   Remember to make all the objectives concrete and measurable. Develop the plan to be implemented, not just read. Objectives that cannot be measured, tracked, and followed up are not likely to lead to implementation. The capability of plan versus actual analysis is essential.

   Sales are easy to track and measure. Market share is harder because it depends on market research. There are other marketing goals that are less tangible and harder to measure, such as positioning or image and awareness.

2. **Get the Product Out: Sales and Distribution.** Begin with how a business will deliver its products or services to customers. Will the business employ its own sales force for direct marketing, or will dealers, distributors, jobbers, or perhaps partners be used? Have any of these been identified or selected? On what basis will they be chosen? How will they be compensated? If the business will rely on its own sales force, what skills and training are required?

3. **Set a Pricing Strategy.** Pricing should be considered part of the overall marketing strategy. Although nonprice factors have become more important in buying behavior in recent decades, price still remains one of the most important elements in determining company market share and profitability. For example, the manufacturer of women's designer apparel might pursue a high-price strategy and then discount the apparel as a means of generating sales. However, this strategy may risk weakening the image of the upscale brand.

   The entrepreneur needs to generate a rationale to explain the pricing strategy and anticipate its impact on gross profit. A detailed price list will be helpful whether the entrepreneur is handling the marketing of the product personally, getting advice from mentors, or outsourcing the marketing to a company that specializes in it.

4. **Raise Visibility: Advertising, Public Relations, and Promotion.** In many instances, public relations will play an important role in attempts to generate sales. Usually, the focus is on the concept and the creative content of the communications campaign, the media used, and the extent to which each will be employed.

   Many start-up or early-stage companies will not have a large advertising budget. For these companies, public relations may be the answer. Entrepreneurs may contact local media—newspapers, radio, and television—that often write or broadcast stories on new businesses in the community. A favorable response may translate into free advertising directed at a large audience. The Dyson case profile in Chapter 8 describes a novel approach using "personality marketing" for a cash-strapped company.

5. **Conduct a Site Analysis.** In some instances, particularly if the business has a retail focus, location must be taken into account in the marketing plan. The entrepreneur must think about the demographic and educational issues of the neighborhood, its environment, its accessibility and proximity to other businesses, and the cost of maintaining a facility there.

6. **Future Marketing Activities.** The marketing plan should consider sales strategies aimed at sustaining growth. For example, a company's immediate plans might involve penetrating only the domestic market, but in the future, the same company might consider a license for its products in some international markets or perhaps even a joint venture or partnership with a company in similar or complementary markets. The Ultrafast case history on this book's web site illustrates how this might be achieved.

7. **Current and Best Customers.** Identifying the company's current clients allows management to determine where to allocate resources. Defining the best customers enables management to segment this market niche more directly.

8. **Potential Customers.** By identifying potential customers, either geographically or with an industry-wide analysis of its marketing area, a company increases its ability to target this group, thus turning potential customers into current customers.

9. **Outside Factors.** Identifying changing trends in demographics, economics, technology, cultural attitudes, and the role of governmental policy may have a substantial impact on customer needs and, consequently, expected services.

Testing Your Marketing Plan Assumption with Digital Tools

Digital marketing techniques can be used to test many aspects of the product or service before committing the business fully to one path. Aspects of the value proposition and what attracts potential customers can be tested via digital advertising. Different pricing strategies and price levels can be tested with landing pages, surveys, or A/B testing. Even the features of the product itself can be determined using crowdsourced data.

Niche or Target Markets

A niche market is a small segment of a large market ignored by other companies. For many firms, niche markets are too small to be attractive to large competitors. Yet a start-up firm can do well within them. The plan is to select a niche market in which the new business can grow and gain a competitive advantage. In the future, additional niches will open up as market efficiency improves.[2]

Target marketing is the strategy used by most successful businesses today. Usually, a company ignores segments that have limited growth because the product will not generate sufficient sales to sustain the company's profitability or allow the company to compete effectively.

ROADMAP

IN ACTION | A new venture or an early-stage business has a high degree of success in a niche market. Niche markets are too small to be attractive to large competitors. Use the marketing plan to select a niche market to grow and gain a competitive advantage.

The market segments are selected and targeted. Marketing tactics are developed for each target market, which is called *strategic market segmentation*. Once markets have been targeted, the entrepreneur should develop a marketing program for penetrating each segment. The business plan will help identify the markets and their segments. Each target market should be treated almost as a separate marketing program.

One new area of marketing related to niche marketing, enabled by digital, is to capitalize on what's now known as the "Long Tail." In a book by Chris Anderson, WIRED magazine editor in chief, he pointed out that the cumulative sales volume of less popular items exceeded the share and value of the most popular books. Amazon made more money and had higher volume on the items that were at the lower end of the demand curve. (The long tail of the curve, hence the name.) While in a brick and mortar retail establishment, the sales velocity of these types of items is not enough to justify carrying them in the selection. Amazon and online retailers, much as catalog merchants did before them, can function as if they have almost zero carrying cost. (In today's digital economy, that can even be the case with the delivery of digital products.) With the advent of digital discovery tools such as search engines and social recommendation and discovery, it has become easy for disparate, geographically widespread demand to discover these long-tail products and purchase them online. Thus, a retail store selling nothing but hot sauce might fail to win enough customers in any given neighborhood, but online can generate tens of millions in sales from spice-loving customers across the country.

One-to-One Marketing

One-to-one marketing requires learning the profile or details about individual customers to identify which are most valuable to the company. By customizing the product or service, the value for the customer can be increased.

One-to-one marketing is rapidly becoming a competitive imperative.[3] As companies learn more about their customers, they can use this knowledge to create and sell products and services to breed loyalty. The key steps to becoming a one-to-one marketer are as follows:

- **Identify Customers or Get Them to Identify Themselves.** Consider all options for collecting names: sales transactions, contests, sponsored events, frequent-buyer programs, 800 numbers, credit card records, simple survey cards, and quick one question polls when customers call and social network scouting.

- **Link Customers' Identities to Their Transactions.** Credit card records are especially useful but not necessary. The best way to build individual customer transaction records is often to adopt a different business approach. Consider membership clubs to make it possible to link information about purchases with people.

- **Calculate Individual Customer Lifetime Value.** Knowing what a customer is likely to spend over time will help the entrepreneur decide which customers are most desirable (because their business is more profitable) and how much to invest in keeping them. In this light, unusual and seemingly expensive offers can make powerful economic sense.

- **Practice Just-in-Time Marketing.** Know the purchasing cycle for the product or service, and measure it in months or years. Time the company's entry into the market to the customer's purchasing cycle. Time the marketing material to meet the customer's needs rather than the company's quarterly sales goals. Send handwritten postcards or marketing materials or use a new catalog for selling.

- **Strengthen a Customer Satisfaction Program.** Survey questions can be tailored to a customer's wish list and buying preferences. Customize responses to meet the customer's demand.

- **Treat Complaints as Opportunities for Additional Business.** Don't ignore customer complaints; follow up with them to identify and correct the problem. By responding quickly, a disgruntled customer may turn into an advocate for the company.

- **Survey Customers to Find Their Points of Pain.** Listening to customers' problems can often lead to new products, services, or business models. The Greif and SmartPak cases in Chapter 2 illustrate this point.

- **Enhance Product Information.** Build in some form of information that will keep customers coming back. For example, the retailer J. Crew provides a $25 electronic gift card when customers make purchases in excess of $200.[4]

The Value of Loyalty Programs

Marketing plans often place a great deal of emphasis on acquisition but not on customer loyalty. The reality is that for a start-up to survive, regardless of industry, it must not only obtain the right customers but keep them. A widely held view is that on average it costs a firm five to six times as much to attract a new customer as to keep one.

Not all existing customer relationships are worth keeping unless you can convert them to valuable client status. Careful analysis may show that many relationships are no longer profitable for the firm because they cost more to maintain than the revenues they generate. At times, firms may want to let customers walk if they prove unprofitable. Of course, legal and ethical considerations will influence such decisions.

In order to know how much the start-up can spend on customer loyalty, one must have a general understanding of what the customers are worth. Generally, customers are worth more with a longer relationship (although this is not always true).

The following factors often underlie hidden profit potential:

- *Profit Derived from Increased Purchases.* Individuals may buy more or consolidate their purchases.

- *Profit from Reduced Operating Costs.* As customers become more experienced, they make fewer demands on the supplier (e.g., they may call the customer service center less frequently).

- *Profit from Referrals to Other Customers.* This saves on acquisition costs.

- *Profit from Price Premium.* Depending on the industry, new customers often benefit from introductory promotional discounts (e.g., phone service, magazine subscriptions). Once loyalty is established, the customer may be sold an upgrade ("upsold") to a premium product which provides a higher profit level to the supplier.

Influencer Identification in Modern Marketing

A key new focus of loyalty marketing is influencer identification and amplification. Prior to digital channels, the only influencers of other consumer that could be easily found were the traditional gatekeepers—the media and press. With the rise of social media, including networks like Facebook, Twitter, review platforms, and other user-generated content—all of which is discoverable and can be analyzed by software—we can now identify influencers among our customers and enthusiasts and work to reward, support, and extend the effect of their positive feelings to other customers. Whereas traditional media marketing is the domain of reach and frequency—spreading a message wide and often to the target audience—influencers are judged differently.

Influencers are not just those with large followings—they also need to have an affinity for the product or topic, and their followers or readership must demonstrate engagement or activation potential. A mom blogging part time about her experiences with different baby products to an avid audience of other moms who comment, trial, and discuss the products she recommends would be an excellent example.

Defining the Market Segmentation

Segmentation divides a market into workable groups or divisions. It divides a market by age, income, product needs, geography, buying patterns, eating patterns, family makeup, or other classifications. Good marketing plans rarely address the full range of possible target markets. They almost always select segments of the market. The selection allows a marketing plan to focus more effectively, to define specific messages, and to send those messages through specific channels.[5]

A market may be segmented in several different ways:

- **Demographic segmentations** are classic. This method divides the market into groups based on age, income level, and gender. Some marketing plans focus mainly on demographics because they work for strategy development. For example, video games tend to sell to adolescent males; dolls sell mainly to preadolescent females. Cadillac automobiles generally sell to older adults, while minivans sell to adults (with families) between the ages of thirty and fifty.

- **Business demographics** may also be valuable. Government statistics tend to divide businesses by size (in sales or number of employees) and type of industry (using industry classification systems such as SIC, the standard industrial classification). If the business is selling to companies, then the focus is on segmenting by using types of business. For example, the business may want to sell to optical stores, CPA firms, auto repair shops, or companies with more than five hundred employees.

- **Geographic segmentation**, another classic method, divides people or businesses into regional groups according to location. It is very important for retail businesses, restaurants, and services addressing their local surroundings only. In those cases, divide the market into geographic categories such as by city, ZIP code, county, state, or region. International companies frequently divide their markets by country or region.

- **Psychographic segmentation** divides customers into cultural groups, value groups, social sets, or other interesting categories that might be useful for classifying customers. For example, First Colony Mall of Sugar Land, Texas, describes its local area group as "25 percent Kids & Cul-de-Sacs (upscale suburban families, affluent), 5.4 percent winner's circle (suburban executives, wealthy), 19.2 percent boomers and babies (young, white-collar suburban, upper-middle income), and 7 percent county squires (elite exurban, wealthy)."

- **Ethnic segmentations** are somewhat uncomfortable for those of us living in a country with a history of ethnic-based discrimination. Still, the segmentation by ethnic group is a powerful tool for better marketing. For example, Spanish-speaking television programming became very powerful in the United States in the 1990s. Chinese and Japanese television stations have also appeared in major metropolitan areas.

- **Combination segmentations** are also quite common. You frequently see demographic and geographic segmentations combined—population groups or business types in a specific area are an obvious example, or ethnic groups in a certain city, or "boomers and babies" within reach of a shopping center. These are all combinations of factors. For example, Apple computer has used a combination of business and general demographics by region, segmenting the market into households, schools, small business, large business, and government. It further divides each group into countries and regional groups of countries.[6]

ROADMAP

IN ACTION

To determine the best segmentation, analyze what specific channel provides the best marketing potential. The goal is to select the right media messages and divide customers in a way that makes it easy to develop a marketing strategy and implementation plan (Figure 4.4).

FIGURE 4.4
Facebook Segmentations
Source: Facebook/online.

Behavioral and Interest Targeting through Digital Communities

With the advent of social media and digital communities, it's become easier than ever to find groups that might be suited to a product or service. Segmentation in the past was based on averages and estimates across an audience, but modern digital marketing allows for very precise targeting based on self-reported or observed interests and behaviors. Facebook, for example, encourages users to self-report their favorite books and films, music, and other media, as well as detail interests as diverse as kayaking and keg stands (although one would assume not at the same time).

Twitter users can be segmented by the feeds they follow, among many other things. One can target older users interested in energy industry issues and right-wing politics, for example, based on the intersection of these two interests as displayed by who they follow on Twitter. Also LinkedIn, the modern professionals resume and industry forum, has groups ranging across a variety of business functions and industry niches.

Conducting a Competitive Analysis

Creating a competitor profile provides the entrepreneur with a detailed assessment of the competitive environment. It is helpful to know the key players, their personalities, and marketed positions in each firm with which the company will be competing. How do they compete for business in terms of product, service, location, and promotion? In many situations, competitors use different methods to gain market dominance. Do the competitors vie for price? Some may pursue price-sensitive market segments, whereas others may seek the business of those who want improved service, quality, convenience, value, rapid delivery, and/or a wide selection of product options.

It is particularly important to identify which businesses will provide the most significant competition and predict what they will likely do. Analyze the situation by asking the questions provided below regarding six key areas of competition:

1. Product or Service

- How is the competitive product or service defined?
- How is it similar or different?
- Does the competition cater to a mass or targeted market?
- What features of the product are superior?
- What strengths or weaknesses of the competition can be exploited?

2. Price

- What is the competitor's pricing strategy?
- Is the competitor's price higher or lower?
- What is the competitor's gross margin for similar products?
- Does the competitor offer terms, discounts, or promotions?

3. Industry Competitors

- Define the competition in terms of new, Internet, or potential threats of existing companies.
- What are the strengths and weaknesses of each?
- How will e-commerce companies affect the business?
- How can the suppliers or buyers affect the competition?

4. Selling/Promotion

- How do the competitors advertise? Analyze their web sites.
- How much do the competitors spend on advertising, web development, and promotions?
- What marketing vision or plan are the competitors selling?

5. Management

- How strong is the competitor's management team?
- What is the team's background or experience?
- How does the company recruit new key employees?
- How does the company compensate its employees?

6. Financial

- Is the competitor profitable?
- What volume are sales and market shares?
- Do they spend money for R&D, Internet, and web development?
- Are they properly capitalized? How strong is their cash flow?

Practical Examples of Digital Tools to Answer These Questions

Fortunately for the new business, tools exist to do extensive and inexpensive research on almost all of these things. Basic Google searches will reveal ads from competitors and how they promote themselves, quickly establishing a competitive matrix and landscape. Google news and other resources can find press articles and web sites that may directly compare products across the industry, or even excerpts from expensive industry reports to get you started. Finally, customer reviews and support forums can yield a wealth of data on product shortcomings and issues that can be attacked by a new entrant.

Pricing can often be established through the same methods and particularly in retail, offers and promotions are tracked by third parties like RetailMeNot and CouponCabin, who compile and disseminate these offers to consumers.

Management teams and employees have a wealth of data available for examination. Search engines can reveal articles and references about a person, and almost everyone is on social media. Additionally, LinkedIn, the professional social network, can be used to understand the size of the competitor's organization and details about where they are being recruited from and even where they go to. Companies like Glassdoor and others maintain independent reviews of workplace benefits and conditions.

Financial information can be easily researched through sec.gov, nasdaq.com, Yahoo, or Google. Finance for larger public companies, and often, detailed info exists for start-ups in CrunchBase, a database of start-up and growth companies that records news, financings, and important hires.

Preparing the Pricing and Sales Strategy

Once the marketing analysis and competition review are established, the entrepreneur should begin to develop the pricing and sales plan. Pricing is the key to the process of controlling costs and showing a profit. It is a very effective marketing tool that must be mastered. The price of a product or service conveys an image and affects demand. Preparing the pricing and sales strategy is also one of the most difficult tasks the entrepreneur must fulfill regarding the product or service.[7]

A number of other factors can influence the entrepreneur's ability to effectively price the product or service: notably, number of competitors, seasonal or cyclical changes in supply and demand, production and distribution costs, customer services, and markups.

Pricing procedures differ depending on the nature of the business, whether it be retail, manufacturing, or service oriented. The general methods discussed below may be applied to any type of business. They also demonstrate the basic steps in adopting a pricing system and how that system should relate to the desired pricing goals. With this general method in mind, the entrepreneur can formulate the most appropriate pricing strategy.

Pricing Methods

Value

Demonstrating value is part of pricing a new strategy. Price should not be based simply on cost plus a modest profit. Rather, it should be based on the value of the product or service to the customer. If the customer does not think the price is reasonable, then the entrepreneur should consider not only a price change but also a new image for the product or service.

Rationale

The entrepreneur must explain why his prices differ from those of the competitors. For instance, does the new business perform a function faster or more efficiently? Lower prices can be justified that way. Or is the new product created with greater care and better materials? A higher cost can communicate this idea.

To determine pricing, you need to know the breakeven point, that is, the sales volume at which a product or service will be profitable. This involves dividing the total fixed and semivariable costs by the contribution obtained on each unit of service.

Example: Calculating Breakeven Points—Hotel Room Pricing

Assume a 100-room hotel needs to cover fixed and semivariable costs of

$2 million/year:

Average room is $120/night.

Variable costs per room are $20/night. Average contribution per room is $100.

2,000,000/100 = 20,000 room nights per year out of 36,500 capacity must be sold. If prices are cut 20 percent (or variable costs rise 20 percent), new calculation is 2,000,000/80 = 25,000 room nights per year out of 36,500 capacity must be sold.

The marketing plan should estimate the following:

- **Fixed Costs:** The overhead for the start-up; the economic costs of running the business even if no products or services are sold (e.g., rent, insurance, taxes, salaries, and payroll taxes for long-term employees)

- **Variable Costs:** The economic costs associated with service for an additional customer (e.g., serving an extra hotel guest, making an additional teller transaction in a bank)

- **Semivariable Costs:** In between fixed and variable costs; represent expenses that rise or fall in stepwise fashion as the business volume increases or decreases (e.g., hiring a part-time employee to work in a restaurant on busy weekends)

- **Contribution:** Difference between the variable cost of selling an extra unit of service and the money received from the buyer of that service

Depending on the start-up, the ratio of fixed costs to variable will vary greatly. For example, an airline has very high fixed costs but relatively low variable costs (and airlines have reduced variable costs recently to compensate for higher fixed costs, such as oil prices). Conversely, the beverage industry would incur high variable costs (e.g., cost of can, beverage, labeling).

This ratio of fixed to variable costs has important implications for pricing. High-fixed-cost industries, such as car rental or airline, are willing to "give away" services, typically as rewards from customer loyalty programs, for many of these firms do not encounter additional costs as a result. Moreover, these industries are most likely to discount their products or services.

High-variable-cost industries cannot discount as readily, especially if their discounted price falls significantly below marginal cost or the cost of producing an extra unit.

Software as a Service (SaaS)

The SaaS model is radically disrupting the software industry in general, and the high-value enterprise software is feeling its effects. Previously, enterprise software involved lengthy sales processes often involving senior-level staff to be involved in deciding multimillion dollar, multiyear contracts. The software itself came in a customized installation that often required extensive training and a multiyear upgrade process that could cost time and money.

Rethinking the deployment of software in the era of cloud computing, companies like Salesforce allow Internet-based access to the full functionality of core software for a relatively small subscription fee. Even small groups within companies, which used to have to go through long procurement and approval processes, can make the decision to adopt based on the low price point amortized over a multiyear subscription. The software itself tends to be much easier to use to attract individual champions, and as it is based in the cloud, it is constantly and consistently upgraded—requiring no effort from customer and corporate IT, and no additional cost, while allowing the software company to avoid the duplicative support costs of multiple enterprise versions in the wild. Best of all, many of these products allow the installation to easily grow and shrink due to the subscription model. If the software provides value, it can grow both in number of seats as new members of the company easily adopt subscriptions, as well as add features to upsell or increase price.

By moving to a much lower price point, simplifying the adoption process, SaaS companies have dramatically changed the game on traditional software companies. This opens up the market to smaller companies that might not have even been able to employ an expensive deployment in the past.

The Freemium Model

Freemium, an amalgam of free and premium, is often coupled with the SaaS model. Since with a cloud-based model, costs of service are often small and variable. While marketing costs can be quite high, the practice of offering a free tier of service to attract users with a premium tier to monetize them has become quite popular. Users adopt the free version for its value and become familiar with the product and can be upsold to the premium tier based on knowledge gained from the very free usage patterns that attracted them!

The freemium model works best when the cost of service is relatively low; there is a clear distinction between the free and paid versions and when there is a natural incentive to upgrade. Additional value can be derived from allowing users to 'earn' more value by promoting the product for the business.

A great example is Dropbox. Dropbox is a company that provides cloud-based computer storage, synced across multiple locations and devices. The free version has a generous storage limit, but once the user adopts cloud storage, the files tend to grow until the space is taken up. The user then faces an easy choice: pay a modest fee and get a very large amount of storage, both monetizing the free user and locking them in further, or earn extra storage by getting others to sign up.

Establishing Pricing Objectives

The marketing plan should be based on a clear understanding of the start-up's objectives. There are three basic categories of pricing objectives:

1. **Revenue Oriented:** The aim is to maximize the surplus of income over expenditures.

2. **Operations Oriented:** Typically, capacity-constrained organizations seek to match supply and demand to ensure optimal use of their productive capacity at any given time (e.g., hotels seek to fill rooms because an empty room is an unproductive asset; theaters want to fill seats). When demand is low, organizations may offer special discounts. When demand exceeds capacity, these firms try to increase profits and ration demand by raising prices ("peak season" prices).

3. **Patronage Oriented:** The aim is to attract customers, even at a loss, typical of grand opening sales. For example, a theater may give away seats for an opening night of a performance to create the image of excitement and popularity.

Furthermore, if advertising is a major revenue draw, giving substantial discounts might pay off in higher advertising rates for the increased exposure.

Another concept that the marketing plan may address is price elasticity. The concept of elasticity describes how sensitive the demand is to changes in price. When a small change in price has a big impact on sales, the demand for that product is said to be price elastic. The converse— a small change in price having little effect on demand—is price inelastic.

Price elasticity affects different industries to varying extents. For instance, the leisure airline passenger market tends to be price elastic. For this reason, airlines are always discounting prices during the off-season to attract more customers. (They also must meet minimum flight capacities to stay profitable owing to their high fixed costs.) Conversely, business airline customers are far less elastic. Usually, a businessperson needs to travel (to conduct important transactions or affairs) regardless of airline prices. Knowing this, some airlines discount fares far more frequently for flights with more consumer than business travelers, typically during the off-season.

Here are some pricing issues to consider:

- How much should be charged?

- Costs to the start-up

- Margin you are trying to achieve

- Breakeven point

- Discounts offered

- Psychological pricing points ($9.95 vs $10.00). What is the basis of pricing?

- Execution of specific task

- Admission to service facility

- Units of time

- Physical resources consumed

- How should prices be communicated to the target market?

The entrepreneur should also consider price bundling as an option. Often, companies will "bundle" a core service with a supplementary one—for example, concessions at a theater and an admission ticket sold under one price. This approach works well for motivating customers to try different types of products or services in addition to those they are already buying from the company.

Using Digital Channels to Create Demand

Creating demand using paid advertising online has a variety of options for the new business. While some are similar to traditional media in branding value and pricing, many are unique to the Internet, and almost all provide smaller businesses and advertisers without deep pockets to nevertheless access pools of potential customers. From search to display, social channels to e-mail, and newer channels like mobile and local, paid channels for advertising allow marketers to reach customers wherever they are. Indeed, advertising is the revenue model powering many of the biggest properties on the Internet.

Preparing an Advertising Campaign

The first thing to determine when planning an advertising campaign is simple: what is the goal? Are you trying to raise brand awareness, generate leads, increase sales, or something else?

Once the overall goal is clear, the next step is to determine the appropriate tracking metric. This is the measure of success—and it's not as easy. For example, how does one measure raising brand awareness online? One could pay for and distribute a survey to an exposed group and a control group—essentially an online focus group—but this can be expensive and difficult. Measuring leads might be easier, for example, through completed forms, but may miss quality measures and the like. Ultimately, the decision must not just be what we'd like to measure, but what we can measure. Easily available and oft-quoted metrics like clicks on an ad or likes on a page may be easy to measure but ultimately are a proxy for a true metric of success.

The most important metric is usually sales, from which we can determine effectiveness of our investment in advertising. If we are unable to directly track this, the best strategy is to resort to a metric as close to the desired goal as practical. For a real-world business like a sandwich shop, the proxy may be visitors to the page with a map and directions; for an e-commerce site, it could be the direct measurement of actual sales by the site.

Search and Pay per Click

Search marketing, or pay-per-click (PPC) advertising, is the primary revenue model of Google, the largest search engine. (Bing, a distant second home to Yahoo's search inventory, should not be overlooked but operates similarly.) Search is unique in that it allows marketers to "harvest intent"—to reach customers exactly when they are searching for a product or service, with a highly targeted and relevant advertisement. Advertisers bid on the cost per click—a performance-based metric ensuring that only interested potential customers are paid for as visitors—and Google displays their ads as the result of a complex algorithmic auction. The advertiser creates the ads and determines the search terms to bid on. When a search on the key phrase "digital cameras" is performed, the ads displayed consist of the winning bidders' creativity, and if the interested party clicks for more information, the advertiser is charged. It is then up to the advertiser's web site or store to do a good job of converting the qualified lead into a sale.

Display Ads

Display ads are most identified with banners. Invented initially as essentially an electronic proxy for magazine ads, the display channel has grown to include rich media like audio, video, and animations. Ads in display come in standard sizes and are priced in a more traditional CPM basis in many cases, that is, by the size and quality of the audience. Most display advertising is placed contextually—that is, based on what the user is looking at and who they are, rather than what they indicated interest in like search. This is similar to traditional media. In digital media, however, unlike Television or magazines, it is possible to target solely the portion of the audience representing the target customers. A seller on men's products advertising on a television show, for example, creates an ad to show to the entire audience, women included. Online, however, the same ad can be shown just to the males in the audience. An advertiser may pay a higher rate but spend less on an absolute basis and see a much higher yield thanks to this kind of targeting.

Display ad prices are generally based on a variety of factors, but in general, the bigger the ads size, the more one will pay. Ads in better placements—higher on the page (and so more likely to be seen)—also get a premium. Interactivity or multimedia raise the price, as does video, and finally, it's worth noting that both the quality of the publisher's audience and the laws of supply and demand also play a strong role. However, with a steady rise of inventory as the "long tail" of web sites make more impressions available for sale, the growth of programmatic trading and the exchanges that facilitate it—in essence, program trading of ads according to rules and budgets by computers in real time—have been phenomenal. Almost half of all inventory in display is now traded this way, opening up huge opportunities for advertisers.

Social media is an area of rapid growth for display ads. Facebook's many ad units fall primarily into this category, for example. With social channels, ads can be shown based on additional data about the viewer that they have shared with the social network. Instead of just targeting males, for example, one can target males who like gourmet food. This level of targeting is unprecedented and coupled with built-in tools for sharing has encouraged many advertisers to begin paid ad campaigns with the hopes of getting additional reach through sharing, liking, or retweeting.

Penetrating the Market and Setting up Sales Channels

The desired market penetration determines specific methods that can be used to sell products and services to customers. Some of the selling options include the following: direct sales, sales agents, and trade shows.

Inbound Marketing

One of the great changes from a world of traditional media to that of digital and social media is the ease of discovery and communication with brands and marketing teams. With search and social channels facilitating a two-way interactive communication between the potential customers and the businesses that are trying to reach them, a new form of marketing that combines a fundamental knowledge of digital discovery with strategic and tactical techniques for facilitating the process, as well as nurturing the lead through the funnel to purchase, has begun to be described as "Inbound Marketing."

Inbound marketing focuses on content creation, used to generate search rankings and social media visibility, to establish a brand or business as an expert in its field with valuable, useful content for potential customers of its products or services. This content is then distributed across customer communities in social media and other channels and leveraged to generate initial leads with potential customers. By establishing a program of regular content creation, businesses raise their profile in search engines with indexable material relevant to their business, as well as create useful or entertaining content about relevant industry issues to encourage sharing and community discussion.

The types of content can vary, but the key is to create consistently valuable content regularly, leverage it appropriately through channels of customer distribution, and over time develop a steady stream of organic traffic from digital channels.

For a consumer brand or a product with a short purchase funnel or low value, this content might simply be entertainment: funny quotes and quips, pictures, and even video. Other techniques include surveys and polls—generating content from the users and reporting back to them, increasing both engagement through the creation and the results. Another technique is timeliness or "meme-surfing" that is trying to tie the brand's content to something already trending like current events. This technique can generate leverage but carries risks of offending people or backfiring if done poorly.

For many business to business or high-value items, this can be an invaluable, modern method of lead nurturing. Buyer's guides and frameworks, white papers and data sets, informative presentations, webinars and videos, and e-books—all are effective tools for generating and nurturing leads. The basic technique is the same: create valuable content likely sought by the target audience and encourage or require e-mail registration or other contact exchange to access or download. This begins a dialogue where content rather than sales messaging is the basis and allows customers to self-identify when they are ready to buy.

For many marketers, the entry point here is the elusive "viral video"—however, a proper inbound marketing content creation strategy has a viral video as the lucky result of a continuous strategy of timely and valuable content. Ultimately, a business must think of this as a long-term strategy to generate a return on an investment into content that makes them the trusted, expert partner for the potential buyer—or the very least entertains them enough to keep the brand top of mind for the next purchase.

Direct Sales Force

The direct sales force is a group of salespeople who work directly for the company and are paid either straight salary, salary plus bonus, or straight commission. The advantage of a direct sales force is that, as full-time employees, they work for the company. The entrepreneur has complete control over training them to sell, price, and service the product. The disadvantage is the added expense in maintaining a full-time sales force. Salaries, travel expenses, office support, and benefits must be paid for each salesperson.

Sales Agents

A sales agent works as a subcontractor to sell products or services. Agents are paid by commission, which is calculated as a specified percentage of the price. They receive their commissions after the company collects from the customers. Sales agents pay for expenses such as product samples, travel, office, telephone, and supplies that are incurred in selling the product or service.

Sales agents usually work a specified territory where they can sell the product or service. In addition, they sign a performance contract, which specifies the minimum number of sales to be executed annually.

The advantage of using sales agents is that sales costs are not incurred until the product is sold. The entrepreneur can quickly build a large sales force and sell the product or service nationwide in a relatively short period of time.

The disadvantage of using sales agents is that they usually sell other products or services as part of a complete line. They tend to push the easier-to-sell products or services and those for which they have already established a large customer following. The entrepreneur has little control over the sales agents since they are subcontractors and do not work directly for the company. Therefore, they can be extremely difficult to manage with regard to pricing, follow-up, and service.[8] An extension of the agent model is to use one or more corporate partners, where there is a closer contractual relationship. Such partners gain additional value from selling your product or service if it helps them sell more of their own products or helps them sell against their own competitors. These issues are highlighted in the Ultrafast case on the web site associated with this book. Similar advantages and disadvantages are met in such partnerships. If you use agents or partners in this way, it is recommended that you also employ some direct selling; this retains close interaction with customers, which may identify new needs or points of pain while making you less dependent on independent sales resources.

Trade Shows

Trade shows are good places to exhibit and sell products. Many trade shows are held year round, but finding the right one can be difficult. The entrepreneur must carefully consider which trade shows to attend to meet target customers.

Selling products at trade shows has five major advantages:

1. Many prospective customers can be identified because they come directly to the trade show booth, rather than incurring additional costs to visit each one individually.

2. It is an excellent opportunity to interact with many people in the industry whom the entrepreneur might not have otherwise met.

3. The company can demonstrate the products and answer any questions from prospective customers about the product or service.

4. The company can initiate a business relationship by inviting the customer to a follow-up meeting.

5. The competition can quickly be assessed.

Prior to the trade show, the company should develop screening questions to identify solid sales leads. This is an excellent method to meet the key players in the industry and learn what is happening. The contracts that are made here can significantly increase business sales and better establish and increase market share. Entrepreneurs should consider the variables of targeted audience, type of product, and cost to help make their choices in determining the type of advertising best suited to let potential customers know about their products or services.

Viral Marketing

The best advocate for a company's products or services is an existing customer. *Viral marketing* is a term used to describe mechanisms by which customers are triggered and motivated to recommend a product or service to other potential customers. These word-of-mouth techniques have been significantly enhanced by the growth of the Internet which makes it easy for one customer to send personal recommendations to several contacts. The advent of Internet social networking and an understanding of how the power of the scale-free networks can exponentially spread information via highly trafficked nodes have led to a number of successful business models that capture the value of viral marketing.[9]

Mini-Case Glue Isobar

The highly creative advertising agency "glue Isobar"[10] executed a viral campaign for the launch of the new MINI Cooper S sports car, using a library of interchangeable video clips combined with a remarkable level of personalized content. With tongue in cheek, the concept centered around the idea that men aren't real men anymore due to the onset of so-called midlife crisis, their target market segment. Visitors to the car web site can nominate friends who may be jokingly demonstrating "soft" characteristics and not showing their "manliness." Using a simple Q&A interface, the visitor can create a highly personalized e-mail. The unsuspecting recipients then receives from the trusted friend a message advising that "someone wants to have a little word with them." They get a personal video message from an "in-your-face" character who seems to know a lot about them including their job, partner's name, and their perceived worst crimes against mankind. They are encouraged to "sort themselves out" and enjoy the visual feast of the MINI Cooper S for inspiration. The ad is very impactive, and those that receive it typically forward it to between five and ten of their closest male friends who automatically match the target group.

SUMMARY

Writing the marketing plan is the first step in the marketing process and a vital component of a full business plan. The marketing plan is an essential of a business because it communicates most directly the nature of the intended business and the manner in which that business will be able to succeed. Specifically, the purpose of the marketing process is to explain how a prospective business intends to manipulate and react to market conditions to generate sales.

The entrepreneur must prepare a marketing plan that is both interesting and thought provoking. The plan cannot simply explain a concept; it must sell a prospective business as an attractive investment opportunity, a good credit risk, and a valued vendor of a product or service.

This chapter provides guidelines to attract new marketing opportunities using digital marketing techniques. Applying digital tools is easier today than ever before to determine the viability of a business also to evaluate the most effective value proposition and refine the offering if it is needed.

Marketing plans to be effective must be realistic with goals set in advance. Market share must be addressed as well as market , penetration, sales goals, and pricing strategies. Pricing strategies must consider such factors as market competition, customer demand, life cycle of products, and economic conditions.

The marketing strategy describes how the business will implement its marketing plan to achieve desired sales performance. This involves focusing attention on each salient marketing tool a company has at its disposal. Elements such as distribution, pricing strategy, advertising, promotion, site analysis, and related budgets all may merit discussion, depending on their importance in relation to the company's overall market strategy. Although meticulous detail is probably unnecessary, it is important that you gain a general understanding of how the business intends to actively market its product or service. Most important, the marketing plan should show that you have spent some time talking to actual or potential customers. This is called *primary research* and is one of the main factors that will influence your ability to raise funds to build your business. (For more details, see the appendix at the end of this chapter.) After all, there *is* no business without customers.

The plan should also detail major competitors, noting their strengths and weaknesses. For the plan to be more strategic rather than mere reporting, it should suggest how the new company will vie within the competition—how it will serve an untapped niche. Perceptual mapping can visually illustrate this in two dimensions. Furthermore, a segmentation scheme of customers can be developed with an emphasis on which customer segments the new product or service seeks to capture.

Once the marketing analysis and competition review are established, the entrepreneur can begin to develop the pricing and sales plan. The crucial step of pricing a product or service is one of the most difficult decisions a business owner must make. A number of factors can serve as guides for pricing a product or service, including the number of competitors, seasonal or cyclical changes in demand, distribution costs, customer services, and markups. The elasticity of demand, or the change in demand given an increase in price, will also influence discounting decisions. Finally, clear knowledge of the breakeven point of the business is crucial in calculating the largest discount the business can afford to give away.

With a marketing plan in place, later chapters will focus on preparing a complete business plan (Chapter 6), setting up the company (Chapter 7), accessing money (Chapters 8), and managing the company's finances and growth (Chapter 9).

Modern entrepreneurship allows discovery with much less risk, both capital and personal time. Let the market help define your business.

STUDY QUESTIONS

Q.1 What are the five steps to formulate a successful marketing plan?

Q.2 How would you apply and use Google digital tools?

Q.3 Describe keyword lists to test the plan.

Q.4 How would you use digital channels to create demand?

Q.5 List three kinds of segmentation. For what kinds of products or services would one kind be more important than another?

Q.6 What are product positioning and perceptual mapping?" (Clue – Search the internet for definitions and examples.)

Q.7 What is viral marketing? Provide an example not referred to in this book. Why do you think a viral effect was created in your example?

Q.8 How can a small company use Google AdWords for market research?

Q.9 What factors determine whether the business would offer discounts?

Q.10 What are the three pricing objectives? Give an example of an industry that would use each.

Q.11 You own a cafe in a large urban area that carries a total of $500,000 per year in fixed costs. Your cafe sells only coffee for $2.50 per cup. The average variable cost per cup (coffee mix, cup costs, etc.) is $1. How many cups do you need to sell per day to break even? If the price of the coffee decreased by 10 percent for a special promotion (with all other costs staying the same), how many cups would you need to sell to break even?

EXERCISES

Marketing Analysis Interview: Customer Analysis

4.1 Interview an entrepreneurial company and prepare the top five reasons people buy (or would buy) its products or services and then answer questions 4.2 to 4.10 inclusive.

Description	Importance (1–10)	Company/product/service strength		
		Low	Average	High
1.				
2.				
3.				
4.				
5.				

4.2 When does a customer buy the product or service?

4.3 Describe a scenario in which a customer buys the product or service.

4.4 Where/how does a customer buy the product or service?

4.5 Describe the target customer (age, sex, income, interests, education, career, etc.).

4.6 How many target customers are within the geographic market (or are within reach of the distribution and marketing mechanisms)?

4.7 What percentage of these people would buy a product or service similar to that offered by the entrepreneurial company?

4.8 Do you expect this number to change? Why or why not?

4.9 Draw three perceptual maps (using two attributes for each map).

Marketing Analysis Interview: Competitor Analysis

4.10 List all of the major competitors, and complete the table with descriptions and figures.

Name	Approximate sales	Target market	Product/service	Price
1.				
2.				
3.				
4.				
5.				

Marketing Analysis Interview: Risk Questions

4.11 Complete the following table by describing the company's exposure to the risks listed on the left and the company's planned response or strategy should these risks be realized.

Area of potential risk	Company	Company response/strategy
Industry		
Product liability		
Economic changes		
Weather		
Legal and government		

INTERACTIVE LEARNING ON THE WEB

Test your skill-builder knowledge of the chapter using the interactive web site:

1. Self-Assessment:
2. Multiple Choice:
3. Matching of Key Terms:

4. Demonstration:
5. Case:
6. Video:

Case Study | Smart Card LLC Marketing Plan

(This chapter does not have a management exercise based on the Neoforma master case, so we have added this case for you to practice your marketing management skills.)

Smart Card LLC uses its expertise in smart cards and magnetic stripe technology to develop applications and solutions to meet the rapidly growing demand for marketing frequency programs. Existing and previous loyalty programs have normally been too expensive, complicated, and paper intensive thus leading to lack of customer participation. As competition increases in retail and other industries, companies are searching for new ways to understand customers and retain them. Smart Card LLC offers a smart card solution for these companies.

Smart Card LLC's strategy is focused on using smart cards for frequency programs that can benefit the customer. The company enables its clients to identify the following:

- Their most profitable customers
- What these customers purchase (how often, how much)
- Their buying preferences

Clients use these smart card solutions to better understand their customers and their purchase habits to introduce new services that create added value. Smart Card LLC also uses a marketing database to drive all aspects of the marketing mix: advertising, promotion, pricing, and site selection. Plus, it can be customized to meet the individual client's needs.

The objective is to establish an ongoing relationship with the client that will enhance the company's return on investment.

Industry surveys have found that 80 percent of revenues are generated by 20 percent of customers. Smart Card LLC can help companies identify that 20 percent segment of their customers.

Review of the Product Analysis

The product's quality and features should be directly compared to those offered by competitors. Unique attributes that are important to customers should be identified and highlighted in the memory of the card. As an example, smart cards can hold one to ten pages of customer-related information.

Other important marketing characteristics for smart cards are as follows:

User-Friendliness: Will customers feel comfortable using the product?

Reliability: Will the card work? Will the user feel 100 percent confident about the card's reliability? What backup system is in place?

Cost-effectiveness: How does delivery cost compare to the customer's perceived value of the service?

Compelling Use: The initial application must be universal and valuable to compel a critical mass of people to accept it. Does the product fit the bill?

Figure 4.5 summarizes the marketing opportunities for smart cards, and Figure 4.6 shows the advantages of smart cards as they relate to the cardholder, merchant, and issuers.

SMART CARD MARKETING OPPORTUNITIES

- **Product**
  - ➤ Compelling use: Application must attract critical mass of users
  - ➤ Versatility: Multiple uses→ more value
  - ➤ Cost effectiveness: Is service's perceived value worth the delivery cost?

- **Price**
  - ➤ Start-up: New high-tech products command price premium
  - ➤ Transition to maturity: Will price cover costs? Eliminate unprofitable services
  - ➤ Maturity: Will competitive price begin cutting?

- **Selling**
  - ➤ Direct salesforce versus distributors for selling smart cards; sale is complex, and direct sales provides better service and control

- **Promotion**
  - ➤ Smart card's promotional issues: industry must create a need for new technology and replace existing magnetic stripe cards

---

FIGURE 4.5
Marketing Opportunities for Smart Cards

Participant	Advantage	Description
Cardholder	Convenience	• No need for correct change • Easier than carrying cash
Merchant	Reduced costs	• Reduced cash handling • Reduced vandalism/theft
Issuer	Additional revenue	• Float/interest • Unused balances • Additional fee income • Expanded cardholder base
Acquirer	Additional revenue	• Additional merchant services charges • Expanded merchant base

FIGURE 4.6
Advantages of Smart Cards

Other issues that the company considered were to use specialists and generalists as salespersons and to strategically assign sales territories. The number of accounts to be assigned to an individual salesperson was determined, and compensation included salary and commission.

To promote smart cards, a complex product, the company used a more sophisticated promotion approach—a combination of trade shows, press kits, web sites, demonstrations, and other promotions.

Summary of the Company's Strengths and Weaknesses

The model in Figure 4.7 measures the company's strengths and weaknesses as they relate to the factors of management financing, product sales, and marketing. The company prepared the factors that affect the business and how attractive each is in terms of high or low priorities.

CASE STUDY QUESTIONS

1. Assess the market feasibility:
   (a) Had the management team done enough research to quantify the size of the market?
   (b) How valid was their assessment of probable market acceptance of the product?
2. Assess the advantages for smart cards as listed in Figure 4.7.

Factor	Attractiveness	
	High	**Low**
Management team	Proven	People with right skills not available
Financing	You have comfortable cushion or can raise capital if needed	You have a narrow time horizon to make money
Product development	Complete product line	One product of limited life
Salesforce	Strong contacts: specialist skills	Limited contacts: generalist skills
Marketing	Deep and tightly focused	Untargeted
Operations	Strategic alliances help improve execution	Learning in a vacuum

FIGURE 4.7
Summary of Company's Strengths and Weaknesses

3. Assess the various outside threats to the Smart Card LLC model.

4. Assume that you are a team member: Would you want to pursue the opportunity? Would you put your own money into it? Why or why not?

| # Marketing Research Techniques

Market Research to Aid Writing the Marketing Plan

Chapter 4 outlines the key parts of a marketing plan. To write a more substantial plan, the entrepreneur may consider marketing research for many purposes, including the following:

Market Dynamics

- To size up a market or industry in terms of annual sales revenue and potential for growth
- To forecast revenue and profit projections for the start-up
- To quantify the strengths and weaknesses of competitors in terms of market share and other competitive metrics
- To quantify untapped niche markets, such as underserved demographic groups, for the product or service

Consumer Behavior

- To gauge potential customers' reactions to a proposed product or service
- To test a name or concept
- To test price points
- To measure customer satisfaction with competing products or services
- To ascertain consumers' perceptions of competing products or services
- To understand customer behavior at different points in the buying experience
- To learn the most effective means of reaching customers
- To gain insight into which advertising appeals are most and least effective

Two Types of Market Research

Market research can be described as information gathered in order to obtain a more comprehensive understanding of an industry, product, or potential clientele. The two basic types of market research are primary and secondary.

Primary market research consists of specific information collected to answer specific questions. A few examples include user surveys, focus groups, phone interviews, and customer questionnaires. Many times, specific studies are commissioned by private or public entities and are conducted for a fee by market research firms that specialize in various methods of data collection. Results are then published and may or may not be considered proprietary and, thus, may or may not be made publicly available.

Primary market research may be accessed directly from the vendor who conducted the research or via various services that collect several providers' reports, called *aggregators*. Many market research vendors, as well as aggregators, make reports and tables of contents accessible via the Internet as well as through database services such as dialogue or profound. Entire reports can range in price from a few hundred dollars to several thousand. Many times, vendors will sell sections of various primary market research reports for much less than the entire report would cost. This is referred to as *cherry picking* and can be a cost-effective alternative to purchasing the entire report. Another cost-effective strategy can be to access the vendor's white papers, which are generally available for free at their Internet site. These are summary papers that are published when a new study is released, and many times, they contain valuable bits of information. A couple of the many potential sources of primary market research are listed here:

- www.ecnext.com (ECNext Knowledge Center)
- www.marketresearch.com (MarketResearch.com)

The dilemma for the small business owner is that, properly done, market research is quite expensive, takes time, and requires professional expertise. Acquiring all the necessary data to reduce the risk to your venture may cost so much and take so long that you may go out of business. The answer is to find a quick and inexpensive way of getting enough data to help you make the right decision most of the time.

An entrepreneur can conduct surveys and focus groups himself or farm them out to a research firm. The cost of conducting primary research, however, may be prohibitive. Therefore, the entrepreneur may consider a quick and dirty study that will not be as statistically reliable but will at least provide some initial insights into the business. Three ways of conducting low-cost research are the following:

1. *Informal Focus Groups.* Gather a group of likely customers for two or three hours and ask pointed questions about the product or service. Ask open-ended questions and probe responses. Use visuals such as competitors' products to gain reactions.

2. *Online Surveys.* Write questions about potential customers' thoughts and reactions to the proposed product or service. Consider a brief consultation with a statistician to ensure that the survey has reliability. (If it were repeated, it would yield the same result.) Purchase e-mail lists of potential customers, and e-mail the survey with incentives to participate. Analyze the tabulated results for key findings. (See the reference section for more information.)

3. *Access Established Communities.* Use an online service such as "ask your target market" (www.aytm.com), which has assembled over 2.5 million respondents that can be reached online. Primary research can be undertaken for less than a $1,000 using the tools provided by this company.

Secondary market research is information that has been gathered and repackaged from already existing sources. At one time or another in its life cycle, most marketing research has been considered primary research; someone somewhere identified the information to be gathered and contracted some entity to collect, repackage, and perhaps distribute or publish the data. Most of the information sources familiar to librarians and their patrons are considered secondary sources of market research.

Secondary market research is by far the most cost-effective information solution and generally the best place to start the information-gathering process. This information is extracted from industry studies, books, journals, and other published resources and is readily available at most public libraries. Many times, the information is accessible for free via the Internet as well. You should look to both sources for a complete picture.

Information to Garner from Secondary Research

- *Basic Demographic Information.* The age, sex, geographical region, marital status, and so on of your existing and potential customers and clients. More in-depth demographic information provides details on their personal preferences and buying habits.
- *Customer Ideas and Opinions.* Information such as product quality preferences, motivators of buying decisions, and color preferences.
- *Buying Cycles or Patterns.* Do they buy weekly, monthly, or yearly? Are the purchases spontaneous or planned? Is the purchase for self or a gift for others?
- *Trends for New or Improved Products and Services.* What needs do they want to have filled? What's missing in the marketplace?
- *Strategic Alliance Opportunities.* Who else is doing what you do? What companies could complement your product or service offerings if you worked together?
- *Opportunities for Beating Your Competition.* What's important to your customers? Price? Quality? Features?

ADDITIONAL RESOURCES

- IAB.net

- Google Knowledge

- HubSpot

- Moz

- **Lexis/Nexis**, Reed Elsevier, P.O. Box 933, Dayton, OH 45401; (800) 227-4908; www.lexisnexis.com/

- **Direct Marketing Association**, 1120 Avenue of the Americas, New York, NY 10036; (212) 768-7271; www.the-dma.org

- **Business Marketing Association**, 400 North Michigan Avenue, 15th Floor, Chicago, IL 60611; (800) 664-4BMA; www.marketing.org

- **Marketing Research Association**, 1344 Silas Deane Highway, Suite 306, Rocky Hill, CT 06067; www.marketingresearch.org/

ENDNOTES

1. The content for this section was provided by Matt Michaux, COO of Halare Inc., in July 2011.

2. See Robert C. Blattberg and John A. Deighton, "Interactive Marketing: Exploiting the Age of Addressibility," *Sloan Management Review 33*, no. 1 (1991): 5–14.

3. See Leonard Fuld, *Competitive Intelligence* (New York: John Wiley & Sons, 1993), 9–10.

4. J. Crew issues gift cards with purchases of specified amounts for specific promotions. Interview with Scott Rosenberg, J. Crew, New York, February 2002.

5. See Leo Jakobson, "Growing Pains," *Alleycat News* (May 2001): 76–78.

6. See Bob Tedeschi, "Spy on Your Customers (They Want You To)," *Smart Business* (August 2001): 58–66.

7. See Philip T. Kottler, *Marketing Management*, 10th ed. (Upper Saddle River, NJ: Prentice Hall, 2000). Kottler indicates that the firm should consider six factors in setting policies: (1) selecting the pricing objective; (2) determining demand; (3) estimating costs; (4) analyzing competitor's cost, prices, and offers; (5) selecting a pricing method; and (6) selecting the final price.

8. See Courtney Price et. al., *The Entrepreneur's Fast Track II Handbook* (Denver: Entrepreneurial Education Foundation, 1997), 109–112.

9. For further examples on viral marketing techniques, see David Silver, *Smart Start-Ups: How Entrepreneurs and Corporations Can Profit by Starting Online Communities* (Hoboken, NJ: Wiley, 2007), L. Weber, *Marketing to the Social Web: How Digital Customer Communities Build Your Business* (Hoboken, NJ: Wiley, 2007), and the section on viral marketing in Albert-Laszlo Barabasi, *Linked: How Everything is Connected to Everything Else and What it Means* (New York: Plume Press, 2003).

10. Other examples of viral marketing campaigns can be found at www.glueisobar.com.

Using the Crowd[*]

5

"Many ideas grow better when transplanted into another mind than in the one where they sprang up."

Oliver Wendell Holmes

OBJECTIVES

- Understand what is meant by "the crowd" and crowdsourcing.
- Recognize that innovation-related knowledge is widely distributed yet accessible and valuable.
- Understand the difference between closed and open innovation.
- Learn the different types of crowdsourcing and when and how to use them.
- Learn the different types of crowdfunding and when and how to use them.
- Understand how the crowd can be central to a business model.
- Understand how crowdsourcing can be used to reduce the need for start-up capital.
- Understand the risks in crowdsourcing including protecting intellectual property.

CHAPTER OUTLINE

Introduction

Profile: Daniel Gulati, FashionStake

Closed versus Open Innovation

Motivations to Be a Contributor to a Crowd

Types of Crowdsourcing

- **Mini-Cases: Flitto, Goldcorp**

Relevant Applications of Crowdsourcing

- **Ideation**
- **Business Model Design**

---

[*]This chapter was written jointly by Professors Marion Poetz and Anthony Warren

"Crowdsourcing is a type of participative online activity in which an individual, an institution, a nonprofit organization, or company proposes to a group of individuals of varying knowledge, heterogeneity, and number, via a flexible open call, the voluntary undertaking of a task. The undertaking of the task, of variable complexity and modularity, and in which the crowd should participate bringing their work, money, knowledge and/or experience, always entails mutual benefit. The user will receive the satisfaction of a given type of need, be it economic, social recognition, self-esteem, or the development of individual skills, while the crowdsourcer will obtain and utilize to their advantage that what the user has brought to the venture, whose form will depend on the type of activity undertaken."

Introduction

The Internet has fundamentally changed the way that ideas are created, expanded, developed, financed, tested, marketed, and sold. No longer is a budding entrepreneur isolated from the world's knowledge, skills, and resources but is immersed in the "crowd" that houses them. The term "crowdsourcing" has emerged to broadly describe a fundamental set of tools that can be used at various stages of creating and implementing new ideas along an entrepreneur's journey.

Jeff Howe and Mark Robinson, editors at Wired Magazine, coined the term "crowdsourcing" in 2005 to describe how businesses were using the Internet to outsource work to individuals. Crowdsourcing may take some part of a function once performed by employees and outsourcing it to an undefined and often large network of people. More importantly, crowdsourcing brings resources to a small enterprise that could not be acquired by hiring individuals in the traditional way. As one investor commented, "why own the mediocre when you can rent the best?"

In crowdsourcing, problems and needs are broadcast to a large and diverse audience in the form of an "open call" for solutions. Members of the public[1] submit solutions, which are then usually, but not always, owned by the originating entity. Sometimes, the contributor of the solution is compensated monetarily, or with prizes or some form of recognition. In other cases, the only rewards may be kudos or intellectual satisfaction.

A subcategory is called crowdfunding in which a need for cash is publicized broadly and contributors in addition to gaining personal satisfaction may receive rewards and even shares in the posting company.

After studying more than forty definitions of crowdsourcing in the scientific and popular literature, Enrique Estellés-Arolas and Fernando González Ladrón-de-Guevara developed an integrated definition shown in the margin.

Crowdsourcing systems are used to accomplish a variety of tasks. For example, the crowd may be invited to expand on a conceptual idea, develop a new technology, carry out a design task, test a market, or fund a project. In addition, intimately incorporating the use of crowdsourcing by entrepreneurs into business models may reduce risk, lower funding requirements, and accelerate revenue growth. In some cases, accessing the "crowd" is a fundamental component and necessary ingredient.

Members of the crowd usually remain anonymous which can lead to other intriguing benefits. All stereotyping is removed. In traditional organizations, the smartest people attended similar universities, with similar courses, and are strongly influenced by the culture and expectations found in their workplace. However, often a lack of experience or exposure to knowledge in another field is a key ingredient required for breakthrough thinking.

More recently, a number of web-based platforms have been created to help entrepreneurs access different "crowds" for specific purposes, and we expect these to proliferate.[2]

The first section of this chapter provides a general background to the rapidly growing field. This is followed by sections that illustrate the different types of crowdsourcing that entrepreneurs may use at evolving stages of their enterprise.

The first of these application sections outlines the way that crowdsourcing impacts innovation. We differentiate between closed and open innovation and outward and inward looking methods.

Once an idea has been honed to represent an actual business opportunity, the entrepreneur needs to develop a business model that may encompass interacting with different crowds. Integrating crowdsourcing into a business model can accelerate time to market and reducing the amount of capital that may be required.

A third application area is accessing skills and expertise from the crowd which may involve help with development and problem solving, or getting to those important early adopter customers.

Finally, we address the topic of crowdfunding, which can provide an entrepreneur access to cash either together with other more traditional funding sources or even as a replacement.

Throughout, we introduce a number of mini-cases where the crowd has been integral to a small, entrepreneurial company. These cases illustrate crowdsourcing at each stage of a company's development from the early ideation activities through the development phases, accessing funds, entering markets, and sustaining innovation in the longer term. Incorporating crowdsourcing into your plans can reduce your need for funding as you access external resources on an "as-needed" basis while accelerating your growth.

ROADMAP

| IN ACTION | The entrepreneur should examine the different types of crowdsourcing and determine which, if any, can be used to accelerate their business growth and reduce the need for cash. |

Profile: Daniel Gulati, Fashionstake[3]

Daniel met Vivian Weng while they were both students at the Harvard Business School. Vivian had worked in the fashion industry and saw how difficult it was for talented designers to promote their collections. It can take years to gain access to large stores, and most do not have the cash to stay in business that long. At the same time, customers are seeking new designs rather than the tired merchandise for sale in their local mall. This mismatch between supply and demand represented an opportunity to the pair of entrepreneurs.

According to Dan, there is an entirely new shopping trend unfolding—a shift from e-commerce (electronic commerce) to p-commerce (participatory commerce), in which customers contribute curation, design, or even funding for the products they eventually buy. A p-commerce web site includes community engagement, user empowerment, discovery, personalization, and supply-side innovation.

The vision of changing the way that fashion designers can reach their customers directly gave birth to FashionStake Inc., which the pair founded in September 2010 located right in the fashion clothing district in Midtown Manhattan, New York.

FashionStake is a marketplace for independent fashion, powered by the community that decides which designers are featured by voting support or otherwise on the web site and is a great way to find the best designers and looks. This creates competition among the best designers while allowing them to get to a large audience. It also reduces the risks that a retailer faces if it makes the wrong choices on inventory while, at the same time, engaging customers with a willingness to buy.

The company charges a small sales commission but does not charge listing fees, thereby aligning its interests with designers.

The company grew rapidly, soon representing over 200 top independent designers from around the world. It eventually garnered the interest of venture capitalists and received growth funding from Battery Ventures, Forerunner Ventures, and others.

In January 2012, FashionStake was acquired by Fab.com, a similarly modeled New York-based company selling primarily home decor from independent designers. In the second half of 2011, Fab grew rapidly, registering 1.65 million users, who purchased 750,000 products. Both companies have a similar mission: to bring independent artists and craftsmen, who make aesthetically appealing and sometimes out-of-the ordinary items to a large marketplace, which represents an engaged "crowd" guiding the choice of products they wish to buy.

Before getting into more detail on the types and uses of crowdsourcing, we need to contrast the difference between closed and open innovation.

Closed versus Open Innovation[4]

The traditional model for new product or service development (NPD) uses internal resources entirely in what is termed the closed model of innovation. Companies have now recognized that searching for and incorporating knowledge from outside the company (outside-in approach) as well as leveraging existing internal knowledge via licensing and other mechanisms (inside-out approach) can be highly effective, using a so-called open model. Figure 5.1 shows the differences between the two models. The open model has a range of options for accessing external knowledge and leveraging internal competencies. The Internet has added a new dimension to this concept, namely, the ability to identify and engage with a "crowd" that can contribute to the generation of ideas, solving problems, undertaking part of the development process, finding applications for existing technologies, and even providing financial backing. Engaging with the crowd is a key activity in open innovation.

Large companies are now embedding open innovation methods into their businesses. For example, Proctor and Gamble, the global consumer goods company, realizing that they could no longer create enough new products using their internal R&D departments, has embraced open innovation for several years. As one illustration, the company created an online social network for mothers called Vocalpoint.com. In exchange for free enrollment by mothers with young children who meet with other such mothers, members receive early notification and free samples of new products. In addition, mothers can suggest new product ideas and vote on new ideas too. Vocalpoint has already generated several new business areas for P&G including an eStore (pgestore.com) for home delivery of detergents bypassing supermarkets and taking away the need to carry heavy products from the store to home. The eStore has also grown as an effective sales channel for other bulky goods including those that customers prefer to have delivered rather than purchase in a store such as adult incontinence pads.

Closed innovation model   **Open innovation model**

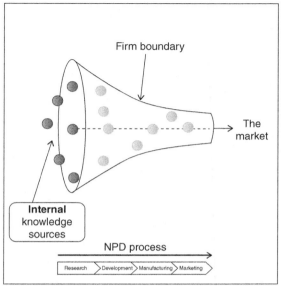
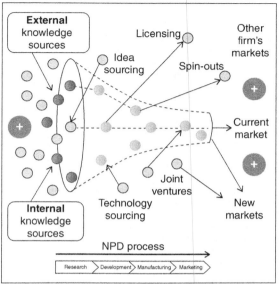

FIGURE 5.1
Comparison between (a) Closed and (b) Open Innovation
Source: Adapted from Chesbrough (2003[4], 2006[5]).

The Internet provides young companies the same opportunities to use the crowd so that they can access knowledge, ideas, customers, and others on the same scale as the large incumbents without investing in large R&D and marketing resources.

Motivations to Be a Contributor to a Crowd

Why do crowd members contribute to company-hosted crowdsourcing initiatives? Research studies[6] indicate that both intrinsic and extrinsic factors play a role. The opportunity to build a reputation, the chance of working on "a cool" project, the fun involved in solving tricky problems, or even some sort of addiction to the platform community were identified as some of the main factors driving crowd contributions. In tournament-based crowdsourcing, the motivation to participate is also driven by the chance of winning a monetary reward, the pride of knowing one is a winner, and being recognized as a winner. Other factors that reportedly influence whether or not crowds are willing to contribute their knowledge relate to the extent to which they perceive the crowdsourcing initiative to be fair and how much they are attached to the product or brand of the firm.

Other personal reasons are spread over this spectrum of behaviors:

- *Philosophy of Life*: In this case, individuals are motivated by a spiritual need to "leave the world a better place" for others. They do not seek attribution or any other benefit. Indeed, they may actively shy away from any attachment to their contribution or any recognition of their work.

- *Altruism*: One step up from here are individuals who, mostly for personal reasons, have reached a stage in their lives in which "giving" in and of itself is sufficient motivation. Perhaps, we all have a philanthropic gene somewhere, and the action here is closely related to this.

- *Bricolage*: This term was first coined by a French social sciences researcher, who observed machinists creating complex and personal ornaments that they placed close to their workplace.

The motivation here seems to be one whereby the satisfaction arises from just exercising one's skills to their utmost—a kind of "celebration of excellence." Bricoleurs do not seek attribution for their work—the sheer excellence of their output is sufficient. This may be the motivation for many hackers for whom the elegant solving of a complex problem provides both challenge and satisfaction. We all like to finish a crossword!

- *Peer Recognition*: In this case, the personal satisfaction comes from having your peers witness the excellent work that you have contributed. This motivation is well known and is common, for example, in academic research, where peer review is central to the process.

- *Fame*: One step further, and the individual wants to be known for the excellence of his or her contribution. Fame may be sufficient in and of itself, or might be a planned step to a coveted and highly remunerated position. In both cases, the contribution is freely offered. An example here is serial reviewers on Amazon. Or again, there is a class of contributors to Wikipedia who have contributed hundreds, even thousands of articles. Are they trying to parade their prowess or build their reputation for future leverage?

ROADMAP

IN ACTION

The entrepreneur should identify possible sources of external knowledge and examples of similar companies to avoid developing what is already known.

Types of Crowdsourcing

It is useful to breakdown the rather broad concept of crowdsourcing into subcategories. The following four types were first described in Jeff Howe's book[7] on the topic.

Crowd Creation

Perhaps, the best-known forms of crowdsourcing are "creation" activities such as asking individuals to film commercials, solve challenging scientific problems, or construct complex software programs—or indeed provide translation services.

Mini-Case: Flitto

Simon Lee was born in Kuwait in 1982 and lived in the United States, United Kingdom, and Saudi Arabia before eventually settling South Korea. He started his first crowdsourcing company, Flyingcane, in 2007 but realized that he needed a broader exposure to global business and spent four years as an investment manager within SK Telecom, a major mobile operator based in South Korea. In 2012, his entrepreneurial drive reemerged and he founded Flitto.

Flitto is a crowdsourcing translation platform that allows you to read any content in your native language or request translations in real time for voice, text, and image. You can also follow and read your favorite celebrities and brands' social media feeds, find amusing comics and cartoons from around the world, or discover deals wherever you go, all in your native language. Simon's exposure to many different languages during his formative years triggered the idea of using crowdsourcing to break down the barriers created by different languages. Frustrated with the poor performance of machine translation and the expense and delays of professional translators, he conceived the idea of using the crowd to provide translations quickly and for free!

The Flitto platform allows anyone to post voice, picture, or text content and have it translated by a native speaker within minutes, often seconds. The originator can rank the responses and the translator of choice gains points in the system, which provides motivation for further involvement. Local companies can reach global markets using Flitto without the costs of promotional materials and advertising in every language. Flitto takes a small percentage of the sales price on any products sold via its platform. Some users are also willing to pay for translations. Cash generated in this way create a fund to redeem points. Avid translators can make a few hundred dollars a month for, say, thirty minutes a day while they are having a coffee break. After just one year of launch, the company was hosting 3,000 translations a day, 2 million users, and had revenues of $100,000 per month and forecasted $8 million in revenue for its second full year of operations. Flitto is an excellent example of a business model where crowdsourcing is a central and fundamental ingredient.[8]

Even government agencies are using crowdsourcing to help solve large social and scientific challenges. For example, the National Aeronautics and Space Administration (NASA) in the United States is using crowd creation for tasks such as identifying locations from over 1 million images taken from space,[9] finding ways to apply its technology in the commercial sector,[10] more reliably predicting the occurrence of solar flares[11], and identifying possible dangerous asteroids.[12]

The crowd may contribute knowledge by their behavior alone, as we saw in the case of Asthmapolis (now known as "Propeller Health"), described in Chapter 12.

Crowd Voting

This mechanism leverages the community's judgment to organize, filter, and rank content such as newspaper articles, music, movies, and even ideas.

The Internet offers various mechanisms to perform voting—ratings of articles by end users or successful search engines are built upon this principle. As we saw in Chapter 3, Threadless.com uses crowd voting to decide which T-shirts to manufacture and sell on its web site. Consequently, the company is able to gauge consumer demand for new products before making investment decisions on production. Both Threadless and FashionStake avoid the costly mistakes that can arise for making the wrong product choices by involving potential customers in the production early decisions in notoriously fickle fashion-driven markets.

Crowd Wisdom

This principle attempts to harness many people's knowledge in order to solve problems or predict future outcomes. It takes the concept of Delphi decision making[13] to a higher level. Howe states that "Given the right set of conditions the crowd will almost always outperform any number of employees – a fact that many companies are increasingly attempting to exploit." Caltech professor Scott E Page's research[14] has shown that even focused groups of highly intelligent people are consistently outperformed by anonymous crowds. According to James Suroweiki,[15] successfully accessing the wisdom of a crowd needs four conditions: (1) there should be a *diversity* of experience and opinion; (2) individuals must be *independent* and not influenced by others in the crowd; (3) individuals must be *decentralized* and immersed in different locations, cultures, and experiences; and (4) there must be an effective mechanism to *aggregate* the inputs. The best-known example of crowd wisdom is the online encyclopedia of knowledge, Wikipedia. And for an example where the wisdom is accessed in real time is the remote audience participation in TV game shows such as "Who Wants to Be a Millionaire?"

Mini-Case: Goldcorp

Another very practical example is that of the Canadian mining company Goldcorp, which was struggling financially and unable to find gold on its land in Northern Ontario. When, in 2002, Rob McEwan came in as a new chief executive, he knew that he had to do something radical to save the company. He was intrigued by the way that the Linux software platform had been developed as an open-source project by combining voluntarily provided crowd knowledge. This prompted him to put all Goldcorp's geological data online, asking for help on where the gold was located. $500,000 was offered in prize money for accurate suggestions. Goldcorp got submissions from 1,400 people from 50 countries, including people using 3D computer modeling techniques. They found $3bn worth of gold on the property, which turned Goldcorp into one of Canada's biggest mining companies.[16]

Studies comparing the quality of crowdsourced ideas and those from within an organization[17] have found, not unexpectedly, that on average ideas generated by external users of a product or service score higher in novelty and customer benefit.

Tournaments, Collaboration, and Open-Source Development

The previous crowdsourcing categories can be enhanced by including the so-called tournaments and multitasking collaboratives. In tournament-based crowdsourcing, only the highest-value solutions are selected either by the crowd using voting schemes or by the solution-seeking firm itself. The firm seeking a solution does not incur the cost of those solutions that do not win. This helps in decision making and resource allocation. Second, in collaboration-based crowdsourcing, a task can be parceled into smaller, less demanding subtasks that crowd members with limited capabilities can perform, improving the likelihood of obtaining higher-value and/or lower-cost solutions.

However, all this does not come for free and an entrepreneur should not underestimate the efforts and possible waste of resources when managing crowdsourcing programs. These may include:

- The internal and external costs (e.g., award for winning solution, internal filtering process in case crowd voting cannot be applied, communication expenses, etc.) associated with crowdsourcing some problems can be rather high, potentially reducing the value created and captured.

- The risk of not obtaining a good solution or a solution at all can be high for some problems, specifically when they are too complex or ill defined.

- The likelihood of a solution being imitated by other members of the crowd is higher.

- The likelihood of the crowdsourcing initiative to not be perceived as fair by potential contributors.[18]

A well-known example of collaborative development is the continual enhancement of the Linux operating system[19]. The software is available to anyone wishing to use it under an "open-source" model. If an independent developer improves or adds to the software, these changes must be documented and made available to everyone for free under the rules of the collaborative. There is some debate on whether open-source collaboration[20] of this type is truly a crowdsourcing activity. Figure 5.2 produced by Chris Grams[21] attempts to contrast the differences between open collaboration which benefits everyone in the community and crowdsourcing which benefits just the challenger.

Successful use of crowdsourcing needs a careful evaluation of the appropriate types of models to use and whether to undertake the efforts alone or to use a commercial web-based platform as an intermediary.

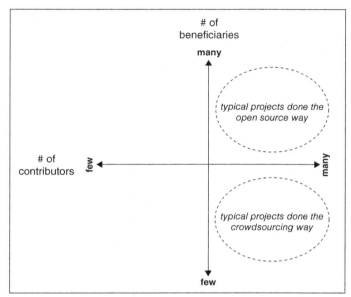

FIGURE 5.2
Comparison between Open-Source and Crowdsource Development
Source: Chris Grams.

Crowdfunding

Crowdfunding circumvents the traditional corporate establishment to offer financing to individuals or groups that might otherwise be denied credit or opportunity. Two groups of typically underfunded populations include individuals in developing nations and amateur musicians. As we see in Chapter 12, Kiva, the microlending portal, offers an example of crowdfunding by providing a marketplace for aspiring entrepreneurs in developing nations to seek financing for projects that is not readily available in their home markets. SellaBand offers a similar value proposition to garage bands that have been turned down by the major record labels in Hollywood. For more conventional funding of new product development, platforms such as KickStarter and Indiegogo help early-stage companies access funds without having to go to the more conventional routes of angel or VC funding covered in Chapter 8.

The inputs of individuals in a targeted crowd are important as they can act as promoters in both triggering the process and influencing outcomes. Sometimes, they may play a donor role oriented toward providing help on social projects or they will become shareholders and contribute to the development and growth of the opportunity. Each individual may disseminate information about projects they support within their own online communities, generating further multiplying support via network effects. The importance of identifying and engaging the "influencers," or "nodes," as members of a crowd was introduced in Chapter 1.

Motivations for participating in funding may be driven by a number of factors such as being part of another's success, or wanting to be part of a communal activity, or for mainly financial benefit. Other motivations may be more altruistically based as discussed more fully earlier in this chapter.

Now that you have a broad background on the different types of crowdsourcing, we will turn to the practical applications that may be used at different stages of your entrepreneurial journey.

Entrepreneurship: Relevant Applications of Crowdsourcing

Ideation: Creating and Building on an Idea

To be a successful entrepreneur, you need to have a good idea. We all have ideas, but are they good? Can they create something of value? The process of idea generation or "ideation" occurs at the earlier stages on your journey—the identification and refining of the central idea of your venture. Most often, the first glimmer of an idea is far from the final version that will form the basis of a new product or service that customers will actually buy. By using the crowd, you can get help in honing your initial idea into something that may have some sustainable value. There are several platforms to aid ideation. Unfortunately, many of them such as Innocentive and NineSigma have been developed to provide open innovation tools for large companies and governmental agencies. For this purpose, they assemble large communities of specialists or the so-called "solvers" from around the world. According to Innocentive's web site, they have 300,000 registered solvers from over 200 countries, which are enhanced through publisher partners to a total of over 13 million contacts. By mid-2014, 1650 challenges had been posted generating over 40,000 responses, of which 1500 or so were deemed of sufficient value to merit a reward from the challenger. Rewards range between $5,000 and $1+ million, the median being about $35,000. These platforms however are not suitable for early-stage companies, as they charge a substantial up-front set-up fee. Innocentive, for example, asks for $50,000 before any rewards are taken into account.

At the other end of the spectrum lie platforms such as AHHHA.com, where entrepreneurs can post their very early ideas, which provide a record of claiming it as theirs, and then others can enhance the concept. Quirky.com has a different model in which you can post your product idea and have it voted on. Those products that are voted likely to be successful are designed and manufactured within the Quirky network and sold via the web site, some percentage of the profit going back to the original inventor. Visit the Quirky web site to view many of the successful product launches. Clearly, these types of crowdsourcing platforms are not suitable for an entrepreneur that wishes to build a company, and they can expose the inventor/entrepreneur to the risk of losing control or even ownership of their idea.

The more advanced and established ideation platforms such as Innocentive and NineSigma have well-defined rules and documentation methods for ensuring that any intellectual property (IP) contributed by "solvers" in response to a challenge becomes the property of the challenger. Innocentive's web site lays out very clearly the processes to ensure clear ownership of IP. This is a highly complex process. As we learn in Chapter 13, in the case of patents, trademarks, and copyrights, ownership resides with the inventor(s) of an idea unless specifically assigned to another person or entity. In addition, the "solver" cannot have found their contribution from another source, as they are then not free to transfer the rights to the challenger.

Fortunately, platforms are now appearing that can provide crowd ideation cost-effectively for early-stage companies. One example is ideascale.com that offers different levels of support depending on the size of the challenging entity. For example, the company onebusaway.com started and operated by students at the University of Washington used a mobile crowdsourcing platform provided by IdeaScale to provide valuable innovation input for their product development.[22]

In some cases, entrepreneurs may already own some technology but lack at least one or potentially more alternative uses for it, that is, they need to find a market application and develop a respective value proposition. Marblar,[23] a crowdsourcing platform founded by young doctoral students in 2012 and meanwhile partnering with electronics giant Samsung, aims at overcoming the problems of traditional tech-transfer offices related to the process of commercializing research results. Instead of crowdsourcing solutions to problems, it uses crowdsourcing-based search mechanisms for finding problems to solutions, that is, applications for patented research discoveries.

Summarizing this section, for entrepreneurs not wishing to grow a company, using one of the idea launching platforms whereby the product launch is carried out by another organization may offer a way to experiment with the entrepreneurial process. There is a risk that the idea is copied in certain settings, but there is little financial risk and probably little long-term financial gain.

However, if the intention is to grow a company, once the first product is being tested in the market place, engaging in crowd ideation can be cost-effective and provide ongoing product innovations and opportunities. In this case, use a crowdsourcing platform that is designed specifically for this purpose, and first talk to a few of the companies that have used the service. Protect your IP prior to making the challenge public.

ROADMAP

IN ACTION	The entrepreneur should explore ways of building on their original idea by accessing appropriate crowds.

Business Model Design

Throughout the book, we have highlighted a number of entrepreneurial businesses in which interaction with the crowd is an inherent and necessary component of the business model. Threadless (Chapter 3) and FashionStake (see the previous text) use the crowd to design and then vote on their products before manufacturing them, Netflix (Chapter 2) uses the crowd to recommend movies to people like them, Asthmapolis/Propeller Health (Chapter 12) uses the crowd to predict asthma triggers and attacks, Flitto (see the previous text) captures the linguistic skills of the crowd to provide real-time translations between many different languages, Kiva (Chapter 12) uses the social motivations of the crowd to tackle poverty using microloans, and Kickstarter (see the following text) encourages the crowd to fund creative projects.

In order to capture crowd value within your business model, you can start with the framework tools described in Chapter 3. In addition, ask yourself these questions to stimulate your thinking as you formulate your plans:

Question	Examples	Reference
• Can I engage my (potential) customers and their crowd contacts in my business in one or more of these roles?	Threadless	Chapters 3 and 5
	FashionStake, BucketFeet	Chapter 5
○ Designing products	OneBusAway	Chapter 4
	MINI Cooper S ad campaign	Chapter 2
○ Providing feedback on my products and services	Netflix, Amazon	Chapter 4
○ Suggesting improvements to my products and services	Facebook Groups	Chapters 5 and 8
	VocalPoint	
○ Bringing new customers to the company	BenchPrep	
○ Providing information on preferences or behaviors that can provide value to other customers		
○ Providing endorsements on social media platforms		
○ Proving focused market research data		
○ Creating customer groups to enhance value to services		

(continued)

Question	Examples	Reference
• Can I access experts in the crowd that can provide valuable knowledge and know-how in areas such as technology, markets, innovation, and so on?	IdeaScale	Chapter 5
• Can I use these experts to undertake specific tasks on an as-needed basis?	Elance, oDesk, LivePerson	Chapter 5
• Can I use social networks for market research and attracting early adopters?	Facebook, Twitter, Google	Chapter 4
• Can I use reward-based crowdfunding to access early adopters?	Kickstarter, Indiegogo	Chapter 5
• Can I design my product or service in such a way that I automatically acquire valuable data on usage, preferences, buying patterns, and so on that will help my company build its knowledge base and establish barriers to competitors?	Netflix, Amazon	Chapter 2

ROADMAP

IN ACTION — Look for examples in business models that you encounter every day and understand how they are using the crowd to enhance their business.

Getting Expert Advice and Help

A small company can now access talent and experience from around the world using one of the platforms designed to make these connections. Engaging with experts can range from just asking a single question, asking for advice on a complex topic, or outsourcing part or the whole of a development task. Accessing the crowd in these cases offers the advantage that the experts are rated on their performance by previous users—the crowd does the vetting for you too by voting. In using these platforms, it is important to be as precise as you can in defining what you want. Charges run from just payment for a single answer only when satisfied to a full project agreement paid in stages of delivery.

The two largest platforms to access experts are oDesk with around 5 million registered experts and Elance with 3 million. Recently, these two goliaths have merged as this sector itself is consolidating. Other smaller platforms include Findanexpert, PrestoExperts, and Freelancer. In addition, if you have a very defined task, say, a software program to be written in PHP, you can search for sites that may specialize in this field such as http://www.teaminindia.com/php-developer.htm which has several hundred specialists on hand. For software or coding-related tasks, TopCoder has become a well-recognized platform, not least because of their collaboration with NASA. Small companies may specifically be interested in yet2 since they also offer access to commercialization experts. For research-based tasks, Zooniverse has become an important platform for crowd science projects, that is, for involving crowds in, for example, the classification of galaxies (Galaxy Zoo), folding proteins by using a computer game (Foldit), or co-determining fields of research within health science (CRIS[24]).

You can also network and access potential advisors by listing on one or more of the social network platforms such as LinkedIn.

As you enter the market, you may need to have 24/7 support for your product or services. Platforms such as LivePerson offer pay-as-you-go live chat services from the crowd and provide other web-marketing tools which can be accessed gradually as you grow your business.

Finding Hires

As you grow your company, you will need to take on more permanent employees. Again, platforms such as LinkedIn can help you network in the crowd to find possible candidates, or you can use one of the job posting platforms such as Monster.com to list your employment opportunities.

Getting to Your First Customers

When you are ready to launch your first product or service, you will need to get to the early adopters. One way is to create a web presence and attract potential customers to the site by accessing the crowd via keywords or joining interest groups. The BreatheSimple smoke-screen example in Chapter 3 describes the techniques used. Recently, young companies in the development stage are using crowdfunding platforms to achieve the same purpose.

Mini-Case: Hello Inc.

James Proud started his first company, GigLocator, when he was seventeen and living at home in London, United Kingdom. GigLocator was a software application that allowed fans to find where their favorite bands were playing and purchase tickets online. He sold the company three years later for a "six-figure" number to Peter Shapiro, a New York-based music entrepreneur. Leveraging this success, Proud moved to San Francisco to start his next company Hello Inc. which has developed a novel sleep monitoring product called Sense[25] (Figure 5.3).

His reputation as an entrepreneur helped him raise over $10MM from 44 investors in January 2014 using an SEC Regulation D filing for an unregistered private placement offering.[26] But in July of the same year, Proud did something rather unexpected. The company launched a Kickstarter campaign to raise a further $100,000; clearly, this was not for funding the company but to engage with early adopters by preselling the product when ready for shipping later in the year. The campaign was extremely successful—over $2.4MM was pledged in a few weeks—more importantly, the 19,000+ contributors were preordering the product at a discount rate, which enabled the company to judge demand and have sufficient money in the bank to fund manufacturing. At the same time, the early adopters being emotionally committed are ready to spread the praises of the products to their own networks. Kickstarter and many of the other crowdfunding sites do not look at the earlier history of the company as they are only managing funding for a specific project. So even well-funded companies can use such platforms for market launch without having to invest in marketing and sales channel development.

Furthermore, you may consider giving the design of marketing or advertising campaigns into the hands of crowds.

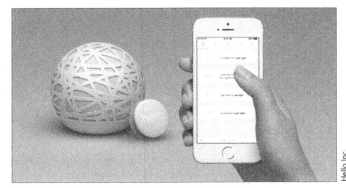

FIGURE 5.3
The Sense Sleep Monitoring System

This table summarizes this section on using the crowd in development:

Task	Platform examples
Asking a question	Ask.com, Yahoo Answers
Getting advice	Findanexpert, PrestoExpert
Accessing experts	oDesk, Elance, Findanexpert
Contracting experts	oDesk, Elance, specialist networks, Freelancer
Hiring	LinkedIn, Monster
Market research	Twitter, Google, Facebook, aytm.com
Market entry support	LivePerson
Accessing early adopters	Twitter, Google, Kickstarter, Indiegogo
Designing marketing Campaigns	Tongal

For an example on crowdsourced market research, see the BreatheSimple mini-case in Chapter 4.

ROADMAP

IN ACTION

When planning your business, have a clear idea how you are going to get your first customers and explore whether they can be accessed at a low cost using crowd-based methods.

Funding

One of the greatest challenges facing a new company, as we will see in Chapter 8, is accessing cash to grow the company. Over the past few years, the use of the so-called crowdfunding has emerged to provide another way to fund an early-stage company. However, crowdfunding is not a panacea. First, the regulations governing crowdfunding are changing all the time and are different in every jurisdiction. There are also risks in controlling IP. And for a company that will require significant amounts of follow-on finance, a crowdfunded history may be a liability. We will deal with each of these issues later in this section.

Despite these problems, crowdfunding is exploding as a valid alternative to more conventional sources of funds as can be seen in Figure 5.4 which shows global statistics.

This table shows a snapshot of global crowdfunding activity in the first quarter of 2014 according to the London-based crowdfunding center[27]; clearly, crowdfunding, already a $5 billion industry, is here to stay. However, the rapid growth may be an indication of a "bubble" and we can anticipate that many of the crowdfunding platforms will fail as the regulatory and legal environments mature.

Total pledges	Total raised	Campaign starts per day	Growth rate
4,057,856	$261,538,013	500	Doubling every 60 days

The earliest recorded use of the word "crowdfunding" was by Michael Sullivan in "fundavlog" in August 2006. But in fact, the concept is hardly new. In 1783, Mozart used the idea to raise money to perform three concertos in Vienna. In exchange for financial backing, Mozart offered manuscripts and 176 backers pledged enough money to finance the performances. The rapid expansion of the concept today is the direct result of network technologies especially the Internet

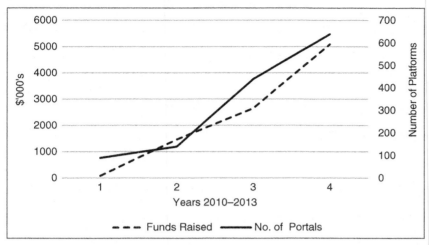

FIGURE 5.4
The Growth in Crowdfunding Activity

which opens up opportunities to a broader audience and reduces the personal efforts needed. To help the process, a number of web platforms or exchanges have emerged; the best known in the United States are Kickstarter and Indiegogo, but there are many, many others.

These crowdfunding platforms serve as "network orchestrators." They create the necessary organizational systems and conditions for integrating resources among different communities, thereby replacing traditional intermediaries such as record companies, film studios, publishers, and even venture capitalists. These platforms link new artists, designers, and project initiators with committed supporters who believe in the persons behind the projects strongly enough to provide monetary support.

Mini-Case: Bragi GmbH, Crowdfunding Goes Global

Bragi was founded by Nikolaj Hviid, who was born in Denmark and trained as a product designer. As head of design at Harman Audio, a global company headquartered in Connecticut, and later as head of his own design agency, Nikolaj witnessed the emergence of "wearable electronics" and dreamed of a product that would deliver a super sound experience with health monitoring sensors so that everyone could enjoy entertainment while exercising. Hence, the earbud "The Dash" was conceived (see Figure 5.5). To quote Nikolaj: "I imagined a discrete assistant that would entertain and take care of me. Help me understand my body, and let me know when I have reached my limit. Help me to get better at what I do."

Courtesy of Bragi

FIGURE 5.5
A Pair of The Dash Earphones

Bragi, located near Munich, Germany, decided to fund product development and market entry using the U.S.-based Kickstarter platform. The campaign was launched on February 9, 2014. Rewards ran from a small cash discount on the "The Dash" when launched to receiving early prototype products or larger discounts later on. The initial funding target of $260,000 was reached in a few days, and eventually, funds raised totaled nearly $3.4 MM in 50 days contributed with 16,000 individual pledges. At that time, it was the most successful European crowdfunding project. Bragi will launch its "The Dash" ear-buds in 2015.

Types of Crowdfunding

There are several categories of crowdfunding; which you choose to use will depend very much on the stage of your company's development, what your ultimate aims are, how much funding you are seeking, and what is legally possible in your environment. Here, we discuss the five basic types:

Reward-based crowdfunding is the most common form as it avoids the regulatory and organizational problems arising from equity-based funding (see the following text). It has been used for a wide range of purposes such as film making, music production, and software development. Within this category, there are two basic models, "Keep-it-All" (KIA) where the entrepreneurial firm sets a fundraising goal and keeps the entire amount raised regardless of whether or not they meet their funding target and "All-or-Nothing" (AON) where the firm sets a fundraising goal and keeps nothing unless the goal is achieved. AON campaigns on average raise twice as much as KIA projects. AON is the model used by Kickstarter and has emerged as the dominant and more successful model. There are usually multiple levels of pledged amounts, with each level getting extra rewards the more that is pledged. Companies can be very creative in their reward offering. However, there is no guarantee that the donor will ever receive a reward. Check out some of them on the Kickstarter and Indiegogo web sites. The average Kickstarter campaign raises $19,000 from 253 people, with about one-fourth of the pledges coming from friends of the founder. This form of crowdfunding is geared to well-defined and usually short-term projects rather than long-term company growth.[28] As we saw in the Bragi case, these types of campaigns can sometimes exceed their targets by many orders of magnitude which can generate other problems for the entrepreneur—what to do with the funds.[29,30] If the campaign is successful, you can expect to pay between 3 and 5 percent commission to the platform and a further 3 percent in transaction management fees. Usually, there are no fees to pay if you do not reach your target.

Donation-based crowdfunding is used to provide support for personal matters such as healthcare costs, educational needs, or charitable causes. It is essentially a philanthropic model, no rewards are provided, and a donor gains no benefit except the personal satisfaction of helping someone in need. GoFundMe is one such platform. Modified versions are platforms in which the donor can choose to fund an individual that they believe will "do something good" but is as yet unspecified; one such platform is Pave.com, based in New York. There is concern that such models are open to abuse and fraud. Fees are about 5 percent commission and a small transaction fee of around 3 percent.

Credit- or loan-based crowdfunding avoids difficulties associated with equity funding (see the following text). A number of platforms exist to match personal lenders to small companies. For example, in the United States, credit-based crowdfunding from nonbanks became more prominent when banks increased their interest rates and reduced their lending activity around 2006. One example is the Lending Club, which, since its founding in 2006, had advanced more than US$6 billion in loans via its web site by December 2014 resulting in nearly $600 million in interest payments to lenders. Prospective borrowers of the Lending Club first submit their requirements and are then matched with pools of lenders who are willing to accept the credit terms. The maximum loan for a business is $100,000, and depending on the grade of a borrower's credit, interest rates range between 7.6 and 25 percent. The funder expects a financial return: primarily the money they initially invested, with interest. This model is particularly attractive to later-stage companies that have fixed assets to pledge against the loan such as "brick and mortar"-based enterprises. Crowdfunding bypasses the usually slow processes that are found with established banks. Fees are typically 1 percent of the loan value. The Lending Club raised $870MM at a valuation of $9BN via a public offering at the end of 2014. Zopa is another large peer-to-peer (P2P) money lending service bringing together individuals who have money to lend and individuals who wish to borrow money.

Equity-based crowdfunding is a mechanism that enables broad groups of investors to fund start-up companies and small businesses in return for ownership participation in the form of shares. Investors provide money to a business and receive ownership of a small piece of that business. If the business succeeds, the value of a share in that business should go up too—the reverse is also true. Research in equity crowdfunding indicates that its potential is greatest with start-up businesses that are seeking smaller investments to achieve establishment, while follow-on funding (required for rapid growth) may come from other sources.

In Chapter 8, we will see how equity-based funding can be rather complex. Issues such as preferences, convertible debt, deal covenants, and so on are negotiated between the entrepreneur and the "lead" investor(s). The entrepreneur is usually working with just one or two such investors experienced in equity investing either as angels or venture capitalists. These communication and negotiating options do not exist for equity crowdfunding. This generally means that the entrepreneur has to set the value of the shares prior to the campaign and adhere to very basic investment rules. This limitation on deal terms usually leads to a lower valuation than might be expected with more conventional equity capital where preferences and rights can be traded for valuation.

Regulatory Issues

Equity investment crowdfunding can breach various securities laws, because soliciting investments from the general public can be deemed illegal, unless the opportunity has been filed with an appropriate securities regulatory authority, such as the Securities and Exchange Commission in the United States, the Ontario Securities Commission in Ontario, Canada, the Autorité des marchés financiers in France, or the Financial Services Authority in the United Kingdom.

The investment contract has to be registered with a regulatory agency, unless it qualifies for one of several exemptions such as, in the United States, Regulation A or Rule 506 of Regulation D of the Securities Act of 1933.

However, several regulatory agencies around the world responding to the inevitability of crowdfunding are creating new legislation to cover equity-based crowdfunding. The United States has been slower than most European countries, but in April 2012, the "Jumpstart our Business Startups" (JOBS) Act was signed into law. The U.S. Securities and Exchange Commission was given nine months to propose specific rules and guidelines while also ensuring the protection of investors. The legislation mandates that funding portals must register with the SEC as well as an applicable self-regulatory organization to operate. The JOBS Act enables equity-based crowdfunding when it is conducted by a licensed broker-dealer or via a funding portal registered with the SEC.

The Act originally limited the value of securities that an issuer may offer and that individuals can invest through crowdfunding intermediaries at $1,000,000 in a 12-month period. Depending upon their net worth and income, investors were permitted to invest up to $100,000 in crowdfunding issues each year. An independent financial statement review by a CPA firm is required for raises $100,000–500,000, and an independent financial statement audit by a CPA firm is required for raises over $500,000.

In March 2015, these SEC rules were expanded to allow a small company to sell up to $50 million of securities in a 12-month period, subject to eligibility, disclosure, and reporting requirements. The 2015 rules, often referred to as Regulation A+, provide for two tiers of offerings: Tier 1, for offerings of securities of up to $20 million in a 12-month period, with not more than $6 million in offers by selling security holders that are affiliates of the issuer, and Tier 2, for offerings of securities of up to $50 million in a 12-month period, with not more than $15 million in offers by selling security holders that are affiliates of the issuer. Both tiers are subject to certain basic requirements, while Tier 2 offerings are also subject to additional disclosure and ongoing reporting requirements.

To add to the confusion, several U.S. states, for example, Kansas, Georgia, Michigan, Wisconsin, Washington, and North Carolina, have recently enacted or are considering their own crowdfunding exemption laws to facilitate intrastate investment offerings that are already exempt from federal (SEC) regulation. As the regulatory frameworks are still uncertain in the United States, entrepreneurs should be cautious if choosing equity-based crowdfunding in their plans. There are a few platforms emerging that offer equity funding from the crowd in the United States such as StartupValley, and it is worth monitoring the situation as the laws become more clearly defined. Crowdfunding platforms such as CrowdFunder in the United States claim to keep up to date with the changing regulatory environment and provide services to guide entrepreneurs through the complexities of equity crowdfunding.

The United Kingdom was earlier in establishing regulations for equity crowdfunding. A leading portal there is Crowdcube (http://www.crowdcube.com) which claims an average campaign raise of $311,000 from 117 people. Another UK-based platform called Seedrs (www.seedrs.com) also pools investors' funds to make selected investments which provide some diversity to investors in much the same way as limited partners in venture capital funds spread their risk across a portfolio.

Hybrid crowdfunding is an extension of the above four categories. However, the usual combination is reward-based leading into equity-based crowdfunding as the needs for the new company change. The rewards phase enables the development of a first product and then growth can be funded using equity; but now, the value of the company will be higher and easier to establish and the risks for investors are lowered and more attractive. The entrepreneur will therefore suffer less dilution of their ownership. One such dual-option platform is fundable.com which offers the opportunity to start with a reward-based program and then use the same platform for follow-on equity funding. Flat rate of $179/month is charged to create a fundraising campaign. Advisory services may add on extra costs. A reward-based campaign has similar fees to the other platforms in this category.

Follow-On Funding The hybrid model is designed to offer a one-stop platform to take the young company through the different stages of cash needs. However, there are risks associated with starting on a route that incorporate equity participation from the crowd.

As we will see in Chapter 8, entrepreneurs usually plan for several rounds of funding to avoid too much dilution of their ownership in the early stages. This is important when the company has significant potential to grow and needs expansion funds. If the early round is via crowdfunding and the crowd cannot meet the need for new capital, the entrepreneur must turn to institutional sources. These usually do not like to invest in a company with a large and largely unknown group of investors because of possible shareholder lawsuits and the inability to make key decisions quickly which may require shareholder approvals. Of course, this issue does not arise if purely reward-based crowdfunding is used.

> "Equity funding through crowdfunding is a legal disaster waiting to happen."
>
> Eric Savits,
> *Forbes Magazine*

When and How to Use Crowdfunding

This table summarizes the pros and cons for an entrepreneur using crowdfunding:

Risks/burdens	Benefits
Loss of reputation if targets are not met	Promotion to a large audience/customers
Loss of IP protection of ideas	Receiving market feedback/beta testing
Fear of abuse under regulatory uncertainty	Accessing the wisdom of the crowd
Inability to raise further funds from existing donors/investors or institutional investors	Access to funds at the early stage of a company
Low valuation when selling shares	Retention of operating control
Heavy commitment to communication to a large crowd	Platform use provides guidance and reduces legal costs

Before deciding whether to use crowdfunding as a source of money for your company, the following factors should be considered:

- If you have a goal to reach a specific target with a clear project plan, and do not plan a high growth company, then consider using either a reward- or donation-based method. Avoid equity funding.

- If you plan to grow a small company and then sell it to another company to create a liquidity event, then consider equity-based funding. In this case, choose a platform that meets all of the regulatory requirements governing such transactions. Check on how other companies that have used the platform found the process and their progress after the funding event.

- If several rounds of funding are required, then consider using a reward-based platform to fund a short-term focused project. This should meet an important milestone as an alternative to conventional equity-based seed funding. If a single funding round can get you to positive cash flow, you may consider equity-based funding, but the risks in this case are high.

- In all cases, identify the platform that has performed well for similar companies or projects. Try to talk to a few of the entrepreneurs that have used them.

- In all cases, have about 25 percent of the funding already verbally committed within your own network prior to starting the campaign. It is important to prime the campaign and create momentum in the early days.

- Have contingency plans if you do not reach your funding target.

- Have plans on what you will do should you exceed your funding needs by a large amount.

- Don't underestimate the amount of time you will have to allot to attract the crowd and communicate with your followers.

- Before investing the considerable time and resources needed to prepare a crowdfunding campaign, check that you can pass the screening rules defined by the platform that you have chosen.[31]

ROADMAP

IN ACTION	The entrepreneur should have a well-designed funding plan for each stage of their company before rushing into using crowdfunding as an easy option. The risks must be carefully balanced against benefits. Always have a contingency plan.

Intellectual Property Issues

One of the challenges of posting new ideas on crowdfunding sites is that there may be no IP protection provided by the sites themselves. Once an idea is posted, it is effectively disclosed to the general public and it can be copied. If it is necessary to protect your ideas before posting them on a crowdfunding site, you should use the methods discussed in Chapter 13 such as early filing of patent applications, use of copyright and trademark protection, as well as a new form of idea protection supported by the World Intellectual Property Organization called Creative Barcode.[32]

"We get asked that all the time, 'How do you protect me from someone stealing my idea?' We're not liable for any of that stuff."

Slava Rubin
*Founder of
IndieGoGo,
a leading
crowdfunding site*

SUMMARY

The Internet has changed the way the companies can be built and operated. For an entrepreneur, using the Internet to access ideas, resources, and funding can significantly reduce the time and efforts needed to start and grow a company. Accessing the "crowd" supports the concept of a "lean" or even "virtual" company. The general term crowdsourcing covers a number of different activities ranging from idea generation and enhancement, accessing expert knowledge, creating powerful business models, and raising funds. Understanding when and how to use crowdsourcing is vital to today's entrepreneur. The entrepreneur must understand the different types of platforms that support crowdsourcing and choose the most appropriate type for specific tasks. Yet crowdsourcing is not a panacea, and it is important to understand the risks of engaging with different anonymous members of the crowd particularly in the areas of IP protection and follow-up funding requirements. Also, the personal efforts required to manage a crowdsourcing project should not be underestimated, and contingencies must be in place should the project fail. Equity-based crowdfunding comes with additional uncertainties with regard to the fluid and ambiguous state of the regulatory rules in different legislations.

STUDY QUESTIONS

Q.1 What are the key attributes of crowdsourcing?

Q.2 What are the main differences between open and closed innovation?

Q.3 Name four different types of crowdsourcing and describe how they differ.

Q.4 What are the advantages of tournament-based crowdsourcing?

Q.5 What is the main difference between open-source development and crowdsourced development?

Q.6 Where would you place on Figure 5.2 a (a) development done entirely by an in-house R&D group and a (b) collaborative development done by a closed group of companies. (Use Sematech as your model.)

Q.7 Name four different applications of crowdsourcing that can be used by entrepreneurs in starting and growing their ventures? How do they differ?

Q.8 Name five different types of crowdfunding and how they differ. What are the advantages of reward-based funding over equity-based crowdfunding? Does the hybrid model remove these disadvantages—explain your answer?

Q.9 Name three risks associated with crowdsourcing and how these can be managed.

Q.10 Describe a business that is not mentioned in this chapter but which uses the crowd as a key part of their business model. Explain how this can create a sustainable competitive advantage.

EXERCISES

5.1 Imagine a business that you would like to start. In what ways could you incorporate the crowd in your business model?

5.2 Visit one of the major crowdfunding sites and select a campaign that you find interesting or intriguing. Why do you think this was successful? Do you think this was the best option for the company or person running the campaign? Argue either for or against the selection of the platform.

5.3 Visit two of the ideation crowdsourcing platforms online. Compare and contrast their methods. What do you like and dislike most about them? What are the risks for an entrepreneur in using these platforms? How could the platforms be improved?

5.4 If used appropriately, crowdsourcing can accelerate the development of a start-up while reducing the need for a high level of funding for growth. Describe the terms lean company, virtual company, and minimum viable product in this context with examples. How do you think the rapid growth in crowdfunding will affect the more traditional venture capital method described in Chapter 8? How might the role of venture capital change?

MANAGEMENT EXERCISE—NEOFORMA IN THE AGE OF CROWDSOURCING

Master-Case Questions: Read the summary of Neoforma and answer the following:

Master question Q1. Neoforma was started before crowdsourcing using the Internet was available. If Wayne and Jeff were to start Neoforma today, how could they use crowdsourcing in their business model?

Master question Q2. Wayne and Jeff were continually at loggerheads with their investors, especially the venture capitalists. In today's world, could their use of crowdfunding circumvent these conflicts? Explain your answer.

Master question Q3. Today, would it be possible for Wayne and Jeff to build Neoforma purely as a virtual company using crowdsourcing? Explain your answer.

INTERACTIVE LEARNING ON THE WEB

Test your knowledge of the chapter using the book's interactive web site.

ADDITIONAL RESOURCES

Here are some links to organizations that can provide you with more information, tools, and examples to help you execute a crowdsourcing project:

Making a convincing video: http://thenextweb.com /dd/2014/09/01/make-crowdfunding-video-sells/.

Up-to-date statistics on crowdfunding sites: http://www .crowdfunding.com/.

For the latest status on the SEC rules for equity crowdfunding, search for JOBS act at www.sec.gov/rules/.

For comments on the SEC rules, see the Harvard Law School Blog at http://blogs.law.harvard.edu/corpgov/2014/03/09 /sec-crowdfunding-rulemaking-under-the-jobs-act-an -opportunity-lost/.

For the latest news and trends in crowdsourcing, visit https://dailycrowdsource.com/.

For an overview of crowdsourcing projects over time, visit http://yannigroth.com/2013/12/31/to-end-2013-some- stats-from-the-crowdsourcing-timeline/.

ENDNOTES

1. The term "public" refers to any external community and may include customers, experts, scientists, as well as members of the general public.

2. According to a 2012 study by Massolution, start-ups offering crowd-sourcing platforms are themselves attracting venture capital. VCs invested $280 million in thirty-five crowdsourcing companies in 2011 alone. The report found that annual revenue from crowdsourcing companies rose more than 75 percent in 2011 to $376 million, topping the 53 percent increase of 2010. Interestingly, the demand for crowd-sourced products and services is highest among smaller companies and start-ups, not big corporations.

3. This profile was partly derived from an interview that Courtney Boyd Myers had with Daniel Galati, in June 2011, and published online as "FashionStake promotes new designers with "p-commerce."

4. See Henry Chesbrough, *Open Innovation: The New Imperative for Creating and Profiting from Technology* (Harvard Business School Press, 2003).

5. See "Open Innovation: A New Paradigm for Understanding Industrial Innovation," in Henry Chesbrough, Wim Vanhaverbeke, and Joel West, eds., *Open Innovation, Researching a New Paradigm* (Oxford: Oxford University Press, 2006), 1–12.

6. See e.g., Allan Afuah and Christopher Tucci. "Crowdsourcing as a Solution to Distant Search," *Academy of Management Review 37*, no. 3 (2012): 355–375; Lars Bo Jeppesen and Lars Frederiksen "Why Do Users Contribute to Firm-Hosted User Communities? The Case of Computer-Controlled Music Instruments," *Organization Science 17*, no. 1 (2006): 45–63; Lars Bo Jeppesen and Karim R. Lakhani. Marginality and Problem-Solving Effectiveness in Broadcast Search. *Organization Science 21*, no. 5 (2010): 1016–1033; Nikolas Franke, Peter Keinz, Katharina Klausberger Does This Sound Like a Fair Deal?: Antecedents and Consequences of Fairness Expectations in the Individual's Decision to Participate in Firm Innovation. *Organization Science 24*, no. 5 (2012): 1495–1516; Johann Füller, Kurt Matzler, Melanie Hoppe. Brand Community Members as a Source of Innovation. *Journal of Product Innovation Management 25*, no. 6 (2008): 608–619.

7. For an introductory text, see Jeff Howe, *Crowdsourcing: Why the Power of the Crowd Is Driving the Future of Business* Random House Press (August 26, 2008).

8. See www.flitto.com. Also as an excellent example of a short investors' pitch, you can see Simon Lee at http://www.youtube.com/watch?v= muhZuXHEDls.

9. "NASA wants to crowdsource 1.8 million images," Carol Christian, Houston Chronical, Aug 20th, 2014.

10. "NASA explores a new world," an interview with David Lockney can be heard at http://www.npr.org/ 2014/06/30/326934037/nasa-explores -a-new-world-crowdsourcing-ideas.

11. "How Open Innovation is Solving Some of NASA's Trickiest Problems," http://knowledge.wharton.upenn.edu/article/how-open-innovation -is-solving-some-of-nasas-trickiest-problems/.

12. "NASA Asteroid Data Hunter contest hopes humans will outsmart dinosaurs," Stuart Dredge, The Manchester Guardian, May 10th, 2014.

13. For an introductory description, see U.S. government document "The Delphi technique" DOCID: 3928741, which can be found at www.nsa .gov.

14. For a deeper look into the research supporting the wisdom of crowds, see Scott E Page, *The Difference: How the Power of Diversity Creates Better Groups, Firms, Schools, and Societies*, (Princeton University Press, 2008).

15. James Surowiecki, *The Wisdom of Crowds* (New York: First Anchor Books, , 2005).

16. For further details, see http://spotopen.blogspot.com/.

17. "The value of crowdsourcing: Can users really compete with professionals in generating new product ideas?," Marion K. Poetz and Martin Schreier, *Journal of Product Innovation Management* 29 (March): 245–256, 2012.

18. Nikolas Franke, Peter Keinz and Katharina Klausberger. "Does This Sound Like a Fair Deal? Antecedents and Consequences of Fairness Expectations in the Individual's Decision to Participate in Firm Innovation," *Organization Science* 24, no. 5 (2012): 1495–1516.

19. See http://en.wikipedia.org/wiki/History_of_Linux.

20. Open-source projects are usually governed by the "free and open-source software" agreements which themselves have been somewhat controversial. See http://en.wikipedia.org/wiki/Free_and_open-source _software for more on this issue.

21. See a discussion on this topic at http://opensource.com/business/10/4/ why-open-source-way-trumps-crowdsourcing-way.

22. See the "OneBusAway" case history available at www.ideascale.com for further details. This web site also has other case histories that may stimulate you on how to use crowd ideation methods.

23. "Crowdsourcing science site Marblar revamps patents-to-products contest," http://blogs.nature.com/news/2013/10/crowd-sourcing-science-site-marblar-revamps-patents-to-products-contest.html.

24. See http://www.openinnovationinscience.at/cris-en.html.

25. More about the product can be found at https://hello.is/ and the Kickstarter campaign at https://www.kickstarter.com/projects/hello/sense-know-more-sleep-better.

26. For those interested in a Schedule D SEC filing, an example for Hello Inc. can be found at http://www.sec.gov/Archives/edgar/data/1598151 /000159815114000001/xslFormDX01/primary_doc.xml.

27. See the "State of the Crowdfunding Nation," available from the Crowdfunding Centre in London, United Kingdom, issued May 14, 2014.

28. Music was one of the earliest fields to attract crowdfunding. For example, Marillion, a UK group, raised money for the production of a number of albums after their fans independently raised funds for an early tour. Film production was also an early use with the feature film "Foreign Correspondents" raising $125K in 1999.

29. On April 17, 2014, the *Guardian* media outlet published a list of 20 of the most significant projects launched on the Kickstarter platform. Here are some of them:

Entrepreneur	Am't raised $'000's	Number of pledges	Date	Project
Amanda Palmer	1,200	24,883	6/2012	New album
Hans Fex	1,227	5,030	3/2014	Mini museum
Rob Thomas	5,700	91,585	4/2013	Feature film
Zach Braff	3,100	46,520	5/2013	Feature film
Spike Lee	1,400	6,421	8/2013	Feature film
Freddie Yong	808	10,612	2/2013	Video game
Marina Abramovic	661	4,765	8/2013	Arts theater
Kano Tech Inc.	1,500	13,887	6/2014	Learning software
Flint and Tinder Inc.	1,100	9,226	4/2013	1-year hoodie

30. The highest reported funding at the date of writing is *Star Citizen*, an online space trading and combat video game claiming to have raised $40,000,000, beating the previous record of $10,266,844 set by *Pebble Watch*. Another highly successful campaign was initiated by the Tile app company that raised US$2.6 million by July 2013 on the Selfstarter crowdfunding platform. The start-up was only looking for US$20,000 to add to the US$200,000 support it had received from Tandem Capital. The Tile product is a small device that helps locate lost items such as keychains, bags, and bikes.

31. As one example of prohibited projects, see this list from Kickstarter: https://www.kickstarter.com/rules/prohibited.

32. Creative Barcode is a method of protecting ideas at an early stage. It uses a unique digital tag which is registered at www.creativebarcode .com. See this web site for more details.

Writing the Winning Business Plan

6

"The biggest change in how entrepreneurship is taught is the switch from writing an academic business plan to doing rigorous fieldwork called customer discovery."

Murray B. Low, Director of Entrepreneurship Education, Columbia Business School

OBJECTIVES

- Understand the value of writing a business plan.
- Explain how a business plan serves as a blueprint for building a company.
- Know the steps toward completing a business plan and when to use the canvas model.
- Learn the detailed components of a lean and full business plan.
- Understand how to write a business plan so that it targets investors.

CHAPTER OUTLINE

Introduction

Profile: Nikolay Shkolnik—Business Plan Turns a Dream into Reality[1]

The Value of a Business Plan

Setting Goals and Objectives

Starting the Process to Write the Plan: Canvas Model and the Five Steps

Determining What Type of Business Plan Is Best

A Lean and Full Business Plan Format and Content

Understanding Why Business Plans Fail

Summary

Study Questions

Exercises

Case Study: Surfparks LLC (Online)

Appendix: The Roadmap Guide for Writing a Business Plan

Interactive Learning on the Web

Additional Resources

Endnotes

Introduction

Smart entrepreneurs recognize the value of a business plan for securing capital and growing their businesses. Business plans are a mode of communication between entrepreneurs and potential investors. In addition, entrepreneurs often find that developing a business plan forces them to introduce discipline and a logical thought process into all of their planning activities. A properly prepared business plan will help entrepreneurs consistently establish and meet goals and objectives for their employees, investors, and management.

Business plans have historically been a necessity for most entrepreneurs, especially for those seeking financing. However, the definition of a business plan has changed recently. For entrepreneurs today, it can mean a traditional or full plan with detailed marketing, financing, and operations content to a few pages showing where and how markets apply to the business.

Additionally, entrepreneurs have complained or concluded that business plans take too long to write and quickly become outdated. Some just focus on the product and marketing and adjust their plan as they proceed.

In this chapter, we'll establish the value of different forms of a business plan and lay out a step-by-step procedure entrepreneurs can follow to create one. We'll also discuss why certain information is required in a business plan as well as how it should be presented.

Once you decide to start a business, you understandably should have a plan to produce products or supply services and to attract the optimum marketing, operations, management team, and financing to get the business off to a good start.

It is important to realize and deal with the various "interest groups" that will be crucial to your success. Each group wants to hear something from your story that provides a comfort factor. Consider these examples:

- Financial interests want to know the risk/reward "formula" and the future "cash-out/cash-in" possibilities associated with your new venture.

- Employees want to feel secure in knowing they have not only a job with your company but also a possible career.

- Marketers need to know the product/service, pricing, placement, and positioning (the four Ps).

- Vendors, suppliers, and associates need to know what your operations will look like so that they can plan to be part of your supply chain.

- Your partners (if any) need to codify their legal and fiduciary rights and responsibilities for their own protection and growth.

- The entrepreneur needs to place his or her ideas beside a companion roadmap to compare and contrast where the business is going to where it was supposed to go. How do you accomplish all of the above in a professional and concise manner?

Profile: Nikolay Shkolnik—Business Plan Turns a Dream into Reality[1]

Dr. Nikolay Shkolonik received an MS from Kiev Polytechnic in 1975, followed in 1984 with a doctorate from the University of Connecticut. An inveterate inventor and winner of the Motorola Award for Creativity, he is also one of a few experts in TRIZ, an analytical system for solving complex engineering problems innovatively. As a senior member of the consulting firm GEN3 Partners in Boston, he taught many companies how to innovate. At the same time, he was intrigued by the inefficiencies of internal combustion engines used in cars and elsewhere. The basic engine had not changed for more than a century, and he gradually evolved a radically new engine concept that can make a truly major improvement in fuel efficiency, a growing issue as petroleum resources decline. But for more than seven years, his ideas remained a dream until, by chance, his son Alex, studying for his doctorate at MIT, met Brian Roughan, Jennifer Andrews Burke, and Vik Sahney, three MBA students looking for some extracurricular work to hone their business planning skills. Alex introduced them to his father, and they agreed to work on a plan for a new company called Liquid Piston, formed to commercialize the new engine. Initially, the team, which now included Alex, thought that this would be a simple exercise, perhaps a few hours a week only, but it ended up consuming their entire lives for more than two months. According to Brian, the hardest part was identifying which markets to enter first because the engine can be configured to fit many opportunities. Indeed, the team changed its market strategy many times, and this important part of the plan absorbed close to half of their effort. The team was fortunate to have Bill Frezza, an MIT alumnus and a partner in the VC firm Adams Capital, as a mentor during the process. (You can see Bill talking about business planning on the book's web site.) Finally, they were ready to enter the annual MIT $50K business planning competition, where they took second place. The prize money of $10,000 was used to file the first patents for the company. The team also won $12,500 in the MIT Enterprise Forum Competition and was in the top four in the GE & Dow Jones Economics Business Plan Competition in 2006. The next year, the company was awarded $75,000 in an SBIR grant competition. Meanwhile, the team was making many presentations to venture capitalists. Did anyone really read the plan from cover to cover? Well, perhaps not. But according to Brian, going through the rigorous process of writing a full plan prepared everyone to answer any tough questions that were thrown at them, first by the judges and later by investors. Nik saw the creation of the plan not just as the production of the final document to be put on a shelf, but as a process through which his dreams of many years finally took shape and became reality. The efforts were rewarded in 2007, when the company, which had matured a lot since the first plan, was able to attract $1.5 million of seed funding, from Adams Capital in Pittsburgh and Northwater Capital in Toronto, to build a prototype of the engine. Based on the results, the investors provided a further $6.5 million of equity capital in July 2013. Now, the company is working hard to fulfill the plan (www.liquidpiston.com).

The Value of a Business Plan

The main purpose of writing a business plan is to test the viability of the business idea and set a path for the entrepreneur to follow. Writing the business plan can help determine if the business has a chance of becoming successful in the following ways:

- **Test the feasibility of the business idea.** The business plan is the best way to determine if the idea for starting a business is feasible. The plan applies rigor and discipline, and the entrepreneur is forced to provide in-depth detail about all aspects of business and how to execute the plan. It should contain solid research to support your opportunity.

- **Act as a safety net.** This can save the entrepreneur time and money if the plan reveals that the business idea is untenable. In many cases, the idea for starting a business is discarded at the marketing and competitive analysis stage because the business opportunity is not viable and the competition is too severe. Having worked on and written down a plan in detail helps an entrepreneur when presenting or discussing the business to be confident and able to answer probing and detailed questions.

- **Increase the likelihood of the venture's success.** Use the learning in writing the plan to evolve, iterate, or pivot. The business plan model will assist in eliminating failure points long before the product or service is launched. Taking the time to work through the process of writing a business plan will make for a smoother start-up period and fewer unforeseen problems as the business becomes established. It is unlikely to be read in detail by investors, except perhaps the important sections on customer/market information and executive summary. Its major value is in forcing an entrepreneur to be thorough and detailed.

- **Provide a platform.** It is valuable in the creation of elevator pitches, executive summaries, and presentations.

- **Attract bank loans and investors.** The plan allows for bank loans and investors to gain insight into the business idea and determine the financial requirements. A solid business plan may be required by venture capitalists and to attract angel investors. A presentation may stimulate their interest, but a well-written document they can take away and study may support any investment commitment. More about how a business plan fits into the range of communication methods you must use is covered in Chapter 10. Both venture capitalists and angel investors will want to conduct extensive background checks and competitive analysis to be certain that the business plan is solid and viable.

ROADMAP

IN ACTION

"Business plans are almost obsolete these days, There's nothing more powerful than customers that are happy."

John Sculley III, Ex-CEO of Pepsico and Apple, and angel investor in early stage companies.

What Is a Business Plan?

A business plan is a 15- to 20-page written document that describes where a business is heading, how it hopes to achieve its goals and objectives, who is involved with the venture, why its product(s) or service(s) is needed in the marketplace, and what it will take to accomplish the business aims. Business plans are becoming more and more concise. If the entrepreneur cannot get the plan down to 15- to 20-page readable and understandable text, then they may not have a full understanding of the business.

There are three essential reasons to prepare a business plan:

1. Entrepreneurs reap benefits from the planning activity itself.

2. The plan provides a basis for measuring actual performance against expected performance.

3. The plan acts as a vehicle for communicating to others what it is that the business is trying to accomplish.

Setting Goals and Objectives

A business plan also serves as a blueprint for building a company. It is a vehicle for describing the goals of the business and how these goals can be reached over the coming years. A business plan provides a means to:

- Determine whether the business is viable

- Raise capital for the business

- Project sales, expenses, and cash flows for the business

- Explain to employees their responsibilities as well as company expectations

- Improve and assess company performance

- Plan for a new product/service development

ROADMAP

| IN ACTION | The biggest problem most business plans have is that they don't include a clear description of the market, competition, and customers. Most plans spend too much time describing the features and capabilities of the new idea rather than how this approach will be better than the current solution. |

However, *the single most important reason for preparing a business plan is to secure capital.* Investors agree that an effectively prepared business plan is often a prerequisite for obtaining future funding. However, in many cases, VCs and angels don't really look for a business plan.[2] The entrepreneur must evaluate and determine that it really depends on the investors—some do and some don't.

The *New York Times*'s Brent Bowers writes about a surprising conclusion of a new study by researchers at the University of Maryland's business school:

"Researchers found that venture capitalists, who screen hundreds or thousands of solicitations each year, pay little or no heed to the content of business plans. Instead, the study said, because they make decisions "under conditions of high uncertainty," venture capitalists rely on instinct and their expertise in ferreting out information by other means to evaluate the prospects of a business.

That means, the study said, that they pay little attention to the documentation from entrepreneurs about their academic credentials, work or start-up experience, previous success in raising equity capital, ability to form a top-notch management team or even how much money they want."

Jeff Fagnan, general partner of Atlas Venture in Waltham, Mass., which provides seed money for young businesses, agrees with the study's main premise. "I've never given funding to an entrepreneur who had a business plan with him when he walked into my office," Mr. Fagnan told The Times. "Never. Most of the information you find there, five-year financial forecasts and so on, is not relevant."

He says he looks for "market validation," hard evidence that the entrepreneur has actually sold his product or at least lined up enthusiastic potential customers. Mr. Fagnan says that, rather than reading a report, he wants to hear the evidence in PowerPoint slides, white board presentations, or "somebody just talking."

Yet writing a business plan is not pointless—far from it. Entrepreneurs say it enables them to think through the logistics, possibilities, and pitfalls of their operations and to clarify their goals. "A business plan can be helpful in identifying opportunities in a competitive landscape," Mr. Fagnan, the venture capitalist, told The Times.

The bottom line is business plans help to define *the who, what, why, when*, and *how* of the business.

Investors need to know parameters, timetables, and expected future revenue streams. Thus, the business plan needs to set goals, but it must be realistic in doing so.

A business plan is a first attempt at strategic planning. The entrepreneur should use it as a tool for establishing the direction of the company and for establishing the action steps that will guide the company through the start-up period.

Many entrepreneurs say that the pressure of the day-to-day management of a company leaves them little time for planning. However, without a business plan, managers run the risk of proceeding blindly through a rapidly changing business environment.

Writing a business plan does not guarantee that problems will not come up. Managers who have a well-thought-out process in place will be better able to anticipate and handle any problems that occur. In addition, a well-constructed business plan can help managers avoid certain problems altogether. This is especially true for entrepreneurs and start-up companies.[3]

Getting Started

The Business Model Canvas (see Chapter 3) is a good place to begin. It is a tool to map out ideas at an early stage and explore both internal and external factors and how they interact. It is flexible and usually is updated and changed before a business model is constructed and before a business plan is started. Its value is in:

- Helping to make sure that you are considering the most important aspects of your business model and how they interrelate.

- Identifying key gaps in your knowledge and who you might talk to in order to fill in some of the blanks.

- Helping to identify questions that you need to ask experts.

- Providing an easily understood, concise, and valuable tool for communicating your business concept to potential investors, lenders, and other stakeholders.

- It does not demand extensive market, technology, and competitor research.

- It does not require detailed financial analysis.

- It is not a substitute for an executive summary, an elevator pitch, an investors' presentation, or a full business plan.

Starting the Process to Write the Plan: Five Steps

As entrepreneurs are bound to discover, they must tell and retell their business's story countless times to prospective investors, new employees, outside advisers, and potential customers. The most important part of the business's story is about its future—the part featured in a business plan. Thus, the business plan should show how all the pieces of the company fit together to create a viable organization capable of meeting its goals and objectives. The business plan must also communicate the company's distinctive competence to anyone who might have an interest. But how does an entrepreneur write a business plan that accomplishes these goals? Let's look at the five steps involved in this process.

Step 1: Identify the Objectives by Using the Canvas Model in Chapter 3

Use the canvas model to explore different business models. Define your key audience(s), what they want to know, and how they will use the information you are imparting to them. For example, if the business plan's audience is a group of investors, they will review the plan to gain a better understanding of the business objectives and to determine whether an investment is worth the risk. Entrepreneurs should use the business plan as an opportunity to develop as managers.

As you use the model as a basis for the business plan, you should think about competitive conditions, new opportunities, and situations that are advantageous to the business. The outline is also an important tool that entrepreneurs can use to familiarize sales reps, suppliers, and others with the company's operational goals.

Step 2: Draft the Outline

Once the objectives have been identified, the entrepreneur must prepare an outline for the business plan. The outline should provide enough detail to be useful to both the entrepreneur and his or her audience. A sample business plan outline is listed later in this chapter in the appendix, "The Roadmap Guide for Writing a Business Plan." The information shown is included in most effective business plans.

Step 3: Review the Outline

Next, the entrepreneur should review the outline to identify areas that should be presented in even greater detail. While doing the draft outline, follow up with research on areas for which you did not have sufficient information. Detailed support for any assumptions and assertions made in the business plan should also be available.

Step 4: Draft the Plan

The entrepreneur will probably need to conduct a great deal of research before there is enough information to start drafting the business plan. Most entrepreneurs begin by collecting historical financial information about their companies and/or industries and by conducting market research (refer to Chapter 4). After they have completed their initial research, they prepare initial drafts of proposed financial statements and projections. By preparing these statements, the entrepreneur will know which strategies will work from a financial perspective before investing many hours in writing a detailed description.

In the financial section of the business plan, the entrepreneur demonstrates the viability of the business; the plan should show first-year projections by each month and quarterly projections for the next two to three years. According to Ralph Subbinono, former partner at Ernst & Young, the biggest problem with most business plans is that they contain unrealistic financial projections. Thus, an entrepreneur should carefully rethink the projected performance and make necessary changes before passing the plan on to others. The entrepreneur should also keep detailed notes on the assumptions being made in the business plan draft so that footnotes to accompany the statements can be added later.

The last element to be prepared is the *executive summary*. Because this is a summary of the entire business plan, its contents are contingent on the rest of the document; thus, it cannot be finished until the other components of the plan are essentially complete. As each section is written, entrepreneurs should refer to the detailed outline included later in this chapter to make sure that they have covered each area adequately.

The executive summary consists of:

1. **Business Concept.** This section describes the business, its products or services, and the market it will serve. It should point out exactly what will be sold, to whom, and why the business will have a competitive advantage.

2. **Success Factors.** This section details any developments within the company that are essential to its success. It includes patents, prototypes, location of a facility, any crucial contracts that need to be in place for product or service development, and results from any test marketing that has been conducted.

3. **Current Position.** This section supplies relevant information about the company, its legal form of operation, the year it was formed, the principal owners, and key personnel.

4. **Financial Features.** This section highlights the important financial information about the business, including its sales, profits, cash flow, and return on investment. (Refer to Chapter 9 for more details.)

Step 5: Have the Plan Reviewed and Updated

Once the entrepreneur has completed a draft of the business plan, he or she should have an independent professional review it for completeness and effectiveness. The plan must then be updated at least every six months and as objectives change. A business plan is not a static document that will sit on your shelf, but one that is continually reviewed and updated. In fact, it is rare that the original plan used to start the business is the one eventually followed. However, without a sound starting plan, an entrepreneur will be unable to acquire a bank loan or any equity investors or have a template against which deviations, both internally or externally from the plan, can be judged and taken into account.

Determining What Type of Business Plan is Best

What type of plan should entrepreneurs prepare to meet their requirements? Three major types of plans exist:[4]

1. **Full Business Plan**
   An entrepreneur should use a full business plan when he or she needs to describe the business in detail to attract potential investors, strategic partners, or buyers.

2. **Executive Summary or "Short" Plan**
   An executive summary plan is a two- to five-page document that contains the most important information about the business and its direction. It is often used to gauge investor interest and to find strategic partners. It can also be used to attract key employees and to persuade friends to invest in the business.

3. **Action Plan**
   An implementation or action plan is a document the management team uses to implement the plan. It consists of a timetable and a list of tasks that should be accomplished within a certain time frame.

"When I judge the business plan competition at Columbia Business School, I first read the executive summary followed by the financial section. Only if the concept is intriguing will I spend more time reading the entire plan. We perpetually review about one hundred plans, and it's quite difficult to read them all. For those plans that capture my attention to receive funding, usually about 5 percent, there is a well-conceived, detailed plan."

Clifford Schorer
Entrepreneur in residence, The Eugene Lang Center for Entrepreneurship, Columbia University Business School

Targeting the Plan to Selected Groups

A business plan could be the perfect tool to reach the target groups listed below.[5] Some investors invest in only certain types of businesses, such as technology, health care, or financial services. Therefore, entrepreneurs must consider which investors or groups are relevant to their needs and send a plan to only the appropriate groups. These can include the following:

- Bankers—to provide loans for expansion and equipment purchases

- Business brokers—to sell the business

- New and potential employees—to learn about the company

- Investors—to invest in the company

- The Small Business Administration (SBA)—to approve business loans

- Investment bankers—to prepare a prospectus for an IPO

- Suppliers—to establish credit for purchases

How Long Will the Preparation Take?

A general rule of thumb is that it takes twice as long to write a good plan as foreseen. A useful benchmark is that it will take at least two hundred hours of dedicated effort to produce a good plan. The best way to reduce this burden is to begin drafting out initial ideas, sections where you have some good input, background information, and so on, before there is an urgent need for a full plan to present to outsiders. This is much easier than sitting down with the aim of writing a full plan in a short period, say, two weeks. Our experience with many entrepreneurs indicates that a sound, well-thought-through, well-researched plan that can be defended under intense questioning will take at least eight to twelve weeks to produce. This assumes that the writing is not continuous, but time is allotted for thinking, discussing alternatives with advisers, and obtaining missing information. Sometimes, entrepreneurs use consultants to help write the plan. While this can be of value and reduce the personal load, particularly for the first attempt, remember that the plan is yours, not the consultants'. If you cannot fully identify with the plan and defend each and every point and claim in the due diligence process, this will be detected by bankers and investors, who will then doubt your ability to lead the venture.

Writing the Business Plan

An effective and complete business plan should answer the following questions:

1. What is the primary product or service?

2. Is there a market for the product or service? Has the opportunity been well defined?

3. Who are the target customers for the product or service, and what value do you provide them?

4. What is the pricing structure?

5. Who is the competition, and what are the barriers to entry?

6. What risks and market constraints are involved?

7. What sales and distribution channels will be needed to sell the product or service? (Note sales and distribution channels are not always identical.)

8. Who are on the management team, and what are their specific talents?

9. What is the current financial cash flow and breakeven plan?

10. What are the immediate financial needs of the business?

11. What are the future financial goals for the business and its founder?

A Lean and Full Business Plan Format and Content

Examples of business plans and executive summaries can be found on the book's web site.

Creating the Title Page and Table of Contents

The title page includes the name, address, and phone number of the company and the CEO. The table of contents provides a sequential list of the business plan sections as well as their corresponding pages.

Writing the Executive Summary

As we noted earlier, the executive summary must be able to stand on its own. It should serve as a synopsis of the business plan. Investors may read only the executive summary; therefore, it must be comprehensive and well written to gain the investors' confidence.

The executive summary should be no more than two to three pages long and should convince the reader that the business will succeed. An example of a targeted executive summary can be found for Leafbusters Inc. in Chapter 10.

Writing the Overview of the Company, Industry, Products, and Services

The company description provides an overview of how all of the elements of the business fit together. This section should not go into detail, however, since most of the subjects will be covered in depth elsewhere.

The section begins with a general description of the legal form of the company, which should take no more than one paragraph. It should present the fundamental activities and nature of the business. This section addresses questions such as:

What is the business?

What customers will it serve?

Where is it located, and where will it do business?

Some further insight should also be offered as to what stage the company has reached. Is it a seed-stage company without a fully developed product line? Has it developed a product line but not yet begun to market it? Or is it already marketing its products and anxious to expand its scale of activity?

Compiling the Marketing Analysis

The marketing analysis section should describe how the business will react to market conditions and generate sales to ensure its success. It should explain why the business is a good investment.

Keep in mind that overcoming marketing challenges is critical to a company's success. Therefore, potential investors pay a lot of attention to the marketing analysis section. In fact, venture capitalists say that the most important criteria for predicting the success of a new company are those factors that establish the demand for the product or service. If a real market need is not presented, all of the talent and financing in the world will not make a company successful.

Some of the most important issues to address in the marketing analysis section include:

Market Opportunity: The marketing section must establish a demand or need for the product or service and should define both the market and the opportunity.

The secondary target market should also be addressed. You should quantify the size of the market as well. Investors like to see a large total available market (TAM), which is the size in dollars if you were able to capture 100 percent of the opportunity.

Competition: The marketing section should describe the market conditions that exist in the business, including the degree of competition and what impact this competition is likely to have on the business. It is also important to address other forces, such as government regulations and outside influences.

Marketing Strategy: The marketing section should define how the business will use its marketing tools. This can include factors such as distribution, advertising and promotion, pricing, and selling incentives. The mission and vision will vary depending on the stage of development.

Market Research: The marketing section should document market research as a part of the marketing plan or in a section by itself. Of most value are data obtained from primary market research, for this is the best evidence showing that if the venture can offer a product of service at the price used in the financial projections, then there are actual customers who will buy from the company. Bankers and investors like to talk to potential customers when undertaking due diligence, and positive responses go a long way to establishing confidence in the business.

Sales Forecasts: Usually, financial projections are presented in the financial section of a business plan. However, it is useful to present sales projections in the marketing section. These forecasts might include projected sales growth, market share, and sales by customer.

Support Material: Include in the appendix materials that will make the plan more credible, such as industry studies, letters of support, brochures, and reviews or articles related to the product or service.

While there is a great deal of flexibility in the writing of the marketing section, the plan should be focused to fit the characteristics of the proposed business.

The *products and services* section of the business plan describes the characteristics and appeal of the products or services. This section may include a prototype, sample, or demonstration of how the products work. The section should include the following:

Physical Description: A description of the physical characteristics of a product usually includes photographs, drawings, or brochures. In the case of a service, a diagram sometimes helps to convey what service the business is providing.

Statement Regarding Use and Appeal: The entrepreneur should comment on the nature of the product or the service's various uses and what constitutes its appeal. This is an opportunity to emphasize the unique features of the product or service and the value proposition to customers and thereby establish the potential of the business.

Statement Regarding Stage of Development: This is a description of the stage of development (prototype design, quality testing, implementation, and so on) of the product or service that the entrepreneur plans to introduce into the marketplace.

Testimonials: Entrepreneurs can include a list of experts or prior users who are familiar with the products or services and who will comment favorably on them. Such testimonials may be included in letter or report form in an appendix.

The company description should detail the objectives of the business opportunity. Perhaps the business is seeking a certain level of sales or geographic distribution. Will it become a publicly traded company in a few years when revenues reach a certain level, or will it become an attractive acquisition candidate? A statement of such objectives is important and may succeed in generating significant interest.

Describing the Marketing and Sales Plans

The marketing and sales strategy section of the business plan describes how the business will implement the marketing plan to achieve expected sales performance. This analysis will guide the entrepreneur in establishing pricing, distribution, and promotional strategies that will enable the company to become profitable within a competitive environment.

Pricing Strategy and Plan

As we mentioned earlier in the book, pricing is an important element in the marketing strategy because it has a direct impact on the business's success. The marketing and sales strategy section of the business plan should address policies regarding discounting and price changes as well as their impact on gross profit (revenue less cost of goods sold). When considering what price to charge, it is important to realize that price should not be based entirely on cost plus some profit. Consider these pricing methods to generate the necessary profits for the business:

Cost-Plus Pricing: All costs, both fixed and variable, are included, and a profit percentage is added on.

Demand Pricing: The business sells the products or services based on demand or whatever the market will bear.

Value Pricing: The business sells its products/services to capture a major part of the overall value that is created for the customer.

Competitive Pricing: The company enters a market where there is an established price and where it is difficult to differentiate one product from another. In this situation, there is limited flexibility to make price adjustments.

Markup Pricing: The price is calculated by adding the estimated profit to the cost of the product. In some industries, such as cosmetics and health care, profit levels may be higher than those in others, such as automotive components.

Entrepreneurs should analyze competitors' distribution channels before deciding to use similar channels or alternatives. Distribution channels include the following:

Direct Sales: Products and services are sold directly to the end user. This is the most effective distribution channel.

Original Equipment Manufacturer (OEM) Sales: An OEM will often bundle or promote its products with yours or pay a royalty on each product sold.

Manufacturer's Representatives: These individuals handle an assortment of products and divide their time based on the products that sell the best.

Brokers: These individuals buy products, often overseas, directly from the distributor and sell them to retailers or end users.

Web E-commerce: Products and services are sold through a web site or through Internet partner alliances.

Advertising, Public Relations, and Promotion Strategies

The purpose of this section in the plan is to describe how you will tell potential customers that you have a product or service that can satisfy their demands, to convince those customers to buy from you, and to successfully compete with similar businesses.

Many start-up companies feel they are unable to pursue advertising, public relations, or promotion strategies until they are more established and have generated significant revenues. However, public relations companies are becoming more willing to partner with start-up companies. Instead of the usual retainer that public relations firms request, they are willing to work on an hourly or budget basis.

Other Elements

The marketing and sales strategy section should also include PowerPoint pie charts, graphs, tables, and other graphics that effectively show how the marketing effort will be organized and how business resources will be allocated among various marketing tools. "A picture is worth a thousand words" also applies to business plans.

Describing Operations

The operations section of the business plan provides a detailed, in-depth operational plan. Creating this part of the plan gives entrepreneurs an opportunity to work out potential problems on paper before beginning operations. The importance of creating an operations plan will depend on the nature of the business. An e-commerce production site will probably require significant attention to operational issues. In contrast, most retail businesses and some service businesses will probably have less operational complexity. Issues addressed in this section of the business plan include the following:

Product/Service Development: It is not unusual to prepare a business plan before a business's full range of products and services is developed. This is especially true of start-up companies. Even after the product has been developed, it is often necessary to continue developing it to maintain a competitive position. It is usually worthwhile to present a summary of the development activities that the company will undertake.

Manufacturing: In the case of a production facility, it is important to discuss the process by which a company will manufacture its products. This usually involves some description of the plant, equipment, material, and labor requirements.

Entrepreneurs should also include a description of the techniques they may employ in combining these resources, including assembly lines and robotics, as well as the production rates and constraints on production capabilities. If some or all of the operations will be outsourced, then details of the subcontractors should be supplied.

Maintenance and Support: The plan should address the level of support a company will provide after a customer has purchased a product or service. This is particularly important in the case of a software or technical product.

Describing the Management Team

The management team's talents and skills should be detailed in the management team section of the business plan. If the business plan is being used to attract investors, this section should emphasize the team's talents and indicate why this management will help the company have a distinctive competitive advantage. Entrepreneurs should keep in mind that individuals invest in people, not ideas. Issues that should be addressed in this section include the following:

Management Talents and Skills: Detail the expertise, skills, and related work experience of the proposed management team and the backgrounds of those individuals who are expected to play key roles in the venture. These include investors, members of the board of directors, key employees, advisers, and strategic partners.

Organizational Chart: After introducing the key participants, it is appropriate to offer an organizational chart that presents the relationships and divisions of responsibility within the organization. In some instances, a brief narrative instead of, or in addition to, a chart may be helpful in providing further detail.

Policy and Strategy for Employees: Include a statement as to how employees will be selected, trained, and rewarded. Such background can be important for investors to give them a feel for the company's culture. A brief reference to the type of benefits and incentives planned may further help define the company's spirit.

Board of Directors and Advisory Board: Describe the number of directors who will comprise the board of directors for the company. The directors can be founders of the company, individuals, or venture capitalists who invested financially or who bring specific business experience to the management team.

Describing the Financial Plan

The financial plan section of the business plan should formulate a credible, comprehensive set of projections reflecting the business's anticipated financial performance. If these projections are carefully prepared and convincingly supported, they become one of the most critical yardsticks by which the business's attractiveness is measured.[6] While the overall business plan communicates a basic understanding of the nature of the business, projected financial performance directly addresses bottom-line interests. This is where the investor discovers the return on investment, performance measures, and exit plans.

The financial plan is the least flexible part of a business plan in terms of format. While actual numbers will vary, each plan should contain similar statements—or schedules—and each statement should be presented in a conventional manner. There should be enough information in these statistics to understand not only the business but also how it relates to similar businesses. In general, the following information should be presented:

Set of Assumptions: The set of assumptions on which projections are based should be clearly and concisely presented. Numbers without these assumptions will have little meaning. Only after carefully considering such assumptions can investors assess the validity of financial projections.

Projected Income Statements: These statements most often reflect at least quarterly performance for the first year, while annual statements are provided for Years 2 through 5.

Projected Cash Flow Statements: Such statements should be developed in as great a level of detail as possible for the first two years. Quarterly or annual cash flows, corresponding to the period used for the income statements, are sufficient for Years 3 through 5.

Current Balance Sheet: This should reflect the company's financial position at its inception. Projected year-end balance sheets, typically for two years, should also be included.

Other Financial Projections: This may include a breakeven analysis that will demonstrate the level of sales required to break even at a given time.

This section should not contain every line item in the financial pro formas; these are better confined to an appendix. Judicial use of charts and graphs can make this section easier to read.

Establishing the Amount of Funds Required

The funds required and uses section of the business plan should describe how much money is required to finance the business, where these funds will be spent, and when they will be needed. To determine financing requirements, entrepreneurs must evaluate and estimate the funds needed for (but not limited to) research and development, purchases of equipment and assets, and working capital. For example, to finance research and development of a product, entrepreneurs might experience a long delay between incurring research expenses and actually generating sales. Thus, it may be appropriate to fund these expenses with long-term financing.[7]

Exhibits (Typical)

- Census data and other population statistics
- Market potential
- Process flow (operations)
- Detailed financials

ROADMAP

IN ACTION	Visit the book's web site to view sample business plans in different markets.

Understanding Why Business Plans Fail

The authors have reviewed hundreds of business plans from entrepreneurs seeking advice or funding and, in so doing, have compiled the following list of factors that differentiate a successful plan from those that fail to attract investments or loans. Remember that there are far more inadequate business plans floating around than good business opportunities. Therefore, any reviewer will try to find a quick reason to *not* read your plan and reject it. Most start-ups fail, not for lack of tech or creativity, but for lack of customers. So engage the customers in developing the plan from the beginning. You have to find a way to sustain interest and to get your plan to the top of the reviewer's pile. Any one of the following factors is likely to trigger a "no thanks" note from a banker, angel, VC investor, or corporate partner:[8]

- The executive summary is unclear, not concise, and not specifically targeted to the intended audience.
- The basic concept of the business has not been researched and validated.

- The business is "so unique that there are no competitors." There are always competitors. They may not be obvious, but they are waiting out there to attack your business.

- The entrepreneur has never spoken to a potential customer. "I will build a new mousetrap, and they will come."

- The financial projections are far too optimistic. Sales and cash flow follow a "hockey stick" curve, with the company turning cash positive after eighteen months of operations and growing at an annual rate of 200 percent thereafter.

- There is no discussion of either how a loan will be repaid or how an investor will get his or her cash out with a satisfactory return.

- The entrepreneur signals that she wants to remain in control come whatever. One indicator of this is not mentioning how a board will be constructed with "arm's length" experts who may challenge the entrepreneur.

- The stated valuation of the company is outrageously high and unrealistic.

- If the company depends on intellectual property (IP) to retain its competitiveness, there is no mention of any IP search showing that there is no conflict with other companies or inventors.

- The management section refers to a group of résumés that turn out to be from friends or merely acquaintances who are not really suitable for the positions but have been included because this is required in the plan. Often, these résumés are barely readable and are in different formats. It is better to be open about the positions that will need to be filled and how this will be accomplished.[9]

- The financials are heavy on irrelevant details, such as weekly postage costs each month for ten years, but have fundamental flaws in the most important assumptions, such as sales and distribution costs or overly high compensation for the founder.

- There is a fact in the plan that can easily be checked independently, and it turns out that the entrepreneur has not been completely honest in the document. Nobody wants to invest in, lend to, or partner with people they cannot fully trust.

ROADMAP

| IN ACTION | Investors will ask the following questions: Will I get my money back before the entrepreneur? Will I have the right to invest in future rounds? What role will I play in the company? Have clear answers. |

SUMMARY

This chapter has established the value of a business plan and the step-by-step procedure involved in its preparation. The business plan has value as follows:

- It applies rigor and discipline when you are forced to provide in-depth detail about all aspects of your business and how you are going to execute the plan. It should contain solid research to support your opportunity. It is unlikely to be read in detail by investors, lenders, or indeed anyone else except perhaps the customer/market information. Its major value is in forcing an entrepreneur to be thorough and detailed. It is valuable in the creation of elevator pitches, executive summaries (which is probably the only thing that will be read), and presentations. Having worked on and written down a plan in detail helps an entrepreneur when presenting or discussing the business to be confident and able to answer probing and detailed questions.

- In any case, business plans are becoming more and more concise. The plan should be limited to a 15- to 20-page readable and understandable text. Venture capitalists and other investors will never start by reading a 50-page business plan and examine a full set of forecast financials—they have too little time for this. But they will read a one-page elevator pitch-style executive summary and, if it stimulates interest, go on to read the executive summary and financial plan.

An entrepreneur can first start with the canvas model filling out the nine sections and then complete the business plan as a guide for establishing the direction of the company and the action steps needed in obtaining funding.

Successful companies demand much more than great products. Marketing channels, pricing partners, and more can be tested long before a launch so that the entrepreneur knows what will work and when the business is ready to go. The executive summary, a part of the business plan, must be able to stand on its own. It should describe the customers, financial requirements, and the expected payback.

- The marketing section of the business plan must establish the demand for the product or service and the potential for the business. This section typically includes a summary of the business's growth potential, the sources of demand, and the ways in which the demand is satisfied.

- The company description section of the business plan begins with a brief, general description of the company. This section should present the fundamental activities and nature of the company. A fine level of detail is not appropriate in this section because it is included in other sections.

- The marketing and sales strategy section of the business plan describes how the business will implement the marketing plan to achieve expected sales performance. In this section, the entrepreneur establishes pricing, distribution, and promotional strategies that will allow the business to succeed in a competitive environment.

The operations section of the business plan presents the potential problems and the ways in which these problems can be resolved. The importance of creating an operations plan will depend on the nature of the business. An e-commerce production site will probably require significant attention to operational issues. In contrast, most retail businesses and some service businesses will probably have less operational complexity.

The management team section of the business plan details the management team's talents and skills. If the business plan is being used to attract investors, this section should emphasize the management's talents and indicate why they will give the company a distinctive competitive advantage. Investors always look for a strong management team before making investments. Many businesses fail because the proper talent has not been assembled. This issue is addressed by describing the objective assessment of the team's strengths and weaknesses as well as the company's requirements for growth. It includes how employees are selected, trained, and rewarded.

The financial plan section of the business plan should formulate a credible, comprehensive set of projections reflecting the business's anticipated financial performance. If these projections are carefully prepared and convincingly supported, they become one of the most critical yardsticks by which the business's attractiveness is measured.

The business plan is essential in launching a new business that will serve as a guide and an instrument for the entrepreneur to raise necessary capital and funding.

STUDY QUESTIONS

Q.1 What are the benefits of preparing the canvas model first before a written business plan?

Q.2 What are the components of a business plan?

Q.3 What are the different types of business plans?

Q.4 How long does it take to write a business plan?

Q.5 Why do business plans fail?

Q.6 Why should the executive summary be written last?

EXERCISES

Please circle the correct answer, either true (T) or false (F), for each question. Visit the book's web site to review your answers.

6.1 Many small companies do not prepare a formal business plan because the major benefit of a business plan is the discussions that occur during its preparation. Therefore, in the absence of adequate resources or time, an oral plan is adequate. (T) or (F)

6.2 List in order of importance the following four purposes of a business plan.
   (a) Explain new technologies
   (b) Guide the entrepreneur
   (c) Avoid competitors
   (d) Provide a historical perspective of the business

6.3 Business plans are planning documents. As a result, they are frequently optimistic and should not be used to assist management in operating the business, nor should they be used as the basis for performance evaluation. (T) or (F)

6.4 Companies need *not* produce a business plan if
   (a) They lack the necessary planning department. (T) or (F)
   (b) There is insufficient time and money to develop a meaningful plan. (T) or (F)
   (c) Management does not know how to prepare a plan and is not aware of the benefits that can be derived from it. (T) or (F)
   (d) Annual sales are less than $50 million. (T) or (F)

6.5 Financial statements are an important part of the business planning process because
   (a) The planning process relates primarily to the financial function of the company. (T) or (F)
   (b) After completing the business plan, the next step is to develop financial projections. (T) or (F)
   (c) Financial statements are commonly used to express business expectations and results of performance. (T) or (F)

6.6 Business planning is primarily a financial activity; therefore, top managers from departments other than finance need not be involved in the preparation of the business plan. (T) or (F)

6.7 Because an outsider would be unfamiliar with a given business, entrepreneurs should not expect a business plan to be meaningful to such outsiders. (T) or (F)

6.8 Review the business plan for Railway Innovation Technologies on the book's web site and answer the following questions:
   (a) What was the intended purpose for this plan?
   (b) What four things do you like best about this plan? Why?
   (c) What four areas require improvement and why?

Master-Case Exercises: If you have not read the appendix for the master case to Chapter 1 at the book web site, do so. Then go to the book's web site and read diary entry Month 23.

Master Case Q1: Neoforma had only a rough business plan when they met Jack and the first investors. Later, to raise more money from more ambitious investors, they were persuaded to use a professional business plan writer, Sasa. What are the advantages and disadvantages of using a consultant to write your business plan?

Case Study ‖ Surfparks llc (online)

This business plan case study was prepared by James Meiselman, Columbia MBA 2002, under the supervision of Professor Jack M. Kaplan as the basis for class discussion on the subject of business plans. Copyright © 2002 by the Lang Center for Entrepreneurship, Graduate School of Business, Columbia University, 317 Uris Hall, 3022 Broadway, New York, NY 10027.

   Note: For competitive reasons, some financial figures—specifically financial costs and marketing figures—have been altered or fabricated.

   The purpose of this case study is to evaluate the business plan of Surfparks LLC. The mission of the venture is to create and operate/franchise the world's first surfing-specific wave pools, targeted primarily at the rapidly growing surfer population. Go to the book's web site and read the case carefully and then prepare answers to the following questions:

1. Does the executive summary describe key elements of marketing, company services, current position, and financial features?

2. Is the proposed offer well written and concise, and are key data included?

3. Where would you place the technology overview section?

4. Are the sections in the business plan listed in the right order?

5. What are the important marketing issues and competitive advantages that should be described in the marketing section?

6. Does the financing section address the funding requirements and how the capital will be used?

7. What are your recommendations for revising the plan to attract needed capital?

Surfparks Business Plan (Online)

| # The Roadmap Guide for Writing A Business Plan

The roadmap guide leads you through a detailed table of contents for preparing a business plan and a framework, which provides the guidelines for writing the sections in the plan. This business plan table of contents was developed by Clifford Schorer at Columbia Business School's Eugene M. Lang Center for Entrepreneurship. Schorer has more than fifteen years of experience working with students and venture capitalists in evaluating business plans. There is no one way to write a business plan, and there are many ways to approach the preparation for and the writing of a business plan. Entrepreneurs will probably find it necessary to research many areas before they have enough information to start writing. Most begin by collecting historical financial information about their company and/or industry and completing their market research before beginning to write any one part.

Initial drafts of proposed financial statements and projections are often prepared next, after the basic market research and analysis are completed. By preparing these statements, the entrepreneur knows which strategies will work from a financial perspective before investing many hours in writing a detailed description. Entrepreneurs should keep detailed notes on their assumptions so later they can include footnotes with their statements.

The business plan framework provides a three-step process to help identify ideas, issues, and research needed to complete the seven sections included in a business plan. The guide is based on the five-phase opportunity analysis described in Chapter 3 and assumes that you have completed preparing the marketing analysis and competition section in Chapter 4.

The following is a sample table of contents that details the eight sections for the business plan.

Business Plan

Table of Contents

Section I. Executive Summary (usually one to two pages)
A. The Business Opportunity and Vision
B. The Market and Projections
C. The Competitive Advantages
D. The Management Team
E. The Offering

Section II. The Company, Industry, and Product(s) and/or Service(s)
A. The Company
B. The Industry
C. The Product(s) and/or Service(s)
D. The Growth Plan

Section III. Market Analysis
A. Market Size and Trends
B. Target Customers
C. Competition

Section IV. Marketing and Sales Plan
A. Marketing Strategy
B. Pricing
C. Sales Plan
D. Advertising and Promotion
E. Channels of Distribution and Sales
F. Operations Plan

Section V. Operating Plan
A. Product Development
B. Manufacturing Plan
C. Maintenance and Support

Section VI. Management Team
A. Organization Chart
B. Key Management Personnel
C. Policy and Strategy for Employees
D. Board of Directors
E. Advisory Board

Section VII. The Financial Plan
A. Actual Income Statements and Balance Sheets
B. Pro Forma Income Statements
C. Pro Forma Balance Sheets
D. Pro Forma Cash Flow Analysis

Section VIII. Funds Required and Uses
A. Financial Requirements
B. Amounts, Timing, and Terms
C. Use of Funds—Capital Expenditures, Working Capital

Appendixes

Financial Data Assumptions Exhibits and Appendixes

Business Plan Framework
The following framework and worksheets will assist entrepreneurs in preparing and writing their business plans by helping them gather their ideas, list the research needed, and identify issues and questions they must address in the key sections in the plan.

Step 1. Business Plan Preparation

Step 2. Business Plan Worksheet

Step 3. Business Plan Financial Planning

The worksheets can also be downloaded from the web site www.wiley.com/college/kaplan. Entrepreneurs can review the business plans on the web site to determine the worksheet that best fits their individual needs.

Step 1. Business Plan Preparation

The business plan preparation framework identifies the market need, competitive advantages, management team, and growth guidelines that should be emphasized in the plan.

Guidelines	List	Questions

1. Focus on Market-Driven Opportunities
- Demonstrate how product/service meets market needs for the venture.
- Establish the size of the market for the product or service and define the specific buyers.
- Analyze the competition and the competitive environment.

2. Stress Competitive Advantages
- Demonstrate the distinct competence that the business will provide.
- How substantial is your advantage in the marketplace?

3. Describe the Management Team
- List the talents, skills, and experience of the management team.
- List how the team will be retained and what incentives will be provided for employees.

4. Support Projections for Growth
- Analyze the market structure and industry.
- Identify the growth rate for the product or service.
- Validate the results of your research by showing the total revenue expended for the business and the total number of current and potential customers.

Step 2. Business Plan Worksheet

The business plan worksheet details helpful tips, research needed, and further questions that need to be addressed. The following are tips to help the entrepreneur get started and make the writing of the business plan easier:

Guidelines	List	Questions

1. Executive Summary
- Make sure that the executive summary isn't more than three pages long.
- Make sure that the executive summary captures the reader's interest.
- Quickly and concisely establish the what, how, why, where, when, and so on.
- Complete the executive summary after all other sections have been written.

2. Company Overview Section
- Describe the business's name.
- Include background of the industry as well as a brief history of the company.
- Define the potential of the new venture and list key customers, major products, and applications.
- Spell out any unique or distinctive features of the venture.

3. Marketing Analysis Section
- Convince investors that sales projections can be met.
- Use and disclose market studies.
- Identify a target market and market share.

Step 2. Business Plan Worksheet *(Continued)*

Guidelines	List	Questions

- Evaluate all competition and specifically explain why and how this business will be better than the competition.
- Describe the pricing strategy that will be used to penetrate and maintain a market share.
- Identify advertising plans with cost estimates to validate the proposed strategy.

4. Marketing and Sales Plan Section
- Describe the features and benefits of the services or products.
- Describe in detail the current stage of development.

5. Research, Design, and Development Segment Section
- State the costs involved in research, testing, and development.
- Explain carefully what has already been accomplished (prototype, lab testing, early development, and so on).
- Mention any research or technical assistance that has been provided.

6. Operations Segment Section
- Describe the advantages of the business's location (such as zoning, tax laws, and wage rates).
- List the production needs in terms of facilities (plant, storage, office space) and equipment (machinery, furnishings, supplies).
- Describe the access to transportation (for shipping and receiving).
- Explain the proximity to the business's suppliers.
- Describe the availability of labor in the business's location.

7. Management Section
- Provide résumés or curricula vitae of all key management personnel.
- Carefully describe the legal structure (sole proprietorship, partnership, S-corporation, LLC, or C-corporation) of the business.
- Describe any expected added assistance by advisors, consultants, and directors.
- Provide information on current ownership and options for an exit strategy such as selling the business or going public.

Step 3. Business Plan Financial Planning

Guidelines	List	Questions

1. Financial Section
- Convince investors that the business makes sense from a financial standpoint.
- Prepare three- to five-year financial projections.
- Prepare first-year projections by month.
- Prepare second-year projections by quarter.
- Include an income statement and balance sheet.
- Include a cash flow statement for years 1 and 2.
- Include a three-year annual forecast.

2. Selling the Plan
- Prepare financial presentation.
- Seek assistance of *outside* experts.
- Identify funding sources.
- Schedule meeting for funding.
- Get started and introductions.

INTERACTIVE LEARNING ON THE WEB

Test your knowledge of the chapter using the book's interactive web site.

ADDITIONAL RESOURCES

- **Biz Plan Software,** www.jian.com
- **Business Plans,** www.bplans.com
- **Business Plans Made Easy,** www.entrepreneur.com

- **Small Business Advancement National Center,** http://sbaer.uca.edu
- **Student Guide to Business Presentations,** http://ideapitch.smeal.psu.edu/

ENDNOTES

1. This profile was prepared using interviews with Shkolnik and members of the MIT business plan team.
2. See "Investors Pay Business Plans Little Heed, Study Finds," Brent Bowers Column, *New York Times*, May 14, 2009.
3. See William A. Sahlman, "How to Write a Great Business Plan," *Harvard Business Review* (July 1, 1997): 2–5.
4. See Jack M. Kaplan, *Getting Started in Entrepreneurship* (New York: John Wiley & Sons, 2001), 95.
5. Ibid., 97.
6. Michael Bucheit (partner, Advanced Infrastructure Ventures Interview), New York, May 2002.
7. See William A. Sahlman, "Some Thoughts on Business Plans," *Harvard Business School*, November 1996, 3–5.
8. Eric Major (angel investor) interview, New York, June 2002.
9. Ibid.

Setting up the Company

7

"The ladder of success doesn't care who climbs it."

Frank Tyger, Cartoonist and Humorist

OBJECTIVES

- Assess the factors in deciding which form of ownership is best suited for a potential business.
- Outline the advantages and disadvantages of a sole proprietorship and partnership.
- Explain the corporate form of ownership and describe how a business is incorporated.
- Understand the S-corporation and the limited liability company (LLC).
- Understand how to register a business with government entities.
- Learn how to choose an attorney.

CHAPTER OUTLINE

Introduction

Some entrepreneurs start businesses and determine the structure of the company with lots of thought and planning. Others find themselves establishing a company without much regard to how the business should be structured. However, one of the most important decisions to make is how to legally structure a business.[1] Before deciding how to organize a company, the entrepreneur needs to identify the legal structure that will best meet the requirements of the business. This is due to the tax laws, liability situation, and ways to attract capital.

Many companies provide added incentives for keeping key employees by offering an ownership or equity interest in the company. This is usually in the form of common stock or options to acquire common stock. In Chapter 9, we will discuss in some detail how companies should establish a qualified stock-option plan and how selected employees receive options to purchase stock in the company.

The legal form of the business—sole proprietorship, C-corporation, S-corporation, partnership, or limited liability company (LLC)—should be determined in light of the business's short-term and long-term needs. In this chapter, we will examine the pros and cons of each of these forms and how to prepare a checklist to start the business. The entrepreneur's specific situation, circumstances, and issues will determine the choice.

Profile: Ethan Wendle and Matt Chverchko—When to Convert from an S- to a C-Corporation

Matt and Ethan met while still undergraduate students in Penn State's College of Engineering, Matt specializing in mechanical and Ethan in civil engineering.[2] Matt is an avid hunter and realized that there was a need for hunters to have a dual carrying capability with their pickup trucks—a lockable section for valuable equipment and a large load-carrying area for hauling large game, ATVs, or other equipment. To meet this need, he designed a unique truck cover that could be retrofitted onto existing trucks, and the prototype won the "best product" award in his class's final year design competition. Based on this success, Matt and Ethan decided to start a company and formed DiamondBack Truck Accessories, Inc. (www.diamondbackcovers.com) as an S-corporation in 2003 ready to sell their first commercial product. The S structure was chosen for simplicity and provided the founders the advantage of a single taxation level. Word of mouth soon created a demand for the company's products, and they turned to friends and family to help out with cash in the form of a 20 percent membership interest for Ethan's father coupled with a small loan. The partners also received $140,000 from the Ben Franklin Technology Partnership, an economic development agency in Pennsylvania, and other help from the commonwealth for locating in a targeted development region in Clearfield. In 2005, the company received its first patent (6883855) and substantially expanded its manufacturing facilities.

As the company grew and moved into new, larger markets such as off-road vehicle transportation systems and building contractors, it needed more working capital. Using their links to Penn State, the founders approached the student-managed Garber Venture Capital Fund, which agreed to invest $350,000 in two stages in the form of a convertible preferred class of stock. However, this created a problem for the university in two regards. First, as a public nonprofit entity, the university cannot participate in a structure that would provide it possible tax advantages. Second, membership in an S-corporation may, under certain situations, imply a liability on its members; in any case, the university could participate at only full arm's length as a passive investor, not even taking a board seat. The DiamondBack board decided to convert to a C status, even though this removed the personal tax advantages for the founders, required a forfeit of tax losses carried forward, and required badly needed cash for the legal fees to make the changes. However, the long-term aim of the company is to create an exit for its shareholders, which will be easier under a C-corporation umbrella. In 2007, the company posted its first profitable year and growth of more than 35 percent. Over 2007 and 2008, the company has established itself as a major industry player in truck cover manufacturing and has procured key partnerships with many large industry leaders including A.R.E., LINE-X, and HUMMER. As the company has continued to grow, so have its financial and corporate structures needed to grow and change. While an S-corp or LLC may have suited the small start-up firm, the C-corp status positions the company for future merger or acquisition opportunities and better reflects the current size of the business.

Identifying What Form of Ownership is Best

In choosing a form of ownership, entrepreneurs must remember that there is no single "best" form; what is best depends on the individual's circumstances. To determine the form of ownership, be prepared to address the following issues[3]:

- How big can this business potentially become?

- How much control do you need in the decision-making process of the company? Are you willing to share ideas and the business's potential profits with others who can help build a more successful business?

- How much capital is needed to start the business?

- What tax considerations are important? What sources of income are there, and how are they to be sheltered?

- In case of failure, to what extent are you willing to be personally responsible for debts created by the business?

- Is it important that the business continues in case of owner incapacity or death?

- Who will be the sole or major beneficiary of the business success? Is the owner the type of person who doesn't mind taking all the risks but expects to reap all the benefits if successful?

- Can you put up with the time-consuming bureaucratic red tape associated with more complicated forms of ownership? What is your emotional reaction to government regulations and their accompanying paperwork requirements?

Forms of Doing Business

The legal form of business (sole proprietorship, C-corporation, S-corporation, partnership, or LLC) should be carefully considered to ensure that the form chosen best meets the short-term and long-term requirements as well as the significant tax and nontax differences. A brief analysis of each form is presented. Because there are significant tax and nontax differences among the forms, the results and requirements of each form should be carefully considered to ensure that the business form chosen best meets the requirements.

Sole Proprietorship

A sole proprietorship is a form of business in which a single owner does business himself or herself and requires only a business license to open. If the plan is to operate a business under a name other than that of the owner, the business name must be filed as a "doing business as" registration with a state and/or local filing authority (e.g., Jack Smith doing business as Jack's SmartCard Consulting). The business can be terminated at any time and always ends with the death of the owner.

The sole owner has the right to make all the decisions for the business. However, the owner is personally liable for all debts and contracts of the business. Because there is no distinction between personal and business debts, if the business cannot pay its bills, the creditors can sue to collect from the owner's personal assets. In matters dealing with taxes, profits, and losses from the business flow directly to the owner and are taxed at individual income tax rates on the owner's personal tax return. If the owner does not plan to take a salary, income is the profits of the business. There is no carryback or carryforward of losses for tax-reporting purposes.

ROADMAP

IN ACTION   Sole proprietorships are popular because they have a number of attractive features.[4]

- *Simple to Initiate Business.* One of the most attractive features of sole proprietorships is how fast and simple it is to begin operations. If a proprietor wishes to operate the business under his or her own name, one simply obtains the necessary license(s), if any, and begins operations. In a sole proprietorship, the proprietor is the business. It is not difficult to start up a proprietorship in a single day if the business is simple.

- *Low Start-up Fees.* In addition to being easy to begin, the proprietorship is generally the least expensive form of ownership to establish. Legal papers do not need to be created to start the business. Rather, if required, the proprietor goes to the appropriate state and/or county government office and states the nature of the new business in his or her license application. The government assesses the appropriate fees and license costs. Once these fees are paid, the owner is allowed to conduct business.

If the proprietorship is to do business under a trade name, a Certificate of Doing Business under an Assumed Name must be filed with the state and/or county in which the business will operate. The fee for filing the certificate is usually nominal. Acquiring this certificate involves conducting a name search of previously filed names to determine that the name to be used is not already registered as the name of another business or as a trademark or service mark for another business.

Advantages of a Sole Proprietorship

Entrepreneurs have a number of legal forms of business to choose from, including sole proprietorship, C-corporation, S-corporation, partnership, or LLC. Entrepreneurs should determine which business form is best for their short-term and long-term needs. In choosing a form of ownership, entrepreneurs must remember that there is no single "best" form; what is best depends on the individual's circumstances:

- *Profit Incentive.* One major advantage of the proprietorship is that after all the debts are paid, the owner receives all the profits (less taxes, of course). Profits represent an excellent scorecard of success.

- *Total Decision-Making Authority*. Because the sole proprietor is in total control of operations and can respond quickly to changes, this becomes an asset in rapidly shifting markets. The freedom to set the company's course of action is another major motivation for selecting this ownership form. For the individual who thrives on the enjoyment of seeking new opportunities and modifies the business as needed, the free, unimpeded decision making of the sole proprietorship is a must.

- *No Special Legal Restrictions*. The proprietorship is the least regulated form of business ownership. In a time when government requests for information seem never ending, this feature has much merit.

- *Easy to Discontinue*. When an owner cannot continue operations, he or she can terminate the business quickly, even though such persons will still be liable for all outstanding debts and obligations of the business.

Disadvantages of a Sole Proprietorship

As advantageous as the sole proprietorship form of ownership is, it does have its disadvantages:

- *Unlimited Personal Liability*. The greatest disadvantage of a sole proprietorship is unlimited personal liability; that is, the sole proprietor is personally liable for all business debts. The proprietor owns all the assets of the business. If the business fails, these assets can be sold to cover debts. If there are still unpaid debts, creditors can seize and sell the owner's personal assets to cover the remaining debts. Failure of the business can ruin the owner financially. Because the law views the proprietor and the business as one and the same, the debts of the business are considered the owner's personal debts. Laws protecting an individual's personal assets to some degree may vary from one state to another. Most states require creditors to leave the failed business owner a minimum amount of equity in a home, a car, and some personal items. The new Federal Bankruptcy Law protects retirement assets from creditors. Bankruptcy or other insolvency protection may be needed to protect a failed business owner. Because laws vary, picking the proper jurisdiction in which to do business is critical.

- *Limited Skills and Capabilities of the Sole Owner*. The owner may not have the needed skills to run a successful business. Each individual has skills and talents reflective of education, training, and work experience. However, the lack of skills and knowledge in other areas is what often causes failure. If an owner is not familiar with an area such as finance, accounting, or law, he or she will tend to gloss over these areas, thinking that they do not seriously impact his or her business or that this is a way to save money by ignoring these services even when needed. The sole owner who fails may have been successful if he or she had had previous knowledge of possible problems in one or more of these areas and had obtained good, timely advice. Sole owners need to recognize their shortcomings and find help in those areas in which they are not proficient.

- *Limited Access to Capital*. For a business to grow and expand, a sole proprietor generally needs financial resources. Many proprietors put all they have into their businesses and often use their personal resources as collateral on existing loans. In short, proprietors, unless they have great personal wealth, find it difficult to raise additional money while maintaining sole ownership. The business may be sound in the long run, but short-term cash flow difficulties can cause financial headaches. Most banks and lending institutions have well-defined formulas for borrower's eligibility. As a result, a proprietor may not be able to obtain the funds needed to operate the business, especially in difficult times.

- *Lack of Continuity for the Business.* Lack of continuity is inherent in a sole proprietorship. If the proprietor dies or becomes incapacitated, the business automatically terminates. Unless a family member or employee can effectively take over, the business could be in jeopardy. If no one is trained to run the business, creditors can petition the courts to liquidate the assets of the dissolved business and the estate of the proprietor to pay outstanding debts.

SETTING UP A SOLE PROPRIETORSHIP

SUMMARY OF PROS AND CONS

Simple to set up
Low cost to set up

PROS

All profits go to owner after taxes
All decisions made by owner alone
Low reporting requirements to the government
Easy to terminate

CONS

Unlimited personal liability
Inability to bring in additional skills by offering ownership rights
Limited access to external capital
No means of continuation on demise of owner

C-Corporation

The C-corporation is a common form of business ownership especially for companies that are growing quickly and are raising funds. Publicly traded companies used this format. A corporation is a separate legal entity apart from its owners and may engage in business, issue contracts, sue and be sued, and pay taxes. The owners of a corporation hold stock in the corporation. Each share of stock represents a percentage of ownership. The actual business of the corporation is conducted by the directors and officers of the corporation.

When a corporation is founded, it accepts the regulations and restrictions of the state in which it is incorporated and of each state in which it does business. Corporations doing business in the state in which they are incorporated are domestic corporations. When they conduct business in another state, that state considers them to be foreign corporations. Corporations that are formed in other countries but do business in the United States are alien corporations. Where and how a corporation does business have an impact on its ability to operate and its tax liability. Also, a corporation may be taxed in every jurisdiction where it is incorporated or doing business.

Generally, the corporation must annually file in its state of incorporation and in every state in which it is doing business. These reports become public record. If the corporation's stock is sold in more than one state, the corporation must comply with federal and state regulations governing the sale of corporate securities.[5] For most small businesses, the selling of stock will not involve registering the stock as a security. However, the law may require the filing of reports showing a registration exemption.

A corporation has three primary sections: the stockholders, the board of directors, and the officers. It is important to understand the specific functions of each section.

The Stockholders are the Owners of the Business

When a corporation is established, its equity is divided among a number of shares of stock that are issued to the investors in proportion to their investment in the corporation. A general protocol for the company's operations, called the bylaws, is adopted by the stockholders. Sometimes, these bylaws can be amended or changed by the board of directors, sometimes only by the stockholders. The ultimate power and control of every corporation lie in the hands of the stockholders.

The Board of Directors Has Responsibility for the Overall Operation of the Company

The stockholders elect the board and have the power to remove board members. The board establishes the general policies of the company and, to a greater or lesser extent depending on the particular corporation, can become involved in various details of the operating procedures. The board of directors elects the officers of the corporation to handle the day-to-day affairs.

The Usual Officers in a Corporation are President, Secretary (or "Clerk" in Some States), and Treasurer

The functions of each officer are defined by the board of directors. The president is in charge of day-to-day operations under the directives of the board of directors. The secretary is charged with handling the paperwork of the corporation, such as preparing minutes of stockholder and directors' meetings, sending out notices, and preparing stock certificates. The treasurer is charged with guardianship of the corporate finances. However, there are differences in the functions of the officers among different corporations.

Additional officers may include vice presidents, who are sometimes charged with a specific aspect of operations such as engineering, finance, production, or sales. There may also be assistants for each of the offices, such as assistant secretary and assistant treasurer.

You do not necessarily need the services of an attorney to set up and maintain a corporation. The days when a corporation was a rigid structure with reams of rules for the precise keeping of records and holdings of meetings are gone. The various states have revised the corporate laws to allow great flexibility in creating and maintaining a corporation. Nevertheless, if you wish to have the benefits offered by a corporation, you must treat the business as a corporation, not as a proprietorship. We'll say more about this presently.

The specific requirements for forming a corporation vary from state to state. The easiest way to start is to request information and forms from the office of your local secretary of state. This will tell you the fees and generally how to prepare the papers for filing.

What State to Register in

Delaware is a popular state for incorporation, so we will use that as a practical example.[6] If you are not a resident of Delaware, you must have an agent in the state who is empowered to accept service in the event the corporation is sued. In other words, if you incorporate in a particular state, the corporation can be sued in that state even if you conduct no other activities there. Such agents represent the corporation for a relatively modest annual fee. A list of acceptable agents in Delaware can be obtained by writing to the Department of State, Division of Corporations, P.O. Box 898, Dover, DE 19901. Similar lists for other states are available from the secretary of state in that state. After obtaining the list of agents, you can then write to them to inquire about their annual fees and the "extra" fees for performing additional special functions.

After selecting a local agent, the next step is to select the corporate name. The name must include an indication that the entity is a corporation. In many states you could not, for example, call your corporation "The SMITH Company." You could call it "The SMITH Company Inc." or "The SMITH Company Corp." You should find out just what corporate indicators are required in your state of incorporation. In Delaware, the permitted corporate indicators are *Association, Club, Company, Corporation, Foundation, Fund, Incorporated, Institute, Limited, Society, Syndicate, Union*, and any of these abbreviations: *Co., Corp., Inc.*, or *Ltd.*

You can ask your agent to check on the availability of the name; this can usually be done by telephone. If the name is available, it can be reserved for thirty days without charge. *Availability* means that no other corporation has a prior registration of the same name or one sufficiently similar that it might cause confusion. If "SMITH Incorporated" is already incorporated in your state, you cannot use the name "SMITH" even if you change the other parts of the name. You can still incorporate in another state where the name has not been used, but this is not likely to be a practical solution because before a foreign corporation (a corporation formed in another state) can do business in your state, it must register there as a foreign corporation. This will not be permitted if another local or foreign corporation has the same or a confusingly similar name.

The next step is to prepare the Certificate of Incorporation (sometimes the Articles of Incorporation). The following is a typical form ready for forwarding to the agent, along with the filing fee and the first annual charge for the agent:

> "To raise capital for early-stage companies, a C-corporation is preferred and provides the most flexible structures for various rounds of private equity investments."
>
> Michael Bucheist
> *Managing Partner, Advanced Infrastructure Ventures*

CERTIFICATE OF INCORPORATION OF SMITH INCORPORATED

A corporation

First: The name of this corporation is SMITH Incorporated.

Second: Its registered office in the State of Delaware is to be located at (here insert the address of the Delaware agent you have selected). The name of the registered agent is (name of registered agent).

Third: The nature of the business and the objects and purposes proposed to be transacted and carried on are to engage in any lawful act or activity for which corporations may be organized under the General Corporation Law of Delaware.

Fourth: The amount of total authorized capital stock of the corporation is divided into 3,000 shares of no-par common (the maximum number of shares with minimum tax).

Fifth: The name and address of the incorporator are as follows: Jane Vista
345 Boulder
Austin, TX 29555

Sixth: The powers of the incorporator are to terminate upon the filing of the Certificate of Incorporation. The name and mailing addresses of the persons who are to serve as directors until their successors are elected are as follows:
Jane Vista 345 Boulder
Austin, TX 29555

Seventh: All of the issued stock of the corporation, exclusive of treasury shares, shall be held of record of not more than thirty persons.

Eighth: All of the issued stock of all classes shall be subject to the following restriction on transfer permitted by Section 202 of the General Corporation Law.

Ninth: The corporation shall make no offering of any of its stock of any class which would constitute a "public offering" within the meaning of the United States Securities Act of 1933, as amended.

Tenth: Directors of the corporation shall not be liable to either the corporation or to its stockholders for monetary damages for a breach of fiduciary duties unless the breach involves (1) a director's duty of loyalty to the corporation or its stockholders, (2) acts or omissions not in

good faith or which involve intentional miscon-
duct or a knowing violation of law, (3) liability
for unlawful payments of dividends or unlawful
stock purchases or redemption by the corporation, or (4) a transaction from which the director
derived an improper personal benefit.

I, the undersigned, for the purpose of
forming a corporation under the laws of the state
of Delaware do make, file, and record this certificate, and do certify that the facts stated herein
are true and I have accordingly set my hand.

Dated: Incorporator

Corporate Stock

The ownership of a corporation lies in the stockholders and is evidenced by stock certificates
issued to the shareholders. There may be several classes of stock. The most usual is no-par-value
common stock. Common stock most often has voting power equal to one vote per share. However,
there may be more than one class of common stock. For example, a Class A stock may have voting
rights, while Class B stockholders own, say, 95 percent of the corporation, but the entire corporation is controlled by the 5 percent of the outstanding stock held by the Class A stockholders.

A specific number of shares of each class are authorized in the Articles of Incorporation,
and more than that amount may not be issued without first amending them. Provision may be
made for converting one class of stock into another. For example, Class B stock might be convertible, at the option of the holder, into Class A stock on a share-for-share basis or any other
specified ratio.

Another class of stock is called *preferred* because it usually has a preferred position with
respect to dividends or receiving distributions should the company go into bankruptcy. More
about different classes of stock is covered in Chapter 8.

There is great flexibility in establishing classes of stock, voting rights, and rights to dividends,
so you can tailor your corporation to best meet the needs of your particular situation.

Par value is an archaic concept that is still applied to stocks; it is the monetary value assigned
to each share of stock in the Articles of Incorporation. Such stock must be issued for an amount
of money, or other property, equal to at least the par value of the stock. If par-value stock is issued
by the corporation without such remuneration, the stockholder could be liable to creditors for the
difference between the par value and the amount actually paid. Once the stock is issued, the par
value of the stock bears no relationship to its actual value. "No-par-value" common stock has no
stated valuation in the corporate charter. In practical terms, the difference between par-value
stock and no-par-value stock lies in the tax area. In some states, as in Delaware, the corporate tax
may be less for par-value stock than for no-par-value stock.

Taxes

Annual taxes are usually based on the number of shares of authorized stock and on whether the
stock has a par value. Currently in Delaware, the minimum annual tax on a company with 500,000
shares of authorized no-par-value common stock is almost $1,770.55. If the stock has a par value,
the minimum tax on the same amount of par-value stock may be as little as $40.00. Before send-
ing in your annual corporate tax to the state of incorporation, read the tax law carefully because
the rules can be somewhat misleading. Delaware, for example, sends the company with 500,000
shares of authorized stock having a par value of $0.01 per share, an official notice in which the
tax is calculated as $1,770.55. The busy businessperson might just send a check for the full
amount. However, the fine print on subsequent pages of the tax notice describes a rather complex

method of computing an alternate tax based on the assets of the corporation. If the corporation has few assets, the actual tax due may be only the minimum of $40.00. If you inadvertently pay the larger sum to the state of Delaware, you can, with some red tape, likely recover the overpayment.

Shares Authorized and Issued

The number of shares you will want to authorize depends on the particular circumstances. Suppose only one or a few people are to be stockholders, then 10 or 100 shares might be sufficient. Usually, some number of shares can be authorized at the minimum tax rate. In Delaware, it is 3,000. The maximum might as well be authorized, so if needed in the future, additional shares can be issued without amending the Certificate of Incorporation.

There may be other reasons for authorizing more shares. If a corporation, for example, intends to issue stock options available to its employees or executives and has only 100 shares issued, an employee getting an option for an amount of stock representing 1 percent ownership of the company receives an option for one share, which doesn't sound like much. If the ownership of the corporation is represented by 2 million shares, then 1 percent ownership is represented by 20,000 shares. There is, of course, no difference, but many individuals may not be aware of that. Even if one does know the difference, one might still rather show 100,000 shares in her portfolio than only one.

Issued Shares

Issued shares are the stock that a company sells to investors to generate capital. It also includes stock given to insiders as part of their compensation packages. Shares that are held as treasury stock are not included in this figure. The amount of issued shares can be all or part of the total amount of authorized shares of a corporation.

The total number of issued shares outstanding in a company is most often shown in the annual report.

Advantages of a C-Corporation

- *Limited Liability of the Stockholders.* The corporation allows investors to limit their liability to the total amount of their investment in the corporation if they adhere to the terms of the Certificate of Incorporation and bylaws. A corporation cannot just be set up and run as if it were a sole proprietorship. Business must be conducted in the name of the board of directors through the officers using books and records separate from those of the shareholders. This legal protection of personal assets beyond the business is of critical concern to many potential investors. Because start-up companies are so risky, lenders and other creditors often require the owners to personally guarantee loans made to the corporation. By making these guarantees, owners are putting their personal assets at risk (just as in a sole proprietorship), despite choosing the corporate form of ownership. However, it is possible to limit the scope of a guaranty so not all assets of a person may be at risk.

- *Ability to Attract Capital.* Based on the protection of limited liability, the corporation has proved to be the most effective form of ownership to accumulate large amounts of capital. Limited by only the number of shares authorized in its charter (which can be amended) and subject to the laws on registration of securities, the corporation can raise money to begin business and expand as opportunity dictates. Professional or "institutional" investors such as venture capitalists (Chapter 8) demand this form of incorporation.

- *Ability of the Corporation to Continue Indefinitely.* Unless limited by its charter, the corporation as a separate legal entity theoretically can continue indefinitely. The existence of the corporation does not depend on any single individual.

- *Transferable Ownership.* If stockholders in a corporation are displeased with the progress of the business, they can sell their shares to another individual, subject only to restrictions on transfer of shares. Stocks can be transferred through inheritance to a new generation of owners. If any person wishes to own some shares in a firm and there is someone who would like to sell his or her interest in that firm, an exchange is possible. During all this change of ownership, the business continues.

- *Skills, Expertise, and Knowledge.* Unlike the sole proprietor who is often the only active member of management, the corporation can draw on the skills, expertise, and knowledge of its officers and board of directors and people whose knowledge and experience can be used to shape the direction of the firm. In many cases, the board members act as advisers, giving the stockholders the advantage of their years of experience.

Disadvantages of a C-Corporation

- *Cost and Time Involved in the Incorporation Process.* Corporations can be costly and time-consuming to establish. The owners are creating an artificial legal entity, and the start-up period can be prolonged for the novice. In some states, an attorney *must* handle the incorporation, but in most cases, entrepreneurs can complete the requirements. However, if an entrepreneur is concerned about the complexity of the requirements, they may feel more comfortable in employing an attorney even in states where one is not required so one does not go afoul of the legal and registration requirements. Failure to properly register and follow the corporate form may cause loss of the ability to limit shareholder liability.

- *Double Taxation.* Corporations are taxed on their profits. Rates range up to 35 percent. In addition, when shareholders are distributed profit in the form of a dividend, taxes on the dividend up to 39.1 percent may be incurred.

SETTING UP A C-CORPORATION

SUMMARY OF PROS AND CONS

- Separate legal and tax entity
- Shareholder liability limited to invested capital
- Existence continues after shareholder's death
- Easier to raise equity capital

PROS

- Limited liability
- Most appropriate structure for an IPO
- Tax benefits such as loss carryforwards and easy-to-set-up stock-option plans
- Ease of transferability of interests
- Structure that a venture capitalist requires

> **CONS**
> - Double taxation
> - High administration compliance costs
> - Directors held accountable
> - Well-defined corporate governance rules and laws to follow

ROADMAP

IN ACTION

Corporations offer limited liability to the owner, which means owners cannot be sued for the debts of the business unless they have personally guaranteed those debts. Therefore, the potential loss for owners is limited to the capital they have invested.

S-Corporation

The S-corporation, often referred to as a sub-S-corporation, is a corporation that elects under federal and state tax laws to be taxed like a partnership. Its profits and losses are recognized for tax purposes at the individual shareholder level. It is the shareholder's responsibility to report the profits or losses on his or her individual income tax returns. To become an S-corporation, the following must occur[7]:

- The company must be a domestic company.

- Only one class of stock is allowed.

- Only individuals and certain trusts may own a stock.

- Shareholders cannot be nonresident aliens.

- There can be a maximum of only 100 shareholders.

- The shareholders must elect to become an S-corporation at the federal and state levels.

Advantages of an S-Corporation

The S-corporation retains all the advantages of a regular corporation, such as continuity of existence, transferability of ownership, and limited personal liability. The most notable provision of the S-corporation is that it avoids the corporate income tax (and the resulting double taxation) and enables the business to pass operating profits or losses on to shareholders. In effect, the tax status of an S-corporation is similar to that of a sole proprietorship or partnership.

Entrepreneur Fanny Chin, who launched Creative Calendar in 1998 as an S-corporation, maintains that form of ownership today. "Since there were no shareholders except me, I didn't see any advantage to C-corporation status since my earnings would have been taxed twice."

Disadvantages of an S-Corporation

An S-corporation has restrictions on use of its losses and tax recognition on sales of its assets different from those of a C-corporation. These may be disadvantages to the owners. Thus, although one may face double taxation as a C-corporation, the loss of flexibility on the sale of assets or stock of the corporation may require one to remain a C-corporation and ultimately gain the most profit upon the sale of a business. In addition, if the entrepreneur's intention is to raise capital from third parties, such as venture capitalists, the company will have to be restructured into a C-corporation before this can occur.

SETTING UP AN S-CORPORATION

SUMMARY OF PROS AND CONS

- Corporation but with "flow-through" tax benefits
- Limited liability for owners and stockholders
- Limited to only 100 owners, one class of stock, and domestic shareholders

PROS

- Offers liability protection
- Enjoys corporation status, but owners pay the taxes

CONS

- Stringent rules to maintain S-corporation status; breaking them can lead to disastrous tax consequences
- Qualification requirements necessitate administrative and cost burdens
- Not eligible for qualified employee stock options
- Investors cannot receive preferred shares, as in a C-corporation

When Is the S-Corporation a Wise Choice?

- **The "S"-Corporation has advantages (vs "C"-corporation) in summary:**
  - **Has the same body of law as "C"-corporations**
  - **One single layer of tax**
  - Very good for businesses that expects to distribute its profits at the end of year
  - Also good for business in which owners can utilize losses
  - **Inherent simplicity (but a double-sided coin)**
- **The "S-"Corporation disadvantages (vs "C-"corporation) are:**
  - **Only one class of stock**
  - **Makes capital raising nearly impossible**
  - **Hard to issue "cheap" stock (except to "true" founders)**
  - **Only certain types of stockholders**
  - **Entities are ineligible**
  - **Nonresident aliens are ineligible**

- **No more than 100 stockholders**

- **NYC doesn't recognize "S" election**

- **Best for closely held businesses that don't require equity financing**

Choosing the S-corporation status is usually beneficial to start-up companies anticipating net losses and to highly profitable firms with substantial dividends to pay out to shareholders. In these cases, the owner can use the loss to offset other income, or the owner is personally in a lower tax bracket than the corporation, thus saving money in the long run.

Small companies with the following characteristics, however, are not likely to benefit from S-corporation status:

- Highly profitable personal service companies with large numbers of shareholders, in which most of the profits are passed on to shareholders as compensation or retirement benefits

- Corporations in which the loss of fringe benefits to shareholders exceeds tax savings

- Corporations with sizable net operating losses that cannot be used against S-corporation earnings

Partnership

A partnership is usually defined as an association of two or more people carrying on as coowners of a business for profit. There are typically two types of partnerships. The first type, a general partnership, requires that each partner participates in all profits and losses equally or to some previously agreed-upon ratio. Normally, a general partner has unlimited liability, which includes personally owned assets outside the business association. A partnership can be created either by a formal agreement or an oral understanding. In addition, it must be banded together for profit-producing motives and is generally not considered a legal entity separate from the partners. A general partnership may not sue or be sued in the firm's name. Each partner shares potential "joint and several" liabilities. See Chapter 8 for partnership charts.

The second type of partnership, a limited partnership, limits the liability of the partners to the extent of their capital contributions. A limited partnership must have at least one general partner so at least one person or entity's personal assets must be at stake. In many instances, the general partner is a corporation so only the corporate assets are at stake.[8]

Advantages of a Partnership

- *(General Partnership) Easy to Establish*. Like the sole proprietorship, the general partnership is easy and inexpensive to establish. The partners must obtain the necessary business license and submit a minimal number of forms. In most states, partners must file a Certificate for Conducting Business as Partners if the business is run under a trade name. Limited partnerships require registration to be official.

- *Complementary Skills of Partners*. In a sole proprietorship, the owner must wear many different hats, and not all of them will fit well. In successful partnerships, the parties' skills usually complement one another. For example, one partner in a software firm says, "My co-owner provides the vision, energy, and enthusiasm needed in a deal situation. I am more negative and careful. Together we're a solid team."

- *Division of Profits*. There are no restrictions on how profits must be distributed as long as they are consistent with the partnership agreement and do not violate the rights of any partner.

- *Larger Pool of Capital*. The partnership form of ownership can significantly broaden the pool of capital available to the business. Each partner's asset base improves the ability of the business to borrow needed funds. Therefore, each individual has more to contribute in equity capital, and together their personal assets will support a larger borrowing capacity.

- *Ability to Attract Limited Partners*. There can be any number of limited partners as long as there is at least one general partner. A partnership can attract investors who, with limited liability, still can realize a substantial return on their investment if the business is successful. A great many individuals find it very profitable to invest as limited partners in high-potential small businesses.

- *Flexibility*. Although not as flexible as a sole proprietorship, the partnership can generally react quickly to changing market conditions because its organizational structure does not stifle its quick and creative responses to new opportunities.

- *Taxation*. The partnership itself is not subject to federal taxation. Its net income is distributed directly to the partners as personal income, on which they pay taxes. General partners are allowed to use partnership losses on their personal returns. The partnership, like the sole proprietorship, avoids the double taxation applicable to the corporate form of ownership.

Disadvantages of a Partnership

- *Unlimited Liability of at Least One Partner*. At least one member of every partnership must be a general partner. The general partner has unlimited personal liability.

- *Capital Accumulation*. Although the partnership is superior to the proprietorship in its ability to attract capital, it is generally not as effective as the corporate form of ownership. This is because the partnership usually has limitations and restriction to raising capital.

- *Restrictions of Elimination for the General Partnership*. Most partnership agreements restrict how partners can dispose of their shares of the business. It is common to find that partners are required to sell their interest to the remaining partners. But even if the original agreement contains such a requirement and clearly delineates how the value of each partner's ownership will be determined, there is no guarantee that the other partner(s) will have the financial resources to buy the seller's interest. When the money is not available to purchase a partner's interest, the other partner(s) may be forced either to accept a new partner who purchases the partner's interest or to dissolve the partnership, distribute the remaining assets, and begin again. When a general partner dies, becomes incompetent, or withdraws from the business, the partnership automatically dissolves, although it may not terminate. Even when there are numerous partners, if one wishes to disassociate his or her name from the business, the remaining partners will probably form a new partnership.

- *Lack of Continuity for the General Partnership*. If one partner dies, complications arise. Partnership interest is often nontransferable through inheritance because the remaining partner(s) may not wish to be in partnership with the person who inherits the deceased partner's interest. Partners can make provisions in the partnership agreement to avoid dissolution due to death if all parties agree to accept as partners those who inherit the deceased's interest.

- *Potential for Personality and Authority Conflicts*. Friction among partners is inevitable and difficult to control. Disagreements over what should be done or what was done have dissolved many a partnership. For example, when the cofounders of a successful communications company got into a dispute over its future direction, the firm lost its edge and momentum in the market. While the partners fought over buyout terms, the business floundered. Ultimately, the business was sold at a very low price.

Limited Liability Company

An LLC is a blend of some of the best characteristics of corporations, partnerships, and sole proprietorships. It is a separate legal entity like a corporation, but it is entitled to be treated as either a sole proprietorship or a partnership for tax purposes, depending on whether there are one or more members. Therefore, it carries with it the "flow-through" or "transparent" tax benefits that corporations do not have. It is very flexible and simple to run. As long as the terms of the governing document, called the operating agreement, are adhered to, the LLC may be operated more like a sole proprietorship or a partnership than a corporation.

The owners are called members, who can be individuals (residents or foreigners),corporations, other LLCs, trusts, pension plans, and so on.

An LLC is formed by filing an Article of Organization form with a secretary of state and signing an LLC operating agreement. The corporation division of most secretary of state offices handles the filing of LLC papers. Most states require that an annual report be filed to keep them apprised of the current status of an LLC. The LLC is not a tax-paying entity. Profits, losses, and the like flow directly through and are reported on the individual member's tax returns unless the members make an election to be taxed as a corporation.

Advantages of an LLC

- Owners do not assume liabilities for debt.

- They may offer different classes of memberships.

- There are no restrictions on the number and types of owners.

Disadvantages of an LLC

- There may be difficulty in business expansion out of state.

- Transferring ownership is restricted. Requirements are different for each state.

SETTING UP A LIMITED LIABILITY CORPORATION

SUMMARY OF PROS AND CONS

- Owned by "members," not shareholders
- A combination of characteristics of corporations, partnerships, and sole proprietorships

PROS

- Liability protection (a separate legal entity as in a C-corporation)
- Not a tax-paying entity (tax benefits to members)
- Statutory meetings are not required

CONS

- Unlikely that a venture capitalist would invest in an LLC
- Cannot take the company public
- Different shareholder interests result in complex operating agreements
- Restrictions on transfer of ownership
- Management and member rules different in each state

ROADMAP

IN ACTION	Different forms of company registration match various stages of development and aims of the founders. Know how and when to change the form as the company grows.

Business Organizational Structure Comparison Chart

Characteristic	C-Corp	S-Corp LLC	LLC
Limited liability for all owners	Yes	Yes	Yes
Owners can participate in management without losing liability protection	Yes	Yes	Yes
Easy to form and maintain without extensive records	No	No	Yes
Number of owners	1 or more	1–100	1 or more
Restrictions on ownership	No	Yes	No
Double tax	Yes	No	Maybe
Able to deduct business loss on individual return	No	Yes	Maybe
Basis for loss includes owner's share of company debt in owner's tax return	No	Yes	Maybe
Can increase basis by "step-up" election	Yes	Yes	Yes
Can specially allocate terms of income and expense	Yes	Yes	Yes
Contributes and distributes property tax free	Yes	No	Yes

Business Start-Up Checklist

Now that you are beginning to understand the legal forms of the organization, a business start-up checklist is presented.[9] This checklist will be your guide for the first thirty days, sixty days, and year-end activities.

This list may seem a little daunting, so you can break it down into monthly tasks as follows:

First Thirty Days

Do a name search in location state to determine if the name is available on Clerks Commission web site. Check whether a web name is available that matches the name. It may be necessary to purchase the web address from a web-name trader. You may have to modify the company name until you find one that is both available to register and you can file the web address.

Determine if the company will be a C-corp, S-corp, or LLC.

- In Delaware: https://delecorp.delaware.gov/tin/EntitySearch.jsp.

- For reference in VA: http://www.state.va.us/scc/division/clk/.

- Obtain an Employer Identification Number (EIN) from the IRS by completing federal Form SS4.

- Select a lawyer.

- Select an accountant.

- Need to show business license #, federal ID, two current IDs for each person authorized, signed corporate resolution allowing for certain persons to make withdrawals, and sign checks.

- SSNs, household location for business owners.

- Business tax ID and SIC code.

- Date business established.

- Business location address.

- Sales and profit for last fiscal year.

- Prepare a business plan. This plan will define the operational details of the company and will include, but not be limited to, items such as budgets, forecasts, capital expenditures, salaries and wages, hours of operation, and market information (products, services, pricing, discounts, etc.). The plan will serve the purpose of giving management direction as to the day-to-day operation of the company.

- Select a banker or banking institution.

- Select an insurance agent.

- Obtain business insurance.

- Order business cards and letterhead.

- Obtain a business license or permit from the city hall or county office.

- Establish bank accounts.

- Establish Merchant Credit Card Service allowing your business to accept major credit cards (if applicable).

- Pick a year-end date.

- Corporations hold an organizational meeting where:
  1. Bylaws are adopted.
  2. A board of directors is elected.
  3. Share certificates should be distributed to shareholders once purchased, and these transactions should be recorded on the corporation's stock ledger.
  4. Company members and/or managers and officers are elected.
  5. Any corporate business that needs immediate attention is addressed.

- An LLC should have an organizational meeting where:
  1. An operating agreement is adopted.
  2. Membership certificates are distributed.
  3. Company members and/or managers are elected.
  4. In some states, publishing is required of your operation or an LLC.

First Sixty Days

- Establish presence on Internet with at least a home page using the URL that you have registered or acquired.

- Contact suppliers.

- If selecting S-Corporation status, file Form 2553 within seventy-five days.

- Obtain business insurance (liability, health and dental, workers' compensation, etc.).

- Join a professional organization.

- Some states such as Nevada require a list of officers and directors to be filed with the state.

By First Year End

- Obtain federal tax forms.

- Obtain state tax forms.

- Pay corporate franchise tax or annual state fees.

- Secure first round of financing from friends/family or angel investors.

- Establish a relationship with a bank in order to acquire a line of credit in the near term.

Selecting Your Attorney

The legal requirements for setting up a company can vary greatly from state to state. An attorney should be consulted to ensure that you meet the legal requirements facing the business. An attorney can provide assistance in formatting the business; filing necessary documents with appropriate governmental authorities; and preparing employment contracts, stock ownership agreements, and other documents for equity holders. An attorney can also assist in preparing documents for the hiring of employees and independent contractors (confidentiality agreements, work-for-hire agreements, noncompetition agreements, nonsolicitation agreements, etc.) and those required for raising capital.[10]

In selecting an attorney, the most important element is finding one that can competently meet your needs. Selecting an attorney based on price is not a good idea. The intricacies of forming and operating a business require that an attorney be knowledgeable in corporate law, securities law, taxation, contract law, employment law, and license and trademark law. Therefore, one should find out how experienced an attorney is in rendering services for a business. One should also get recommendations from other business owners and consult guides that list attorney credentials and rate their abilities. An attorney should always be interviewed before being engaged for his or her services. A competent attorney should be able to answer all of your questions in your initial interview. The attorney should also be able to give an estimate of cost for establishing a business. If you are not satisfied with the answers received, then you should consult another attorney. As you grow your business, you are likely to need additional legal advice in specialist areas such as exporting, franchising, and patenting. Ask your first corporate attorney what affiliations he or she has with specialist legal offices.

Selecting Your Accountant

The accountant should be a practical business adviser who can set up a total financial control system for the business and render sound financial advice. At the outset, the accountant should work to establish accounting and reporting systems, cash projections, financing strategies, and tax planning. In addition, as the company matures, the following services can be provided[11]:

- Vendor services and payment options

- Cash management or fiscal accounting

- Cost reduction planning using invoices

- Compensation plan for employees

- Merger, acquisition, and appraisal assistance

- Management information systems to determine the accounting software requirements

Name Registration

A business that adopts an assumed business name must register the name with the state of incorporation and with each state in which the business is doing business. This should be done before taking any other steps to do business in the state. The registration will protect the name from infringement. The amount of registration fee varies by state.

In most states, a corporation's name must include the word *corporation*, *company*, *incorporated*, *limited*, or an abbreviation of one of these words. Limited liability companies must include *LLC* as part of their names. A competent attorney can assist with this phase of establishing a new business.

Federal Identification Number

A business must obtain an identification number from the Internal Revenue Service, except for a sole proprietorship that has no employees other than the owner. An identification number can be obtained by using Form SS-4, "Application for Employer Identification Number."[12] One may get an EIN by calling the IRS or going online.

Insurance Issues

Most businesses require insurance of one form or another. In addition, state law may require some forms, such as workers' compensation. The entrepreneur should shop around to find the insurer who offers the best combination of coverage, service, and price. Trade associations often offer special rates and policies to their members.

Even though not required by law, the entrepreneur should consider the following forms of insurance to protect the business:

- Fire

- Employee health and life

- Crime coverage, which reimburses the employer for robbery, burglary, and vandalism losses

- Business interruption, which compensates the business for revenue lost during a temporary halt in business caused by fire, theft, or illness

- Key man insurance, which compensates the business for the death or disability of a key partner or manager

- Liability, which protects the business from claims of bodily injury, property damage, and malpractice

- Product liability

   Other issues the entrepreneur should address in the business are as follows:

- Directors and officers insurance may be required as the company grows to protect against personal lawsuits associated with the company's business activities.

- State registration.

- Most state taxing authorities require a business, whatever its form, to register. The purpose of this registration is to receive sales tax registration numbers or exemptions and to receive the proper forms for filing wage withholding. Each state in which an entity does business must be contacted to determine how to do this registration.

- Web site registration.

- Domain name registration is a separate form of registration from registering a business name with a government entity. One should register a domain name as soon as possible. If a name is already registered, a business cannot use it on the Internet. Domain names can be bought and sold. This is an expensive alternative to direct registration. One should "reserve" one's domain name prior to filing with any government authority. This will prevent the costly process of changing the name on government registrations to the domain name after one has registered with government authorities.

SUMMARY

This chapter provides a good beginning for understanding the legal forms of the organization. It presents guidelines on the best legal form most appropriate for a particular situation.

In choosing a form of ownership, entrepreneurs must remember that there is no single "best" form; what is best depends on the individual's circumstances. Ask the questions that will help determine which form of ownership is best:

- How big can this business potentially become?

- How much control do you need in the decision-making process of the company? Are you willing to share ideas and the business's potential profits with others who can help build a more successful business?

- How much capital is needed to start the business?

A sole proprietorship is a form of business that has a single owner and requires only a business license to open. If the plan is to start a business under a name other than that of the owner, one must file a name to operate as "doing business as" (e.g., Jack's SmartCard Consulting). The business can be dissolved or closed at any time, and it always ends upon the death of the owner.

The C-corporation is the most common form of business ownership. It is a separate entity apart from its owners, and it may engage in business, issue contracts, sue and be sued, and pay taxes. When a corporation is founded, it accepts the regulations and restrictions of the state in which it is incorporated.

The S-corporation is a corporation that is treated like a partnership for tax purposes in that profits and losses are typically taxed directly to the individual shareholders. It is the owner's responsibility to report the gains or losses on individual income tax returns.

A partnership is usually defined as an association of two or more people carrying on as coowners of a business for profit. A general partnership requires that each partner participate in all profits and losses equally or to some previously agreed-upon ratio. A limited partnership limits the partners' liability to the extent of their capital contributions. Both types of partnership must have a general partner whose liability is unlimited.

An LLC is a blend of some characteristics of corporations, partnerships, and sole proprietorships. It is a separate legal entity like a corporation, but it is entitled to be treated as a sole proprietorship or a partnership for tax purposes and, therefore, carries with it the "flow-through" or "transparent" tax benefits that corporations do not have. It is very flexible and simple to run, and, like a sole proprietorship, there is no statutory necessity to keep minutes, hold meetings, or make resolutions, which can trip up many corporations' owners.

The chapter summarizes the major forms of the legal business organization. The advantages and disadvantages of each are discussed, and a list of questions is highlighted to help you decide which form of ownership is best for you. In addition, a checklist has been prepared to assist you in the first thirty-day, sixty-day, and year-end periods to maximize the best performance for the business.

You should also seek legal advice to assist in preparing charters, name registration, and other documents to ensure the proper registration of the form of business.

STUDY QUESTIONS

Q.1 What are the factors in deciding what form of ownership is best suited for the potential business?

Q.2 Briefly describe the advantages and disadvantages of a sole proprietorship and partnership.

Q.3 Explain the corporate form of ownership and how a business is incorporated.

Q.4 List the differences between the S-corporation and the limited liability company.

EXERCISES FOR DETERMINING BEST FORM OF OWNERSHIP

There is no master-case exercise associated with this chapter.

Exercise 1: We have therefore created two hypothetical cases, A and B, for you to explore the best form of ownership, an LLC, sub-S-, or C-corporation. In each case, suggest a name and then select the form of the company that you think is appropriate. Give your reasons for this selection.

When you have done this for both A and B, compare your two answers and explain the differences and whether in either case there are other possibilities. What are the advantages and possible disadvantages of the forms you suggest?

Case A: A new medical device company is being formed and will be owned by two Americans and a French citizen. They are planning to raise angel capital initially and institutional capital eventually. The team plans to the granting of equity to compensate first employees.

The business will be located and based in Rochester, NY.

Case B: A new fast casual restaurant franchise outlet is being formed. The owner will finance the franchise fee and build out with debt using her personal savings. She will operate the restaurant and will derive her livelihood from its operations. Employees will include kitchen and waitstaff initially and will expand in the future.

Exercise 2: Starting a new health-care service company. In September 2014, Peter, the chief technology officer for a midsize health-care technology company, resigned from his position. He then contacted Jennifer, who was a hospital's director of marketing, in charge of advertising and promotions. Both discussed an idea to start a company that offered health-care providers claim processing services. Peter and Jennifer agreed to start a new company called New Health Claim Processing. This name was important, for it would carry great weight in the industry. Peter and Jennifer had developed a unique business model to process claims at a very low cost while providing a high degree of customer service. The company would lease all the back-end hardware and write the software necessary to operate the business. The company would also provide all implementation, maintenance, and other ongoing support that would be required to use the service.

Peter and Jennifer invited Andy and Grace to join their effort. The four had met in Professor Jack Kaplan's course at Columbia Business School. They were all technologically savvy and had outstanding grades and extensive relevant work experiences. Their credentials would look good for raising capital. This core group of four refined Peter and Jennifer's initial ideas and started drafting a business plan.

As part of the business plan, the group decided that they needed a CEO to attract the venture capital they needed. Before the business plan was complete, they called their friend Michael with a proposition. They promised that they would make it worth his while if he would lead the company as the CEO. Two months later, the business plan was complete. The group of five was very excited as Michael took the lead in seeking funding for the venture. Michael's early contacts were successful. Within weeks of completing the business plan, he had lined up a venture capital firm that expressed interest in the company's plan and the team was invited to present at the next monthly partners' meeting.

During the presentation, the partners became interested in the company's vision, strategy, and the business processes for delivering services to planned customers. However, as the questions delved deeper into the organization and corporate governance structure, Michael became quiet as the partners asked him about the type of company formed and the ownership of the business. A moment of silence occurred when one partner asked who owned the company. Michael had not yet settled how the ownership would be divided.

At the end of the session, one of the venture partners told Michael in frank terms that he had handled the ownership questions poorly. He referred Michael to Cathy, a partner at a local law firm who was a close friend of his. Michael immediately made an appointment with her for the next day.

Cathy was an expert in company organization and stock incentive plans. She began by asking for a retainer fee which Michael paid out of his personal funds. He gave her a brief overview of the situation and arranged to bring all the members of the team in for questioning.

She soon uncovered the following information:

- Jennifer had left her previous company three months ago but did not tell Michael that she was still on retainer. She had also signed a nondisclosure agreement on the day she left.

- Peter had taken his client list and index of all his personal contacts from his previous job. He also took a notebook and articles on health-care products. Peter had received a letter from his previous company stating, "It has come to our attention that you may have in your possession confidential documents belonging to the company."

Based on the foregoing information, please answer the following questions:

(a) Identify the issues raised by the conduct of the start-up team.

(b) Identify the legal structure and issues that need to be resolved by the start-up team before going back to the VC firm.

(c) Identify three ethical business issues that are raised in the case.

(d) Should Michael proceed at this point or not? What are the key points that he must agree with the company if he decides to proceed?

INTERACTIVE LEARNING ON THE WEB

Test your knowledge of the chapter using the book's interactive web site.

ENDNOTES

1. See Amar V. Bhide, "The Questions Every Entrepreneur Must Answer," *Harvard Business School Review* (November 1, 1996): 8–9.

2. Ethan and Matt were engineering students at Penn State. This profile was developed using a number of interviews and class visits by Ethan Wendle. You can learn more about their company at www.diamond-backcovers.com.

3. Robert Katz, Esq. (Cooper & Dunham LLP) interview, New York, May 15, 2002.

4. Sole proprietorships are very common for single owners and home-based businesses. See interview with Ann Chamberlain of Richards and O'Neil LLC law firm, New York, March 10, 2001.

5. For most companies that require financing, David Cohen, CPA, at J. M. Levy suggests a C-corporation.

6. "To increase business within a state, entrepreneurs should file for a certificate of incorporation in the state where they conduct business. The state of Delaware has attractive advantages for companies and should be investigated." Alan Brody, Esq. (Buchanan Ingersoll Inc.) interview, Princeton, NJ, February 2001.

7. See Andargachew Zellcke, Jay Lorsch, and Katharina Pick, "Unbalanced Boards," *Harvard Business Review* (February 2001): 1–2.

8. See Gordon B. Baty, *Entrepreneurship for the Nineties* (Englewood Cliffs, NJ: Prentice Hall, 1990), 219.

9. David Cohen (CPA, J. M. Levy and Company) interview, New York, June 2002.

10. Robert Katz, Esq. (Cooper & Dunham LLP) interview, New York, May 15, 2005.

11. Kurt Hoffman (consultant, Financial Services) interview, Princeton, NJ, July 2004.

12. Ibid.

FUNDING THE VENTURE

Part 2, "Funding the Venture," focuses on a key resource of the company—cash. Without this element, you cannot survive, grow, and prosper. This chapter teaches an entrepreneur without financial training the fundamentals of entrepreneurial finance for a startup. These are substantially different from techniques and methods taught in more conventional corporate finance courses. The chapter deals with different sources of early and growth financing as well as the financial structures of a growing company. In Part A, we start with methods of financing that are more applicable to very early-stage companies before they are ready for major infusions of funds. It also examines techniques for growing a closely held company—one in which the founders retain control. These techniques are often referred to as *bootstrapping*. References to Chapter 5 where crowdfunding is explored are pertinent here. In Part B, we address later-stage sources such as venture capital, including how to find and work with them, as well as the vexing question of valuation.

8 Funding the Venture

"Very early on, the founders of start-ups make an important choice. Do they want success or control? Neither is bad so long as the choice is explicit."

Joe Kraus, Founder of Excite and Jotspot

OBJECTIVES

- Understand bootstrapping methods and their importance.
- Learn the role of milestones in stage funding.
- Identify the different methods of early-stage funding and how to access complementary resources.
- Learn the problems and issues in taking money from friends and family.
- Identify and work with angel investors.
- Understand virtual company design, microequity, and microloans.
- Learn when and how to use personal bank loans.
- Identify and obtain government loans and grants.
- Understand the appropriateness of the different types of private equity investments.
- Learn when and how to find super-angels.
- Learn how venture capital partnerships work.
- Describe how to attract venture capital financing and use a private placement.
- Learn the process of finding investors and targeting the right firm.
- Learn how to construct a capitalization table.
- Understand the due diligence process.
- Prepare a term sheet.
- Learn what is needed for a corporate loan.
- Balance the pros and cons of a corporate partnership.
- Learn the different methods of valuing a business.

CHAPTER OUTLINE

Part A

Introduction to Part A

Profile: James Dyson—Bootstrapping out of Necessity

The "Virtual" Company

Securing Early-Stage Funding

Self-Funding—Example: BenchPrep Inc.

Moonlighting and Part-Time Consulting

Bootstrapping Methods—Example: Injection Research Specialists

Family and Friends

Angels

Microequity and Microloans: A Little Money, a Lot of Help

Bank Loans, Factoring, and Supplier Lines of Credit

Managing Your Personal Credit Rating

Government Sources of Funding

How to Qualify

Summary of Part A

Endnotes

Part B:

Introduction to Part B

Profile: Jason Cong, Vivado-High Level Synthesis, Super-Angels, VC, and Corporate Investors

The State of the Venture Capital Industry

Super-Angels

Equity Investment Fundamentals

Using Private Equity for Fundraising

Understanding the Venture Capital Process

Guide to Selecting a Venture Capitalist

Private Placements

Home Runs or Singles?

Corporate Debt

Strategic Partnerships and Corporate Investments

How to Value a Business at the Early Stage

Summary

Introduction to Part A

Chapter 1 discussed the personal attributes of entrepreneurs and the management skills that need to be developed within the context of a new business. Therefore, it is important that every entrepreneur examine at the outset and choose one of two fundamentally different routes for the proposed company. If control and remaining the chief executive of the company are of paramount personal importance, then the company should in no way seek funding by selling part ownership to outside investors and remain "closely held." Raising money by selling ownership participation is called equity investment. Equity investors provide money to companies in exchange for part ownership in the form of shares to get a financial return on their money. Early-stage companies are risky investments, and investors typically seek an annual return on equity investments of 30 percent at a minimum. This is clearly well more than the 2–3 percent or so they can earn by putting their money into treasury notes or bank CDs.

To provide investors with a return on their investments, the company must create a *liquidity event*. Otherwise their money stays locked up in the company and is *illiquid*. To unlock the value, the stock of the company must be purchased by another company through an acquisition (the most usual way) or by a sale of stock to the public through an initial public offering (IPO). In very rare cases, the company is generating so much cash that there is enough left after internal funding requirements that it can afford to buy back the stock from outside investors. If the founders wish to retain control of the company, they have no incentive to create such a liquidity event and, therefore, are unable to provide a real return to their investors. This misalignment of objectives between founders and investors is the principal reason that start-up companies end up with major conflict problems. If control is your prime objective, then equity financing should not be pursued. In this case, other means of attracting resources, both financial and otherwise, are required. The techniques for doing this are broadly referred as *bootstrapping*—a term deriving from "pulling oneself up by the bootstraps."

ROADMAP

| IN ACTION | Before starting a company, be completely honest with yourself. How much personal risk will you take? Are you building a lifestyle? Do you wish to remain the chief executive, or are you willing to forgo some control if it means greater wealth in the long run? |

Family-owned businesses are a special type of "closely held" company which have their own unique issues, and these are dealt with separately in Chapter 14 found on the book web site. These businesses are usually grown using the bootstrapping techniques discussed in the first part of this chapter.

If, on the other hand, an entrepreneur is comfortable with trading control with an interest in acquiring significant personal wealth, then seeking outside investors should be considered. This may even lead to stepping aside as CEO should the entrepreneur not have the appropriate skills to manage hectic growth. Raising outside equity investment can be roughly divided into two categories: (1) private individuals including friends, family, and so-called business angels and (2) organized institutional investors such as venture capitalists.

Even if the eventual aim is to seek institutional equity investment, however, bootstrapping is highly relevant. The further a start-up company has progressed successfully with its plans before seeking venture capital, the higher the value of the company is likely to be and, therefore, the lower the percentage of the company that must be sold to raise an equivalent amount of institutional money. Typical milestones that can trigger a jump in the value of the company include developing a working prototype, gaining a few paying customers, having a patent awarded, receiving a government grant, signing up a larger company to test the results of the development, and getting some paying customers. Table 8.1 shows approximately how the value of Ultrafast Inc. (refer to the case on the book web site) increased with each milestone. It always makes sense for entrepreneurs who plan on seeking outside investors to delay this event until as late as possible. Also, investors like to see that entrepreneurs are not totally dependent on their funding but know how to complement their money with other resources. Every entrepreneur, therefore, needs to learn how to bootstrap her company whether for reasons of control retention, increasing valuation before taking in equity investments, or perhaps out of necessity. We will examine a number of options for financing a company in its earliest stage, including self-funding; various forms of bootstrapping; family, friends, and angel investors; early-stage loans; and government grants. Another bootstrapping alternative that has emerged recently is crowdfunding; this is dealt with separately in Chapter 5. Finding the source that is best will depend on many different factors, including the amount of funding required, when it is needed, and when it can be repaid. It is important to remember to plan ahead and not let financial requirements be a surprise. Arranging financing takes time, and rushing decisions can be costly to the entrepreneur and the new venture.

Table 8.1 How Milestones Can Increase Value: The Ultrafast Case

	Value, $'000K
Patent filed	0
Corporation formed	10
Partnership with TMF, a technology management company	10
Awarded $50K SBIR NASA funding + testing	75
Proof-of-principle demonstration with PSU	150
Market segmentation analysis and BM creation	200
Signed licenses with Atlas Copco, Bosch, and Toyota subsidiary	1,000
Raised angel rounds A	1,200
Pilot production established in the United States	4,000
Raised angel rounds B	10,000
Signed up beta customers in Europe	20,000
Raised economic development funding in Germany for plant	50,000
Raised tranched private equity funding for growth	80,000

Running out of money is the most common reason for small companies to fail. Generally speaking, it takes twice as long as anticipated to raise money. Forecasting cash requirements is, therefore, very important and is dealt with in detail in Chapter 9. Starting early to make sure that the funds are available when they are needed and having contingencies in place are extremely important considerations and cannot be overemphasized.

dyson

Source: Dyson

Profile: James Dyson—Bootstrapping out of Necessity

James Dyson[1] studied at the Royal College of Art in England, focusing on furniture design. While there he invented several new products such as the Ballbarrow and the Sea Truck boat (see www.dyson.com). His first and only job was as a sales manager for a small company in England called Rotork (www.rotork.com). He advanced rapidly to a directorship of this engineering firm, furthering his skills in product engineering. Yet he felt confined in this position and left the company in 1978 to branch out on his own, using some cash that he had earned from his college ideas. While vacuuming his old cottage, he noticed that sucking power was quickly lost as the paper bag filled. He had observed a point of pain and decided to tackle the problem of making a bagless cleaner. His idea was to spin the air flowing through the cleaner, throwing the dirt to the outside, where it was collected. He built 5,127 prototypes (!) in his basement workshop before he felt he had reached a satisfactory outcome. Now was the time to cash in on these efforts, so he filed a number of patents on the invention. His initial business model (refer to Chapter 3 for more discussion on this topic) was to license his ideas, and he took to the road, providing demonstrations to all of the existing vacuum cleaner companies worldwide. Surely they would readily grab the opportunity to make and sell his "much better" products. After two years and no interest, he decided to start manufacturing and selling cleaners. He was unable to raise any venture funding, however. The idea of breaking into a well-established but dull market dominated by large companies with deep pockets was hardly alluring to venture capitalists when there was a lot more fun to be had with high-tech, dot.com start-ups, in fashion at that time. Moreover, Dyson did not match the profile of a supertech highflyer living in one of the start-up hotbeds in the United Kingdom. He was simply seen as a country boy inventor playing around with vacuum cleaners.

The constant process of learning and refining led to several cash shortages before the product was launched in the United Kingdom in 1993, forcing Dyson to sell the patent rights in Japan for just $70,000 in 1986 and the U.S. rights for $100,000 in 1988. He later bought back the rights for both countries but at vastly inflated prices. Dyson paid $2 million in 2002 to buy back the U.S. rights after having success in the U.K. market. With little money left, he had to be creative in how he introduced the first "cyclone" product to the market in 1993. A combination of cameo appearances on popular television programs such as *Friends*, which triggered word-of-mouth recommendations, helped to raise sales. He also decided to price the product well above the entrenched competition that on average sell for $150; Dyson's cleaners sell in the range of $399 to $1,500. The distinctive bagless vacuum cleaner has managed to grab a 25+ percent share of the $2.3 billion U.S. market in just more than four years, leaving Hoover trailing with only a 16 percent share. In 2003, Dyson had only a 4.5 percent share of the U.S. market, but sales of 891,000 units—a threefold increase—over the next year catapulted it to the top. These strong U.S. sales, which now make up 40 percent of worldwide revenue, helped Dyson to grow profits to

$450 million, while sales grew to $1.5 billion in 2012. To date, more than $20 billion worth of Dyson's cleaners have been sold worldwide.[2]

So why didn't one of the existing companies take up the offer when Dyson was just starting out? Perhaps their reticence had something to do with the large profits they were making on the disposable bags, which, without any marketing or selling expenditure, provided revenues of $500 million every year. Hoover was locked into a business model that prevented it from responding. According to Mike Dutter, a Hoover executive, "I do regret that Hoover did not take the product technology off Dyson; [in our hands] it would have lain on the shelf and not been used." As Dyson states, "Hoover wouldn't give me the time of the day. They laughed at it. They said, 'Bags are best. Bags will always be best.' Then they copied it." This copying, which came after Hoover realized that this little start-up was beginning to take away its market and profits, forced Dyson to sue for patent infringement. Again straining his cash for payment of legal fees, he won the case after eighteen months of litigation.

Dyson is not satisfied yet with his success. With the cash now coming in, he has repurchased the Japanese business, which, as in the United States, has also accelerated sales in Asia. Sales in 2004, which were running at 14,000 units a month there, rose fourfold. Expansion in Japan demonstrates Dyson's continued focus on research and his ability to shape his technologies to new markets. Since Japanese apartments tend to be smaller than those in the United Kingdom or United States, his team has devised a compact vacuum cleaner that uses a digital motor rather than a traditional mechanical one. The resulting machine is not only half the weight and size and more powerful than its larger contemporaries, but the digital technology allows customers who have problems with the unit to hold the machine up to the phone and have faults diagnosed online. In this way, Dyson is embedding services into his products. The company is selling in China, too. The company has branched out into other areas such as "silent fans" and hand dryers and is also planning to launch a new washing machine. It takes a few minutes to wash by hand, so why must it take longer than an hour for a washing machine to do the same thing? Watch out Bosch, Maytag, Whirlpool, and GE!

Dyson's company, which he and his family still own completely, employs twelve hundred people in the United Kingdom. Recently Dyson paid himself and his wife approximately $30 million, a prize worth waiting for after facing bankruptcy on more than one occasion.

ROADMAP

| IN ACTION | There are many ways of accessing resources, including cash, without taking major risks or selling part of your company. Be creative to find ways to bootstrap. Take the company as far as you can before bringing in investors or putting your personal assets at high risk. |

The "Virtual" Company

One way to conserve cash and to maintain flexibility in your plans is to reduce the level of monthly fixed costs to a minimum. The growth of the Internet with the number of freely available management tools that can be accessed online can support a "virtual company." This is a company that has no offices, very few employees loaded with associated costs and benefits, no communication costs, low legal costs, and so forth. A virtual company will use providers like Skype for videoconferencing, Basecamp or Dropbox for project team and document management, ADP for payroll and tax management, online basic legal documents for protection, and Salesforce.com for sales tracking. The move to so-called cloud computing provides start-ups with access to highly sophisticated management tools on a free or a low pay-as-you-go basis. The virtual company finds experts on the Internet or through personal recommendations. These experts work on an hourly basis under a standard work for hire contract and can be turned off at a moment's notice. Virtual companies, sometimes referred to as "lean start-ups," move quickly, change direction without disruption, and use the best resources without taking on long-term liabilities.

One of the most important techniques used by lean start-ups is called the Minimum Viable Product (MVP).[3] This is best described as that version of a new product which can collect the maximum amount of validated learning about customers with the least effort. It requires judgment for any given context to decide what MVP makes sense. This concept is discussed in detail in Chapter 3. At the simplest level, just using a "smoke screen" web site test may provide sufficient market knowledge. At a minimum, a simple AdWords campaign can reveal how utterly bad a concept might be. In other cases you may need at least a simple minimum product features to test the market. For software companies, early incomplete "beta" versions are made available to customers for testing and feedback. Google, for example, uses this method for many of its new products. In this way, companies can find out quickly whether anybody actually wants the product or get feedback on what features consumers like and dislike. Customers become part of your development team, thereby multiplying your intellectual assets at no cost. Refer to the section on inverse commons and open innovation in Chapter 5 for more on this topic.

Securing Early-Stage Funding

Most entrepreneurs and business owners know when the company requires financing. However, it is much more difficult for entrepreneurs to judge what type of financing is appropriate and realistic for the business. In addition, after a string of record-breaking years in which public and private companies have created high wealth, investor interest in entrepreneurial companies was at its height in the early years of this century. Bank lending was readily available and affordable. Now with the capital and debt markets being highly uncertain, what are the best financing prospects for entrepreneurial companies? Raising funds can be confusing, so careful review and analysis are necessary to learn the process.

The various sources of funding available to the entrepreneur are listed in Table 8.2.

Table 8.2 Sources of Early- and Later-Stage Funding

More suitable for the early stages (covered in Part A)	More suitable for the later stages (covered in Part B)
Self-funding	Super-angels
Moonlighting and consulting	Institutional venture capital
Bootstrapping	Private placements
Crowdfunding	Company debt
Family and friends/angels	Strategic partnerships
Microequity, microloans	Mezzanine finance
Personally secured bank loans	Initial public offerings
Factoring and supplier financing	Government programs

Self-Funding

This form of financing is usually available to entrepreneurs who are highly motivated and committed to using personal resources to launch a venture. The majority of new businesses are usually started with funds that come from personal savings or various forms of personal equity of the founder(s). This form of capital reflects the business founder's degree of motivation, commitment, and belief. Personal investment can also include what is called *sweat equity*, where owners either donate their time or provide it at below market value to help the business get established. Sometimes it is possible to pay the first hires with some ownership in the company rather than with a salary. However, it is important that the aspirations of these hires be in line with those of the founder(s); otherwise a conflict may arise later similar to that which arises when investors seek an exit. Also, in some cases, entrepreneurs use profits from previous endeavors to invest in their new enterprises.

When considering self-funding, carefully decide how much financial risk you are willing to take. This is a very personal decision and should involve other family members. Some entrepreneurs will stretch themselves to the limit and use every cent they have, including pledging all of their assets—their house as well—to the bank. Others are much more cautious. However, investors and lenders alike expect entrepreneurs to put some of their own assets at risk, so entrepreneurs must learn to be comfortable with this scenario.

Source: Benchprep.com

Self-Funding—Example: Benchprep Inc.[4]

As Ashish Rangnekar was preparing for the GMAT while having a full-time job, he was frustrated by the lack of resources to help him study. In 2008, he teamed with Ujjwal Gupta, a friend from college, then a chemistry PhD student at Penn State, forming a company, Watermelon Express. The company began with an iPhone app, but the founders soon realized that the real opportunity was to become a one-stop shop for mobile and online learning. It has now matured to be "a publishing platform, called BenchPrep, delivering interactive learning courses on multiple touch points—smart phones, tablets and Web—that focus on social engagement, adaptive learning and game mechanics."

To get to this stage however, the pair operated as a virtual organization, no offices, geographically apart, and carefully guarding every cent that they had. Initially in their "spare time," Rangnekar and Gupta worked on the first course—250 sets of GMAT problems and solutions—and released the iPhone app in just three months. It soon became one of the best-selling test-prep apps for the iPhone, generating sizable cash. The founders reinvested the income to expand into more courses including LSAT, GRE, and SAT and added social networking capabilities. They used low-cost programmers in India/Pakistan to accelerate development, meanwhile both continuing with their other full-time commitments.

Once they had completed their studies and could devote more time to the company, they moved to Chicago, colocating with Groupon. In July 2010, they obtained their first outside equity investment from Lightbank, the fund operated by Groupon cofounders Eric Lefkofsky and Brad

Keywell. This initial small investment provided the resources to further develop the product and establish partner relationships with major publishers such as McGraw-Hill, Thomson Learning, and John Wiley—the key to them becoming the best resource for students worldwide studying for important tests. Exactly two years later, when the company had acquired 250,000 student customers, a further $6 million of institutional financing was made by New Enterprise Associates (NEA) together with Revolution Ventures in order to accelerate growth and drive the number of customers rapidly to 1 million before the end of 2012. Bootstrapping the first stages of the development has allowed the two founders to retain a significant ownership position, even after this large infusion of venture capital.

Moonlighting and Part-Time Consulting

Many businesses are begun while the founder is still working a full-time job. The income from the job can both help support the owner during negative or low cash flow and provide working capital to augment the business's cash flow. Usually, when the business begins paying as well or better than the regular job, the entrepreneur can leave the job and devote all her time to building the new business.

Similarly, most people have skills that are valuable to existing companies on a part-time basis, perhaps as an advisory expert. Skills can include deep technical knowledge, design skills, the ability to write computer code, or the like, which are currently in demand on a part-time basis. Perhaps the existing employer is willing to have the work performed for six months or so in a part-time capacity, continuing the current work while a replacement is found. This may be a better solution for both parties than just leaving the company. Having a source of "survival" income while the company is getting started removes a lot of stress and improves the chance of success. If a technical consulting assignment is available, the entrepreneur must make it clear who owns the result of the work—usually the client. Therefore, document what areas are considered the property of the entrepreneur, so the future opportunity is not stymied due to questionable ownership of the intellectual property.

Bootstrapping

Bootstrapping, a type of self-funding often applied in a small business, can reduce costs from the current operation and overhead. It is usually overlooked as a source to business owners. The process of analyzing the operation to save and improve efficiencies will also allow the entrepreneur to learn more about the company. By becoming more efficient and cost conscious, the entrepreneur will be in a stronger position to qualify for additional financing. A multitude of bootstrapping techniques is available, and it is not possible to catalog all of them. Indeed, an entrepreneur can be just as innovative in developing her own methods as in developing the original business opportunity. The following discussion describes some bootstrapping techniques that may suit your own and your company's needs[5]:

No or Low Rent. Start by using a residence for office and workspace. Paying extra rent to a landlord takes away cash that can go directly into the company. The term *garage start-up* is not a myth. Hewlett-Packard was started by two fresh graduates in a now-famous garage in Silicon Valley. When it comes time to move out and have a separate location for the business, avoid signing long-term leases in expensive locations. Often incubator space is available, which may be subsidized by an economic development grant for just this intermediate phase. Incubators usually have shared services too, so money need not be spent on copiers, conference room furniture, and full-time office support staff since they are shared with other start-ups (see the appendix to this chapter for more details on incubators). Investors and lenders like to see that "unproductive overhead" spending is being kept to a minimum. Unless the business is a beauty parlor or a wealth management consulting firm, opulence is usually a waste of hard-to-find funds. If a lease for more space is signed, make sure subletting is available to offset some of the costs.

Bartering for Goods and Services. Perhaps you can trade some web site development work with a local small engineering firm in exchange for their machining the first prototypes of a product. (Note: Some bartering activities may have tax implications.)

Trading Intellectual Property Rights. Dyson traded international rights when he desperately needed cash. At that stage in his company, he could not enter overseas markets anyway, so using these "sleeping assets" was one way to continue. Alternatively, you may be developing technology that has multiple applications, perhaps a new glue for rapidly assembling metal parts. Your interest may lie in the high-value but smaller aircraft market. You could sell the rights for the automotive sector to an existing company to fund your field of interest. The Ultrafast case in Chapter 10 and on the book web site provides another example of this method.

Renting or Leasing Equipment. Often an expensive piece of equipment may be needed in only the start-up phase. Rather than buy, rent or lease the equipment only while it is needed.

Used Equipment. Usually the latest high-speed machines are not needed in the early stages of manufacturing and test marketing. It is often possible to find a piece of used equipment, often at a scrap price, that with a little work will fill short-term needs. The same applies to office furniture. Look for large companies that are moving or companies in bankruptcy; they will often give away or sell for a song perfectly good furniture they no longer need.

Access to Expensive Equipment. Check out university and government labs. They often have programs to help small companies and may allow access to equipment that an entrepreneur could only dream of owning.

Suppliers' and Customers' Help. Suppliers may be willing to help in many ways with the hope that, in the future, a new company will become a major customer. Help may include access to experts, supplies of test materials, introduction into their supplier and customer networks, technical support, sharing of market data and reports, and perhaps even an option to license some of their proprietary know-how. They may also be willing to help with funding inventory until you have been able to receive payment from your customers. Establishing a close and honest relationship with suppliers will help.

Similarly, engaging with customers early on can provide a range of benefits, even financial, by prepaying on a future delivery or paying for product development work to meet their specific needs. Also, a purchase order from a large company in good standing, even if it is contingent on the delivery of product or service to a defined specification, may help in securing a working capital loan.

Cooperative Purchases. As companies begin to scale up, often they can find ways to work with other small companies to create a buyers' club. The first area to look at is health insurance costs, which are exploding. Often professional society membership can provide access to reduced costs in a range of areas.

Outsourcing. A new, growing company will need a number of professional services that are not required full time and, indeed, may make sense to outsource entirely. These include payroll services, bookkeeping, and tax return preparation, which can usually be found as a service or by using part-time workers. Legal, accounting, and other consulting services will always be purchased as needed. These professions are usually accommodating with regard to payment schedules.

Credit Cards. Credit cards have always been a source of funding for a new venture. If the options of equity or bank loans are not available, the entrepreneur may contact all the major credit card suppliers to compare prices and options. As with a bank, the entrepreneur should ensure that there are opportunities to increase the borrowing limit (and add on other financing sources, such as equipment leasing) as necessary, once the company has proven to be a good customer. Credit card funding is quick funding of the business and is more viable now than ever before. MasterCard or Visa cardholders with good credit now often receive credit limits of at least $10,000. By carrying more than one credit card, the entrepreneur can considerably boost the total amount tapped into at any given time. Entrepreneurs may also take advantage of the regular offers of "no interest for six months" and keep rolling over their credit.Unfortunately, use of credit cards in this way can adversely affect personal credit ratings if done too often. Credit card interest rates on cash advances vary considerably, from as high as 21 percent to 10 percent or lower. Annual fees can also range from more than $50 down to zero. Therefore, when obtaining credit cards, it is wise to investigate getting the best deal. It may be advantageous to cancel one or more of the high-interest cards and transfer the balances to lower-cost credit cards. The disadvantage is that it costs much more to obtain funds through credit cards than through bank loans. If the enterprise is not successful, the credit card payments will continue and may place the entrepreneur in a personal financial squeeze.[6]

Contingent Litigation. A small company does not usually have the financial resources to fight a major lawsuit against a large infringer of its patent rights, such as James Dyson faced. If the case looks as if there is a good chance of prevailing, then there are some patent law firms that will take the case "on contingency," whereby the settlement, if the case is won, is shared by the legal team and the company filing the case. Some major law firms specialize in such cases, and just signing up with them can send a strong message to the alleged infringer, perhaps prompting an early settlement.

The above is a short list of the many bootstrapping techniques entrepreneurs use to get through their early stages either to defer the search for equity funding or to retain control of the company.

Bootstrapping Methods—Example: Injection Research Specialists

Ron Chasteen[7] was awarded a patent for a fuel injection system for snowmobiles in the late 1980s. He and his partner, John Balch, approached Polaris Industries in Minnesota about a possible supply agreement. "When we first met with their chief engineer, he told us we had made a massive leap in technology," states Chasteen. Initially, Polaris wanted to buy rights to the system outright. But Chasteen didn't want to sell. Eventually, a deal was struck, and Polaris agreed to purchase the system. After about a year of collaboration, Polaris claimed it was not going to proceed in selling fuel-injected snowmobiles, and so the relationship ended.

Chasteen was shocked when, soon after, Polaris launched a fuel-injected snowmobile. Examination of the product immediately showed that the snowmobile was very similar to the product Chasteen had developed. "We were furious; they'd simply cloned ours." Chasteen and Balch decided to sue not only Polaris but their component supplier, Fuji Heavy Industries. It took several years, a lot of money, and five different patent law firms before they found one that agreed to take the case on a contingent-fee basis. "They were all happy to just take our money with no end in sight," Chasteen says. "We got nowhere, just a lot of bills." The case was eventually taken by the Chicago law firm of Niro, Scavone, Haller & Niro. According to Joe Hosteny, a partner at the firm, "Contingent-fee litigation is for individual inventors and small to medium-size businesses which would have trouble affording normal patent or trade-secret litigation. Without contingent-fee litigation, big corporations could steal solo inventors' ideas with no one to stop them."

After almost eleven years, Chasteen and Balch finally got their justice—a check for $70 million. Other well-known cases include $120 million paid by Microsoft for using the "Stacker"[8] data compression software developed by Stac Electronics and a payment of more than $10 million from Ford Motor Company to Robert Kearns, an individual inventor, for infringing on his patent on intermittent windshield wipers.[9]

Family and Friends

Friends and family members are a very popular source for start-up capital because they are not as worried about quick profits as are professional investors. However, there are problems associated with this method. Usually friends and family do not investigate the business very well and are not familiar with all the risks of the business. In many cases, friends and family accept the word of the entrepreneur without any analysis or detailed review of the business venture. To guard against the risks of failure and to avoid being blamed for not disclosing all the important information about the proposed venture, the best method is to provide the same disclosure to a friend or relative that would be provided to the most sophisticated investors. Entrepreneurs should always resist the temptation to keep the venture on an informal basis and not document the details of the company's risks and financial requirements.[10]

Angels

Angels[11] are an excellent source of raising capital and sometimes represent the best method for the entrepreneur to pursue when self-funding and friends are not a viable option. Angels are high-net-worth individuals who have some funds they are willing to risk in start-up companies. They usually invest locally because they like to have personal interactions with the entrepreneur. Often they look for investments in areas that they know well, which could range from retail stores to health products and from real estate management to high-tech manufacturing. They may have a social agenda attached to their investments. For example, one group in Central Pennsylvania invested in a Pyramid Healthcare, a chain of drug rehabilitation centers,[12] and Schoolwires, a company that provides software for school districts to help the No Child Left Behind program. Angels are often willing to become actively involved, and they are usually well networked into the local professional service firms. They may operate individually; more often they work as an investment partnership. Angels are usually less rigorous in their due diligence and their push to reach an exit strategy. However, as the venture capitalists (VC's) are moving to the later-stage investment and angels take over more of the earlier-stage funding, they are themselves becoming more professional and demanding in their style and governance.[13]

Angels are different from venture capitalists in that they invest their own money, in the range of $50,000 to $500,000 that companies need to get started. However, when acting as a group, the investments can be significantly higher. VCs, by contrast, invest institutional funds, and typically they are likely to invest later in a company's life, supplying $1 million or more to both early-stage and midstage companies. Angels review potential deals carefully. They review business plans, require a strong management team, and perform financial review and analysis. Angels also expect the companies they invest in to go public or to be acquired in five to seven years, but not one to

Table 8.3   Typical Profile of Angel Investors

Average number of members in an angel group	10–25
Average group investment per year	$2 million to $5 million
Average group investment in a start-up	$350,000
Percentage of companies funded, out of all that presented	<33 percent
Estimated total invested per year by angels in the United States	$54 billion

two years. Angels require an equity stake and a return of 20 to 35 percent on their investments, and some require a seat on the board of directors (Table 8.3).[14]

The best method to locate angel investors is through word of mouth. It is preferable to come recommended or to seek a referral from a friend or business associate. Another option is to receive an invitation to present to a local angel group. Angel groups offer an opportunity to present the company to several angels in one session and determine the financial viability quickly. Entrepreneurs should explore friends, acquaintances, chambers of commerce, and any local entrepreneurial groups. Angel networks and matchmaking services set up by universities and state development agencies are other sources. Sometimes for a small fee ranging from $100 to $300, your company can be listed in the organization database. (Investor contacts and angel networks are listed in the resource section at the end of this chapter.) Many angel groups use the management tools provided by Angelsoft. This is an excellent gateway for you to search for angel groups and make your initial contact (see gust.com). Also, Keiretsu angel network connects entrepreneurs to a global network of angels via a number of local chapters. (See http://www.keiretsuforum.com/.) Angels are always looking for new deal opportunities, called *sourcing*. The best angels are those that can bring contacts, experience, and long-term financing. Contacts means helping the company find customers, employees, and partners. For experience, the angel should understand the business and be able to assist the company in deals and important issues. The financing of the business may require additional funds in the future; the ideal angel will have the financial wherewithal to continue to support the company. Remember that it may take over six months to actually get funding from an angel after the initial contact, so start early with your networking.

The number of angel investors grew 60 percent during the stock market boom years, but since then they have become more reticent in investing as their own net-worths have significantly declined; with the recent increase in the public stock markets, angels are again becoming more active and are an exceedingly important source of funds, many times larger in aggregate than professional venture capital firms.

MicroEquity and MicroLoans: A Little Money, a Lot of Help

A relatively new form of help organization for entrepreneurs has emerged over the past few years. Recognizing the tremendous value that mentors can provide to young founders, angel investors are banding together and creating regional networks of advisers. Two examples are YCombinator with offices in Boston, Massachusetts, and Mountain View, California, and DreamIt based in Philadelphia, Pennsylvania.[15] Without a full-blown business plan, an entrepreneur can submit an idea on the web sites of these "microequity" organizations. For a small percentage ownership of your company, typically 4 percent of common stock, they will provide you with sufficient cash to live for a few months near their offices. During this period, your team can develop plans and work on a prototype. Most important, you will be introduced into their network of other entrepreneurs, potential employees, angel investors, attorneys, bankers, and venture capitalists who will meet you on a regular basis to prepare you for your first round of investment.

xobni

Source: Xobni

Mini-Case: Xobni Inc.[16]

Matt Brezina graduated from Penn State in electrical engineering in 2003 and moved to the University of Maryland to study for a graduate degree in engineering. He met Adam Smith, a computer graduate student at MIT, on the Internet while looking for a roommate. Adam was excited about starting a company "doing something in e-mail" and convinced him to join him. Matt dropped out from college and moved into Adam's dorm room. Adam had already contacted the Boston office of Y Combinator, and the pair soon received $12,000 to help them live for a few months while they worked on their ideas. After the three-month program, Y Combinator suggested that they move to California, where they were promptly immersed in the local advisers' network where they made a presentation to a group of more substantial angel investors, resulting in an $80,000 investment. This allowed them to create a very good demonstration of their e-mail management software, and after another six months, they were ready to present to institutional venture capitalists, raising a further $4 million led by Khosla Ventures.[17] According to Matt, "Without YCombinator's mentoring and investing network, Xobni would not exist." The $4 million allowed the company to launch its product to much public enthusiasm from notables such as Bill Gates. Having money in the bank has also helped in hiring great people, including Jeff Bonforte, who joined them from Yahoo! to take up the CEO's role. "We realized we needed really good operational management skills, with that neither Adam nor I had much experience." Within two years, Adam and Matt had built a fifteen-person company; raised more than $4 million in investment; hired top talent away from leading companies such as Google and Yahoo!; built a product used by thousands of people; appeared in *Newsweek*, the *Wall Street Journal*, and *Entrepreneur* magazine; and struck a partnering relationship with LinkedIn. Early in 2008 Microsoft offered them approximately $20 million for their company, which they felt was too low. Xobni has since raised $16.2 million from a syndicate of venture capital investors including First Round Capital, Cisco, BlackBerry Partners Fund, Atomico Investments, Baseline Ventures, and RRE Ventures. That done, Matt and Adam handed over to their new leaders and are planning their next venture. Meanwhile Yahoo purchased Xobni for over $60MM in 2013 and decided to close down the service a year later. It is not unusual for large companies to pay a high price for an innovative small company and then fail to integrate its products effectively.

Microloans were introduced initially to help alleviate poverty in Bangladesh in 1976 by Professor Muhammad Yunus, now a Nobel laureate for his work. He formed Grameen Bank to lend small amounts of money to people that could offer no collateral.[18] This model has spread around the world enabling anyone to lend money to budding entrepreneurs in poverty.[19] For another example, refer to the Kiva case in Chapter 12. The microloan concept is beginning to spread to developed economies. For example, the U.S. Small Business Administration (SBA) offers microloans for certain categories of businesses.[20] Loans may be up to $50,000 with the average being $13,000. Microloans may be used for the following purposes: working capital, purchase of inventory or supplies, purchase of furniture or fixtures, and purchase of machinery or equipment. There are also nongovernmental sources of microloans.[21] Both categories promise management help and advice, but, unlike Grameen loans, you will have to provide personal guarantees.

Bank Loans, Factoring, and Supplier Lines of Credit

Bank Loans

It is important to understand debt financing and its appropriateness for the business. The primary advantage of debt financing is that the entrepreneur does not have to give up any part of ownership to receive the funds. However, the loan has to be paid back with interest and may require the entrepreneur to personally guarantee part or all of the money. In addition, many loans have certain conditions ("covenants") that come with them. Often these conditions are tied to certain milestones or events that the company must make in order for the loan to remain in place and not be recalled. These covenants are not so different from conditions that might be applied by equity investors, and therefore, they often remove some control of the company from the founders until the loan is repaid. Bank loans therefore are more suitable for companies that have a track record of sales and growth, and for this reason, we will discuss corporate loans in Part B. For the formative stages of a company, before any substantial sales, an entrepreneur will almost certainly have to secure the loan with personal assets or seek out loan programs underwritten by federal, state, or local economic development agencies. Even if you are not willing to provide personal guarantees or cannot secure a bank loan at the outset, you should nevertheless identify a local bank that has provided support for small companies and begin to develop a relationship with their in-house business banker. This will be invaluable later as your company grows and you are able to secure loans based on the performance of the company. Bankers like to get to know you early on, and monitor your track record, before lending.

ROADMAP

IN ACTION

The entrepreneur will generally be required to have some type of collateral to support a loan. The types of securities used for collateral include endorsers or cosigners, accounts receivables, real estate, stocks and bonds, and personal savings.

Factoring and Supplier Funding

These are alternatives to conventional bank loans. If you are unable or unwilling to provide personal or asset-backed guarantees but you have purchase orders from reputable customers, it may be possible to use these orders to secure funding from so-called factors. These are private lenders that provide funds for your operations using purchase orders as security for the loan. They lend only a percentage of the sales orders and charge very high interest rates. The payment goes directly from your customers to them before the lenders provide you with any cash that may be left over after their fees and any interest payments are paid. Suppliers may also give you a line of credit, in exchange for getting your purchase orders.

Source: Best Lighting Product

Mini-Case: Best Lighting Products

Alvin Katz,[22] after a number of unfortunate business ups and downs brought on by the circumstances out of his control, found himself at the age of sixty-two with $200,000 in a bedroom closet and only Social Security checks and a small state pension to support himself and his wife.

Undaunted, he decided to start a company in California, Best Lighting Products, to manufacture recessed lighting fixtures. He and his partner were unable to get a bank loan, so they used a factoring company, Altres Inc., in Salt Lake City, to finance the purchase of components. Cash from all sales went directly to Altres; after deducting 10 percent the remainder was forwarded to the company. With no personal credit or a sound company balance sheet, this was the only financing source Alvin could find. Gradually sales climbed, the first year being $450,000 and $2.6 million the next. This level of business allowed the company to move from punitive factor financing to a more conventional small bank loan. However, this was not sufficient to buy new equipment to diversify into new markets. He found a small toolmaking company that was willing to defer payment for the tooling for two years in order to obtain the sale. This so-called supplier financing avoided the need for external capital. To further finance the rapid growth, an Asian supplier gave an unlimited line of credit for product purchases with a One-hundred-and-fifty-day payment cycle, allowing the company to receive payment from customers *before* it had to pay suppliers, thereby using suppliers' cash to fund the company. This supplier-financed model allowed Best Lighting to take off, and when Alvin was 72, Wafra Investment purchased control of the company from Alvin and his partner for $31+ million, a value of 7.2 times annual sales.

Managing Your Personal Credit Rating

When an entrepreneur applies to a bank to acquire a loan for a business that has few or no assets as collateral, the banker will turn to the credit history of the founder as an indication of the likelihood that the loan will be secure. A track record of meeting personal financial obligations, although not being sufficient to secure a loan, will help considerably in the application. It is, therefore, important that an entrepreneur establish a sound credit record with a score greater than 700 well before any loans either personally or for a business are contemplated. This is achieved by paying all bills on or before due dates, keeping any borrowing levels down to less than around 50 percent of established borrowing limits, and refraining from continually changing sources of credit such as credit cards. Long, stable records count for a lot. There are three major personal credit rating agencies in the United States: Equifax, Experian, and TransUnion. Under the federal FACTA of 2003, everyone has the right to access their credit ratings from each of these companies annually for free through the web site www.annualcreditreport.com. You should monitor your ratings every four months by rotating the free requests and correcting any habits that are impacting your rating. Additionally, if you have credit refused at any time, make sure that you follow up to determine the reason; often mistakes are made in data entry, such as an incorrect address record, that can seriously impact your rating unwittingly.

Government Sources of Funding

Federal Agencies

The major source of government financing available to small businesses is the SBA. The SBA was established in 1953 to "aid, counsel, and protect the interests of the nation's small business community." The agency works with intermediaries, banks, and other lending institutions to provide loans and venture capital financing to small businesses unable to secure financing through normal lending channels. The agency's web site, www.sba.gov, provides much information about sources of loans, as well as many helpful reports on starting and managing a new company. The funding programs, and the rules for obtaining support, change often, so it is best to seek the latest information on the web site.

Many other federal programs are operated through government departments and agencies. The Small Business Innovation Research (SBIR) Program (www.sbir.gov) and the Advanced Technology Program (www.atp.nist.gov) are among other federal programs that provide funds to small businesses to develop new technologies.

Small Business Innovation Research Program

One of the best opportunities for obtaining early-stage funding is participation in the federally funded SBIR Program. The program allocates in excess of $1 billion annually to businesses with proposals for developing scientific innovation, and it has three phases[23]:

Phase I: There is a grant award up to $150,000 for the purpose of investigating the feasibility of an innovation. The award recipient has six months to prepare a feasibility plan that includes prototypes, market research, and report development.

Phase II: The report is reviewed, and if feasible, a grant of up to $1 million can be awarded for operating expenses. There is a two-year deadline to complete this phase, which can include further testing and market research. A report must be prepared to review the results that were achieved and how the funds were spent.

Phase III: This is not a funded stage of the program but includes selling the developed products or services to a federal government agency. Funding for development and commercialization must be obtained through private financing, which may be helped by having on hand a purchase order from a creditworthy customer.

ROADMAP

| IN ACTION | Consider using government sourcing as a method for financing a venture. Review federal and local government options and the Small Business Administration. Also, state governments provided funding for businesses through their state departments. |

How to qualify

To begin the process, the entrepreneur should remember that the SBIR receives more than eight thousand proposals each year with fewer than one thousand grants being approved. Under the Small Business Innovation Development Act, applicants must be independently owned companies with five hundred or fewer employees and be able to demonstrate the capability for scientific or technological research. Through the first eight years of SBIR grants, award recipients have had, on average, fewer than thirty-five employees, with nearly half of all initial phase I grants awarded to companies with fewer than ten employees. The SBIR grant program provides operating money to companies and is not a loan. There is no assumption to repay the amount of the grant. A single company can be awarded more than one SBIR grant simultaneously. One problem the SBIR Program presents for entrepreneurs is the time it may take for the relevant agency to make a decision on grants, leaving a gap in cash flow. For more information on the SBIR Program and award announcements, visit the SBIR web site at www.sbir.gov.

Small Business Technology Transfer Program

The Small Business Technology Transfer (STTR) Program is similar to the SBIR Program in that it fosters research and development (R&D) by small businesses. The major difference between the programs is that funding from STTR is provided to joint ventures or partnerships between nonprofit research institutions and small businesses. Like the SBIR, the STTR Program has three phases. An award of $100,000 is made during the yearlong phase I. Phase II awards are up to $500,000 in a two-year expansion of phase I results. Funds for phase III of STTR must be found outside the STTR Program. By this time, however, the research project should be ready for commercialization. The STTR Program began making awards in fiscal year 1994 and is ideally suited to entrepreneurs wishing to start companies based on research at universities through a technology transfer program. Details can be found at the SBIR web site.

Financing for Minorities and Women

The definition of a minority-owned business is one that is 51 percent or more owned by one or more owners who are either minorities or women. Federal assistance is available, for example, to Native American-owned businesses and programs that promote the business and economic development of reservations.

The SBA division of the Office of Minority Enterprise Development (MED) assists certain business owners. The act provides assistance, through the Division of Management and Technical Assistance, to "socially and economically disadvantaged individuals and firms owned by such individuals, businesses located in areas of low income or high unemployment, and firms owned by low-income individuals."

Other federal offices and agencies that give assistance to minority firms and individuals for business expansion and development are the Bureau of Indian Affairs, the Office of Small and Disadvantaged Business Utilization, and the Minority Business Development Agency.

State and Local Small Business Financing Initiatives

Most states have programs that provide financial assistance or incentives to small businesses. Such programs are administered by departments and agencies within state and local governments. Many different programs are available in each state, but most states have a department of trade or commerce that runs loan assistance, investment, procurement, and other programs. Small business assistance at the state level can be in the form of direct financial assistance through grants or loans, tax benefits, subsidized rents, technical assistance, or small business incubators.

Contact city and county or township governments for assistance. In many areas local development authorities can also be useful resources in locating financing for new or existing businesses.

Summary of Part A

Depending on funding needs, the entrepreneur faces a number of options. To increase the chances of success, the entrepreneur must know what sources are available and understand the requirements of any financial partner. Preparing a business and financial plan with important milestones laid out, before beginning the search, helps the entrepreneur determine which sources would be most likely to assist in capitalizing the business.

This part examined the many sources of early-stage funding. Determining which source is best will depend on many different factors, including amount required, when it is needed and for how long, and when it can be repaid. The development stage for the company and the goals and objectives must be considered. Entrepreneurs become expert at using a range of bootstrapping methods to bridge the gap from starting the company to the stage where either they can acquire equity or bank loan funding for growth or the company becomes self-financing through retained profits from sales. The longer the entrepreneur can survive without selling ownership, the greater the value that can be retained. This is most important if the entrepreneur intends to remain fully in control, when sale of equity is no longer an option.

It is never too early to cultivate relationships with potential angel investors, bankers, and other funding sources long before you need their help. Accessing funds takes much longer than planned; longevity is a powerful recommendation.

In today's economic climate, commercial loans to small businesses must be secured. As early-stage companies are unlikely to have any assets that can be valued by a bank, this means personal guarantees from the entrepreneur or others are required. To overcome these issues, other sources of cash may be explored such a factoring and supplier lines of credit.

The SBA is the most active federal agency in assisting small businesses. Loans guaranteed by the SBA (up to 80 percent) are the prevalent means of obtaining government support, but direct loan assistance is available under certain programs.

The SBIR Program provides direct grants to businesses engaged in scientific development. With an SBIR phase I grant, entrepreneurs are provided up to $100,000 for developing feasibility plans; phase II grants can be as much as $1 million for the commercialization of their innovations. Many local governments have a range of programs to support early-stage companies.

Introduction to Part B

This part describes the financing options for entrepreneurial companies that are ready for rapid growth. They have already received funding from the sources discussed in part A. The first sections describe the three main sources of attracting significant equity funding, namely, "super-angels," "institutionalized" venture capital (VC), and formal private placements of stock. We also introduce the concept of crowdfunding, which is in its early stages of development. Equity funding means selling part of the ownership of the company to investors through the purchase of shares. Once an entrepreneur sells part of her company, her life fundamentally changes. Outside shareholders' primary objective is to earn a substantial return on their investment. The anticipated return will depend on the stage of the company when the investment is taken; usually the earlier the investment, the riskier the venture and, therefore, the higher the expected returns. Investors can derive the benefit of their investment only when a liquidity event occurs and an exit strategy is fulfilled. This means that a new entity agrees to buy the stock in the company held by the current shareholders. The most common way for this to happen is for the company to be sold to a larger firm, referred to as a merger and acquisition (M&A) exit. Alternatively, the company may be sold to the public via an IPO, although this is relatively rare now. Figure 8.1 shows how many companies are acquired compared to those that exiting through an IPO. The effects of the dot.com bubble in 1999 and the 2008–2009 recession can be clearly seen.

The master-case company for this book, Neoforma, provides a good example of a company that first managed to have an IPO when the public markets were buoyant but was eventually sold to a larger company.

Clearly, if the founders' intention is to retain control of the company and manage it for their own benefit and lifestyle, there will be a fundamental conflict of interest between the inside entrepreneurs and the external shareholders. So the golden rule is *do not take cash from external shareholders unless you intend to build the company for sale*. Note that this is irrespective of *how much* of the company you sell; sale of only 1 percent of the company fundamentally changes the way the company must be run. Many entrepreneurs starting out make the mistake of thinking that if they sell less than 50 percent of the company, they are still in control. As we shall see, investors with a minority interest can still determine how the company is run.

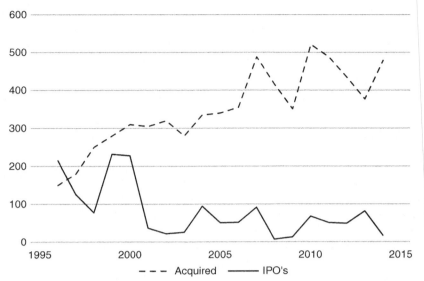

FIGURE 8.1
Comparison between Exit Methods for VC-backed Companies, 1996–2014
Source: National Venture Capital Association

ROADMAP

| IN ACTION | Entrepreneurs wishing to retain control of their company, come what may, should not accept equity financing from outsiders. |

We also discuss the pros and cons of having corporate partners make an investment. We also look at how a company is valued using the different methods such as earnings and asset valuation, adjusted book value, discounted cash flow comparatives, and market valuation. A discussion for evaluating investment opportunities using the time value of money that addresses net present value and internal rate of return (IRR) is also presented.

Source: Xilinx

Profile: Jason Cong, Vivado-High Level Synthesis, Super-angels, VC, and Corporate Investors

Jason Cong is Chancellor's Professor and Director of the "Center for Customizable Domain-Specific Computing" at the University of California in Los Angeles (UCLA).[24] He is a leading researcher in software tools used in the development of specialized integrated circuits. These tools help chip designers save time and ensure accuracy in the ever-increasing complexity of laying out very high-density, multilayer circuits on silicon. Not satisfied with a totally academic life,

Jason has always interacted with outside corporations in his field and has become a serial entrepreneur. His first spinout from UCLA was Aplus Design Technologies, founded in 1998, entirely grown using bootstrapping until it was acquired by Magma Design Automation in 2003. After the sale, Jason remained closely in contact with Magma acting as a consultant to them. Three years later, in 2006, after a few years of basic research at UCLA, another breakthrough emerged that seemed to be too big an opportunity not to create another spinout. Jason cofounded AutoESL and took his second license from UCLA for the "xPilot" technology. This time around, he realized that to get into the marketplace quickly, he needed some external funding. Using his past contacts, and now having a track record, he was able to raise nearly $1 million in a seed round from so-called super-angels to launch the company; several of his graduate students took the first jobs. The company soon needed more cash, and in 2008, it was funded in a preferred equity "A" round by Adams Capital Management (ACM), a midsized nationwide VC firm, together with a small amount from the seed round super-angels and a corporate investor, Xilinx Inc. Although Xilinx's cash contribution to the round was relatively small, they participated because they had an interest in the technology. Perhaps of more value was the fact that the design team at AutoESL could work closely with a company that really understood the market they were targeting. Now that the company was headed for rapid growth, the investors saw the need to bring in a full-time experienced CEO and hired Atul Sharan, a seasoned executive in the field, to take over the reins. Jason moved over to the role of chairman and chief technology officer, enabling him to spend more time back in the UCLA labs with his research students. The company hired engineers in China and California to accelerate the software tool development. Before the technology was ready to market test, the company needed more funding, and ACM led a preferred stock "B" round totaling $4.5 million in 2010 with over half the round taken by syndicated coinvestors, Xilinx, National Semiconductor, and Magma Design Technologies. In January 2011, when sales were just beginning, the company was acquired outright by Xilinx with most of the design team becoming Xilinx employees and Jason returning to his professorial role at UCLA. The investors received two to three times their invested capital at the exit. Because Jason had been diluted three times in the seed, "A" and "B" rounds and by stock options that were offered to Atul, Jason actually ended up with a somewhat lower payout than the CEO. On the other hand, without experienced investors and management, he might have ended up with much less or even nothing. "In both spin-outs," Cong says, "it was an exciting experience for the students to see firsthand their research results making a direct contribution to society."

The State of the Venture Capital Industry

The venture capital industry is going through a major restructuring. At the height of the dot.com bubble, any company with ".com" in its name could raise enormous amounts of capital. Before there were any profits on the horizon, they were taken public at outrageous prices giving the venture capitalists that had funded them staggering returns. Based on this success, VC firms were able to raise new funds to manage. Figure 8.2 shows this clearly, and it is easy to see the correlation with the bubble in Figure 8.1. Of course, all this new money had to be invested, but the bubble had burst, and the new companies were unable to command high prices upon sale or IPO, and the numbers of exits fell drastically (see Figure 8.1). The high returns vanished and most venture firms for the last decade have been unable to provide acceptable profits to their funders. In many cases, it has been more profitable to put the money in the bank than have it managed by VC firms. The resulting current restructuring has radically impacted the availability and suitability of venture capital for most entrepreneurs for the following reasons:

- With the influx of large amounts of cash in 2000, VCs moved their investments to later stages in start-ups. New companies just did not need enormous amounts of capital, and if they took it, of course, the owners would rapidly lose their ownership percentage. It became increasingly harder to find seed and early-stage money.

- The dearth of exit opportunities meant that the VCs had to continue to support their existing portfolio companies diverting funds away from new companies. This "put-aside" money is referred to as reserves.

- Moving to the later stages reduced the risk and length of time to get to an exit event. But even so, the lack of highly valued exit opportunities seriously impacted large returns on the investments.

- The sum of these problems has led to fewer VC firms, dropping from 860 in 2000 to 790 in 2010 where it has now stabilized. More worrying is that the funds being raised for new investment has dropped precipitously (see Figure 8.2 and note these figures do not allow for inflation).[25]

The net sum of these changes means that new entrepreneurs need to bootstrap their ventures and be extremely frugal with their resources, perhaps using virtual business models. They must extend the life of their company until they are far enough along to fit the with the limited VC funds that are available. In many cases, entrepreneurs now prefer to stay with angel investors and avoid taking institutional venture capital.

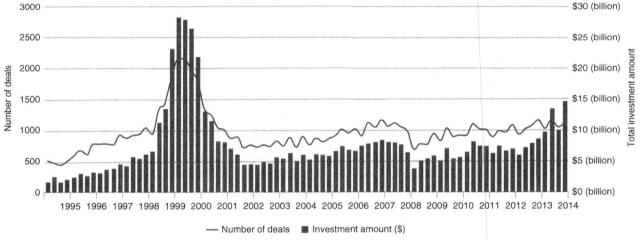

FIGURE 8.2
New Capital and Number of Deals in the VC Sector, 1995–2014
Source: PwC/NVCA MoneyTree™ Report. Data: Thomson Reuters

Super-Angels

Super-angels are an emerging group of investors that sit between conventional private angel investors and the venture capitalists. Like the angels discussed in part A, super-angels also invest their own personal funds, rather than managing money for others. Super-angels are individuals with very high personal net worth, often gained from selling their own companies. Whereas the conventional angel may invest up to perhaps $100,000, super-angels typically invest over $1 million and, most importantly, through their own networks and reputation, can bring other like-minded super-angels along with them. Some super-angel groups are even raising money from others and managing both their own money and others. They are now competing directly with VC firms.[26] From an entrepreneur's perspective, identifying super-angels in your community and making them aware at an early stage of your plans can open doors later on when you might need an alternative to VC funds. It is best if one of your early angel investors has a relationship with a super-angel investor and can make the introduction at the appropriate time. Remember it takes time to build a trusting network.

Equity Investment Fundamentals

Public Stock

There are two basic classes of ownership in companies. The first, with which most people are familiar, is by holding shares in publicly traded companies. Usually associated with larger, well-known corporations such as Ford Motor, Johnson & Johnson, and Citibank, public companies trade freely on stock exchanges, such as the New York Stock Exchange and NASDAQ, both of which are designed for trading the stock easily and transparently. In fact, many smaller companies also trade on these exchanges, which provide a "liquid market" in their stocks. Any member of the public can buy and sell these shares in this type of company. This liquidity enables inside shareholders to turn their shares into cash. When a privately held company "goes public," several benefits result. The private stock can now be traded openly, and insiders can convert their illiquid assets into cash. The company can also sell some of its own stock to raise further money for growth and acquisitions. This also provides an easy way, should more cash be required, to sell more stock later in a secondary offering. No wonder most entrepreneurs dream of going public. We will return to the topic of IPOs in more detail in Chapter 11.

Private Equity

In contrast to public stock, the term *private equity* actually covers a broad range of investment categories that come into play at different stages of a company's, and even an industry's, life cycles:

- **Venture capital** is a broad subcategory of private equity that refers to equity investments made, typically in less mature companies, for the launch, early development, or expansion of a business. Venture capital is often subdivided by the stage of development of the company, ranging from early-stage capital, sometimes called seed money, used for the launch of start-up companies to late-stage and growth capital that is used to fund the expansion of an existing business that is generating revenue but may not yet be profitable or wants to generate cash flow to fund future growth.

- **Leveraged buyout**, also known as **LBO** or **buyout**, refers to a strategy of making equity investments as part of a transaction in which a company, business unit, or business assets are acquired from the current shareholders, typically with the use of financial leverage. The companies involved in these transactions are typically more mature and generate operating cash flows. In fact, LBO can be a method by which outside investors can sell their equity to new investors, with the management team remaining to share in the future of the company. (See the reference to Pyramid Healthcare in part A.)

- **Growth capital** refers to equity investments, most often minority investments, in more mature companies that are looking for capital to expand or restructure operations, enter new markets, or finance a major acquisition without a change of control of the business.

- **Distressed** or **special situations** refer to investments in equity or debt securities of a distressed company or a company where value can be unlocked as a result of a one-time opportunity (e.g., a change in government regulations or market dislocation).

- **Mezzanine capital** refers to subordinated debt or preferred equity securities that often represent the most junior portion of a company's capital structure that is senior to the company's common equity.

Private equity firms generally receive a return on their investments through one of the following avenues:

- *IPO*. Shares of the company are offered to the public, typically providing a partial immediate realization to the financial sponsor as well as a public market into which it can later sell additional shares.

- *M&A*. The company is sold for either cash or shares in another company.

- *Recapitalization*. Cash is distributed to the shareholders (in this case, the financial sponsor) and its private equity funds from either cash flow generated by the company or raising debt or other securities to fund the distribution.

The category that is of most interest to an entrepreneur, at least at the midstages of the company, is venture capital. When an entrepreneur starts a company, she and perhaps a few other cofounders agree how the company should be owned and issue stock in the company (see Chapter 7). They own private equity in their company, usually in the form of common stock, or participate as members in a partnership or LLC. For brevity, this is now referred to as private equity.

When a company is founded, legal contracts called membership or shareholders' agreements must be in existence as soon as there is more than one owner. An attorney should be hired for preparing these contracts. They should clearly state how ownership can be transferred under different situations and how the company will be valued in these cases. For example, if one of the owners should die, there must be a way that the ownership position can be valued both for probate reasons and to set a price for which this ownership can be bought back by the company or other designated shareholders.

Private equity has limited liquidity. Trading is usually confined to the existing shareholders of the company, and this internal trading may also have restrictions. So ownership in a private company has real value only when a liquidity event occurs.

Using Private Equity for Fundraising

One way that a privately held company can acquire funds for its operations and growth is to sell an ownership position in the company to willing investors. Usually a company will not need all the money to reach its goals immediately, and therefore, investments are divided into stages or "rounds." The entrepreneur and investors have to balance several factors in choosing the size and timing of each round:

- The earlier in the company's life that the investment is sought, usually the less a company is worth. Therefore, to raise, say, $250,000 when there is little more than an idea and a business plan could cost the founder 50 percent of the company, for the idea at this stage is worth only $500,000. Clearly using the bootstrapping techniques described in part A to move the company further along its development path will reduce this early loss of ownership. This loss in percentage ownership is called "dilution." In this case, the entrepreneur will have "suffered a 50 percent dilution on the first round."

- This dilution will discourage the entrepreneur from asking for more funding, even if the plan really needs $1 million to reach a key milestone.

- On the other hand, raising very small amounts of money in dribs and drabs can be a tremendous drain on the founder's time, leaving little time to actually build the company.

- Not raising enough money in the first round and, therefore, being unable to meet a key milestone could actually damage the company's reputation and make it even more difficult to raise money in the next round. In fact, it is not unusual in these cases that the investors demand a "down round"—that is, one in which the company's value is lower than in the previous round. This, of course, creates an even greater dilution of the ownership for the company's founder, who can end up with little ownership if things go wrong. Even in what is seen as a successful venture such as AutoESL, profiled earlier, the founders usually end up with only a small part of the company when it is sold.

- The investor may not insist on too low a valuation, however, because once the ownership position of the founder is diluted down to a few percentage points, then there is no motivation left for the insiders to work hard to create value, little of which they will ever see. Smart investors are careful to leave enough on the table for the entrepreneur(s), so there is enough alignment of objectives left for both parties.

These complex forces are at play every time an entrepreneur raises equity finance, and it is advisable, if possible, until sufficient experience is gained, to find a trusted adviser who has gone through the process several times to guide the negotiations. Before seeking private investments, it is vital that a sound business plan (as outlined in Chapter 6) has been prepared, stating clearly when funds are required, the key milestones, and how the funds will be used. This enables the entrepreneur to determine the right time, amount, and potential sources for the funds. Table 8.4 shows the likely target investors at different stages of a company's growth.

The fewer rounds of investment that a company must go through prior to exit, the less dilution both the founders and the early-stage investors will experience. If the company needs large amounts of capital to fulfill its plans, different investors will likely be required for later stages. It is usual for investors to work together to share the risk if the cash demands get too high for their risk profile. This is called syndicating. Investors like to choose their own syndicating partners and usually have relationships in place for this role. Entrepreneurs should question potential investors about their own appetites for funding and their access to syndicating partners if this is required in later rounds.

The table indicates that friends and family are usually undemanding on the annual return (IRR) that they expect. They are usually helping out for personal, not financial, reasons. It is rare, however, that they have deep enough pockets to see the whole venture through. Other professional investors expect high rates of returns for the risk they are taking.

Table 8.4   Rounds of Equity Finance

Round	Status	Likely sources of Funds	Expected IRR
Preseed	Barely an idea, rough business plan	Friends/family, bootstrapping, grants, and microequity funds	1–40 percent
Seed	Prototype or proof of principle, no sales	Angels, grants, possibly a local VC firm	20–40 percent
A round	Development nearly complete, first trials with customers	Angels, early-stage VC	30 percent +
B round	Customers, first growth phase	VC or other institutional sources of funds	30 percent +
C/D rounds	Sufficient to get to cash flow neutrality or exit	Late-stage VCs in syndicate	20 percent +
Mezzanine	Prepare for sale or IPO, acquisitions	Large private equity funds	15–20 percent

Classes of Stock

Once an entrepreneur seeks equity funding beyond her close friends and family, the structure of the investment becomes more formal. Any professional investor will require that an LLC or partnership be converted into a full corporation, usually a C-corporation. The founders and any employees who own stock will have common shares that carry few rights except their ownership position. Investors will demand a different class of stock, known as convertible preferred stock. These shares carry with them certain preferences, the most important of which is "preference on liquidation." This means that if the company is sold at a low price or files for bankruptcy, once any debt is paid off, the preferred shareholders receive their investment back before any distribution to the founders holding common stock. Different classes of stock may also have different voting right powers, rights to choose one or more board members, preferential votes on key issues, and so forth. In some cases, investors may insist on having a participating preferred position, which means that they receive a multiple of two or three times their investment before others see any return. Usually preferred stockholders also have some protection against dilution should the company experience a down round with only the founders experiencing dilution. Once the preferences have been paid off, the stock is converted to common shares and participates *pro rata* with the founders.

Another form of investment often used is convertible debenture or loan. In this case, the initial investment is made as debt. The loan will carry interest, typically a few percentage points above the current prime rate. The interest is normally accrued and not paid to the investors but, of course, increases the debt owed by the company. The loan can be converted usually at the investor's option to a defined class of preferred stock within a given time and at a valuation of the company that has normally been agreed to beforehand; the interest becomes part of the debt that is converted to equity at the time the option is taken. This form of investment is often used at the earliest stage of a company, when it is very difficult to agree on a value. The loan then will convert at a discount ranging between 20 and 40 percent to a value established at the first substantial equity round, usually the "A" round. If the conversion is not requested, then the investor usually has the right to recall the loan plus interest. This gives the investor greater flexibility. If the company does not appear to be meeting its growth objectives and moving toward a liquidity event, then the investor can get the original sum plus interest out of the company. This is also a protection for the investor in the case that the founding entrepreneur(s) run the company as a "lifestyle" business. Calling the loan can effectively give the investor control should this happen, for it is unlikely that the company is financially strong enough to pay back the full sum owed. On occasion, there can be a forced conversion, when the loan must be converted to equity, this conversion being triggered by a key milestone, or a stipulated level of new investment.

As the company moves forward, additional rounds of investment will likely be required. The first investors will have insisted that they have the first right to make investments in subsequent rounds. Thus, the entrepreneur will enter into a negotiation before the funds are needed to try to reach mutually agreeable terms. This can result in the following scenarios:

• The investors are pleased with how the company is developing and wish to take all of the next round of investment. In this case, it is usually easy to reach satisfactory terms. However, the entrepreneur also has the right to find other investors who might be willing to invest at a higher valuation of the company, thereby reducing the dilution experienced by the existing shareholders. The existing investors are entitled to be informed of this intention and meet the terms that the entrepreneur finds. It is important to be open and retain a good relationship with the current investors.

- The investors do not want to make the full investment in the next round but are willing to coinvest with new sources of funds. Coinvestment is common in later rounds and is called "syndication." It allows investors to diversify their risk portfolio much in the same way that individual investors are advised to do for their retirement funds. In this case the entrepreneur should negotiate the terms of the next round and approach other investors to see if they wish to participate on these terms or perhaps better terms. Asking the existing investors to find other sources of funds through their own networks is by far the best approach.

- The investors decline to invest in the next round. It is important to understand the reasons for this decision. If they do not have sufficient funds to go to the next level or their investment objectives are not to invest at later stages, then having them talk to new investors can help raise the next round; there are legitimate reasons for no further participation. On the other hand, if they are dissatisfied with the company's performance, the entrepreneur may have difficulty attracting further investments. New investors will insist on talking to the existing external shareholders, and this will make them very cautious in making an investment. In this case any new investor will likely view this as high risk, and the round will be at a lower valuation than the previous round. This will significantly dilute all the old shareholders, and the new money will dictate the terms of the deal. Often, in this case, the earlier investors will lose their preferences and downgrade to a common stock ownership position. Clearly this is a bad situation for the entrepreneur and is to be avoided if at all possible.

Warrants may also be negotiated by investors when making an investment. Warrants convey a right to purchase a certain number of shares, common or preferred as defined, within a given time period and at a stated price. The exercise of the warrants is at the option of the investor, not the company. For example, assume that an investor purchases 10 percent of a company for $1 million by buying 100,000 preferred shares at $10 each. Each share purchased may have an attached warrant to allow the investor to buy one-half of an additional share of common stock for $6.00 within two years from the original investment. Within a two-year period, the investor may exercise all or part of this right and buy more of the company at a slightly higher valuation than the original investment—$12.00 a share rather than $10.00. In this case this new stock is common rather than preferred, and therefore, the investor will have to feel pretty confident about the company's progress to buy it. On the other hand, she has two years to watch the company before this decision is made. If the company is not doing well, the investor is unlikely to come up with the extra funds, and the warrants will expire.

An often asked question is: "How much more is a preferred share worth than a common share?" The answer depends on the actual preference terms and the health and stage of the company's development. As a rule of thumb, in the very early and uncertain stages, the ratio can be as high as ten times. As the company approaches a suitable exit point for investors, this ratio approaches unity. Thus, in the warrant case above, the investor would take into account how far the company had moved forward toward an exit plan before exercising the warrants. If there was little progress, then the warrants would be worth as little as $1.20 a common share, and the purchase of the warrants would not be attractive. The company may have to raise money in a down round, which would be a better opportunity for the investor's participation.

Pre- and postmoney valuations are commonly used at the time an equity investment is made. The premoney valuation is the value that the entrepreneur and the investor agree the company is worth prior to any investment. The postmoney is the valuation of the company immediately after the investment is made. The simplest way to reconcile these two numbers is just to add the premoney valuation to the amount of the investment. For example, a company that is valued at

$10 million just before receiving $5 million in equity investment will now be worth $15 million—the original company plus the $5 million cash now in the company's bank account. Of course, now that the money is in the bank, other possibilities for the company have opened up, and the postmoney valuation may be considered higher than this number for various reasons. However, the simple calculation is a good guideline to use in most cases.

Capitalization or "cap" table shows the total amount of the various securities issued by the company. This typically includes the amount of investment obtained from each source and the securities distributed—for instance, common and preferred shares, options, warrants, convertible loans, and shares set aside in an option pool for current and future employees. It is customary to provide a pre- and postinvestment "cap" table as part of the negotiation of the terms of an investment. Table 8.5 shows a simple cap table example. The left-hand side shows the capitalization of the company with two equal founders who have set aside an option pool of 10 percent of the company's outstanding shares for future employees. The share price is nominally $.05 per share. This is the premoney cap table. On the right-hand side, an investor has provided $400,000 to purchase common stock at a $1.00 per share and owns 26.67 percent of the company postmoney. Each partner has been diluted from a 45 percent to a 33.33 percent ownership after this seed round investment. The company authorized additional shares for the sale. As a company grows with several investors, warrants, convertible notes, and different classes of stock, the cap table can become very complicated.

ROADMAP

IN ACTION — Investors will undertake a detailed analysis of your company before providing any cash. Reduce the chance of future antipathy by being completely open with them and carefully checking out whether they are the best partners for you.

Table 8.5 Example of Pre- and Postmoney Cap Tables

Premoney cap table

Share Ownership name	Shares	value	price
Total = 1,000,000		$50,000	$0.05
45%	Founder A	450,000	$22,500
45%	Founder B	450,000	$22,500
10%	Option pool	100,000	$5,000

Postmoney Cap Table

Share Ownership name	Shares	Value	price
Total = 1,500,000 $1,500,000 $1.00 33.33%	Founder A	500,000	$500,000
33.33%	Founder B	500,000	$500,000
6.67%	Option pool	100,000	$100,000
26.67%	Investor	400,000	$400,000
100.00%			

Due Diligence

The term *due diligence* refers to the investigative process that prospective investors undertake prior to making an investment. This is usually broken down into at least two phases. The first is a quick evaluation on key claims made by the entrepreneur. Investors are loath to spend significant efforts until they have made some checks to see whether there are any obvious showstoppers. They may want to do some background checks on the principals, make sure they own title to any intellectual property, do a short analysis of existing and potential competitors, and talk to some existing or future customers. If these check out, then they will start a complete and detailed investigation on all aspects of your business and plans. Appendix 1 to this chapter can be found on the book web site. It shows a due diligence checklist that is typical for a professional investor. (A similar list may be used by a bank before approving a loan.) It is broad and thorough. It is mandatory that the entrepreneur provide full and complete access to this information and offer any other information that may be relevant. This is called "full disclosure," and it is a legal responsibility imposed on anyone seeking funds from an investor or bank. (The ethical importance of disclosure is discussed in Chapter 9.)

In addition, the entrepreneur should undertake due diligence on the potential investor(s) to make sure that the deal is a good fit to their investment criteria, that they have deep knowledge in the business area, that they will take an active role to help and be there for a follow-up round or can provide access to a network of future investors, and, most important, that they will be easy to work with during times of stress. There will be such times for sure, and investors should be good partners, not enemies, when this happens. The best way to check this is to call the CEOs of companies who have already received investment from the investors and question them on the quality of the relationship. Usually the investor's web site has a list of prior investments. Poor due diligence and an entrepreneur's unrealistic expectations when seeking equity investment are common causes of future conflict. Building a company is difficult enough in any case; doing it with misunderstanding and with a misalignment of objectives between an entrepreneur and investors makes it impossible.

Bridge Financing

Timing investments to match a company's plans is extremely difficult. In today's climate, the time between identifying the need for additional funds and actually getting money in the bank can range from a minimum of six months to more than a year. There is always the danger, therefore, that a company may fail to raise the funds needed before running out of cash. In this case it may be appropriate to seek bridge funding. Remember: a bridge spans the area between two places and does not hang in midair. Bridge deals require an event to happen that terminates the interim financing. A well-known example is a bridge loan that allows someone to own two homes at the same time during a move. If there is a contract to purchase your original home from a qualified buyer, then the bank will provide bridge financing for the period between buying the new home and selling the first home. The bridge loan is secured by the first house, and the loan is repaid precisely when the first home is sold. Bridge loans are expensive but convenient. For a company strapped for cash, current investors may agree to provide enough funding until the company has closed a new round of funding. The bridge financier must be relatively confident that the new money will be secured, so the bridge money can be extracted or at least the investor made safe.

As expressed in the bridge loan offer in Table 8.6, the current investor, BVP, is not willing to continue to fully fund this company, which requires $16 million of additional financing. It is willing to invest a maximum of $7 million. In order to bridge the company to its next "C" round, it will lend the company an interest-bearing sum of $4 million in stages. In addition to the interest, which will be paid in stock and not cash, the company will have a right to further invest at a very

Table 8.6 Bridge Loan Example Terms for $4 Million Bridge Loan for Acme Inc.

Amount	A total of up to $4 million to be done in an initial closing of $1 million and a secondary closing of $1 million and, if necessary, a third closing of $2 million
Institutional support	Beta Venture Partners LLC
Interest rate	6 percent simple interest to be paid in stock
Repayment	At the earlier of Series C close or December 31, 2008
Security interest	UCC filings on all assets (and if applicable in the Patent and Trademark Office)
Warrant coverage	Note: holders will receive a warrant to purchase one share of common stock for every $2.50 invested in the bridge note
Warrant term	Five years
Warrant exercise price	$0.01
Commitment to Class C Round	BVP will commit $7 million to the Series C financing and will work with management to secure the $9 million follow-on financing to fill out a $16 million Class C round
Conditions of closing	Satisfactory completion of customer reference checks
Date of closing	The date of the first closing will be August 15, 2007; the date of the second closing will be October 1, 2007; and the date of the third closing, if necessary, will be November 1, 2007, unless otherwise agreed upon by the company and BVP

low rate for five years by exercising warrants. Both of these terms significantly dilute the owner-ship of the founders. The loan is secured by all of the company's assets. BVP will, however, commit to providing nearly half of the next round, which will greatly help the company raise the rest of the money. Clearly the company has not achieved its expectations, and the deal is punitive for the company and the founders. However, they have little alternative at this stage.

Preferences and covenants are terms negotiated by investors when making an investment. They contain several protective provisions that provide certain advantages over the common stockholders and certain rights to protect their interests. Private equity investment terms can become rather complicated, and the company will require the services of an attorney specializing in venture investments to guide it through the negotiations and contracts. The following list describes some of the more important terms that are encountered:

- *Board Membership.* Investors usually request a board seat in the company. If several investor groups or VCs participate (i.e., the deal is syndicated), then one investor will be the lead. This means that they will negotiate the terms of the investment, agree on it with the coinvestors, and usually take on the board representation. Investors look for a balanced board, not control of the board. Other investors might request "board visitation rights," which enable them to observe but not participate in board meetings or have voting rights.

- *Management Decisions.* Investors owning preferred stock may request a right to change the management team if certain conditions are not met. This is often an emotional topic. However, it offers a wonderful chance for each party to understand its objectives. A smart entrepreneur will know whether she is the right leader to take it all the way or her management skills will be sorely tested once the company reaches fifty employees, for example. Often it is better to step aside for more seasoned management to be brought in with mutual consent and take on a chairperson or technology officer role. Remember: control is not equivalent to ownership or wealth creation. Have this discussion up front, before the investment is made. It will avoid major problems later.

- *Registration Rights.* Investors will insist on having registration rights should the company go public. This means that, in this event, their shares will convert automatically to common shares and have the same rights to be included in the public offer.

- *Later Rounds.* A right of first refusal to participate in future investment rounds is granted. Investors fear that they will be diluted out of the company ownership or the company will bring in investors that the original investors do not like or trust.

- *Antidilution Rights.* These protect an investor from the company not meeting its objectives and from a subsequent round of investment being made at a lower valuation (i.e., a down round). In this case, the investors are freely issued an amount of common stock to bring their ownership position back up to their original stake so they do not suffer dilution. The dilution in this case then falls onto the shoulders of the founders. This arrangement is also referred to as a *ratchet* clause.

- *Forcing Exit.* The investors may request a *forced buyout* term, which means that if the company has not created a liquidity event within a stated time frame, the investors can take independent action and find a buyer and impose it on the board of the company. This is intended to protect investors from the founding entrepreneurs wishing to preserve the company as a lifestyle firm and not to lose their perceived control. If this clause is invoked, then clearly there is significant animosity between the insiders and the investors. A similar clause, called "demand registration rights," allows the investors to force an IPO on the company by an agreed-upon date. These clauses are rarely exercised in full, as the ability to create a viable exit may depend more on externalities. However, the existence of these clauses does enable investors to force the board to take action.

- *Piggybacking.* This gives all shareholders holding such rights to sell their stock at an IPO. An IPO may be used to sell the company's stock (treasury stock) only in order to raise further funding for the company. It is not automatic that shareholders can offer their stock at the same time. Normally the investment banker managing the IPO makes these decisions.

These terms and conditions may sound very complicated; indeed, they can be. However, there is one guiding principle in private equity financing that must be remembered: at each new round, *everything* can and usually is renegotiated. For example, if an investor in an "A" round does not have enough capital to invest when the company looks for a "B" round investment, the new investor will often require the first investor to forgo all of their preferences and rights, converting their shares to common. In the parlance of private equity, "last money in calls the shots." If the company is exceeding everyone's expectations, then the entrepreneur may be in a good position to negotiate great terms on later rounds. Unfortunately, this is not usually the case, and the entrepreneur takes the brunt of the dilution and loss of rights before any investor.

This happens for the following reason. To get investors to finance the company, an entrepreneur, always the optimist, will write a business plan that looks fantastic—*if* everything goes according to plan. The financial forecasts will have a hockey-stick sudden rise in sales and positive cash flow in Year 2. If the plan is not so aggressive, then it is unlikely to attract investment. The entrepreneur knows this, but so do the investors. They are already discounting the plan when they evaluate the investment. The overenthusiastic plan, therefore, can be used to the detriment of the entrepreneur when the company does not reach its goals by the time the next round of investment is required—usually earlier than planned. A better approach is to have a conservative plan as well as a more aggressive plan, which the company can follow if things go better than expected. Funding should be sought for only the first phase of the more conservative plan. This leaves space for slippage, and yet the situation has been set up for raising more capital at a much higher valuation should things really take off. Investors are always ready to continue funding if an entrepreneur is exceeding the plan. Start-up companies rarely, if ever, follow their business plans; they will change direction many times as they learn about their environment and understand more about the opportunities they are creating. Investors welcome this flexibility and can be reflected in the structure of the capital raising.

Understanding the Venture Capital Process

How VC Firms Work

Nearly all venture capital firms are organized as partnerships.[27] A group of professional managers gets together to manage high-risk private equity investments for investors who wish to participate in this sector of the investment market. The managers form a legal partnership and assume the role of general partners. This means that they have the authority to make decisions on investments that the partnership makes. The partners prepare a prospectus describing in detail how much money they are trying to raise for their VC fund and how the money will be used. It also details how the profits from the fund will be distributed back to the limited partner investors. A typical VC fund has a defined life, typically ten years; this is called a "closed-end fund." At the end of this period, all the assets held by the partnership must be converted into liquid assets and the proceeds distributed according to the terms of the partnership agreement. There may be a provision by which certain assets can be held for up to, say, three years further to create a higher value for the fund, but after ten years, no further investments can be made.

The general partners use the prospectus to solicit commitments to their funds. Typical sources of money are corporate, state, and university pension funds and endowments; high-net-worth individuals; and large funds under the management by other money managers. All of these sources of money are looking to diversify their own investments by putting a small percentage of their cash into a high-risk, high-gain fund managed by professionals who understand the small company environment. The size of funds raised has grown significantly, and now a fund of $500 million

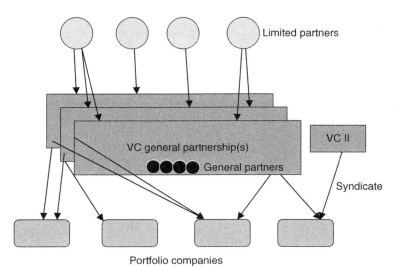

FIGURE 8.3
The Structure of a VC Partnership and Its Investments

would be considered a small- to midsized fund. As the size of funds has grown, it has resulted in VC investments moving toward later-stage opportunities. This is a direct result of the difficulty of putting so much money to work; it takes just as long to undertake due diligence for a $250,000 investment as for a $10 million investment. If the partnership has raised $500 million, then there is just not enough partner time to make many small investments and sit on a myriad of boards. Thus, these funds look to put a total investment of more than $10 million into one opportunity, even if it is in two or three rounds. Figure 8.3 shows the structure of a typical VC partnership. A group of "limited partners" commits to provide funds to VCI, a partnership managed in this case by four "general partners," responsible for finding and investing in young companies. These general partners may actually be managing several funds and may have different limited partners subscribing to each fund, as shown. The family of funds invest in portfolio companies, some of which may receive investments from different funds in different rounds. We also show that one company has money from independent VCII, through a syndicated round.

Once the partnership has commitments for the amount it was seeking by having sufficient subscription agreements signed, the partners then actively look for opportunities for investment. Usually any VC firm is very focused on what sort of companies it seeks. When an opportunity is found, one or two of the partners undertake a full due diligence exercise, perhaps taking several months, before an investment decision is made. (See Appendix 1 to this chapter on the book web site for a complete due diligence checklist.) Prior to making this large investment in time and resources, the VCs agree on the terms of a possible investment, which is memorialized in a "term sheet." Although this is a good faith rather than a binding document, it does restrict the entrepreneur from seeking other investors during the period of the agreement. Most VC firms use a standard form of term sheet. A typical pro forma is shown in Appendix 2 to this chapter to be found on the book web site. If the due diligence meets the partners' requirements, a vote is taken; usually a majority or sometimes a unanimous agreement is sought before the investment is made. Attorneys then draft the final shareholders' agreement, and the investment is made. Figure 8.4 shows how the money flows at this stage. The VC general partner makes a "call" for funds on the limited partners, who have a short time to transfer the funds to the company. Should they default, they lose all rights, including the value of the investments in which they may already have participated. At the same time, each general partner is usually required to invest

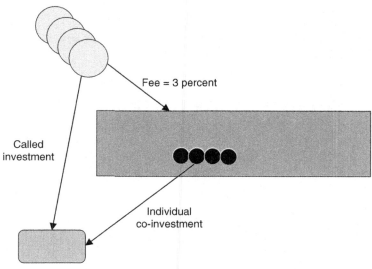

FIGURE 8.4
The Flow of Money in a Single VC Investment

personally alongside the limited partners, thus aligning their interests and making sure they have some skin in the game.

In order to pay for the running of the VC office, including partners' salaries and expenses, the investors pay a fee of typically 2.5 to 3 percent of funds invested annually. When a liquidity event occurs and one of the investments is turned into cash, the distribution agreement determines how the proceeds will be used. Typically, the limited partners receive all of their investment back first; then the rest is split 80:20 between the limited partners and the general partners. As an example, let us assume that an investment of $10 million has been made in Acme Inc. and the company is sold, returning $100 million to the VCs. Then the limited partner investors would receive $10 million "off the top" and $72 million of the remainder. The general partners would share $18 million among them. Figure 8.5 shows how the money flows after a liquidity event, in this case, an acquisition by a larger company of one of the portfolio companies.

The most important thing for an entrepreneur to understand about a VC firm is that all interests are focused to maximize the return on investment; there is no other agenda. If the company is successful and achieves a high value upon exit, then everyone wins. If the VC firm fails to help the company and does not make sure that the management is well motivated, they and their investors lose, too. So negotiating with a VC firm becomes easier if the entrepreneur understands these motivations and realizes that the aim is to make the pie bigger for everyone rather than to make the entrepreneur's slice smaller.

Venture capital firms look for generally larger deals and more impressive returns than do angel investors. Also, angels will invest in the early stages of a company, whereas venture capitalists usually do not invest until a product or service can be demonstrated or a prototype is ready for commercialization. Some venture capital firms specialize in very early-stage funding, but this is the exception rather than the rule. Many venture capital firms want to invest where the time horizon is relatively short, since they must liquidate their investments and provide cash returns to their investors over a comparatively short period of time. Some venture capital firms focus on specific industries or stages of investment, such as bridge financing. In addition to raising capital, venture capitalists can be a valuable asset to the company in terms of their contacts, market

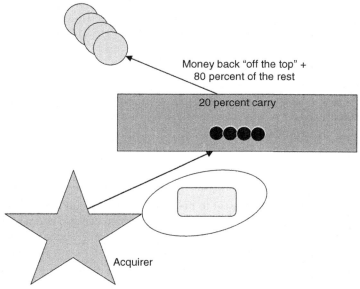

FIGURE 8.5
How Funds Are Distributed at a Liquidity Event

expertise, and business strategy. As with angels, it is imperative to locate potential investors whose skills, experience, and reputation complement the entrepreneur and the company. The most critical element in a successful venture capital relationship is the close alignment of the entrepreneurs' objectives with those of the venture capitalists. The entrepreneur should reach an agreement on several key aspects when negotiating a deal with venture capitalists, including the following: What are the investment objectives? How much control will be given up? And are the entrepreneur's needs compatible with the venture capitalists' for a successful result?

The factors that might influence a venture capital firm's funding decisions are as follows:

Specialized Industries for the Venture

Many venture capitalists specialize in a narrow set of industries. Some specialize in semiconductors, others in health-care devices, biotech, or Internet services. Still others invest in low-tech businesses such as retail stores and service businesses. Knowing what industries a venture capital firm invests in will help in locating appropriate funding and demonstrate past performance in similar cases.

The Location of the Venture

Some venture capitalists are located in Silicon Valley, California, because traditionally, a large number of technology start-ups began in this geographic area. Others are located in large cities. This does not mean the firm will invest in only their area. Although venture capital firms prefer to invest in companies that are located near them, others have a national or even global scope. However, entrepreneurs will fare better if they are located within two hours' driving time of the VC head office, for they are likely to receive more help and attention from the senior partners than from more junior staff.

Stage of Fund

In a ten-year life fund, investments made early on have a longer time to mature to an exit, and the VC firm will have more patience. As the fund nears the termination date, it is unable to make longer-term investments. This would not be a good fit with, say, an early-stage biotech opportunity that may take ten years of patient investment to reach an exit. However, late-stage funds may be suitable for a short bridge finance.

Stage of Development

Although some firms like to invest in a start-up company, others like to invest in later stages of development. The key stages of development that venture firms consider are divided into three sectors—early stage, expansion, and acquisitions/buyout—and are based on the type of financing each requires.

ROADMAP

IN ACTION

Venture capitalists can also be a valuable asset to the company in terms of their network of personal contacts to attract customers, to assist in building partners, and as board members to participate in business strategy. Make sure to find potential investors whose experience and reputation complement the venture.

Note that angels actually invest *more* than professional VC firms. Together, however, they represent only a minority of the funding accessed by early-stage companies, indicating the importance of the financing methods discussed in part A.

Guide to Selecting a Venture Capitalist

1. *Scrutinize your business with a critical eye.* Can the business give the returns that a venture capitalist demands? Work out solid financial projections to prove the results to the venture capitalist.

2. *Beef up management.* Venture capitalists invest in start-ups, but they usually don't want unseasoned executives. Everyone has strengths and weaknesses. Hire staffers who can make up the deficits.

3. *Keep a high profile so the VCs will visit.* For example, Edison Venture Fund, a venture capital firm in Lawrenceville, New Jersey, initiates contact with about 35 percent of the companies it funds. "We've already heard good things about the company and have researched their potential," says managing partner John Martinson, who has also served as chairman of the National Association of Venture Capitalists. Edison Ventures requires companies to have sales of at least $5 million annually before they will invest.

4. *Target the search.* Look for firms that specialize in the industry and the size of investment.

5. *Keep a lookout.* Look for smaller VC firms that may be more flexible and more receptive to investing in a company.

6. *Investigate possible venture partners.* One should treat the method of locating venture capitalists as though they were a customer. Find out what the needs are for the venture capitalist, so when a visit is made, the meeting can be more successful.

Venture capitalists like to invest in companies that include some bootstrapping techniques in their plans as a way of reducing their investment and risks.

"The single best thing any start-up can do is to find a beta customer or a customer sponsor as early as possible. This immediately gives you legitimacy in that you have moved from a business concept in a plan to solving a real problem. It also makes you smarter about what real customers want and will pay for. Ideally these beta sites become references and sources of funding."

James B. Sanders
President, Columbia Group, investor and consultant to high-tech start-ups; adjunct professor of entrepreneurship, University of Maryland

Private Placements

A private placement memorandum (PPM) is another alternative for raising capital and, as with VCs, involves selling stock in a private company to investors. Federal and state laws regulate these activities and determine how the offerings are made. The investors are solicited with a PPM that involves a business plan and a prospectus explaining the risks, issues, and procedures of the investment. Private placements should be done with the advice of an attorney who knows the federal laws as well as the laws of the state in which the new business will be run. There are registered agents that manage money for a network of clients. Your accountant or law firm may be able to introduce you to one of more. They will require a fee based on raising the capital for your company. Private placements are less expensive and take less time to achieve than a public offering. Each state has standardized disclosure and offering documents that must be followed. Some states require a registration process, and others do not. Also, private placements are not exempt from the issue of antifraud provisions. This means that the company must give potential investors the information they need to make a well-informed decision.[28]

The Securities Act of 1933 states that securities may not be issued unless they are registered or an exemption from registration is available. The typical exemption would be Regulation D, adopted by the SEC in 1982. This details the SEC rules governing the exemptions from registration for private placements and limited offerings. The intent was to make capital markets more accessible to businesses and to simplify the private offering process for investors who met the requirements. The exemptions under Regulation D used for a private placement are commonly referred to by their rule number as follows:

Rule 504: Sell up to a $1 million limit in twelve months' time to a number of investors, whether or not they are sophisticated. No requirement of disclosure and no advertising restrictions on resale of stock are required. *Sophisticated* refers to investors who must have sufficient knowledge and experience in financial and business matters to make them capable of evaluating the merits and risks of the prospective investment.

Rule 505: Sell up to $5 million in twelve months of unregistered securities. There can be no more than thirty-five nonaccredited investors, no requirement of disclosure to accredited investors but disclosure to nonaccredited investors, no advertising, or restrictions on resale.

Rule 506: There is no limitation to selling stock. There is a maximum of thirty-five "sophisticated" investors who must have sufficient knowledge and experience in financial and business matters to make them capable of evaluating the merits and risks of the prospective investment.

Many of these rules for private placements have been found to be overly restrictive and difficult for early-stage companies. The advent of the Internet has led to a concept called "crowdfunding" which should provide an easier path for early-stage companies to raise money from angel investors. In March 2012, the so-called JOBS Act was signed into law in the United States. As part of the bill, the requirements for raising private equity from individuals were relaxed in order to help entrepreneurs raise early-stage money and to make it easier to go public more quickly. The Act provides small businesses needing capital with many options previously out of reach.

Although the law is aimed at helping fast-growing operations like biotech and tech companies, mom-and-pop shops may benefit as well. For the first time ever, members of the public may invest in private start-up companies using the Internet and social media. This is called crowdfunding, a way for entrepreneurs to raise up to $1 million online each year from individual investors with minimal financial disclosure. Investors with annual incomes of less than $100,000 are limited to $2,000, while those who make over $100,000 are limited to $10,000.

The bill requires crowdfunding sites to provide educational materials to make investors aware of the risks. The law has its critics, who say it removes too many of the protections in Regulation D, referred to earlier, that were put in place for investors without experience. The legislation also does away with the 500-shareholder rule, which puts a cap on the amount of shareholders a company was allowed before having to register with the SEC.

At the time of writing, it is too early to predict whether this new law will really bring a major change to entrepreneurs when seeking funds. The SEC has not yet published the reporting rules, but we can anticipate the emergence of a number of Internet-based brokerage sites where young companies can solicit funding.

There are some dangers too for the entrepreneur. Having a large "crowd" of unknown investors may bring management headaches when it is time to have a shareholders' vote on key issues, and the chances of a frivolous shareholders' lawsuit will increase. In addition, if your company is highly successful and needs a lot of capital, more than allowed by the new law, institutional venture capitalists are unlikely to fund a company with a "crowd" of shareholders for the same reasons. One way to avoid this problem is to have individuals invest via a "voting trust" whereby an independent trustee takes actions on behalf of the shareholders. As yet, it is not clear whether and how such mechanisms will be possible. But just as the Internet and social media have created entirely new forms of business models, it is certain that it will also impact venture funding in ways that we have not yet experienced. Stay tuned as the wrinkles get ironed out. Crowd-funding is discussed in greater detail in Chapter 5.

Home Runs or Singles?

The previous sections illustrate the potential tensions between institutional venture capital and angel investors. The structure of a VC partnership implies that in order to get a high return for the limited partners, there has to be a home-run investment to cover for the inevitable poor performers in the portfolio and to provide the limited partners an incentive to participate in a new fund. This drives the VCs toward investing more and more capital over a long period, chasing this home run. As we have seen, this strategy has not really worked, and the investment returns are poor. Chasing the home run can really hurt the founders and early angel investors by continual dilution of their ownership position. Entrepreneurs therefore are looking more and more at capital efficient "virtual businesses," as described in Chapter 3, as a better route to creating a higher return on the early-stage funding. The limited funds are used to build the "essential" assets for an early sale to a larger company in two to three years, thereby "hitting a single"—rather than waiting and taking high risks for a VC-driven—home run, which may take seven to eight years.[30]

Corporate Debt

As we saw in part A, at the early stages of a company, it is unlikely that there are any assets to collaterize a bank loan and any loan must be underwritten by the entrepreneur personally. An unsecured loan is a personal or signature loan that requires no collateral; it is granted on the background and strength of the borrower's reputation. But as the company grows, and has quantifiable assets and customers, it is worth exploring a commercial loan for a working capital. Such loans are made at fair market interest rates if the borrower can demonstrate that the business is sound. To most banks, that will mean having an operating history of at least two or three years. Banks often require that the borrower maintain appropriate deposits with them. In most instances the entrepreneur must seek loans through community banks that make it their business to serve the small business sector. Talk to the owners of other small companies locally to learn about the most receptive banks for small companies and to get an introduction if possible.

If no local institutions are available, reference to the SBA publication for friendly, out-of-state banks. Many of the 567 banks that make business loans of less than $100,000 cross the state lines in the process. Also, the entrepreneur should reference the SBA's report on small business lending in the United States, which ranks about nine thousand commercial banks by state based on their lending practices. Other reports are available at www.sba.gov. The entrepreneur may also want to visit www.entrepreneur.com/bestbanks for a recent listing of the banks friendlier to small businesses.

Preparing a Loan Proposal

A loan proposal consists of seven key parts, not unlike the structure of a business plan covered in Chapter 6:

1. *Summary.* State your name and title, company name and address, nature of business, amount sought, purpose, and source of repayment.

2. *Management Team Profiles.* Provide the background experiences of the key managers.

3. *Business Description.* Define the products and markets as well as customers and competitors along with the inventory in terms of size, rate of turnover, and market acceptance. Provide the status of your accounts receivable and accounts payable and a list of fixed assets.

4. *Financial Projections.* Include forecasts for the next three years with fallback plans. Bankers compare these with the industry's practices and trends.

5. *Financial Statements.* Include a balance sheet and income statement for the past three years (if available). Bankers are more comfortable with audited statements. If the entrepreneur cannot afford a full audit, he or she should ask the accountant for a financial "review." Two sets of projected balance sheets as well as income and cash flow statements should also be prepared, one predicated on receiving the loan and the other on proceeding without it. Bankers match projections against published industry standards, searching for padded earnings and meager cost estimates. Personal financial statements, including tax returns for the past three years, must also be submitted because the entrepreneur's own net worth is a factor. Bankers check the entrepreneur's personal credit rating in addition to the company's.

6. *Amount and Purpose.* Bankers want to know how much you're asking for and why. Detail how the funds will be used.

7. *Repayment Plans.* Show how you will generate the cash to provide payments of both the interest and principal.

The Four Cs of Lending

When lenders consider a loan request, they concentrate on what are sometimes referred to as the "four Cs" of credit: character, cash flow, collateral, and (equity) contribution:

Character which includes such traits as talent, reliability, and honesty

Cash flow to cover debt service must be available throughout the term of the obligation

Collateral to support at least part of the loan should the company be unable to meet its obligations

Contribution by the entrepreneur toward the funding requirement

ROADMAP

IN ACTION

The entrepreneur will generally be required to have some type of collateral to support a loan. The types of securities used for collateral include endorsers or cosigners, accounts receivables, real estate, stocks and bonds, and personal savings.

Establishing the Terms of Debt

The term of the debt (the length of time over which the obligation is amortized or paid off) usually depends on the life of the asset financed. If a lender really wants to make a deal, he or she can give some latitude to structure the debt in a way that makes sense economically, and so cash flow is sufficient to amortize the debt. Working capital loans are usually paid off over the shortest periods of time, and real estate loans are usually paid off over the longest. Remember: the longer the term, the lower the monthly payment (principal and interest) will be, but there will be more monthly payments, more interest accruing, and more money paid in total to meet the debt requirements. Failure to meet interest payment typically constitutes loan default. Normally, on default, the entire principal amount outstanding becomes immediately due.

Rates

Most business debt today is provided at a variable interest rate, usually fluctuating with the prime rate (the rate banks charge their "best" customers). This rate is usually quoted as "prime plus" multiplied by percentage points, often 0.5 to 2 percent, but it can be as much as 3 or even 4 percent greater than prime, depending on risk and other variables that motivate the lender. This rate can change as often as the prime rate changes; therefore, each monthly payment can be different.

There will also be other covenants, rules, and restrictions to the loan, which may constrain the entrepreneur's management freedom. This can include not giving raises to senior management without the lender's approval or obtaining further financing or reaching certain sales milestones.

Building a Relationship with a Banker

Setting up a checking account at a bank is one of the first steps in building a relationship with a lending institution. It will provide the opportunity to meet a loan officer, who can be crucial in developing the business. The best borrowing relationships often depend on a loan officer who knows the business and will take a personal interest in the entrepreneur and his or her company. The entrepreneur should consider the following questions before making a choice:

- How much lending authority does the banker have, and what is the approval process?

- Can the banker understand the business? Is there any personal excitement about the business potential?

- What experience does the banker have with similar companies?

ROADMAP

| IN ACTION | Another method to secure capital or debt financing is to structure a strategic partnership that may include an equity investment. When the entrepreneur is rejected from traditional financing methods or is unwilling to accept the equity valuations assigned by potential investors, this option is often used. |

Strategic Partnerships and Corporate Investments

Structuring a strategic partnership that includes an equity investment is an excellent alternative for many companies to raise equity funds. This usually occurs when ventures find that they are rejected from traditional financing methods or are unwilling to accept the equity valuations assigned by potential investors. Funding associated with strategic partnerships is usually at a more attractive valuation than it might have been with a traditional financing deal. A strategic partner assigns other nonfinancial values to the transaction that relate to the impact on its own operations and competitive positioning.

Although any financial equity structure is possible, a typical strategic partnership involves the sale of a minority interest in the business to a larger company. In addition to the partner providing equity, the partner may also expect to benefit from the entrepreneurial venture itself. The partner might gain access to technology, add a new product to its product line, or profit from a business opportunity that is identified. From the small company's perspective, such an arrangement can provide access to resources such as development facilities, complementary technologies, fast access to the market, and reputation. An investment from a corporation may make it easier to attract VC funding in parallel. The profile of Jason Cong at the beginning of this chapter illustrates the use and value of corporate partners as investors.

There may be significant downsides, too, as the objectives of the small company, the VC investors, and the larger corporation might not coincide.

Here are some points to consider:

- The corporation is usually seeking only access to intellectual property and know-how rather than a direct return on the investment it makes in the entrepreneur's company.

- The corporation may perceive that the small company is financially weak and use this fact to take advantage (refer to the Chasteen case on contingent litigation in part A).

- The relationship may *reduce* the chance of receiving VC funding, particularly if the corporate investor is considered to be a prime target to buy the company later. The value may be depressed as the ability to have an auction to gain the highest price could be compromised.

- Corporations are usually slow in making decisions and may hinder the growth of the smaller firm.

- Corporate management often changes, and the champion supporting the relationship may suddenly disappear or be moved to another position. This can be disastrous for the smaller firm. Always have numerous contact points at different levels to mitigate this common problem.

On the other hand, many VCs are comfortable with coinvesting with a corporate partner, realizing that they can bring value other than just the funding. Balance is required, however, and an entrepreneur should enter into relationships with major corporations being aware of the downside. The best solution is to have a VC lead the investment round, take a board seat, and negotiate the relationship with a known and trusted corporate partner. Many corporate VC funds welcome this arrangement, not wishing to be the lead investor. Examples include the internal venture funds of Dow Chemical and Intel. Establishing an expression of strategic interest with such a fund may lead to the introduction to VC partnerships with which they have already coinvested.

A minority investment by a larger company is only one way to structure a strategic alliance. Other forms of such alliances include setting up a separate legal entity (joint venture), establishing cooperative arrangements (e.g., to fund R&D or to exploit an idea or strategy), and instituting a variety of cross-licensing or cross-distribution agreements.

Such relationships can ease cash flow constraints and lower the amount of funding the venture must obtain from other sources.

Unfortunately, in many cases, large companies make uncomfortable partners as their objectives and decision-making methods may not align closely with the faster-moving, innovative, smaller firm, so the relationship usually requires a lot of skilled management time. The master-case has many instances where these issues occur, and there are management exercises based on this topic at the end of Chapter 3.

Investments from larger firms usually fall in the range of two to 25 million dollars, gaining ownership of up to 25 percent. UPS, for example, has established a venture fund and receives more than one hundred plans a year to review; no more than 5 percent receive any funding. The investments are strategic; UPS invested in Vidco networks, a digital document security company, a clear fit to UPS's core business. As with the case for venture capitalists, approach a corporate investment office only if your business has a clear strategic fit to the company.

How To Value a Business at the Early Stage

Any private equity investment requires that the entrepreneur and the investors reach an agreement on the premoney value of the company, for this determines how much of the company the investors will own on closing the transaction. A number of valuation methods can be applied. The later the stage of the investment round, when there is likely to be a history of sales and operations and it is easier to predict future performance, the more precise the valuation. In this case financial analytical techniques can be used. These cases are dealt with in Chapter 11. However, in early rounds, when there is little history on which to base future performance and there are still many unknowns to be explored, it is much harder to establish a valuation. This section describes the various valuation methods and when they are applied.

Early-Stage Investments: The Venture Capital Model

This is the most appropriate method for an entrepreneur when seeking funding. The first step taken by investors looking at a seed or early-stage company is to estimate the company's future value at the planned exit date of usually three to five years. Remember: outside shareholders can make a return on their money only when the company is sold or a liquidity event occurs. There are two fundamental ways of making this calculation:

1. *Cash Flow Estimates.* By looking at forecasted earnings (profits) and multiplying those earnings by a factor that is relevant to the industry, a value can be computed. In growth industries, such as computing or telecommunications, investors might use an earnings multiple between 15 and 25. In a consumer-oriented business, a multiple of 2 to 10 might be used. For example, a health-care company forecasts annual sales of $3 million at the end of three years, with a profit of just greater than $1 million. Multiplying the forecasted profit by 10 yields an estimated value of $10 million. This is the value one could assume for a company if it went public or were offered for sale.

2. *Strategic Sale.* For the same strategic reasons that major corporations make investments in small companies, they also purchase later-stage companies. They will often pay a premium price if they think that the acquisition will have a major effect on their competitive position. Indeed the company may have little or no positive cash flow now or in the foreseeable future, and the first method is not applicable at all. In this case, the valuation has little or nothing to do with cash flow and much more to do with the potential impact on market share, perceived stock market price, competitive positioning, and other aspects of the acquirer. This was the case when Xilinx bought AutoESL when there was no track record

of commercial sales. Estimates of values that might be attained in a strategic acquisition are usually calculated on the basis of comparison with other purchases that have taken place recently in the same industry sector. These are referred to as "comps."

Early-Stage Investments: Milestone Methods

As we discussed in part A, value is perceived when observable milestones are met. Examples are working prototypes, patents issued, first customers, strong management and advisory boards, and so forth. One simple form of this method has been developed by Dave Berkus.[29] His list of key milestones is shown in Table 8.7.

Another interesting method developed by Cayenne Valuation Consultants[30] uses twenty-five questions about the business, many of which are milestone related, while others focus on the size of the opportunity. Take a look at the questionnaire and experiment with different answers to see which factors are likely to be more impactive on value.

Whichever method is used, investors use the potential exit values to indicate whether a company will be large enough someday to make their investment worthwhile and to determine whether their percentage of ownership in the company would be commensurate with the amount of their investment. Taking the health-care company (example 1) as an example, assume the investor seeks a compound annual IRR of 30 percent after three years. This is equivalent to an increase in value of 2.2 times over this period. Thus, the present value of the company to provide this level of return is $4.55 million, postinvestment. If the investors provide $1 million for the company now, they need to own 22 percent of the company to meet their goal. This calculation provides the investor with a starting point for negotiating the value. However, they will discount the exit value, knowing that the company will probably fall short of its plans, which are optimistic. Therefore, the exit may be later than anticipated and the amount of ownership demanded commensurately higher. More details on how to calculate an IRR can be found in Chapter 9.

The investors will consider other factors regarding exit valuation. As illustrated in the CoreTek case at the end of the chapter, the valuation at exit of $1.35 billion was high not because of any earnings forecast, but because the oligarchical structure of the market sector drove the value up. An everyday analogy is the price that an owner of a key piece of real estate might capture if it is the last house blocking a large subdivision development by a major real estate investor. The value is related to the overall project and not the simple value of the house as a dwelling. Thus, an investor is likely to look at the structure and dynamics of the industry sector targeted for an exit to determine whether this might provide a premium over a purely financially driven sale. Concentrated markets where there are well-defined and intense competitive forces produce higher valuations than unstructured sectors where there are no clear competitive factors at play.

Table 8.7   The Berkus Valuation Milestones

If exists:	Add to company value:
Sound idea (basic value)	Up to $500,000
Prototype (reducing technology risk)	$500,000 to $1,000,000
Quality management (reducing execution risk)	$500,000 to $2,000,000
Strategic relationships (reducing market risk)	$500,000 to $1,000,000
Quality board (reducing governance risk)	Up to $1,000,000
Product sales (reducing production risk)	Up to $1,000,000

Investors will also look for similar transactions ("comps") where a comparable company in the same field has recently been acquired or been taken public and can be used to benchmark a potential exit price. Entrepreneurs must also realize that certain fields become hot when valuations greatly exceed any that can reasonably be quantified on purely financial calculations. This was certainly the case with the dot.com bubble, where companies with no believable plans to ever be profitable still attracted enormous valuations in a feeding frenzy by investors and acquirers. We are now well past this phase, and valuations have returned to levels that can be more soundly justified based on purely financial grounds.

In the end, all of the valuation methods, though helpful in establishing a basis for discussions, are overridden by the negotiations between the company's board and the investors where other factors come into play. We deal with valuations at a later stage of a company's life in Chapter 11, dealing with exiting.

SUMMARY FOR PART B

Entrepreneurs seeking significant funds for growth may seek out investors who wish to purchase an ownership position in the company. Recognizing that this implies giving up some control in the company, you should not approach investors unless you intend to create a liquidity event for them to give a cash return on their investment. Selling equity dilutes the ownership for the entrepreneur; combining sale of stock with bootstrapping and debt financing methods can reduce the dilution. There are many different types of investors, and they must be carefully matched to the company business, needs, stage of investment, and personal chemistry. The entrepreneur should research sources of funds and approach only investors that are a good fit. Angel investors are typically less demanding than venture capital and other institutional professional investors. They are more patient and less demanding as to terms. However, they may not have sufficient funds to take you all the way. Super-angels may be able to fully finance the company. Other alternatives include selling stock to accredited investors using a private placement, seeking funds from venture capitalists, or attracting corporate partners. In every case a valuation of the company must be agreed to prior to the investment. This valuation can be calculated in several ways. At the earliest stages of a company, it is usual to base today's value by discounting a future exit value at a rate equal to the IRR that the investor is seeking. More mature companies may be valued using more exact methods based on assets, earnings, or future cash flow. However, in the end, it comes down to negotiating a satisfactory deal depending on the current investment market for your type of opportunity. Valuation is only one part of the transaction, and often it may be better to accept a lower current valuation in exchange for a better long-term relationship with investors. Investors will undertake detailed due diligence prior to making an investment after the terms of a transaction have been agreed to and memorialized in a term sheet. An entrepreneur should also thoroughly research investors prior to accepting their money.

STUDY QUESTIONS FOR PART A OF THE CHAPTER

Q.1 What sources of funding are available to entrepreneurs at the early stage of the company?

Q.2 What are "virtual" companies? What tools help them function? Why are they of interest to an entrepreneur?

Q.3 Describe seven techniques for bootstrapping that you could use if you started a company.

Q.4 Why is bootstrapping important for (1) closely held companies and (2) early-stage, high-growth companies seeking equity investors?

Q.5 What is meant by factoring of purchase orders?

Q.6 How can suppliers help in providing working capital?

Q.7 What is an angel investor? How would you locate an individual angel and an angel group?

Q.8 Describe three government funding programs.

STUDY QUESTIONS FOR PART B OF THE CHAPTER

Q.1 What are various sources of equity investment?

Q.2 What are the main differences between an angel, a super-angel, and a VC investor?

Q.3 What guidelines should entrepreneurs follow when they are selecting a venture capitalist?

Q.4 What is a private placement? How does it differ from a VC investment?

Q.5 What are the difference between a single-hit and a home run business?

Q.6 What are the four key factors that a banker seeks before providing a corporate loan?

Q.7 What are the advantages and disadvantages of corporate investors?

Q.8 What are the main ways an entrepreneur can value a business before it has significant sales?

EXERCISES FOR PART A

8.1 Refer to the Dyson profile in this chapter and consider the following questions:
   (a) What personal attributes led to Dyson's success? (*Hint*: Revisit Chapter 1.)
   (b) Give three reasons you think Hoover rejected Dyson's offer of a license.
   (c) Describe three ways that Dyson creatively bootstrapped his company when he did not have enough cash to proceed.
   (d) Name two other large consumer companies with household brand names that are still privately owned and were, therefore, bootstrapped from their very beginning.

8.2 With regard to establishing early-stage funding:
   (a) Select and briefly describe a business idea that will require early-stage funds to get started.
   (b) Establish the amount of start-up capital needed to fund the venture for one year.
   (c) Describe where the venture will get sources of funding and other resources it may need. Use a mix of personal funds, family, friends, bank loans, creative bootstrapping, and any other sources.
   (d) Prepare an oral presentation to an angel group.

Master-Case Exercises: If you have not already read master-case summary on the book web site, do so. Then go to the book's web site and read the diary entries Months 0, 2, 12, 14, 15, 18, 19, 21, and 23 and view the video selections "Your Money, My Life: The Pros and Cons of Bootstrapping" and "Angels, More than Just Investors."

Either as a team or individually, produce a short presentation on each of these questions for discussion. Only one or two slides for each are required to state the key points.

Master-case Q 1: Bootstrapping allows founders to have more control and give up less of their company to investors. Yet in a rapidly changing world, living on limited resources and continually worrying about money can slow the growth of a company. What are the pros and cons of bootstrapping generally (include control issues, lifestyle questions, dilution in ownership, speed to market, habit forming, personal risk taking, and so forth)?

Master-case Q 2: List the range of bootstrapping methods used by Wayne and Jeff. What were the pros and cons for each of these?

Master-case Q 3: Linda chose to retain control of her company for personal reasons, whereas Jeff and Wayne were willing to give up control. Who do you most identify with and why?

Master-case Q 4: Money and/or advice, is there a trade-off? Angels provide funding *and* mentoring. Is one fine without the other? What are the most important factors that you should take into account when (a) finding and working with angel investors? Include networking, champions, deep pockets, and others in your discussions.

EXERCISES FOR PART B

8.1 Calculate the net present value using Table 9.2, "Present Value of $1 Due in n Periods." What is the present value of $100 received at the end of seven years if the required return is 12 percent?

8.2 Examine Table 9.2, "Present Value of $1 Due in n Periods." Discuss why the numbers decrease as you move from left to right and why the numbers decrease as you move from top to bottom in a given column.

8.3 Assume you will receive $300 per year for the next three years plus an extra $300 payment at the end of the three years. Determine how much this prospect is worth today if the required rate of return is 12 percent.

8.4 Refer to Table 8.2. What is the premoney and the postmoney valuation of the company? How much percentage dilution was suffered by the founders by accepting the investment? If they needed an additional $3 million investment after another year, with a premoney value of $6 million, how much more dilution would they suffer? What percentage of the company would the first investor of $400,000 now have? What would the postmoney valuation be after the second investment?

8.5 Refer to Figure 8.3. Indicate a situation where one portfolio company has been funded from two of the funds managed by the same general partners and in which the limited partners in the funds are not identical. that in the second or "B" round, the investment fund is not the same as the earlier "A" round. The general partners have a contractual obligation to try and maximize the value created for *all* their limited partners. Yet in this case, if they strike a deal with the portfolio company that benefits the second fund, by investing at as *low* a value as they can, this automatically devalues the ownership position of the limited partners that were only in the "A" round. Is this a conflict of interest? And, if so, how can the general partners fulfill their obligations to *both* groups of limited partners?

8.6 Read the earlier profile on AutoESL and answer the following:

(a) Why was Jason able to get an early angel investment in the company?

(b) What were the pros and cons of bringing in competing corporate investors in the A and B rounds?

(c) The VCs brought in a professional CEO when they made their first investment. He ended up with slightly more cash at the exit than the founder. Is this reasonable or not? Provide reasons for your response.

(d) UCLA licensed its research results to AutoESL and received a small payment when the company was sold. Do you think universities should benefit from their research results in this way or provide access freely to the private sector? Give reasons for your answer.

Master-Case Exercises: If you have not yet read the appendix in Chapter 1, do so. Then go to the book's web site and read the diary entries Months 18, 19, 23, 25, 26, 36, and 42 and view the video selection "VCs and Investment Bankers: When the Stakes Get High, the Ethics Get Low."

Either as a team or individually, produce a short presentation on each of these questions for discussion. Only one or two slides for each are required to state the key points.

Master-case Q 1: VCs need deal flow, which often comes from angel investors. Yet they often abuse the very people who are providing them with opportunities. Discuss the reasons for potential conflicts between angel investors and institutional VC firms. How can these impact (a) the start-up investment field and (b) the operations of a start-up company?

Master-case Q 2: VCs benefit by creating the highest value for the companies they invest in. However, they often act as if they are willing to destroy the company. Was Venrock working in its best interests in driving a wedge between Wayne and Jeff? State your reasons.

| Case Study | Coretek Inc. |

A physicist by training, Dr. Parviz Tayebati received a BSc with first-class honors from the University of Birmingham, England, in 1982, followed by a master's degree from the University of Cambridge in theoretical physics and a PhD in quantum electronics from the University of Southern California in 1989.[31] Parviz then joined Foster-Miller Inc., near Boston, a small firm that in the past had derived much of its revenues by undertaking government-funded research using the SBIR Programs (see Chapter 9). While there, Parviz led research in optical computing and, most important, learned much about the process for winning technology development awards from the federal government.

Throughout the 1990s, Internet bandwidth and information applications grew dramatically in a kind of virtuous circle, with more bandwidth making new applications practical and acceptance of these new applications driving demand for even more bandwidth. Recognizing the opportunity to apply his technical and management skills to this area, Parviz formed CoreTek Inc. in 1994 with the vision of developing truly innovative, enabling technologies to support this growth. Continued expansion of the Internet required components and architectures enabling the bandwidth to grow faster than costs. CoreTek's tunable laser technology was important because it could address cost growth in two ways: it reduced manufacturing and inventory costs for the source lasers, and it provided an essential element of the wavelength-managed network, which promised to reduce costs by dramatically increasing network use and efficiency. He initially secured government funds for the development of what was viewed as a speculative technology. Between founding the company and 1998, CoreTek received more than $5.5 million in SBIR grants, nine phase I awards, and five phase II awards.

Parviz soon realized that to make his dream come true in this fast-moving field, he would have to accelerate his development program. Therefore, in 1999, CoreTek raised $6 million in an "A" round of preferred stock from a syndicate of three VC firms, led by Adams Capital Management (www.acm.com), valuing the company at $11.5 million prior to the investment. The VCs were attracted by the fact that the company was in a hot field and was able to secure significant amounts of

government funding. For his part, Parviz chose this investor group not only on the attractive deal that he was offered (in fact, another group of VCs offered a higher valuation) but by witnessing the speed with which they could make decisions and their deep knowledge of the telecommunications industry—the fit was excellent. Parviz and his team were now working 24/7. The development proceeded rapidly, as CoreTek built its first manufacturing line. But the money was still not enough, and only nine months later, the company closed on a "B" round of $20.5 million at a premoney valuation of more than $52.5 million from an extended syndicate of four VC firms. In 2000, a number of the major telecommunication giants expressed an interest in acquiring CoreTek. At that time, the telecommunications industry was anticipating major growth, and technologies such as that developed by CoreTek were seen as vital for them to reach their targets. The oligarchical structure of the industry worked to CoreTek's advantage—a breakthrough in cost/performance in components could radically shift market share. Finally, in June 2001 Nortel Networks purchased CoreTek for $1.35 billion paid in Nortel's publicly traded stock. Parviz joined Nortel as vice president of business development. At that time, Parviz and the other insiders of the company still owned approximately 30 percent of the company.

CASE STUDY QUESTIONS

1. Why did the VC firms like the fact that the company had received significant government grants? Assume that this had not happened and that all the funding for the company had come from VCs. Add an earlier seed round to replace the government funds, and make an estimate of the dilution that Parviz and the founders would have had to take in this case if the VCs were to retain their IRR. Approximately how much less would the founders have in their pockets when the company was sold?

2. Draft a short-term sheet (no more than two pages) for each investment round under the new circumstances of question 1.

3. Give three reasons Adams Capital Management, the lead VC firm, was a good fit for this opportunity.

| *Appendix* | Guidelines for Selecting an Incubation Program |

Track Record

- How well is the program performing?
- How long has the program been operating?
- Does it have any successful graduate companies, and if so, how long have they been in business independent from the incubator?
- What do other clients and graduates think of the program?

Graduation Policy

- What is the program's graduation policy; that is, what are the incubator's exit criteria?
- How flexible is the policy?
- How long, on average, have clients remained in the program? (Incubators typically graduate companies within three years.)

Qualifications of Manager and Staff

- How long has the current staff been with the program?
- How much time does the staff spend on-site?
- Have they had any entrepreneurial successes of their own? Do they actively engage in professional development activities, or are they a member of a professional/trade association to keep them up to date on the latest in incubation best practices?

FOR MORE INFORMATION

Information about Joining an Incubator

The National Business Incubation Association's web site has resources to help you manage an incubator or to become an incubator tenant. This site will also help you find an incubator near you. See www.nbia.org/.

Additional tips can be found at www.smallbusinessnotes.com/.

For information on a network of incubators focusing entirely on renewable energy companies, see www.xmarks.com/site/www.nrel.gov/technologytransfer/entrepreneurs/inc.html.

A number of research reports on business incubators can be found at www.kauffman.org/.

For a list of "for-profit" incubators, see www.capital-connection.com/privateincubators.html and www.idealab.com.

Research Articles

Adkins, Dina, Chuck Wolfe, and Hugh Sherman, *Best Practices in Business Incubation*. (For a list of "for-profit" incubators, see http://capital-connection.com/privateincubators.html and www.idealab.com 2000.) Study performed for the Maryland Technology Development Corporation (TEDCO). www.marylandtedco.org.

David S. Chappell and Hugh Sherman, "Methodological Challenges in Evaluating Business Incubator Outcomes," *Economic Development Quarterly* 14 (1998).

Hansen, Morten, Henry Chesbrough, Nitin Nohria, and Donald Sull, "Networked Incubators: Hothouses of the New Economy," *Harvard Business Review*, September 1 (2000).

McKinnon, Susie, and Sally Hayhow, *State of the Business Incubation Industry* (Athens, OH: NBIA Publications, 1998).

Lawrence A. Molnar, Donald R. Grimes, and Jack Edelstein, *Business Incubation Works* (Athens, OH: NBIA Publications, 1997).

INTERACTIVE LEARNING ON THE WEB

Test your knowledge of the chapter using the book's interactive web site.

ADDITIONAL RESOURCES

There are many articles and case reports of entrepreneurs' bootstrapping ideas published by popular magazines. You can search for articles for ideas and tips at the following sites:

- www.entrepreneur.com
- www.inc.com
- www.fastcompany.com

The following web sites provide further information about certain aspects of government grants:

- www.nttc.edu/ has details of all ten units of SBIR and five units of STTR sources.
- www.winbmdo.com lists all contact information, has links to relevant web sites, and so on. This agency, now known as MDA, has traditionally funded riskier projects.

- http://www.grants.gov/web/grants/search-grants.html lists all active federal grant programs.

- www.acq.osd.mil/osbp/sbir/ covers most SBIR and STTR documents.

- www.acq.osd.mil/osbp/sbir/solicitations lists solicitations from the DOD, which includes Army, Navy, Air Force, DARPA, and MDA with contact information. The DOD constitutes about 50 percent of the total SBIR/STTR funding, more than $500 million.

- grants1.nih.gov/grants/oer.htm is a link to grant opportunity, policy and guidelines, and contact information for the National Institutes of Health, the second largest funding source. At this site, click on "Small Business (SBIR/STTR)."

- www.nsf.gov/funding/ is a link to grant opportunity at the National Science Foundation.

- www.nsa.gov/research/math_research/index.shtml refers to the National Security Agency Mathematical Sciences Program, which funds high-quality mathematical research in the areas of algebra, number theory, discrete mathematics, probability, statistics, and cryptology.

- For finding technologies available at government labs, see www.nttc.edu/.

  - **American Banker's Association** 1120 Connecticut Avenue, NW, Washington, D.C. 20036; (800) 338-0626
  - **Annual Statement Studies** Robert Morris Associates, 1650 Market Street, Suite 2300, Philadelphia, PA 19103; (800) 677-7621
  - **Dun & Bradstreet Corp.** 3 Sylvan Way, Parsippany, NJ 07054; (973) 605-6000; www.DNB.com
  - **National Association of Small Business Investment Companies** 666 11th Street, NW, Suite 700, Washington, D.C. 20001; (202) 628-5055
  - **Polk World Bank Directory, Polk Bank Services** Thompson Financial Services, 1321 Murfreesboro Road, Nashville, TN 37217; (615) 889-3350
  - **Thomson Bank Directory** Thomson Financial Services, 4709 W. Golf Road, 6th Floor, Skokie, IL 60076-1253; (847) 676-9600

WEB RESOURCES

Companies looking for funding or ways to attract the attention of venture capitalists have plenty of places to look on the Internet. Searches on the web will find most venture capital firms and their portfolio companies, as well as local angel groups. For starters, bookmark these sites:

- www.mycapital.com/companies/resources_companies.php—a comprehensive venture capital resource library

- www.nvca.org—headquarters for the National Venture Capital Association

- www.techcapital.com—online magazine dealing with venture capital

- www.garage.com—assists start-ups wishing to acquire funding

NETWORKS

Many angel and VC investors participate in networks. You can find them through your local chambers of commerce, your local Small Business Development Center, and your local SCORE office and by searching on the Internet.

The Kauffman Foundation in Kansas City has several programs to help entrepreneurs and also undertakes research on matters affecting start-up companies. For example, a 2002 report on business angels has valuable information for entrepreneurs seeking angel investments. Web links into the Kauffman Network can be found at www.kauffman.org and www.entrepreneurship.org.

The following table lists a few of the many local angel investor networks in the United States. Others can be located by contacting your local chamber of commerce.

Georgia Capital Network	(404) 894-5344
Investors' Circle	(708) 876-1101
L.A. Venture Network	(310) 450-9544
Mid-Atlantic Investment Network	(301) 681-0162
Northwest Capital Network (serves only businesses located in Oregon)	(503) 282-6273
Pacific Venture Capital Network	(714) 856-8366
Seed Capital Network Inc.	(615) 573-4655
Technology Capital Network (formerly the Venture Capital Network at MIT)	(617) 253-7163
Texas Capital Network	(512) 794-9398
Venture Capital Network of Minnesota	(612) 223-8663
VentureLine	(518) 486-5438
Washington Investment Network	(206) 389-2559

APPENDIX 1: DUE DILIGENCE CHECKLIST[34] (ONLINE)

APPENDIX 2: MODEL VENTURE CAPITAL TERM SHEET—SERIES A PREFERRED STOCK (ONLINE)

ENDNOTES

1. Materials for this profile were obtained from www.dyson.com and a series of interviews at a series of on-line published interviews.

2. See www.newsweek.com/how-james-dyson-revolutionized-vacuum-67039.

3. See Eric Ries, "Startup Lessons Learned," www.startuplessonslearned.com/2009/08/minimum-viable-product-guide.html, where some notes, a video, and a presentation exploring this concept further are available.

4. This case was derived from the interview with Ujjwal Gupta in August 2011.

5. For a comprehensive review of bootstrapping techniques, see "Boot-strapping Finance," Chapter 8 by Lynn Neeley and Harold P. Welsch, ed., *Entrepreneurship, The Way Ahead* (New York, NY: Routledge, 2004).

6. See Ellen Paris, "David vs. Goliath," *Entrepreneur Magazine*, November 1999.

7. "Microsoft Loses Patent Suit," Associated Press Announcement, February 23, 1994.

8. Edmund Andrews, "Patents, an Inventor Wins but Isn't Happy," *New York Times*, December 14, 1991.

9. See Eric Rosenfeld, *Credit Where Credit is Due: Using Plastic to Finance*, August 1, 1999, www.entreworld.org.

10. From an Interview with Rick Smith, 2002. Smith is an entrepreneur who received funding from his family when he started Smith and Solomon Training School.

11. The Kauffman Foundation has studied angel investing and networks. See, for example, their report that can be downloaded from http://www.kauffman.org/entrepreneurship/angel-investment-guidebook.aspx.

12. See Pyramid Healthcare, www.pyramidhealthcarepa.com. The company was recently purchased by a private equity fund providing the angels with a satisfactory return on their investment.

13. Two examples of large, professionally managed angel groups are the Band of Angels in Silicon Valley (www.bandangels.com) and BlueTree Allied Angels in Pittsburgh (www.bluetreealliedangels.com).

14. See Carl Simmons, "Every Business Needs and Angel," *Inc. Magazine*, Summer 2002. *Inc.* publishes a list of angels annually.

15. See Y Combinator, www.dreamitventures.com and www.ycombinator.com.

16. See www.Xobni.com.

17. See www.Khoslaventures.com, the latest partnership started by Vinod Khosla, a long-time and highly successful venture capitalist, formally with the famed VC firm of Kleiner Perkins. For Khosla's and well-known investors, see U. Gupta, ed., *Done Deals, Venture Capitalists Tell Their Story* (Boston: Harvard Business Press, 2000).

18. See www.grameen-info.org/.

19. See www.kiva.org, a social entrepreneurial nonprofit organization that manages microloans.

20. See www.sba.gov/content/microloan-program.

21. See http://frugalentrepreneur.com for a comprehensive list of micro-loan sources.

22. Alvin Katz was introduced to one of the authors by his nephew. The case was used for analysis when Mr. Katz visited a class at Penn State.

23. You can find details on all federal funding programs for small companies for all government agencies, including topics of interest, available funds, direct contacts, etc., at the LARTA web site, www.larta.org.

24. This profile introduces a number of important concepts and terms that are explored later in the chapter. You should therefore return to the profile as you become more acquainted with the terms. These include *spinout, seed, A and B rounds, super-angels, preferred stock, syndicate, dilution,* and *stock options.*

25. *Source*: Thomson Reuters annual report on the VC industry, 2010. This can be found at www.NVCA.org with more supporting data.

26. See Pui-Wing Tam and Spencer E. Ante, "Super-Angels Alight," *The Wall Street Journal*, August 16, 2010.

27. An excellent source for data and news on the venture capital sector can be found at www.nvca.org. This site reports on surveys such as the Pricewaterhouse annual "MoneyTree" report.

28. See Stephen C. Bowers, *The Ernst & Young to the IPO Value Journal* (New York: John Wiley & Sons, 1999), 97–99.

29. See Berkonomics—Business Insights from Dave Berkus, http://berkonomics.com.

30. See Cayenne Consulting, www.caycon.com.

31. Interview with Parviz Tayebati, June 2005

32. This list was derived from one used by Adams Capital Management, a VC firm located in Pittsburgh.

BUILDING AND EXITING

Part 3, "Building and Exiting" covers several topics that are important as you grow the venture. Chapter 9 explores several management issues that can make or break the success of a company. The first is the management of money. Many companies fail because they just run out of cash to manage their day-to-day operations. They may be making a profit on every product they sell, but there is not enough money in the bank to fund manufacturing and sales efforts. As we saw in Chapter 8, it always takes longer to raise capital or get a loan than anticipated, so planning your cash needs well in advance is vital. You will also have to find, interview, hire, incentivize, manage, and, yes, even fire people as you build the organization. In a large company, a nonperforming employee may not be such a big issue; in a small firm, just one bad hire can be fatal. As you bring in more employees, you need to build a culture that encourages everyone to contribute fully, to persevere when the going gets tough, and to enjoy their time with your company. This cannot be taken for granted; you have to work at it every day. Finally, this chapter deals with the management of stress and conflicts of interest. You will be faced with complex decisions as the company grows, and you need a framework that enables you to think clearly and get to the right answers.

Chapter 10 will help you develop your communication skills. No idea has any value until you can communicate it effectively to all stakeholders whether they are partners, hires, investors, bankers, or, eventually, buyers of the company. This chapter and the associated tools will help you in this regard.

Finally, Chapter 11 focuses on the sensitive issues regarding "exiting" the company or creating a "liquidity" event for your shareholders. We explore different alternatives including selling all or parts of the company to its employees as well as transferring ownership to family members or a new management team. Of course, a lifestyle company may not plan an "exit," but eventually, nearly all companies need to find a way to create tangible liquid wealth, perhaps at retirement, a family emergency, or just a desire to do something new. It is, therefore, a sound strategy to have exit options in place for just these situations, even if the original plan did not call for an "exit event."

9 Managing Resources—Money and People

"The secret of success in life is known only to those who have not succeeded."

J. Churton Collins, Literary Critic

OBJECTIVES

- Understand financial statements.
- Prepare financial projections such as the budget, cash flow forecast, burn rate, and runway.
- Calculate and interpret return on investment.
- Prepare a breakeven analysis.
- Analyze an investment decision.
- Calculate the lifetime value of a customer.
- Manage the timing and stresses of fundraising.
- Understand the importance of managing the team every day.
- Learn how to build a strong creative culture.
- Learn how to hire and fire employees.
- Know how to deal with a resignation.
- Create frameworks for dealing with ethical conflicts.
- Learn basic legal requirements.

CHAPTER OUTLINE

Introduction
Profile: Paul Silvis—Conserving Cash While Building an Embracing Culture
Financial Statements
The Value of the Balance Sheet
The Value of an Income Statement
The Value of a Cash Flow Statement
Preparing Financial Projections

Introduction

This chapter focuses on the day-to-day management skills you will need as you grow your company. There are two key resources that are very important to a young company—cash and people. They are far more important than in a larger established company where a slip or two can be overcome; failure to pay close attention to either can be fatal in a start-up. Executives used to the well-established procedures found in mature companies have great difficulty in adapting to a fragile, young organization. Yet, most first-time entrepreneurs have little experience of the unique skills and knowledge required to take care of these critical resources. Although formal qualifications in financial accounting or human resource practices are not mandatory, it is imperative that you acquire at least a basic knowledge in these areas.

The first part of the chapter is devoted to the tools needed to analyze a company's performance, to manage the day-to-day financial activities, and to prepare financial statements for investors and lenders. The company uses these tools to communicate its financial condition to others, to manage the day-to-day cash, to forecast future cash needs, and to aid in investment decisions. Financial statements should reflect the operation of the business in the same way that the management views its business.

The second part of the chapter deals with building a cohesive team culture. This is often taken for granted, but, in fact, what you do every day in your interaction with your colleagues (how you hire, fire, celebrate, compensate, and set values) is vital. Ask yourself: why are some companies seen as great places to work and others not so? Great companies don't just happen; they are led and managed to be the best.

Profile: Paul Silvis—Conserving Cash While Building an Embracing Culture

Before founding Restek in 1985, Paul Silvis worked at Supelco Inc. as the supervisor of the capillary research group and for the federal government's Mining and Safety Enforcement Agency.[1] He received a bachelor's degree in chemistry/life science from the University of Pittsburgh in 1977 and later took chemical engineering courses at Penn State. Not satisfied with just working for a company, Paul decided that he had some ideas for a new business. He took the plunge in 1985 and started Restek Corporation in an old schoolhouse in State College, Pennsylvania. At the outset, Paul had a modest target of reaching $3 million in sales in five years. However, the company continually innovated new products and was able to finance its growth from the retained funds from sales of products. Paul managed to retain full ownership by extremely careful cash management in the early days of the company. During this time, he kept control of the company as he wanted to grow a "family" and not just personal wealth. He never took outside equity investment. As the company grew, he carefully used bank loans to fund working capital. Restek (www.restek.com) is now a leading manufacturer of chromatography laboratory supplies with annual sales of greater than $40 million and offices and distribution centers in more than sixty countries.

Paul's title—head coach (rather than president or CEO)—reflected his leadership philosophy. "The head coach puts the right players in the right positions; provides training, tools, and opportunities for them to become star players; encourages an atmosphere of support and honesty; helps to define the team's strategy for winning— all for the sake of creating a championship team of which each member can be proud!"

Restek has grown every year since its formation and has always been profitable. It has been ranked among the top fifteen companies in the United States to work for by the *Wall Street Journal*. Paul sends clear messages to his top managers regarding hiring and firing, which is consensus driven. "Hire the best, even if you have to pay them more than yourself. Intensively mentor new hires to assimilate them into the culture. Always give someone help to improve their performance before firing them—give them a chance, help them if they have to leave, and make sure everyone's self-esteem is preserved. Celebrate when you lose someone that you want to retain and tell them that they will always be welcome back." These clear statements from the top of the organization have enabled Restek to establish an embracing culture in which everyone pulls together, works hard, and is ready to give that little extra when the inevitable problems arise. Paul elected to sell the company to the employees using an ESOP (see Chapter 11) in order to preserve this unique culture and not have it threatened by being acquired by a larger company. Paul uses the sports metaphor often: "Embracing problems and overcoming insurmountable obstacles is the key to any successful venture. Envision 'problems' like a track and field event, in which the relay team that jumps hurdles faster than the competitor wins the race. It is not the number or magnitude of the problems you have, but how fast you can jump over them and embrace the next one that wins the race." Having successfully transferred ownership and culture to a new set of coaches, Paul spun out a new technology from Restek and is starting all over again with his new company, SilcoTek Inc.

Financial Statements

There are three standardized financial documents that you should become acquainted with:

1. The balance sheet (also called the statement of financial position)

2. The income statement, or profit-and-loss (P&L) statement

3. The statement of cash flows (also called source and use of funds)

The Value of the Balance Sheet

The balance sheet provides a picture of the business' financial position at a particular point in time—generally at the end of a financial period (e.g., month, quarter, or year). It encompasses everything the company owns (assets) or owes (liabilities), as well as the investments into the company by its owners and the accumulated earnings or losses of the company (equity).

The balance sheet equation is

$$\text{Assets} = \text{liabilities} + \text{shareholder equity}$$

Assets are current if they can be converted into cash within one year and liabilities are current if they must be paid off within one year; otherwise, they are considered long-term. Inventory is considered current because it is sold within one year from the date of receipt; however, certain business inventories can be further segregated into work-in-process (WIP), raw materials, or finished goods inventories.

The sample pro forma balance sheet in Table 9.1 shows shareholders' equity, or the net worth of the company, projected to be $182,200 in Year 1 and $462,600 by Year 5. Equity is calculated by subtracting the total liabilities of $323,800 (Year 1) from the total assets of $506,000 (Year 1).

Table 9.1   Sample Pro Forma Balance Sheet (in $,000's)

Assets	Year 1	Year 2	Year 3	Year 4	Year 5
Accounts receivable	180.7	174.2	209.1	250.9	301.1
Inventories	168.6	158.6	190.3	228.3	274.0
Current assets	382.3	372.7	447.3	536.7	644.1
Net fixed assets	107.6	130.1	156.1	187.3	248.8
Other	16.1	18.2	21.8	26.1	31.4
Total assets	$ 506.0	$ 521.0	$ 625.2	$ 750.2	$ 900.2
Liabilities and net worth					
Accounts payable	53.7	61.0	73.2	87.8	105.4
Accrued expenses	24.4	28.5	34.2	41.0	49.2
Current portion, LTD	1.0	1.0	1.0	1.0	1.0
Current liabilities	288.8	259.4	310.3	366.8	436.6
Long-term debt	5.0	4.0	3.0	2.0	1.0
Convertible debt	30.0	30.0	30.0	–	–
Net worth = total assets − total liabilities	182.2	227.5	281.8	381.4	462.6

When analyzing a company's balance sheet, managers and investors view it in terms of its type of business. For example, fixed assets account for a greater percentage of total assets in a manufacturing operation as opposed to a distributor or professional services company. The balance sheet should be analyzed with respect to the volume of the company's business. For instance, receivables should be compared to sales to determine how quickly the company collects its cash or current liabilities compared to expenses to see if the company is paying its short-term obligations in a timely fashion.

Book Value

Book value is derived through an analysis of the *balance sheet* by taking the original cost of fixed assets less their accumulated depreciation. Divide the book value by the number of shares outstanding, and you'll know the value each share would have were the company to go out of business. Book value does not include intangible assets such as patents and other forms of intellectual property, and it does not take into account the value of a company's business relationships, or *going-concern value.*

When a firm is acquired, the difference between its book value and its going-concern value is called *goodwill.* Goodwill includes factors that add value but cannot be easily liquidated or sold, such as brand, market share, the "learning curve," and human capital.

ROADMAP

IN ACTION   The entrepreneur should also use the income statement to evaluate the business' financial condition. The income statement shows how the business made a profit by displaying how much money it generated in sales and how much money it cost to run the business.

The Value of an Income Statement

The statement of operations, also known as the income statement or P&L statement, summarizes the revenue (or income) and expenses of a company on a monthly basis for one year or on an annual basis for several years. It divides expenses into broad categories, such as cost of goods sold and operating expenses. The cost of goods sold would represent the resources that went into production of the products ultimately recognized as sales. These are sometimes referred to as *direct costs.* These costs would include materials, labor, and manufacturing expenses. Two more terms for costs of goods sold are shown here:

- *Inventory costs*—costs that are assigned to inventory before being sold

- *Production costs*—costs that are identified with the product

Operating expenses are costs that are not identified with the product. The major categories include research and development expenses; selling, general, and administrative (SG&A) expenses; and financial expenses.

The income statement in Table 9.2 shows how the business made a profit by displaying how much money it generated in sales and how much money it cost to run the business. The equation used to determine net profit or loss is

$$\text{Net profit (or loss)} = \text{gross sales} - \text{total expenses}$$

Table 9.2   Example of a Pro Forma Income Statement (in $,000's)

	Year 1	Year 2	Year 3	Year 4	Year 5
Sales	$ 605.0	$ 726.0	$ 871.2	$ 1,045.4	$ 1,254.5
Cost of goods sold	349.5	406.6	487.9	585.4	702.5
Gross profit	255.5	319.4	383.3	460.0	552.0
Research and development	100.4	108.9	130.7	156.8	188.2
General and administration	106.9	123.4	148.1	177.7	213.3
Income from operations	48.2	87.1	104.5	125.5	150.5
Interest expense	19.7	19.0	20.0	21.0	23.0
Profit before taxes	28.5	68.1	84.5	104.5	127.5
Taxes	10.0	23.8	29.6	36.6	44.6

Note that operating income is not the same as net profit. Operating income is determined by subtracting costs from sales and does not include taxes or interest charges. Operating income is the amount the business earns after expenses but before taxes and other income, such as interest. It is sometimes referred to as earnings before interest and taxes (EBIT).

The EBIT-to-interest ratio is calculated by dividing the EBIT by the interest. For example, if operating profits were $10,000 and interest was $10,000, the business would break even. This is risky, as a slight downturn in sales or an increase in interest rate would cause losses.

A Rule of Thumb: The ratio should be at least 3:1. Monthly trends might fluctuate (building up inventory for seasonal fluctuations, awaiting payment on large receivables, etc.), but in the long term, it is important that this ratio hover in the 2.5+ range.

ROADMAP

| IN ACTION | The entrepreneur should use a monthly cash flow statement to plan future fundraising activities. He or she should be aware of the monthly "burn rate" and the "runway." |

The Value of a Cash Flow Statement

An income statement may show that the company is profitable over a given period but does not give any information about the cash position of the company. A seemingly profitable company can go bankrupt if its short-term cash position is insufficient to meet its short-term liabilities such as salaries, interest payments, and other receivables. This is particularly true with early-stage companies, which, more often than not, are cash strapped. Therefore, this statement and its use to predict cash availability to pay bills are the most important for the entrepreneur to understand and use. It is advisable to have a month-by-month cash flow forecast for the first two to three years of a company as cash reserves will fluctuate wildly. Table 9.3 shows a cash flow statement for one year's operations of Acme Inc., a company selling course management software to two-year colleges. The company has two products, A and B, and is just ramping up its sales force. At the start of the year, the company has $21,000 in the bank and an angel is investing $400,000 in January for 25 percent of the company. The company is expecting to be cash flow neutral at the end of 2014, at which time it will have no cash reserves. Typically, cash forecasts are optimistic, and it usually takes at least six months to raise further funding. This forecast suggests that despite

Table 9.3   Acme Inc. Cash Flow Forecast for the Year Ending December 31, 2014($)

	J	F	M	A	M	J	J	A	S	O	N	D
Product A price	4,560											
Product B price	25,000											
New client sales:												
Michelle	4,560	4,560	4,560	4,560	4,560	4,560	4,560	4,560	4,560	4,560	4,560	4,560
Heidi	4,560	4,560	4,560	4,560	4,560	4,560	4,560	4,560	4,560	4,560	4,560	4,560
Richard	4,560	4,560	4,560	4,560	4,560	4,560	4,560	4,560	4,560	4,560	4,560	4,560
New sales hire 1		0	4,560	4,560	4,560	4,560	4,560	4,560	4,560	4,560	4,560	4,560
New sales hire 2				4,560	4,560	4,560	4,560	4,560	4,560	4,560	4,560	4,560
New sales hire 3						4,560	4,560	4,560	4,560	4,560	4,560	4,560
Total	**13,680**	**13,680**	**18,240**	**22,800**	**22,800**	**22,800**	**27,360**	**27,360**	**27,360**	**27360**	**27,360**	**27,360**
Old client upgrades:												
Level one	18,750	18,750	18,750	31,250	31,250	31,250	37,500	37,500	37,500	37,500	37,500	37,500
Level two	0	0	0	0	0	0	24,750	24,750	24,750	41,250	41,250	41,250
Basic renewal	0	0	0	0	5,000	10,000	1,080	13,200	3,000	7,440	19,200	38,560
Sponsorship	0	0	0	0	0	0	0	0	20,000	20,000	20,000	20,000
Custom development	5,000	5,000	5,000	5,000	5,000	5,000	5,000	5,000	5,000	5,000	5,000	5,000
Overall total	**37,430**	**37,430**	**41,990**	**59,050**	**64,050**	**69,050**	**95,690**	**107,810**	**97,610**	**138,550**	**150,310**	**169,670**
Projected cash receipts	27,360	3,7430	37,430	48,240	59,050	59,050	64,050	104,609	95,689	116,061	114,110	138,780
Projected expenses	93,807	9,7824	96,962	107,121	105,019	97,620	102,280	111,989	109,706	125,380	138,174	138,658
Cash in bank January 1st	21,000											
Investment	400,000											
Monthly cash flow	333,553	−60,394	−59,532	−58,881	−45,969	−38,570	−38,230	−7,380	−14,017	−9,319	−24,064	122
Net cash position	**354,553**	**294,159**	**234,627**	**175,746**	**129,777**	**91,207**	**52,977**	**45,597**	**31,580**	**22,261**	**−1,803**	**−1,681**

receiving a $400,000 investment in January, it is not time to relax; the entrepreneur must immediately begin fundraising before running out of cash sometime later in the year.

Burn Rate and Runway: The burn rate is the rate at which a new company uses up its cash to finance overhead before generating positive cash flow from operations. In other words, it's a measure of negative cash flow. Burn rate is usually quoted in terms of cash spent per month. A related number is the *runway*, which is the number of months the company has before running out of money. In Figure 9.3, Acme Inc. has an average burn rate of about $35,000 per month and a runway of eleven months based on January's cash on hand (COH).

COH is the cash in all bank accounts *plus* expected cash from customers, suppliers, and other accounts. If the business intends to borrow to access cash (e.g., bank credit line or revolving fund) or receive cash from investors, you should include the amount of any interim payments due. Additional considerations include quarterly or semiannual payments, such as tax installments or advertising. Include a pro rata of these expenses in the calculation. The burn rate is determined by looking at the cash flow statement. The cash flow statement reports the *change* in the firm's cash position from one period to the next by accounting for the cash flows from operations, investment activities, and financing activities. Compared to the amount of cash a company has on hand, the burn rate gives investors a sense of how much time is left before the company runs out of cash—the runway.

Preparing Financial Projections

Entrepreneurs need to be able to plan operations and evaluate decisions using financial accounting information. Budgets, cash flow forecasts, and breakeven analyses are not only important management tools, but they are also usually required information for potential investors or lenders.

One of the first steps in any business is to establish a financial plan to measure financial performance. There are three widely used methods of measuring financial performance:

1. **Measuring Sales Volume.** The first perspective is to view performance in terms of sales, such as percentage of increased sales or new business. Many Internet companies measure success in terms of increased sales volume. However, if the expectation is that additional sales mean higher profits, which may not always be the case, certainly increasing sales is part of the financial plan. But to stop at that point is shortsighted.

2. **Measuring Profits.** The second perspective is to measure profits, that is, the difference between revenues and expenses as reported in the income statements. Sales must be profitable for the business to succeed. A firm can determine the profitability of either products or customers. It can also provide incentives to its sales force to encourage more profitable sales.

3. **Measuring Cash Generated.** Just because a company has an income statement that shows it is profitable does not necessarily mean it is generating cash. If the company uses accrual accounting, a sale is recognized when, as an example, a customer takes title to the product even though the cash may not be collected for some time. Accrual accounting does not recognize that cash may have been required to purchase materials, labor, and other resources in advance of the sale. Frequently, businesses, though profitable, run out of cash because when a sale occurs, the cash from the sale is not collected until a later date. It is important, especially for an undercapitalized company, to project cash flow and to note any periods where it will have inadequate cash, so the company can secure outside financing; otherwise, the company may be forced into bankruptcy. A major cause

of failure of start-up companies is poor cash management rather than a lack of customers willing to pay.

Preparing an Annual Budget

The annual budget presents a month-by-month projection of revenues and expenses over a one-year period. The budget is the foundation for projecting the other financial statements. It presents a more detailed accounting of expenses than what the income statement does. In a budget, expense details are usually grouped by department or functional area, such as general, administrative, and research and development. The details of a standard budget are divided into eleven major categories[2]:

1. **Sales.** The budget detail should include all or some of the following: sales by product line and by customer, geographical region, and goals for each sales representative.

2. **Cost of Goods Sold.** The detail should include both materials and shipping costs, as well as any allocated overhead if the company is a manufacturer. If sales are identified by product line, the cost of goods sold for each product line should be calculated to determine gross profit by product line.

3. **Gross Profit.** The detail should include, where possible, the gross profit by whatever categories the sales are classified (e.g., product line, geographical region). Gross profit is defined as sales less those costs directly incurred to achieve the sales (such as component pieces and assembly labor in the sale of a computer).[3]

4. **Operating Expenses.** The detail should classify expenses by research and development and SG&A. Within these categories, the detail should reflect the budgeted expenses by category, such as salary, benefits, rent, and telephone. Some expenses should be further categorized by such items as salary by employee and allocation of rent expenses.

5. **Operating Profit/Loss.** If operating expenses can be identified by sales category, an operating profit/loss for each sales category should be calculated.

6. **Other Income and Expenses.** This category usually includes interest expense, which should be detailed by each type of debt (e.g., leases for computers and copying equipment, lines of personal credit, and bank loans), and other income and expenses not related to the normal operations of the business, such as a legal settlement or loss due to fire.

7. **Pretax Income.** Income before taxes is calculated by taking operating profit and factoring in other income and expenses. It denotes the income that will be subject to corporate income tax.

8. **Income Taxes.** This is the management's estimate of what taxes will be owed on its earnings. Detail should reflect amounts owed for federal and state taxes.

9. **Net Income.** This is the amount available for dividends or reinvestment in the company.

10. **EBIT.** This is the earnings (net income) before interest expense, interest income, and income taxes. It measures the profitability of the company's current operations as if it had no debt or investments.

11. **EBITDA.** This is the earnings before interest expense, interest income, income taxes, depreciation, and amortization. It measures the profitability of a company's operations without the impact of its debt, investments, and long-term assets.

Preparing a Cash Flow Forecast

Reasons to Prepare a Cash Flow Forecast

As stated earlier, one of the major problems that start-up companies face is cash flow. Lack of cash is one reason that profitable companies fail. Cash managers, however, can anticipate temporary cash shortfalls and have sufficient time to arrange short-term loans if needed.

A cash flow forecast shows the amount of cash coming in (receivables) and cash going out (payables) during a certain month. The forecast also shows a bank loan officer (or the entrepreneur) what additional working capital, if any, the business may need. In addition, it provides evidence that there will be sufficient COH to make the interest payments on a revolving line of credit or to cover the shortfalls when payables exceed receivables.

Computer spreadsheet programs such as Microsoft Excel or any variety of full-faceted business software can be very useful for generating a cash flow worksheet. Reliable cash flow projections can bring a sense of order, well-being, and security to a business. The most important tool that owners and/or managers have available to control the financial liquidity of their businesses is the cash flow worksheet.

Getting Started

Step One: Consider Cash Flow Revenues Find a realistic basis for estimating sales each month. For a start-up company, the basis can be the average monthly sales of a similarly sized competitor's operation, which is operating in a similar market. Be sure to reduce your figures by a start-up year factor of about 50 percent a month for the start-up months. For an existing company, sales revenues from the same month in the previous year make a good basis for forecasting sales for that month of the succeeding year. For example, if the trend in the industry predicts a general growth of 4 percent for the next year, it will be entirely acceptable to show each month's projected sales at 4 percent higher than the actual sales of the previous year. Include notes to the cash flow to explain any unusual variations from the previous year's numbers.

Step Two: Consider Cash Flow Disbursements Project each of the various expense categories beginning with a summary for each month of the cash payments to suppliers as well as wages, rent, and equipment costs.

Each month shows only the cash that is expected to be paid that month to the suppliers. For example, if suppliers' invoices are paid in thirty days, the cash payoffs for January's purchases will be shown in February. If longer terms are obtained for trade credit, then cash outlays will appear two or even three months after the stock purchase has been received and invoiced.

An example of a different type of expense is insurance expenditure. Commercial insurance premiums may be $2,400 annually. Normally, this would be treated as a $200 monthly expense. However, it will not be recorded this way on the cash flow statement. Rather, the cash flow records show how it will be paid. If it is to be paid in two installments, $1,200 in January and $1,200 in July, then that is how it must be entered on the cash flow worksheet. The same principle applies to all cash flow expense items.

Step Three: Reconcile the Revenues and Disbursements The reconciliation section of the cash flow worksheet begins by showing the balance carried over from the previous month's operations. To this, the net inflows/outflows or current month's receipts and disbursements will be added. This adjusted balance will be carried forward to the first line of the reconciliation portion of the next month's entry to become the base to which the next month's cash flow activity will be added or subtracted.

Making the Best Use of the Cash Flow Statement

Cash flow statements must constantly be modified as new things are learned about the business and paying vendors. Since this cash flow forecast will be used regularly to compare each month's projected figures with each month's actual performance figures, it will be useful to have a second column for the actual performance figures alongside each of the "planned" columns in the cash flow worksheet. Look for significant discrepancies between the planned and actual figures.

For example, if the business' actual figures are failing to meet cash receipt projections over a three-month period, this is a signal that it is time to revise the year's projections. It may be necessary to apply to the bank to increase the upper limit of a revolving line of credit. Approaching the bank to increase an operating loan should be done well in advance of the date when the additional funds are required. Never leave cash inflow to chance.

Designing a Cash Flow Worksheet

A cash flow forecast can be presented in a variety of ways. The best way is to show only revenues from operations and the proceeds from sales.

The format should be a double-width column along the left side of the page for the account headings and two side-by-side vertical columns for each month of the year, beginning from the planned opening month (e.g., the first dual column might be labeled *April Planned* and *April Actual*). (See Tables 9.3 and 9.4 for examples.) From there, the cash flow worksheet is divided into three distinctive sections: The first section (at the top left portion of the worksheet, starting below and to the left of the month names) is headed *cash revenues* (or *cash in*). The second section, just below it, is headed *cash disbursements* (or *cash out*). The final section below is headed *reconciliation of cash flow*.

Table 9.4   Sample Cash Flow—Planned versus Actual

Item	April planned	April actual	May planned	May actual
Cash revenues/cash in	$22,000	$18,500	$24,000	$22,500
Cash disbursements/cash out				
Wages	$10,000	$11,500	$11,000	$12,000
Commissions	$2,000	$1,500	$2,000	$2,000
Rent	$3,500	$3,500	$3,500	$3,500
Equipment payment/computers	$12,000	$12,000	$12,000	$12,000
Total cash out	$27,500	$28,500	$28,500	$29,500
Reconciliation of cash flow				
Opening cash balance	$5,000	$5,000	($500)	($5,000)
Add: total cash revenues in	$22,000	$18,500	$24,000	$22,500
Deduct: total cash disbursements out	$27,500	$28,500	$28,500	$29,500
Closing cash balance (Carry forward to the next month)	($500)	($5,000)	($5,000)	($12,000)

Preparing a Breakeven Analysis

The breakeven technique is a decision-making model that helps the entrepreneur determine whether a certain volume of output will result in a profit or loss. The point at which breaking even occurs is the volume of output at which total revenues equal to total costs. The technique can be further used to answer the question, "What is the profit associated with a given level of output?" To use this technique, you need only to know the fixed costs of operation, variable costs of production, and price per unit.

Fixed costs are expenses that do not change in the short run, no matter the levels of production and sales. Variable costs differ according to the volume produced; they are usually expressed in terms of per-unit variable costs. Total costs are the sum of fixed and variable costs. Price is the total amount received from the sale of one unit of the product. Multiplying the price by the number of units sold yields the amount called revenue. Profit is what remains when the total costs are subtracted from the total revenues. The breakeven point is the level of output or sales at which total profit is zero—in other words, where total revenues equal to costs.

Example 1

Suppose the company spent $10,250 of variable material cost and $20,000 of variable labor cost in the month prior, when the company sold 10,000 units. How much variable cost should the company plan on for the current month if it is expected to increase by 20 percent? Assume costs change in proportion to changes in activity.

Note that although the total variable cost increases from $30,250 to $36,300 when production changes from 10,000 to 12,000 units, the variable cost per unit does not change. It remains $3.02 per unit. With a variable cost of $3.02 per unit, the variable cost increases by $6,050 (i.e., $3.025 × 2,000) when production increases by 2,000 units. This is illustrated in this table:

	Prior month		Current month	
Units	10,000	Per Unit	12,000	Per Unit
Variable costs				
Direct material	$10,250	$1.025	$12,300	$1.025
Direct labor	20,000	2.000	24,000	2.000
Total variable costs	$30,250	$3.025	$36,300	$3.025

Example 2

Suppose that in the prior month, the company incurred $22,500 of fixed costs, including $10,000 of depreciation, $7,500 of rent, and $5,000 of other fixed costs. If the company increases production to 12,000 units in the current month, the levels of depreciation, rent, and other fixed costs incurred should remain the same as when it was only 10,000 units. However, with fixed costs, the cost per unit does change when there are changes. When production increases, the constant amount of fixed cost is spread over a larger number of units. This drives down the fixed cost per unit. With an increase in production from 10,000 to 12,000 units, total fixed cost remains $22,500. Note, however, that fixed cost per unit decreases from $2.250 per unit to $1.874 per unit. This is illustrated in the next table:

Month	Prior month		Current month	
Units	10,000	Per unit	12,000	Per unit
Fixed costs				
Depreciation	$10,000	$1.000	$12,300	$0.833
Rent	7,500	0.750	7,500	0.625
Direct labor	5,000	0.500	5,000	0.416
Total variable costs	$22,500	$2.250	$22,500	$1.874

Using the Breakeven Formula

A quick way to calculate the breakeven point is to use the following formula. The price per unit (P) multiplied by the number of units sold (X) is equal to the fixed costs (F) plus the variable costs (V) multiplied by the number of units produced:

$$P(X) = F + V(X)$$

As an example, if fixed costs are $40,000, the variable costs per unit are $15, and the price per unit is $20, the breakeven point can be calculated by plugging these values into the equation:

$$20(X) = 40,000 + 15(X)$$
$$20(X) - 15(X) = 40,000$$
$$5(X) = 40,000$$
$$X = 80,000 \text{ units}$$

The breakeven point is one measurement of your business' "time to profitability." This measurement can be used in different ways during, for example, the start-up phase or the expansion phase. What if the business wants to expand its production? We can readily calculate the additional capital needed to fund this expansion, but a few very important questions must be asked: "Are the customers there and ready to buy, and what will it cost to capture them?" and "If I can capture these new customers, will it be profitable?" These questions can be answered by employing a second measurement of viability—the lifetime value of a customer (LVC).

The LVC is the net profit customers generate over their lifecycle. You should not spend more to get customers than their lifetime value, or you might lose money.

Example

When many businesses look at customers, they see the value of the first sale. If Jeffrey bought a product worth $99, many companies would see Jeffrey as being worth $99 in revenue. Then if, and only if, later on Jeffrey buys another product worth $99 will he be seen as worth $198 in revenue. Let's assume X Company looks at customer value this way.

A better approach would be to let the above model also reflect the element of the time value of money. The true value of Jeffrey is the value of all the purchases he has made plus the value of all the purchases he is likely to make in the future (discounted to the present). This is called the lifetime value. Do not be afraid to spend more than the profit on the first sale to acquire a customer, however. As long as your cash flow is healthy enough to support it, spend whatever you need to acquire that customer, as long as it is less than the average lifetime profit plus your current customer acquisition cost. Increasing the lifetime value of your customers comes down to three objectives: increasing the length of time a customer buys from you, increasing the amount customers spend on each purchase, and decreasing the time between purchases. Such techniques as loyalty programs, discount offers, recommendation software based on collaborative filtering as used by Amazon and others, and "sticky" web sites are used to increase the LVC.

Analyzing an Investment Decision

In evaluating whether to make an investment, for example, in a piece of expensive equipment, an entrepreneur must consider not only how much cash the company must give out but also whether the investment will earn a suitable return for the company. The *time value of money* approach recognizes that it is better to receive a dollar today than it is to receive a dollar next year or any other time in the future. This is because the dollar received today can be invested so at the end of the year, it amounts to more than a dollar. It also considers the decrease in the value of a dollar over time due to inflation.

In making an investment, a company invests money today in the hopes of receiving more money in the future. Obviously, a company would not invest money in a project unless it expected the total amount of funds received in the future to exceed the amount of the original investment. But by how much must the future cash flows exceed the original investment? Because money in the future is not equivalent to money today, we must develop a way of converting future dollars into their equivalent current, or present, value.

Net Present Value Method

The net present value (NPV) method is an alternative method for determining whether to make an investment. It is usually applied to later-stage investments or in making investment decisions within a company on whether to undertake a planned project or purchase a piece of machinery. To illustrate the method, let us evaluate an investment opportunity using the NPV method. A trucking company wants to purchase engine-testing equipment. The equipment will have a five-year life. Each year, it will save the company $2,000 in wasted current operation, and it will also reduce labor costs by $20,000. It is estimated that the engine equipment will require maintenance costs of $1,000 per year. The equipment costs $70,000, and it is expected to have a residual value of $5,000 at the end of five years. Management has determined that the rate of return required on any new initiative is 12 percent. Should the company invest in the new equipment?

The Steps Involved in the Net Present Value Method

The first step in using the NPV method is to identify the amount and time period of each cash flow associated with a potential investment. Investment projects have both cash inflows (which are positive) and cash outflows (which are negative).

The second step is to equate or discount the cash flows to their present values (PVs) using a required rate of return, which is the minimum return that the management wants to earn on investments.

The third and final step is to evaluate the NPV. The sum of the PVs of all cash flows (inflows and outflows) is the NPV of the investment. If the NPV is zero, the investment is generating a rate of return exactly equal to the required rate of return. Thus, the investment should be undertaken. If the NPV is positive, it should also be undertaken because it is generating a rate of return that is even greater than the required rate of return. Investment opportunities that have a negative NPV are not accepted because their rate of return is less than the required rate of return.

Refer to Table 11.2, which shows the PV for each year cash flow total. Consider first the $70,000 cash outflow created by purchase of the equipment. Note that the PV factor associated with the $70,000 purchase price is $10,000. Because this amount is going to be spent immediately, it is already expressed in terms of its PV. Now consider the cash flows in Year 1. In this year, the net cash inflow is $21,000. The PV factor for an amount received at the end of Year 1 using a 12 percent rate of return is 0.8929 (see Table 11.2 showing the PV of $1). Multiplying the PV factor by the cash inflow of $21,000 indicates that the PV of the net cash inflow in Year 1 is $18,751. The NPV of the investment in testing engine equipment is found by summing the PVs of the cash flows in each year. This amounts to $8,538. Because the NPV is positive, the company should go ahead with plans to purchase the equipment provided the cash is available.

Internal Rate of Return

An alternate way of analyzing internal investments is using the internal rate of return (IRR) method. IRR equates the PV of future cash flows to the investment outlay. If the IRR of a potential investment is equal to or greater than the required rate of return, the investment should be undertaken. Like NPV, it takes into account the time value of money.

Consider a simple case in which $100 is invested to yield $60 at the end of Year 1 and $60 at the end of Year 2. What rate of return equates the two-year $60 annuity to $100? Recall that when we performed PV analysis for previous annuities, we multiplied a PV factor by the annuity to solve for a PV. Because the $60 is to be received in each of two years, we use the annuity table to look up the IRR. In the row for two periods , we find a PV factor of 1.6681 (very close to 1.6667) in the column, for a 13 percent rate of return. Thus, the IRR on this investment is approximately 13 percent. If the required rate of return is 13 percent or less, the investment should be undertaken.

Taxes and Filing

The entrepreneur is required to withhold federal and state taxes from employees. Each month or quarter (depending on the size of the payroll), deposits or payments need to be made for funds withheld from wages. Generally, federal taxes, state taxes, Social Security, and Medicare are withheld from employees' salaries and are deposited later. If payments are late, high interest and penalties will be assessed. In addition to withholding taxes, the company may be required to pay a number of taxes, such as state and federal unemployment taxes, a matching FICA and Medicare tax, and other business taxes. These taxes will need to be part of the plan since they will affect cash flow and profits.

The federal and state governments also require the company to file end-of-year returns of the business, regardless of whether it earned a profit. A tax accountant should be consulted for advice on handling these expenses. The accountant can also assist in planning or budgeting appropriate funds to meet any of these expenses.[4]

The Stresses of Managing Money

The topics covered in the previous sections are, for the nonfinancially trained entrepreneur, rather complex. Yet, managing the money is one of the most important aspects in building a company securely. As early as possible in the activities of the company, you must engage a financial adviser that you can trust to help you set up the systems *before* it is too late. Not knowing precisely whether you have sufficient funds to execute your plans is one of the most stressful and danger-ous threats to a company. As we learned in Chapter 8, raising money whether from investors or corporate partners, or getting paid by customers, *always* takes longer than anticipated. Yet, your employees and suppliers expect to get paid promptly. Sound financial accounting systems and forecasting can help manage these stresses. Highly profitable and fast-growing companies can go bankrupt from not managing money carefully. As you can observe in the master-case, making sure that Neoforma had sufficient access to cash, particularly in the earliest stages, put enormous strain on the founders and their families.

Managing Human Resources—Introduction

Now that we have studied how to manage one key resource, money, we turn our attention to managing people. We started this book by emphasizing the importance of learning management skills to become a successful entrepreneur. One of the greatest challenges entrepreneurs face is the day-to-day management of human resources. A young company is not a set of independent activities, such as marketing and sales, money management, or product development, but a com-plex and changing interplay among all functions made more complicated by the individual aspi-rations and behaviors of creative, high-energy employees. The company is more like a fragile spider's web than a solid building supported on individual pillars. The next sections detail how to manage, on a daily basis, the ever-changing and unpredictable events met when hiring and moti-vating employees. Of course, we cannot foresee all the challenges that one might encounter, but by introducing some key concepts and tools, illustrated with examples, entrepreneurs can gain confidence to guide a team through the inevitable stormy seas.

Often an entrepreneur will feel overwhelmed by the seemingly unending and unpredictable problems she must face. But these must be tackled and the sooner, the better. Letting things slide by hiding will only make things worse. Prioritize them and deal with them promptly, seeking help from mentors if necessary. The stress to manage the business every day will be reduced by creating a supporting culture and employee expectations that in many cases will actually deflect problems before they develop. One of the most important leadership tasks, therefore, is to create an organization in which everyone understands the core values that underpin decision making.

Developing a Strong Corporate Culture

A successful entrepreneur must demonstrate strong leadership skills and the ability to engage everyone in pulling together toward a single defined goal. As we have seen, innovation, not only in products and services but also in the all-encompassing business model, is an important factor for success. Companies with seemingly identical financial assets, products, brand recognition, and the like may perform entirely differently—one is highly successful, while the other gradually declines. The successful one is judged as innovative, motivating, and exciting; the other, dull and unable to get its innovative ideas executed smoothly. Why is this? Michael Dell was not the first person to experiment with the direct model for computers. Why did he succeed where others had failed for more than twenty years? The ability to lead an organization on a mission where everyone is involved every day in moving toward clearly defined goals makes the difference between success and failure.

ROADMAP

IN ACTION

Two companies competing in the same markets with the same resources may have very different success rates. Learn how to develop a corporate culture to provide a key advantage.

Much research has been done in this area, and many business books have been written about the field. On one point at least, there seems to be a consensus: a culture supporting innovation requires leadership from the very top of an enterprise. It is never too early to start, and this section will provide guidance in shaping a winning culture for the company. Getting it right from the start is *much* easier than trying to change an old, unsuitable, and deeply embedded culture.

We have narrowed the leadership attributes down to ten factors, which should be practiced and demonstrated *in nearly everything that is done*. We have tried to make these factors largely independent of each other so areas can be identified to improve a management style without concerns that changes in one area will create other problems.

Table 9.5 provides definitions of these ten cultural attributes,[5] together with illustrative statements that might be casually overheard within a company. We suggest that you review these factors and ask yourself whether your leadership style exhibits these attributes. Imagine what you might hear if you could be a fly on the wall in the offices of a company you are leading. If you cannot imagine hearing these statements, start modifying your behavior and adopt a leadership style in which such factors would become more evident. This will help you build a flexible, innovative organization where everyone is valued and willing to contribute their utmost efforts daily.

It is easy to imagine successful entrepreneurs encouraging these behaviors. When you next see or read an interview with a successful entrepreneur, you will not find it difficult to imagine how she would have run her own organization along the lines of these attributes.

We now turn to three key functions of a founding entrepreneur: hiring, firing, and dealing with employee resignations. The way that you carry out these vital tasks will clearly demonstrate to the world what your personal and, hence, corporate values are.

ROADMAP

IN ACTION

Companies *are* the people and the way they work together. Find, keep, and motivate the best teams.

Table 9.5   Cultural Attributes of a Successful Innovative Company

Attribute	Definition	Example statements
Honesty	The degree to which each employee has total confidence in the integrity, ability, and good character of others, and the organization, regardless of role	"I trust the people I work with. I find it easy to be open and honest with people from other departments."
Alignment	The degree to which the interests and actions of each employee support the clearly stated and communicated key goals of the organization	"We have clear aims and objectives, which everyone understands. We build consensus around key objectives. We recognize and reward loyalty."
Risk	The degree to which the organization, employees, and managers take risks	"I am encouraged to experiment. We take calculated risks. We encourage trial and error."
Teams	The degree to which team performance is emphasized over individual performance	"We promote teamwork; it is the center of everything that we do. There are usually people from other departments in my team. We have both problem-solvers and 'out of the box' thinkers in our teams."
Empowerment	The degree to which each employee feels empowered by managers and the organization	"As a manager, I am expected to delegate. We have a 'no blame' culture. We allow staff to make decisions."
Freedom	The degree to which self-initiated and unofficial activities are tolerated and approved throughout the organization	"I am allowed to do my own thing. We encourage people to take initiative. We recognize the individual."
Support	The degree to which new ideas from all sources are welcomed and responded to promptly and appropriately	"We encourage fresh ideas and new approaches. We reward innovative individuals and teams."
Engagement	The degree to which all levels of the organization are engaged with the customer and the operations of the organization	"Management understands the operations of the company. I can share problems with my managers. I know why my job is important."
Stimuli	The degree to which it is understood that unrelated knowledge can impact product, service, and operations improvements	"I am encouraged to search externally for information and obtain data from many sources. We listen to suppliers' suggestions."
Communication	The degree to which there are both planned and random interactions between functions and divisions at all levels of the organization	"I am kept in the loop about how we are performing. We have excellent formal channels of communication. We use best practice knowledge transfer between departments. We actively manage our intellectual assets."

Finding and Hiring the Best People

It is easier to build an exciting, trusting, and supportive corporate culture if the people you hire have personal values that match. In a small company, one bad hire can do a lot of damage quickly. There is no room for misfits, so the hiring practices need to be excellent. Here are some guidelines that will help you in this important task:

NEOFORMA INC.

You've heard the buzz; now join an exciting, energetic company that is changing the way that lives are saved.

We are seeking ambitious self-starters to join our management team as we move into the next phase of our rapid growth. If you have strong leadership skills, are not afraid of hard work, and enjoy intense teamwork, then we may be the place to save you from boredom.

Specifically we are looking for:

- **Sales Leader:** Someone who can establish high-level relationships with the top suppliers and purchasers in the health-care industry and convince them that the Neoforma Web-based marketplace is *the* future in health-care supply chains. You must be passionate about improving access to affordable health care anywhere in the world and believe that the latest technology is the means to achieve this. Ability to succeed in adverse situations, create your own opportunities, and earn the respect of your fellows is more important than direct experience in the health sector—*if* you are a quick learner.

- **Operations Leader:** Neoforma is one of the fastest-growing companies in the Valley. Our management structure and organization is always trying to keep up with our unbounded acceleration. If you think you can grab a raging bull by the horns and tame it into a behaved beast, you may be the person to manage the company to its next platform of success and beyond. The ability to work with some of the most creative and passionate folks on earth, providing them the infrastructure that supports, not hinders, them in their quest for the best is more important than being a number-cruncher or form-filler. Show us how you can achieve the impossible and join us on the ride to fame and, yes, fortune.

Searching: Look for people in places where you might expect their personal values to match the company's culture. Personal networks and recommendations are best. However, be careful when bringing friends into the company. Of course, you are more likely to know their values and skills, but the personal relationship may cloud your judgment and send the wrong messages to the company, and if things don't work out, you will have a tough decision to make. For very key positions, it may pay to use a professional recruiter. These tend to be expensive, but remember, a bad hire can be fatal. If you advertise, choose the appropriate medium and make sure the copy clearly reflects the values of the company. Don't have a stodgy ad if you are seeking creative people who are interested in a real challenge. For example, above is part of an ad that Neoforma might have placed to attract two key hires.

These positions are not for the fainthearted. There are generous benefits for those who can stand above the rest, including a stock-option pool, free health care, and much more.

Neoforma is a privately held Internet marketplace that removes the inefficiencies from the health-care supply chain to bring quality and affordable health care to everyone. We are partnered with several major companies and funded by the best of Silicon Valley's VC firms.

For more information, call Wayne or Jeff at 1-800-NEOFORMA anytime.

Once you have a short list, you will need to interview the candidates. Do not treat this lightly; it is a difficult skill that will take time to learn. Hire for cultural fit if the other skills are good. Err toward culture if in doubt. Skills can largely be trained; values cannot. If in doubt, don't hire even if under pressure to fill a position. Table 9.6 provides a useful guide to the interview process.

You will probably need a second interview with someone you would like to make an offer to. A more relaxed environment, say, over dinner, may be more appropriate.

Ask for and check references. Then reach a decision as quickly as possible and make an offer. In a small company that is usually short of cash, it is customary to keep salaries as low as possible

Table 9.6 Interview Guide

Establish culture	The way you interview reflects on the culture of your company.
Have a two-way communication	Taking a new position is just as important a decision to the interviewee as to you. Create a level-dialogue playing field.
Be punctual	Stop whatever you are doing at least fifteen minutes before the scheduled time, review the applicant's background, and think through carefully what you are looking for and how you are going to learn about the fit. Be overly prepared. It is an insult to an applicant if you are late and you have not read their résumé and background.
Be prepared	If more than one person is going to interview the applicant, say you and your partner, then agree beforehand on the areas that each of you is going to explore. It is insulting to be asked the same questions twice and indicates poor internal communications.
Relax	Start the interview by talking about the company, your background, and what excites you about being there. This allows the interviewees to relax, so they can more easily open up later in the discussions.
Invite input	Ask them to tell you a little about themselves and what attracts them to the position. If they know little about the company and have done no research, it is a bad sign. A great candidate should tell you something about your company, competitors, and/or trends that are new to you.
Explore values	Most candidates rehearse standard questions such as "Tell me about something in your past work that you are really proud of." This will allow them to be expansive. Follow this up with a question such as "And what are you less proud of, what did you learn from it, and what would you do this time around?" Such questions highlight personal values (do they blame others, do they think they are perfect, etc.?). Other pairs of such questions are: "What do you most like doing when at work, and what do you least like doing?" and "If you go home at the end of the day feeling on top of the world, what might have happened, and if you feel really down at the end of the day . . .?"
Explore creativity	Pose a real challenge you are confronting. How would they tackle it?
Explore ambitions	"Where do you see yourself in three years?" "Would you like my job?" You should be hiring to grow, and you need to delegate.
Now ask me	Prompt their questions. These will be rehearsed, so use them to probe. "How many weeks' vacation?" or "What is the pay?" may indicate misaligned values for a small company.
Summarize	Be clear at the end of the interview what the process is and how quickly you will get back to them with an indication of the next steps.
Record	Write your notes on the meeting immediately after the interview and compare these as soon as possible with the other interviewers.
Act	If turning someone down, do it quickly, be honest, and preserve their self-esteem; create ambassadors, not enemies.

and enroll key employees in a stock-option program. (See the legal section of this chapter for further details.) Options provide the owner the right to purchase stock at an agreed-on price, usually current or even below current price, over some future time period, typically ten years. Any appreciation of the value of the company allows the option owners to exercise their rights and buy stock at a low price and sell it to a buyer at a much higher price. The company often retains the right to be first in line to buy these shares. Stock options then allow an employee to become a shareholder in the company over time. Indeed, investors usually welcome these programs, allotting a certain amount of shares to be in the "option pool" for motivating and retaining key people. These plans, if managed correctly, can be an excellent way of building a strong culture and team values. Typically, the pool will be between 10 and 20 percent of the total equity of the company. New hires do not get all of their options at once but earn them over a vesting period, say, three years, based on their performance. They may get some options issued as a joining bonus, but these can be taken back if they are fired within a certain time for nonperformance or real cause. In addition, certain positions, such as sales manager, may have part of the compensation based on measurable performance.

- Once you have reached an agreement on compensation and role, you will execute the appropriate legal documents (see this chapter's section on legal issues) and set up a starting date.

- Mentoring and assimilation into the culture is an important part of the hiring process. On the first day, make sure you take the time to introduce the new person to everyone and put a plan in place to train and support the new hire. Over the first few months, it is a good idea to set up a regular time each week, even if for only fifteen minutes, to review progress and to deal with any misunderstandings or emergent problems.

Dealing with Firing an Employee

Unfortunately, it is highly likely that you will have to terminate the employment of one or possibly several employees as the company evolves. The reasons for this decision fall into the categories described in Table 9.7.

All good companies mishire; all great companies correct their mistakes quickly. The way that someone is terminated is a strong indicator of the company's culture. Not taking appropriate action promptly is bad for the company *and* the employee. In all cases, terminating the employment of someone you have hired is one of the most difficult tasks for any manager. According to Paul Silvis of Restek Inc., "The day that you enjoy firing someone is the day you should leave the company." Here are some guidelines to help with this task:

Implement a system for catching problems early and working with the employee to correct them. If possible, it is better to help someone perform better, perhaps in a different role, than to have him or her leave and risk hiring an inappropriate new person. Give feedback early; provide timelines for improvement and keep to them. But when it is clear that it is not going to work out, make the decision to end the relationship.

Table 9.7   Reasons for Terminating an Employee

Funding shortage	The business is suffering a downturn, and you do not have sufficient funds to pay all salaries. This could be from failure to raise sufficient funding using the various sources described in Chapter 8, a loss of a major customer, a costly lawsuit, the emergence of a strong competitor putting pressure on prices, and so on. You have to trim down your payroll to match the lower income or cash reserves.
Change of direction	The company needs new skills and experience as it matures. Some of the early-stage employees are no longer needed and are to be replaced by new hires.
Performance	The employee is not performing adequately and needs to be replaced.
Disruptive	The employee is disruptive and possibly untrustworthy.
Cause	The employee has broken a contract or behaved illegally in some way.

- In all circumstances, it is vital that employees retain their self-esteem. Give the reasons for the decision, and provide guidance and help if possible. If the company can afford it, be generous in benefits to soften the financial impact on the employee.

- Do not allow anyone you have decided to fire to remain on the company's premises. Make the break clean. Make a final payment contingent on the former employee not causing any disruption or maligning the company to third parties.

- Remind the employee of his or her continuing contractual obligations to the company regarding the protection of confidential information. If a noncompete contract is in place, agree on the companies, customers, and/or others to which it applies. Do not be overly restrictive.

- Keep discussions professional and try to maintain a level of trust between you and the employee. Remember, it is to the company's benefit too if the former employees believe they were treated fairly and with respect. It is best if they tell others that the company has great values and that any grudge that may be there dissipates quickly.

Dealing with a Resignation

An entrepreneur will likely have to deal with a situation in which one of the most important employees decides to leave and join another company. First, try to convince him or her to stay, but do not enter into a bidding war with the new company regarding compensation. There may be some small adjustments that can be made, but being held hostage will lead to many problems later. Once it is clear that the employee cannot be convinced to stay, follow the steps outlined in Table 9.8, trying to make the process as open and as painless as possible for everyone involved.

ROADMAP

| IN ACTION | Understand how to analyze conflicts of interest and ethical dilemmas and deal with them clearly and fairly. |

Table 9.8   Handling a Resignation

Agree on procedures	If there is a notice period, then insist that this be respected and do not pay any outstanding benefits if it is not met.
Keep doors open	If the company would really like the employee to come back if things do not work out, then make this clear. Do not let a feeling of betrayal prevent rational thinking.
Celebrate	Have an office party to celebrate moving on and treat him or her like a star.
Conduct exit interview	Learn why he or she made the decision. Ask for honest feedback. Take this opportunity to explain ongoing legal obligations with regard to confidential information and any noncompete conditions. Ask the employee where he or she is going. If he or she declines to tell, indicate that he or she should inform his or her new employer of these obligations. If he or she does disclose this information, write to the new company, complimenting them on a good hire and stating the ongoing constraints that apply to the move.
Analyze	What triggered the move? A good leader knows if someone is unhappy *before* he or she starts looking around.

Conflicts of Interest and Business Ethics

We all find it difficult sometimes to know what is right and wrong, particularly when the boundaries are not clearly drawn and the situation is complex and perhaps ambiguous. There seems to be a gray area where we can tread a path that allows us to have it both ways. These situations abound in the business world, and it is important for you to have some guidelines that help you analyze such issues so they do not get out of control and begin to undermine your personal values and the culture of the company that you are building. Let us consider a case that could relate directly to this course.

Mini-Case: Teachers Helping Students outside of Class

In your entrepreneurship class, you and two team members come up with a great idea for a new business. In fact, the whole class and your professor urge you not to wait but to start a company and work on its development while still at college. You really value the experience of your teacher so you approach her and ask whether she would act as a mentor. Of course, you have no money to pay her, so you decide to offer 5 percent of the equity of the company to pay for the extra time that you are demanding. Should she accept this offer? Before jumping to a conclusion, consider some of the issues involved here:

- She is already being compensated by the college for performing her duties as a teacher of entrepreneurship.

- At the end of the course, she is required to give you a grade for your work. Will a deeper involvement in your project bias her in this regard?

- Will the extra work that she undertakes to help your team take away from efforts that should be devoted to other class members who are entitled to equal attention?

  - Does it make a difference if only two of the three team members want to participate in the new company? How would you handle this?

  - What policies are in place at the college to govern such issues? For example, it is common for professors to agree in their employment contract that any invention that they make while in employment will be the property of the college. What if he or she invents something valuable while in the role of company mentor? Who owns it? Some colleges allow professors to consult for up to one day a week for extra compensation. Would this case come under this arrangement? Does it make a difference if the class has ended and grades have been submitted, or must the students in the team have graduated fully from college?

As you see, the picture is rather more complicated than it first appears. There are a number of conflicts of interest between different groups of stakeholders—those with some interest in any decision that is made. These include teammates, classmates, the college, and individual teachers. There may be contractual agreements in place, and college policies that must be taken into account. For example, professors at Columbia University may be compensated to help students in company formation once course grades are entered, whereas at Penn State, the students must have graduated from the university.

Let us now take this a step further. As before, you have decided with your teammates to actually form a company to take your class idea further, and you indicate this to your teacher. She then asks to see you after class and indicates that she can help you but only if you are willing to allot 10 percent of the shares of the company to her. You would certainly value the input, and you are worried that if you refuse, then this might adversely affect your grade. How do you respond?

The case has taken on a rather more serious tone. Whereas before you have to decide how to avoid conflicts of interest, now you are faced with an ethical issue in addition. You have the gut feeling that this is not appropriate, but you are caught in a dilemma. If you flatly turn down the offer, then you may suffer repercussions; if you accept, then you may be breaking rules and even existing contracts. You like the teacher and feel that she, herself, may not be aware of all the issues that come into play in this situation.

This is the time to invoke the full disclosure principle.[6] If you sense that everything is not in order, then you must disclose it fully and honestly to *all* the key stakeholders and ask for their comments. Failure to fully disclose makes you a party to unethical behavior. So in this case, you could raise your concerns with the teacher and ask her for the mechanisms for full disclosure of the situation. If she understands the issues, she is likely to withdraw her offer and help you anyway. If not, she can take it to the appropriate authority in your college, perhaps the dean, who will clarify the situation and make sure that the conflicts of interest are resolved.

The Three Principles to Resolve Ethical Dilemmas

1. **The Gut-feel Test.** We all know the feeling when we sense something is wrong about an action. If you get this feeling, then most likely there is something amiss. Don't ignore it; stop and consider the issues surrounding the problem. Ask yourself, "If one of the stakeholders finds out later what happened, could this be embarrassing or worse, create serious problems, even legal repercussions?"

2. **Analysis of Conflicts.** As we saw in the case earlier, things are not quite as they seem at first blush. There can be multiple levels of interests from a range of stakeholders. You must find out who they are, what their interests are, how they are governed, what rules apply, and what contracts may be in place. Only when you have these data can you actually draw out the lines between the stakeholders and expose all the real or potential conflicts of interests.

3. **Full Disclosure.** Once you understand the complexities of the conflicts of interest together with the ethical and legal issues, you will be able to determine whom you should inform about the situation and its potential outcomes. This is called full disclosure. You should not edit or color your disclosures; overdisclosing is far better than restricting information. Let the interested recipients tell you what the problems might be.

With these three principles, you will find it easier to spot and resolve ethical issues quickly.

Legal Issues

Unfortunately, you will not be able to grow your company without dealing with some basic legal issues. Indeed, failure to manage the legal affairs of your company can result in serious consequences. In Chapter 7, we dealt with the formation of the company, and in Chapter 13, you can learn about the management of your intellectual property; here we address the day-to-day management of your legal affairs. You should incorporate these procedures from the first day. Correcting mistakes after they occur may be costly or even impossible. We provide templates for legal documents in the appendix to this chapter which can be found on the book's web site. (In each case, NUCO is the name used for the issuing company.) These will enable you to become acquainted with the way that these documents are framed. However, you should always check with the company's legal counsel before issuing and signing anything. Laws and their interpretations change over time and will certainly differ depending on location. Here we describe the basic legal documents that you will require for any company.

ROADMAP

IN ACTION

The best employment agreement serves as an incentive for the employee and provides protection against the employee damaging the company subsequent to employment. Incentives may include stock options, payments for inventions, or bonuses.

- **Employment Agreement.** It is important to establish employment agreements for your management team and key employees in the company. The agreement describes the obligations of the employer and employee and varies widely among companies and even among employees within the same company. Usual provisions included in the agreement should emphasize the following employee issues:

- They cannot disclose any confidential information about the company either during or subsequent to employment.

- They must return all materials that belong to the company at the time of termination of employment.

- They cannot engage in a new business during the period of employment without the consent of the employer.

- They will not compete with the company for a period of time subsequent to employment.

- They will disclose and assign to the company all inventions during their employment.

Employment agreements can present an element of coercion. The employee may assume that because he or she is given the agreement for signature, the employee has little choice but to sign it or seek employment elsewhere. If the employer tries to enforce an agreement, the sympathies of the court usually lie with the employee. Seldom will a court enforce an employment agreement if it deprives the ex-employee of the means of making a living. For these reasons, employment agreements should be drafted, read, and agreed to prior to actual employment.

- **Consulting Agreement.** You are likely to use consultants for certain tasks as you build the company. These should be subject to a work-for-hire agreement. Without such an agreement, the work that consultants do would become their property. For example, you might be paying for people to design a web site. Without such an agreement, they would own the site and its content.

- **Separation Agreement.** It is important when someone leaves the company, voluntarily or otherwise, that the conditions and expectations of their leaving be clearly laid out and understood. These agreements usually contain a "general release" protecting your company against later legal actions.

- **Sales and Marketing Agreement.** A growing company may not have the resources to reach all markets simultaneously, and entering into an agreement with a marketing partner is a common alternative. It is important to specify the responsibilities of both parties. The example we provide relates to a U.S. firm partnering with a Canadian company.

- **Confidentiality Agreement.** You will need to enter into exploratory discussions with third parties before any definitive agreement is made. To protect the disclosures that you make, you must execute this agreement. These can be one-way or perhaps two-way agreements if there is a need for both parties to protect against disclosure of confidential information.[7]

Setting Up Stock-Option Agreements

Many young companies provide added incentives for keeping key employees by providing an ownership or equity interest in the company. This is usually in the form of common stock or options to acquire common stock. Companies should consider establishing an incentive stock-option plan under which selected employees receive options to purchase stock in the company. Incentive stock options (ISOs) are restricted to employees and are not available to others. The ISO and nonqualified stock option (NQSO) are used in the following manners:

1. **ISO** is a type of stock that qualifies for preferential tax treatment provided that the option holder holds the stock for one year and one day after exercise and two years after the date of any renewal, whichever is later. Under current tax laws, the employee pays no taxes at exercise and will be subject to capital gains tax if the holding requirements are met. Exercise of ISOs may subject the employee to alternative minimum tax (AMT). The company does not receive a tax deduction for this form of compensation. ISOs are for the holder only and cannot be transferred.[8]

2. **NQSO** is an option that does not receive preferential tax treatment and is considered the equivalent of cash compensation. The option holders pay payroll and income taxes at the time of exercise and, if they hold on to the stock, are subject to capital gains treatment when the stock is sold. The company takes a tax deduction on the difference between the grant price and the fair market value upon exercise.[9]

Any plan must be adopted by the board of directors and approved by the stockholders of the company and can be effective from the next annual shareholders' meeting or within twelve months.

The plan must state the aggregate number of shares being set aside for the options and the employees or class of employees (e.g., "key employees") for which options will be made available. The option cannot be transferable.[10] When setting up a plan, you should consult with an expert in the field as there are complex legal and tax issues to consider.[11,12]

SUMMARY

The two most important resources for an entrepreneur to manage are cash and people. He or she should examine financial statements, including the balance sheet, P&L statement, and cash flows, which can help analyze and monitor overall performance. These important accounting statements show the company's financial picture either at a given time or for a given period. The balance sheet itemizes assets, liabilities, and shareholders' equity at a given time and gives a detailed picture of where a company stands. The income statement is an itemized statement of revenues and expenses during an accounting period. It basically shows revenues minus expenditures, resulting in income or loss. The cash flow statement is an itemized statement of receipts and expenditures, resulting in increased or decreased cash. Both the income and cash flow statements uncover important trends and overall performance, giving management direction as to what adjustments need to be made to the business' operations. Entrepreneurs must also value different groups of customers to determine how much should be invested in procuring and managing them over time. Financial management is a key attribute of an entrepreneur and one that is often underestimated. Too many good companies fail because the founding entrepreneur was not adequately concerned with managing cash, assets, and profits. Budgets, projections of cash flow, and breakeven analyses must be monitored on a regular basis and evaluated when changes occur.

A company is not an assembly of individual functions, such as marketing or human resources, to which you can turn your attention when needed, but a complex and ever-changing interplay between many activities that continually combine in new ways. Just as a conductor guides an orchestra through a symphony, an entrepreneur must lead and impose personal values on the organization every day. In this way, a collective culture can be created, one that is able to deal with adversity and respond to new opportunities without the need for micromanagement.

Guidelines and procedures for hiring, firing, and dealing with conflicts of interest and ethical transgressions all help to build and sustain such a culture. These must be underpinned with a basic set of legal documents and contracts that provide a firm foundation on which to build. Without these basic financial and human resource management structures in place, it is too easy for things to get out of control and overly stressful, leading to chaos.

STUDY QUESTIONS

Q.1 What financial measurements should be prepared to measure company performance?

Q.2 What are the categories and steps in preparing a financial budget?

Q.3 What are the major categories and steps in preparing the projected cash activity?

Q.4 Describe the breakeven technique in the decision-making model to determine profit and loss.

Q.5 Why are some customers more valuable than others? How can these differences be measured and used for decision making?

Q.6 Why is building a corporate culture to match a company's mission important?

Q.7 Select six leadership attributes that you feel are the most important when building a strong culture. Why?

Q.8 Name three important factors that you must take into account when hiring key people.

Q.9 Name three important factors that you must take into account when firing key people.

Q.10 How do you treat someone who resigns from the company?

Q.11 What are the three principles for resolving conflicts of interest and ethical problems?

Q.12 What are the five basic legal agreements needed for day-to-day management? What are the key features of each?

Q.13 What is a qualified stock-option plan, and what is its purpose?

EXERCISES

9.1 List four items that entrepreneurial companies should show on a balance sheet.

9.2 Prepare a breakeven analysis for the following example: David Falk, the vice president of business development, wants to determine the breakeven point for the company's gift card product. The analysis will help David determine the possibility of incurring a loss for the product. The company will sell the product for $200 per customer. Variable costs are estimated to be $185,000 per month, composed of $95,000 for producing the product and $65,000 for fixed selling and administrative costs. How many units must be sold to break even?

9.3 Calculate the pretax income and the return on investment for a company with the sales and expenses as follows:

Sales	$40,000,000
Cost of goods sold	$25,000,000
Selling and administrative expense	$5,000,000
Interest expense	$1,000,000
Income taxes	$5,850,000
Shareholders' equity	$800,000

Comment on the company's profitability.

9.4 Joe Flicek of SIP Commendations is considering investing $79,137 in a computer storage room. He will rent space to customers and expects to generate $22,500 annually net after miscellaneous expenses other than depreciation. (a) Assuming Joe wishes to evaluate the project with a five-year time horizon, what is the internal rate of return on the investment, ignoring any taxes to be paid? (b) Should Joe make the investment if his required rate of return is 12 percent?

Master-Case Exercises:

Financing and Stresses. If you have not yet read the appendix for the master-case in Chapter 1 on the book's web site, do so. Then go to the book's web site, read the diary entries Months 0, 14, 15, 18, 21, 23, 26, 36, 42, and 46 and Four Years Later, and view the video selection, "Balance Your Business or Your Life."

Either as a team or individually, produce a presentation on each of the following questions for class discussion. Only one or two slides for each are required to state the key points, which will then be expanded in the class.

Master-Case Q 1: List the sources of funds that Wayne and Jeff used to finance Neoforma. How long after the anticipated date was each of these funds actually received? Why was this in each case?

Master-Case Q 2: Anni and Wayne started out with a dream that nearly became a nightmare for their family. Chart the key stressful events in the story of Neoforma that threatened their relationship. What lessons can be learned from these events regarding how to balance work passion and personal lives?

    Corporate Culture. If you have not yet read the appendix for the master-case in Chapter 1 on the book's web site, do so. Then go to the book's web site, read the diary entries Months 4, 27, 29, 31, 37, 39, 40, 50, and 52, and view the video selection, "Culture: Invisible, Intangible, Important."

    Either as a team or individually, produce presentations to address the following questions for class discussion (refer to Table 9.5 as needed).

Master-Case Q 3: How do you maintain a vibrant and successful culture as the company grows rapidly and the founders have no time to engender new employees with the value systems that they consider important? Consider the following attributes often referred to by the managers in Neoforma: honesty, freedom, and empowerment. Which attributes were most prevalent earlier in the company, and which became important later?

Master-Case Q 4: A great corporate culture seems to just happen; forcing it is counterproductive. How was the unique culture of Neoforma developed? Despite coming under stress due to fast growth and mistakes in hiring, it seemed to survive and be almost indestructible. Why do you think this was? What other culture threats can you name? Put them in the order of most potential culture damage, and argue why you chose this order. If you were a manager, what would you do to embed a great culture and militate against its erosion?

Master-Case Q 5: Companies use acquisitions to accelerate growth and gain skills. Yet, acquisitions rarely meet their expectations because of culture clash. Was Linda right in not selling her company to Neoforma? After all, Neoforma survived, and Galatia did not. Why did she choose to remain separate? Did Neoforma make the right decisions regarding GAR and Pharos? Why?

Master-Case Q 6: Using the culture table, Table 9.5, compare Varian and Neoforma.

    Conflicts of Interest and Ethics. If you have not yet read the appendix in Chapter 1, do so. Then go to the book's web site, read the diary entries Months 18, 25, 26, 26–36, 42, and 46, and view the video selection, "VCs & Investment Bankers: When the Stakes Get High, Ethics Get Low."

    Either as a team or individually, produce short presentations to address the following questions for class discussion.

Master-Case Q 7: Do you consider Bret's behavior reasonable? Ethical? Defensible? Argue for your position. If you were Wayne in this situation, what steps would you have taken to resolve the conflicts? (*Hint:* Refer to the three principles in the section on ethical dilemmas.)

Master-Case Q 8: An IPO is often priced low by the underwriters so there is an immediate rise in value even though this hurts the company. When Neoforma went public, the stock price went from $13 to $52 on the first day of trading. Why did Merrill Lynch price the offering so far below the market demand price? This resulted in less money going into the company and the internal shareholders suffering more dilution. Discuss the ethical issues concerning this "bounce" in the first day of trading.

    Hiring and Firing. If you have not yet read the appendix for the master-case in Chapter 1 on the book's web site, do so. Then go to the book's web site, read the diary entries Months 3, 5, 27, 31, 32, 39, 40, and 50, and view the video selection, "Hiring and Firing: Using Your Head and Trusting Your Gut."

    Either as a team or individually, produce short presentations to address the following questions for class discussion.

Master-Case Q 9: Is it better to hire someone you know than a total stranger? How do you avoid the Cassandra problem when you are under pressure to hire quickly?

Master-Case Q 10: Imagine you are Jeff and Wayne. Create an interview guideline for *each* founder separately for hiring key people. What will each explore? How will you cross-check? How do you test for tenacity, honesty, values, and innovativeness?

Master-Case Q 11: (Paradox) You hired all good people, so how do you choose which to fire? Do you think Wayne did the right thing regarding the firing of Thalia over Sheila? Give your reasons.

INTERACTIVE LEARNING ON THE WEB

Test your knowledge of the chapter using the book's interactive web site.

ADDITIONAL RESOURCES

- **Dun and Bradstreet Information Services**, www.dnb .com

- **Hoover's Corporate Information**, www.hoovers.com

- **NASDAQ**, www.nasdaq.com

- **Small Business Advisor**, http://www.isquare.com/ prologue.htm

- **ThomasNet Register of American Manufacturers**, www.thomasnet.com

APPENDIX LEGAL DOCUMENT TEMPLATES (ONLINE)

ENDNOTES

1. This profile was developed from several interviews with Paul Silvis as well as from presentations he made to classes at Penn State.

2. See Robert C. Higgins, *Analysis for Financial Management*, 3rd ed. (South Bend, IN: Irwin Press, 1992), 346 ff.

3. Gross profit as a percentage of sales is an excellent indicator of a company's ability to compete profitably. A sustainable gross margin of 60 percent implies that product or service pricing is not under pressure and the company has a strong competitive position and, in the long term, can be highly cash positive. Many venture capitalists will not consider investing in companies that cannot generate this margin after three years of operations.

4. For a more detailed analysis, see Stephen C. Blowers, Peter H. Griffiths and Thomas L. Milan, *The Ernst and Young Guide to the IPO Value Journey* (New York: John Wiley & Sons, 1999), 132 ff.

5. See Nimal Pal and Daniel Panteleo, eds., *The Agile Enterprise* (New York, NY: Springer Press, 2005), 118 ff.

6. The term *full disclosure* is defined as "the ethic to tell the full truth about any matter that the other party should know to make a valid decision." This is a legal requirement in many cases, such as when seeking investors or lenders. It is considered fraudulent if you do not disclose *all* relevant information prior to taking funds from investors or borrowing money from a bank. The concept also applies when analyzing conflict-of-interest issues and ethical dilemmas where all stakeholders should receive full disclosure of all the facts in order to seek a just resolution.

7. The sample nondisclosure agreement provided by the Richards and O'Neill law firm, New York, 2001.

8. Kurt Hoffman (consultant in Financial Services), interview, Princeton, NJ, August 2004.

9. David Cohen (CPA, Jacques M. Levy and Co.), interview, New York, June 2003.

10. See J. L. Nesheim, *High-tech Start-up* (New York, NY: The Free Press, 2000), 59–60.

11. See Dwight B. Crane and Indra Reinberg, "Employee Stock Ownership Plans (ESOPs) and Phantom Stock Plans," *Harvard Business Review* (November 2000): 5–6.

12. See Brian Hall, Carleen Madigan, and Norm Wassman, "Stock Options at Virtuanet.Com, a Case Study," *Harvard Business Review* (November 2000). This paper describes the issues that founders of a high-tech firm face in negotiating equity and stock options.

Communicating the Opportunity 10

"I have made this letter a rather long one, only because I didn't have the leisure to make it shorter."

Blaise Pascal, Mathematician, Inventor, and Philosopher

OBJECTIVES

- Understand how to target the business to investors, lenders, or purchasers.
- Prepare oral and visual presentations to external stakeholders.
- Learn the investor evaluation process.
- Prepare the teaser.
- Prepare the opportunity presentation.
- Prepare a video.

CHAPTER OUTLINE

Introduction

No idea or company, however good it is, will attract resources to help it grow or attract purchasers unless the entrepreneur can communicate the opportunity clearly to potential stakeholders whether they are investors, bank loan officers, corporate partners, potential acquirers, suppliers, or employees. (In this chapter, we use the term *investors* broadly to encompass all external stakeholders that may provide resources to help the company grow or eventually acquire it.) Communication skills are, therefore, key to successful entrepreneurship. This chapter will help you gain those skills.

These skills are necessary any time you present your company to outsiders. In this chapter, we will largely focus on locating and engaging with potential investors to fund the company as it grows. In the final chapter, we will show how these skills can be extended to the case where the company is executing an exit for its shareholders.

ROADMAP

IN ACTION

Entrepreneurs need several prepared documents and verbal presentations to communicate their opportunities to interested parties. These are an executive summary, a short-form or full business plan, and both a short and long presentation. All of these must be adjusted to take into account the specific needs of the audience.

Any communication, whether verbal or written, must be customized to the target audience. One message does not fit all. For example, when seeking a bank loan, entrepreneurs have to show how the risk is minimized for the lender, whereas, if talking with a venture capitalist, the entrepreneur will need to show how the business fits with the VC's investment profile, how it can grow quickly, and how an "exit" for the investors will be created. When approaching a potential acquirer, it is necessary to show the value that can be created by the purchase.

Any commitment from an investor will not come quickly. There has to be an exploratory period during which the two parties get to know one another. This "dating" period requires different levels and types of communications as the process proceeds. The first communication should be in the form of an executive summary, or "teaser." The purpose of this short document is merely to gain the attention of the targeted audience. Most investors receive a torrent of business plans and teasers, so it is important that their attention be grabbed quickly.

The verbal equivalent of the teaser is the so-called elevator pitch. The name describes an imaginary situation in which an entrepreneur finds herself by chance in an elevator with a potential investor/lender and has his/her ear for just the length of the elevator ride. In the minute or two available, a crisp, compelling message that engages the recipient must be conveyed.

If the teaser is successful, it is likely that a business plan will be requested for review. If this plan continues to appeal to the investor, the next step is usually an invitation to give a full "investors'" presentation.[1]

Think of these stages of more and more engagement with potential investors as similar to trout fishing. A good angler will choose her bait carefully to match what she thinks the fish are feeding on at that moment. After setting the appropriate bait and the fish takes it, the angler plays the fish, gradually bringing it closer and making sure that nothing happens to allow the fish to get off the hook.

Furthermore, it is becoming more usual to create a short promotional video, either for showing to potential investors or seeking crowdfunding (see Chapter 5 for further details on these methods). We include a short section on tips for making such a video in this chapter.

Chapter 6 has already shown you how to produce a winning business plan. Now is the time to get it in front of the right stakeholders and convince them to participate in your venture. In this chapter, you will learn how to approach stakeholders, prepare the appropriate documents and presentations, and move toward closing a negotiation.

Profile: Craig Bandes—Matching Presentations to Investors

A graduate of Babson College, Craig Bandes now has more than nineteen years of experience as a CEO, entrepreneur, venture investor, and investment banker, building companies in the defense, telecommunications, and professional service industries with particular emphasis on raising capital and creating exit strategies.[2] Bandes has negotiated more than $300 million in financial transactions and completed strategic partnerships in the United States, Asia, and Europe. According to Craig, "the key ingredient in raising capital is to clearly and effectively communicate the investment opportunity. I've found that the biggest mistakes most often made in an investor presentation are spending too much time on the 'widget' rather than the market strategy and not tailoring comments to the audience and what drives their ultimate investment decision." For example, when Craig was the chief financial officer for a telecommunications start-up that needed to raise at least $200 million to fund the expansion of both a nationwide network and an extensive sales force, he used a two-pronged strategy. He first approached strategic investors, both telecom equipment manufacturers and fiber cable operators, and followed that by contacting private equity sources. The providers of the equipment and the network operators had a completely different set of objectives from the private equity funds, so two very different pitches were developed. The equipment manufacturers and network providers that were targeted were asked to lend the company about $150 million to purchase hardware and network bandwidth from them in the future and invest an additional $25–$50 million in equity for working capital. Rather than a pure return on their investments, what these corporations cared about was the ability for the company to pay back the debt and to buy more equipment and network resources in the future as the company grew. The presentation to them primarily focused on equipment purchase schedules and increasing bandwidth needs. The targeted private equity groups that provided the balance of the capital cared solely about how they would gain a 30 percent rate of return on their capital and the timing of when they would realize that return. In these presentations, Craig focused on revenue growth rates, when EBITDA was expected to turn positive, comparable company valuations, and expected exit strategies for them.

He knew that the strategic investors would give the private equity groups confidence because they were perceived as the experts and that the corporate investors would view the private equity fund managers as validating their assessment, both of which worked in tandem to enhance the value of the company and encourage two types of investors with very different agendas to work together.

Craig's most recent venture is as CEO of Pixelligent Technologies Inc. He is funding this company using a combination of government grants, corporate partnerships, and a recent venture capital funding of $3.8MM (see http://www.pixelligent.com/).

Locating Investors

Once the entrepreneur has prepared a business plan, a presentation that contains ten to sixteen slides (discussed in more detail later in this chapter), and an executive summary, it is time to contact potential stakeholders to see if they may be interested in funding the business. (Chapter 11 deals with the specific case of locating acquirers.) Investors are busy people, and it is important that the entrepreneur contact only those who are likely to be interested in the opportunity. This requires some research before making an approach. One way to do this is to speak with other entrepreneurs in similar business fields who have been successful in getting investment, closing loans, or entering into a corporate partnership. The Internet is valuable here in locating and learning about the interests for different investors and finding the correct contacts.

To locate active investors, one should first look within the industry where the business is focused. Investors prefer involvement in a business they know, which will require less explaining or selling the concept. Locating the right investor can add value in a number of ways besides investment. This can include identifying and helping to recruit key management team members and providing key industry and professional contacts. The investor can serve as a mentor, confidant, and sounding board for ideas and plans to solve problems. In some cases the investor helps to establish relationships with key customers, suppliers, and potential corporate partners.

Another less obvious alternative to finding active investors is to pursue passive, or arm's length, investors, who will have little or no involvement in the business. This could include companies that wish to diversify or groups of investors formed for tax advantage reasons. In general, this route is not recommended. "Smart money" brings not only funding but knowledge, help, and contacts, and is far more valuable. Entrepreneurs, however, may feel that hands-off funding is preferable as they won't have interference in their businesses while growing them. This thinking is misguided, and finding sources of funding coupled with real help is *always* the best choice.

The initial conversation with the investor is to present a summary of the plan describing the business and the type of financing needed. The entrepreneur should also prepare a list of potential investors and phone them for an interview. If an investor asks for a business plan, one should explain that a meeting is preferred before handing over a formal plan. Investors invest in people, not plans. The entrepreneur should arrange to send the business plan or preferably only the executive summary prior to a face-to-face meeting. Send the plan or summary with a cover letter. One should try to be as specific as possible in the letter and refer to matters discussed in the initial telephone conversation, so the letter is not perceived as a mass mailing. A follow-up call in two weeks should be made to answer any questions.

ROADMAP

IN ACTION	Entrepreneurs should use a "rifle" rather than a "shotgun" strategy for engaging with potential investors. Imagine that there are only twenty *people* (not just organizations) who might have interest. Research them and contact them after knowing precisely what is likely to interest them. Blasting your idea out to everyone wastes time and devalues your opportunity.

Here are some tips on finding the right contact:

- If an entrepreneur thinks that the opportunity is best fitted to an angel investor or angel investor group, go to any local entrepreneurs' networking function. Often angels go to these meetings to seek out new deals. Many local angel groups now have web sites where your opportunities can be listed; these sites can easily be found by searching the web. There may be someone in the local community who has been successful in a similar field whether in retail, software, construction, or technology. He or she may be investing privately in new opportunities or know individuals who are; they are often willing to make introductions. Introductions can also be made through accountants and lawyers. As entrepreneurs build their businesses, they will need such services, and it is wise to choose professional service firms that are able to access strong local networks. Chapter 8 lists several useful places to enter the angel networks.

- If the target is a VC firm, then it is important to narrow down the targets to just a few. VC firms are usually very focused and do not look at opportunities that do not pass through their tight filters, which usually have the following important categories:

  - *Stage of company.* Taking an early-stage company opportunity to an expansion-stage investor is futile.
  - *Domain or field.* Many VCs invest in only businesses that sell to other businesses (B2B); others focus on retail opportunities. Others may prefer technology-based businesses, software companies, or franchises.
  - *Size of investment.* If $250,000 is sought, there is no point in talking to a firm that invests only upward of $5 million.
  - *Location.* The majority of VC firms have a bias to invest in a local region, which they can reach within, say, a three-hour drive.
  - *Stage of fund.* VCs usually have a ten-year horizon to invest their money. If it is getting near to the end of their fund life, it is unlikely that they will invest in a biotech firm that will take seven to eight years to mature to an exit.

A match can be found by first accessing "Pratt's Guide to Venture Capital" online or at a local library.[4] Once a short list of potential VC firms has been made, each can be researched in greater detail by visiting its web site. VC firms are looking for matching deals and, therefore, are usually very clear in their communications as to what they are looking for. In addition, their past investments (portfolio) will be listed on their web sites. Reviewing these will determine whether there is a good fit with your company. Calling the CEOs of the portfolio companies most closely aligned with your new opportunity can provide more insight and may lead to a personal introduction, which always helps. Venture capitalists are much more likely to review an opportunity that is referred to them by someone already in their network rather than looking at unsolicited business plans.

> "If an entrepreneur cannot locate me and send me a compelling executive summary that is a close fit to what I am looking for, then they have already failed the first test of being an entrepreneur![3]"
>
> Bill Frezza
> *venture partner,*
> *Adams Capital*
> *Management (www*
> *.acm.com)*

ROADMAP

IN ACTION   If a small business loan is sought, then there are probably several local banks that seek such opportunities. Calling them and asking if they have a small business loan officer can start the conversation. They may participate in the federal lending programs to support small companies.

Preparing a Teaser

Once a target has been identified and researched, the bait needs to be set. This requires a well-written executive summary, or "teaser." This document must be impeccable in its appearance, short and to the point clear in both the description of the opportunity and what benefit is offered to the targeted investor or partner. Writing a compelling teaser can take an experienced entrepreneur a full day. Do not underestimate either the importance or difficulty of this task.

Writing a clear, concise, elegant, and engaging short document is extremely difficult and requires considerable practice. Although everyone has a personal approach to writing, we find that it is best to create a draft rather quickly and then wait a couple of days before going back and reading it critically *as if you were the recipient*. Edit this document to a second draft and again wait. This is a good time to have someone not closely involved in the company, but with business experience, read the document and provide criticisms and suggestions for improvement. It must flow logically and smoothly; every sentence should be carefully constructed and grammatically correct; there must be no typos or spelling errors. Avoid repetition, long sentences, jargon, and short forms. Avoid "woolly" words, such as *hopefully*, *maybe*, and *we believe*, and the conditional verb forms, such as *should, might, could*, and so forth. Keep away from overused hyperbole such as *major breakthrough, revolutionary, cutting edge, best-of-breed*, and so on. Finally, go through the document with a fine-tooth comb and be ruthless in removing every word that is not absolutely necessary and could be seen as padding. It is usually possible to remove 30–50 percent of the text between the first draft and the final versions.

Mini-Case: LeafBusters Inc.

The idea for this new business was triggered by an entrepreneur reading an article about how farmers in the Midwest do not own their own combine harvesters, but use crews with their own equipment to take in the wheat crop.[5] These crews move from north of the Canadian border and follow the harvest time south as the climate changes. This makes sense for the farmers who cannot justify the high cost of a combine and/or do not have the skilled labor available for just a short harvest period. For the crews, the cost of the equipment can be justified much more easily as it is in use two to three months a year, not just two weeks. The entrepreneur recognized that leaf collection has much the same issues, and so she conceived a company to provide leaf-collecting services to local municipalities. After researching the opportunity and creating a business plan, the entrepreneur decided that the $3 million required to fully finance the start-up should come from two sources. Since half of the money would be for leaf-collecting equipment, a bank loan could be used for the purchases as there would be hard assets with which to secure the loan. The rest of the money would be best raised from angel investors. This size of investment would most likely require more than one angel, so an angel network was sought—one that was local to the region where the entrepreneur lived. After meeting one of the angel group members at a local networking meeting, the following teaser was supplied to the angel group for discussion.

EXECUTIVE SUMMARY

THE OPPORTUNITY

LeafBusters Inc. offers leaf-collection services to municipalities in the Northeast region with a significant cost savings over their current operations. Our research has shown that municipalities use their own workforce and equipment, spending as much as $1 million per year to perform this service for residents. Our service offer municipalities a 10 to 20 percent cost reduction. Our business model has tremendous growth potential since we will be able to perform this service at a 30 to 40 percent lower cost than the municipalities can for themselves.

THE MARKET

Leaf collection is a major activity performed ten to twelve weeks every fall in virtually every town and city in the United States with hardwood trees. Municipal employees normally perform this activity with a variety of leaf-collection equipment owned by the municipalities. Our research estimates the expenditures on leaf collection to be $250–$500 million/year throughout the United States and southern Canada. Budgets for leaf-collection range from $100,000/year for small towns to $1 million/year for large suburban counties. Municipalities are under significant pressure to reduce costs. Outsourcing of the leaf-collection process will provide them with a very attractive cost-cutting solution to their budget pressures.

THE COMPETITION

We are surprised to find that no significant business competition currently exists for this activity. Individual municipalities perform an estimated 98 percent of the leaf collection in this market with no significant sharing of resources. Small local subcontractors perform the remaining leaf collection primarily for business properties.

Although we do expect our success to draw the attention of potential entrants, our business model will provide us with the flexibility and economies of scale to remain the consolidated market leader.

BUSINESS MODEL

LeafBusters Inc. intends to become the premier supplier of seasonal curbside leaf-collection services throughout the United States and Canada. All contract services will be provided from regional service centers, with more efficient collection cycles than those currently available from local municipalities. Shorter collection times will allow LeafBusters Inc. to cover more areas with less equipment and staff than are currently used. Our business model will create an outstanding opportunity for investors such as the Network Angel Group. Based on our projections, we believe that we can capture 20 percent of the market within the first five years of operations.

LeafBusters Inc. will provide the staff and equipment necessary to perform those services currently provided by local governments for curbside leaf collections. While the length of annual leaf-collection programs varies (depending on weather and the volume of leaves), the normal program length is ten to twelve weeks. Our business model involves moving leaf-collection equipment and operations from north to south, following the leaf fall patterns, which will allow us to expand the collection season. For example, the first regional rollout will begin in New England and end in North Carolina, with a total collection period of at least fourteen to sixteen weeks. Instead of the usual eight to ten hours/day staffing by most municipalities, LeafBusters Inc. will operate for approximately twenty hours each day. The goal is to use less equipment and staff to cover more areas by migrating them based on scheduled collections. While the transportation of equipment is extremely important, particular care will be taken in recruiting and retaining seasonal staff. Transportation and accommodations will be provided, as well as a competitive hourly pay rate and per diem.

The collected leaves will be turned over to local recycling and composting facilities in an effort to assist communities in achieving their solid waste reduction goals. Some optional services available from LeafBusters Inc. are scheduling services, communications services (to notify home owners of collection days and times), and compost distribution services.

OPERATING SUMMARY

During its first year of operations, LeafBusters Inc. will acquire equipment and obtain at least thirty contract awards for leaf collection in its first targeted region. In each ensuing year, one additional region will be added to operations until all four are operational.

The regional rollout of services will be the Northeastern states, the Midwestern states, and the West Coast, with final expansion into Canada. This approach will allow LeafBusters Inc. to properly manage growth while providing a high level of service to customers. In addition, proving our concept in stages will allow us to deliver success stories as a part of the bid submission process. We already have two orders from municipalities that we will service as soon as our financing is in place.

Although the focus during the first regional rollout will be on those municipalities that currently offer leaf-collection programs, those that do not do so will be targeted during the next phase. We intend to offer our services as a means for municipalities to save money on solid waste removal efforts and to improve their recycling efforts.

In addition, each rollout phase will include the exploration of additional lines of business such as tree-trimming services, street sweeping, solid waste removal, and composting facilities. These additional services will allow us to further utilize our seasonal staff and equipment, keeping our staff employed and improving our return on assets.

PRELIMINARY FINANCIAL SUMMARY

The following table summarizes the preliminary five-year forecast of revenue, expense, and net income for LeafBusters Inc.

Pro Forma Income Statement LeafBusters Inc.
(in Thousand USD)

| | For the year ending December 31 | | | | | |
	2007	2008	2009	2010	2011	2012
Revenues	$0	$6,075	$13,669	$30,755	$69,198	$107,001
Direct labor	0	1,519	3,417	7,689	15,224	23,540
Gross profit	0	4,556	10,252	23,066	53,974	83,461
SG&A	500	2,126	4,784	10,764	22,143	34,240
Other expenses		911	2,050	4,613	10,380	16,050
EBIT	(500)	1,519	3,417	7,689	21,451	33,170
EBIT margin		25.0%	25.0%	25.0%	31.0%	31.0%
Net income	($600)	$1,063	$2,392	$5,075	$14,158	$21,892
Profit margin		18%	18%	17%	20%	20%
Cumulative Income/(Loss)	($600)	$463	$2,855	$7,930	$22,088	$43,980

FUNDING REQUIREMENTS

LeafBusters Inc. is seeking initial financing of $2.5 million, of which $1.5 million will be a bank loan secured against equipment and $1 million will be the equity in the form of preferred stock from angel investors. These funds are sufficient to initiate the establishment of a leaf-collection fleet and begin operations. These funds will finance the equipment, marketing activities, labor expenses, organizational costs, and working capital for the first year. Since we expect that contracts will be in place for the fall 2011 season with the profitability shown above, no additional external funding will be needed after the 2012 season.

EXIT STRATEGY

There are several possible exit strategies. The most attractive option will likely be selling the business to a major municipal service company such as a solid waste removal company after three to four years of operations. We anticipate providing our first-round investors with an internal rate of return exceeding 40 percent.

For further information contact:
LeafBusters Inc.
Main Street Any town, USA
www.leafbuster.com 1-800-Leafbust

Normally, the document would be provided with a short personal cover letter highlighting the opportunity and expected outcome. Note the following points in this document:

- The summary has a clear identity and image. It looks like something from a company, not an individual. The company has a name, relating directly to the opportunity.

- The opportunity, market size, and the customer "value proposition" are spelled out clearly at the outset.

- Competition, business model, and how the company will be operated are described.

- Six-year financial projections are summarized.

- Expectations from investors, including the expected payback and the method of achieving liquidity, are all stated unequivocally. There are no "woolly" terms such as *might*, *hopefully*, and *could*. Such words convey doubt and, hence, high risk; edit them out. Anything beyond this content detracts from its impact. Keep it brief and to the point.

The Elevator Pitch

An elevator pitch (so named in reference to the short time you may have to describe your opportunity during a chance meeting in an elevator) is essentially a verbal version of the teaser.[6] For an example of an actual elevator pitch, visit www.wiley.com/college/kaplan where Ankit Patel pitches an idea for how to reduce the operating costs of major U.S. freight railroads.[7] This relates to the full business plan for Railway Innovation Technologies that you can find on the book's web site. Again, making all the points in a one- to two-minute presentation is extremely difficult. You have time simply to state the problem you are solving and the value that your company will bring when solving that problem. It must be easy to understand with no jargon, leave no major uncertainties in the audience's mind, and show how the investor will make money; everything else must be left to later. Elevator pitches must be rehearsed, first alone, then in front of an audience. Pay attention to the following factors:

- Speak clearly, do not mumble, and do not rush. Modulate your voice and make the presentation pleasant and engaging.

- Get the audience involved and interested as early as possible. A good way of doing this is to relate your opportunity to something that the audience already knows. This is particularly important if your idea is rather obscure or highly technical.

- Be enthusiastic. If you are not excited about the opportunity, how can you expect someone else to be?

- Enthusiasm is also reflected in body language. You should be comfortable with your posture; hands in pockets, masking your face, or other involuntary movements detract highly from the impact.

- Do not be overanxious or overact. Take a few deep breaths before starting, and be determined to enjoy the experience yourself. Avoid theatrics.

- Finish on an up note and let your closure focus on the next actions.

Get into the habit of watching professional presentations and analyzing what is powerful, natural, and engaging about them.

Investors' Presentation: Preparation for the Meeting

After reviewing the executive summary or hearing the elevator pitch, the investors, if interested, will ask for a copy of the business plan. Follow up with a phone call a few days after submitting the plan to test reactions and to deal with any immediate questions. In reality, most investors do not read business plans in detail; they read just enough to determine whether they wish to go to the next step.

Note on Confidentiality

Most investors will not sign a confidentiality agreement at this stage. Put in the plan only materials that are not considered proprietary. If the business is based on new technical inventions, the inventors are justifiably concerned about disclosing proprietary information. Indeed, doing so can jeopardize the patent filing process. On the other hand, we find that scientists and engineers are only too eager to disclose their invention in looking for professional recognition or kudos for their baby. Remember that investors are interested in the *business* opportunity, not the invention itself.

Therefore, the entrepreneur has to state only *what the invention can do*, not *how it does it*. For example, "I have invented a new fuel injector for cars that increases the efficiency of existing gasoline engines by up to 7 percent. It has been tested at an independent test facility, and I can share the results with you. The market for such a product is $900 million annually. I am willing to disclose the details of the invention with you under a confidentiality agreement at a later date should you choose to enter into full due diligence for making an investment in my company." This statement does not threaten the proprietary nature of the invention, yet it gives the potential investors comfort that, should they proceed, they will learn more but under a full confidentiality agreement.

A further intermediate step can be taken to protect both parties. They can agree to let an independent third party review the invention and comment on its status, viability, originality, and so on without disclosing the invention to the investors. This is called escrowing the IP and is often used when investors want to get an opinion that the invention is likely to be patentable. No details are provided to the investors, only an opinion on the status and likelihood of success in getting patents granted.

ROADMAP

IN ACTION

An investor's presentation is a key event. It needs extensive preparation and rehearsal. Try to think of every difficult question you are likely to be asked and prepare answers for them beforehand.

If the investors wish to proceed after a review of the plan, they will usually require the entrepreneur to make an oral presentation. This is an important event. This presentation is more formal than the teaser or elevator pitch and is normally made to a group of investors, perhaps the senior partners of a VC firm, an angel investment board, two or three loan officers at a bank, directors of a local enterprise development board, a road show before an IPO, or several executives within a corporation deciding whether to become a partner with your company. Like the teaser, it should be tailored to the audience.

It is as much about personal chemistry as the opportunity. This is the chance to establish a rapport with investors as partners in the future success of the company. At this presentation other members of the management team should be prepared to answer questions. The entrepreneur should strengthen the oral presentation with the use of presentational aids such as prototypes of products and web sites.

Early arrival at the venue, allowing time for setup, is important. Survey the room and arrange it to suit the presentation. Start with personal introductions, exchange business cards, and some general small talk to relax the atmosphere. Ask how long the investors have for the meeting, and tailor the presentation to allow for questions. Try to determine who the key decision influencer is in the group, and make an extra effort to answer any questions or uncertainties this key person expresses. Don't get sidetracked by questions if they are to be dealt with later in the presentation, but answer relevant questions promptly and move on. If the answer is not readily at hand, don't bluff; indicate that an answer will be provided within, say, two days. If several persons are presenting, have one "director" of questions. Avoid interrupting others on the team, and do not disagree among yourselves.

An investor's presentation will follow the same general pattern of the teaser but will fill in many of the details. You can find a comprehensive guide for the creation of your presentation at http://ideapitch.smeal.psu.edu/. Your pitch should last no more than twenty minutes without questions, using about twelve to sixteen slides covering the opportunity overview, customer value proposition, market, competition, products/services, business model, management, and financials. Table 10.1 shows eleven basic slides and their contents. The topics here are typical for an

Table 10.1 Template for an Investors' Presentation

Slides	Notes on contents
SLIDE 1: OUTLINE • Market • Product or service • Customers • Intellectual property • Development plan • Distribution plan • Team • Competition • Financial projections • Exit strategy	This slide provides an overall guide to your presentation and a roadmap for the audience. You can title each slide to relate to this guide

SLIDE 2: MARKET
 	
• What market will your company serve with its *first* product or service?
• How large is this market?
  ○ Is it existing or emerging?
  ○ Show third-party market research data: historical and forecasts
• Name entrenched or potential competitors
• What market(s) might your company serve with potential future products or services?
	Starting with this topic will engage your audience and enable you to put your best foot forward. Describe who you are going to serve. How large is the market you are attacking? Is it mature, developing, or must you create it? Show a third-party research to support your claims. Name your first product or service and how you will add to this later

SLIDE 3: PRODUCT OR SERVICE • What product/service will your company develop and sell *first*? • What competitive advantage does your *first* product/service have over alternatives? • After the *first* product/service gains traction in the market, what future offerings will you develop and sell?	Describe in detail your first product or service. 80 to 90 percent of your presentation should be based on this "market entry" offering, as this is where you will spend your initial money. Show how you can build on this later with new products or services as a "roadmap" for expansion

SLIDE 4: CUSTOMERS
 	
• Who are the target customers for your *first* product/service?
  ○ Name at least two specific prospective customers and include contact information
• Why will they buy from you, and how much do they say they will pay?
  ○ Describe your economic value proposition to these customers
• What alternatives do your prospective customers have besides buying from you?
	Name the customers showing interest in your product/service. Name the person(s) you spoke to and describe what they said. Why are they going to buy from you, and how much are they willing to pay? Describe the value proposition of your product/service—how is the customer going to make and save money by buying from you rather than buying from someone else?

(continued)

Slides	Notes on contents
SLIDE 5: INTELLECTUAL PROPERTY • State the form(s) of IP you will use (trademarks, patents, copyrights, trade secrets) • Describe the competitive benefits they will provide • Describe how you plan to obtain, develop, expand, and protect your IP • If your company uses new technology, give a general overview, state the stage of development, and describe any risks remaining in its implementation.	Here is an opportunity to talk about your special attributes. Keep the discussion at a high level. How are you protecting your intellectual property? Have you filed patents, or are you planning on filing patents, trademarks, and so forth? How long do you think your IP will protect you from competition?

SLIDE 6: DEVELOPMENT PLAN
• Outline the timetable under which your *first* product/service will be brought to market
• Specify the resources required and when you need them, defining milestones:
  ○ Personnel and materials
  ○ Capital equipment
  ○ Third-party products, services, or IP
  ○ Corporate partners
	How long will it take, and how much is it going to cost, to get your first product or service out and producing income? How many people is it going to take? Will you need to buy capital equipment?

SLIDE 7: DISTRIBUTION PLAN • Describe the company's business model • Describe the company's sales model: ○ Direct, indirect, web-based, IP licensing, franchising or other • Describe any partnering plans with other companies	How are you going to sell your product/service? How are you going to get it to your customers? Will you sell direct, through distribution, use licensing or franchising, and so forth? Describe your business model and how that will provide you with healthy profits
SLIDE 8: MANAGEMENT TEAM • Describe the ideal characteristics of the rest of the senior management team that you are going to have to fill as you build the company and/or get funding • Describe team members. Include founders, identified or committed follow-on hires, and the advisory board • Describe the additional skills and key management personnel required to build a company and when you need to add them: ○ CEO, CFO or controller, VP marketing, VP sales, VP engineering, and so forth	Who are you? Who are the founders? Provide relevant background information on your team and their roles. Boast a little here

Table 10.1 (continued)

Slides	Notes on contents

SLIDE 9: COMPETITION
 	
• Describe incumbent competitors:
 	
  ○ Number, size, market shares, growth rates, IP, product/services positioning, likely roadmap
 	
  ○ Can any of these competitors be turned into customers or partners?
 	
• Describe emerging or potential competitors:
 	
  ○ Stage, backing, technology, product positioning, likely roadmap
 	
  ○ Why will you be the winning start-up in your market?
	This is a very important slide. You are never unique. You will have competitors, and you must understand who they are, their strengths and weaknesses. Are they big or small companies, are they competitors you might be able to turn into a distribution partner or customer and why? What is your strategy to win against these competitors?

SLIDE 10: FINANCIAL PROJECTIONS
 	
• Describe the amount and phasing of the capital you need to raise to reach exit:
 	
  ○ Are federal or state grants included?
 	
• Show pro forma annual financials for five years:
 	
  ○ Include gross margin forecasts
 	
• Describe the potential enterprise value of the company you hope to build
	State how big a company you can build and how quickly you can do it. Give financials at a high level by year, showing revenues, expenses, and sources of capital, highlighting the breakeven point. Show use of federal or state grants supplementing bank or equity funding. It is important to state your expected gross margins after two or three years, how the value of your company will grow, and what it might be worth when you are ready to sell it. When do you need different amounts of funding? Are there third-party products/services or other partners needed for your success? Do you have a bootstrapping plan to minimize the amount of cash you will require?

SLIDE 11: EXIT STRATEGY
 	
• Is your company an IPO candidate?
 	
  ○ If so, explain why and show comparables
 	
• Who are your likely acquirers?
 	
  ○ How much might they pay, why, and when?
 	
  ○ Have they completed similar acquisitions in the past?
 	
  ○ What will compel them to buy you rather than see you bought by a feared competitor?
	Investors need to know not just how much money they need to put into a company but also when they are going to get it back out with a profit. This will occur when you sell or take your company public. What companies like yours can serve as benchmarks either by looking at their public stock price or knowing how much an acquirer paid for them? Describe how, in four to six years, investors are going to earn a return on their investments

early-stage company presenting to angel investors. However, the flow of information is similar for all stages of investment, loans, or an exit. Up to five more may be added for extra clarification. It is useful to anticipate probing questions and have backup slides that address these points. It impresses investors if they come up with a difficult question such as "Isn't Global Inc. a major competitive threat to this business?" and the presenter can immediately show an analysis of Global Inc. and illustrate the new company's advantages over that company. A well-prepared presentation of twelve to sixteen slides may have as many again anticipated backup slides. All the comments made above regarding making an elevator pitch apply here as well.

PRESENTATION TIPS

- Goal is to offer a high-level, summarized view of the company.
- Presentation is not a business plan on screen.
- Have only one or two speakers, no more.
- Limit material to twelve to sixteen slides.
- Slides should contain concise ideas, not sentences.
- Use no more than five bullet points per page.
- Choose Arial typeface, twelve-point font (simple, noncurlicue font).

- Dark background with white letters is easier read on the screen.
- Minimize the use of bullet points, check marks, boxes, and other noninformation symbols.
- Never read from the slides.
- Do not turn your back on the audience.
- Have back-up slides covering more detail to address anticipated questions.
- If you have video materials, then either link them into the presentation or host them on a free public site such as YouTube or Vimeo.

In addition, consider the following:

- Do not hand out copies of your presentation prior to the formal part of the meeting. Indicate that you will leave copies afterward for reference. If you fail to engage all the participants, you will be distracted by one or more reading forward from the handouts and perhaps even participating in side conversations about points that you have not yet reached. You will have lost control of the situation.

- Do not read from the slides. Use the slides to raise points and add to the content with your presentation.

- Face the audience, not the screen.

- Do not overrun your time for the formal presentation. This may leave you no time for more personal engagement, and the opportunity will be lost.

- Fewer slides are better than too many. Fewer words are better than many.

- Design the presentation around a clearly articulated and visual roadmap.

Since prospective investors are often taking an unsecured position in the company, the presentation must include a financial plan that describes data to make an informed decision. Sophisticated investors will rigorously evaluate the abilities of the management team, the financial strength of the company, and the commercial viability of the business. Prior to the "real event," the entrepreneur should make the presentation before several people to get feedback and to make sure a compelling case is made for the new company.

A full investors' presentation based on the elevator pitch and business plan for Railway Innovation Technologies referred to earlier is available at www.wiley.com/college/kaplan. The presentation is accompanied by a commentary and the slide presentation.

After the Presentation

The entrepreneur should contact the investors a few days after having completed the presentation to see if additional questions need to be answered.

Create Excitement about the Investment

If investors have expressed any degree of interest, the entrepreneur should move interest into action and investment. He should set a realistic deadline for the investment and notify investors that the supply of available equity is rapidly dwindling. Once investors have put money into a company, the relationship isn't over; it's just beginning. To state the obvious, investors have a vested interest in seeing the business succeed. The company should always make a point of involving investors in the success of the business by keeping them updated on new business opportunities and sales and financial targets. Good communication is vital throughout the life of the investor–company relationship. This is particularly true when the company goes through some disappointments, as undoubtedly it will.

Learn the Investor Evaluation Process

During the evaluation period, investors analyze the business into four fundamental sections:

1. **Management Team**   Investors like to review the experience and previous successes of the management team and the entrepreneur. They like to know a team is in place to run the business.

   The entrepreneur does not have to hire an entire team immediately, but she should indicate the types of individuals the company will hire to operate the business. In cases where the entrepreneur has been involved in previous successful ventures, investor confidence in providing immediate funding is made easier. Also, other investors, advisers, and board members who have a stake in the business are reviewed.

2. **Business Model**   The business model, market size, and customers are examined along with the timing of the opportunity. It is important to emphasize that the company has sales or can obtain sales through a solid sales plan. The emphasis for investors is that the longer it takes to achieve sales, the longer it will take for investors to get their money back.

3. **Context**   Both internal and external factors that affect the business, including customer reactions to the product, competitors, economic regulation, and the stage of technology, are analyzed.

4. **The Deal**   The deal and the price structure relate to the valuation. *Structure* refers to the terms and timing of the deal, and *price* is the stock, cash, or debt that will complete the transaction. This can include a silent investor, active participation, or an adviser. A final valuation is generally made three to six months following the presentation, after the investors have conducted full due diligence along the lines explored in Chapter 8.

Dealing with Rejection

The entrepreneur can view the experience of finding investments as a positive, even if the investment is rejected owing to inadequate answers regarding the risks of the business. The entrepreneur should always inquire if the investor knows another interested party or under what conditions the investor would reconsider. Therefore, the entrepreneur should always ask, "Who else may be interested?" "Do you have a contact name?" "If we do not receive funding now, can we count on you for later financing?" The entrepreneur must learn to turn negative experiences into positive opportunities.

The Financing Agreement

Once an offer is accepted, the entrepreneur will begin to negotiate the final financing agreement that includes ownership, control, and financial objectives. This is called a *term sheet* (see more on term sheets in Chapter 8), and it sets out the initial investment and understanding between the issuer and investor. The ownership for investors can range from 10 percent (profitable companies) to 90 percent (financially troubled firms). Most investors, however, do not want to own more than 50 percent of a business. Voting control usually remains with the entrepreneur and his management team. However, the investors will generally ask for representation on the board of directors to have some say in important decisions. Therefore, the actual control exercisable by the entrepreneur is usually greatly curtailed after an equity investment.

The financial objectives of the investors are either a corporate acquisition or a public stock offering within three to five years of their initial investment. These objectives are discussed when long-term financial goals are negotiated with the investors. A major concern for the investor is in determining the valuation of the business and the returns, which will be dictated by the value of the business. Investors price a business on the potential capital return in the future. The share an investor expects to gain in return for the investment depends not only on the amount of money contributed but also on the time and opportunity costs (missing investments in other businesses). The entrepreneur wants the investor to value the company for what it will be worth in three to five years (i.e., a corporate acquisition or an initial public offering). This is important in determining how an investment today will be worth more tomorrow. Investors usually value a company at a lower price than the entrepreneur would. For example, an early-stage company has a great idea and a young management team but no sales. From the investors' viewpoint, ideas are cheap, and an inexperienced management team might not be able to execute or implement the plan. Investors are always interested in maximizing the return on their investments. See Chapters 8 and 11 for more on term sheets and deal structures, business valuations, and the methods and procedures used.

Creating a Promotional Video

Increasingly entrepreneurs are using video technology for promoting their ideas and engaging with potential investors and stakeholders. With the emergence of crowdfunding as one option for raising start-up funds, video promoting is becoming an important tool. And now, with the latest low-cost technology, the cost and skills required for producing such a video clip are available to almost everyone. Many smart phones have high-quality inbuilt cameras, some with antimovement correction software which removes the need for even a tripod. Also simple-to-use video-editing software such as iMovie, Magix MoviePro, Pinnacle Studio, or Adobe Premium Promo make the postprocessing easy. And you can publish your video on platforms such as Vimeo, YouTube, and so on and provide links to these sites or use them on one of the many crowdfunding sites. Some of these sites also have guidance on how to create an engaging video.

Here are a few tips to help you make a good video clip:

- Go online and watch several short videos that are in a field similar to the one you wish to develop. Note what you find good about them and how you might improve them.

- If you become bored while watching, note why. On the other hand, note what you really find attractive. Watch without the sound track to gain additional insights.

- Choose a simple font that is easy to read and only use one.

- If you have to use fancy cuts, such as rollbacks, then your material is probably rather boring—keep it simple.

- Write a storyboard before starting to show how different parts of the video will link smoothly. Make sure your message is clear, consistent, and easy to follow.

- If you are going to be part of the video, get help when recording these sequences.

- Keep scripts short and to the point.

- Do not exceed three minutes in total length.

- Don't use the canned free music backgrounds that come with editing software, choose appropriate music, and make sure that you can use it without breaching a copyright. You can also access good background tracks, images and video clips at sites such as AudioMicro, Freesound and Shutterstock.

- If you are looking for crowdfunding on sites such as Kickstarter, IndieGogo, and so on have a clear statement of your reward structure or payback plan (see Chapter 5 for more details).

  Here are a couple of examples that meet most of these rules and are worth watching for tips:

- Precision Gyroscope on Kickstarter

- Alter Ego on IndieGogo

ROADMAP

| IN ACTION | Remember: the questions to be answered are as follows: Will the investors get their money back before the entrepreneur? Will the investors have the right to invest in future rounds? There is also the issue of what role investors will play in the company. |

SUMMARY

No idea or opportunity can create value unless the entrepreneur can communicate it effectively to all classes of potential stakeholders in the venture, including investors, lenders, customers, suppliers, agents, advisers, partners, and employees. Entrepreneurs must learn to lead others so they can become as excited and driven by the opportunity as the founders themselves. Communicating, then, is vital.

Every communication medium must be tailored to fit the targeted audience. The entrepreneurs must become used to putting themselves in the role of recipient so they can craft a message that will directly appeal to the individual needs and aspirations of the audience.

Entrepreneurs use oral, written, and presentation media to communicate. The short forms of an elevator pitch, introductory letter and teaser, and executive summary require a surprising effort to make them lucid, concise, and engaging. It is often more difficult to express yourself in a limited time or space than in a full business plan or full-blown presentation. These shorter forms are used to create initial interest and must be followed up with a more detailed presentation, which highlights all the key points of a business plan. These skills need practice, and entrepreneurs should take every opportunity they have to present to an audience and to write brief summaries of their opportunities for different targeted stakeholders.

The advent of simple-to-use low-cost video production and publishing tools is making video promotion methods much more prevalent, whether for crowdfunding or engaging with potential investors.

STUDY QUESTIONS

Q.1 What are the various types of communications that an entrepreneur uses, and what are their main purposes?

Q.2 What key points would you make in an investor's presentation to the following audiences: bankers, angel investors, VC partners, suppliers, and potential key employees?

Q.3 What are the major content items in a teaser?

Q.4 Name the eleven foundation slides for an investor's presentation.

Q.5 Name five common mistakes made by entrepreneurs when making a presentation.

Q.6 How does an entrepreneur handle the situation when an investor refuses to sign a confidentiality agreement?

Q.7 How can you use short video clips to promote your business?

EXERCISES

10.1 Read the Surfparks case study posted on the book web site. Prepare a teaser for this business targeted at one of the following audiences: a banker, a venture capitalist, or a corporate partner. Identify the actual entity that you are targeting and the appropriate person, by name and title, to whom you wish to send the teaser. Write a one-page accompanying letter of introduction as if you were the CEO of Surfparks.

10.2 Read the Surfparks case study on the book web site, and prepare a twelve- to sixteen-slide presentation for a group of angel investors.

10.3 Prepare five backup slides for difficult questions that you anticipate will be asked in the presentation referred to in question 10.2.

10.4 View Ankit Patel's elevator pitch on the book's web site. What three things do you like best about this, and why? How would you improve it?

10.5 View the investor's presentation by Ankit Patel for the railroad opportunity mentioned in the previous question. What are five key points that he makes? How would you improve the presentation, and why?

10.6 Produce a short video sequence promoting a new idea that you have.

10.7 Read the ChemStation case in Chapter 3. Represent the business model on the canvas in Figure 3.2. Use this as a basis for a short presentation to a banker seeking a loan for working capital for the business.

Management Exercise

View Denis Coleman's comments in the video on the book's web site entitled "Angels, More Than Just Investors."

Then individually or as a team, produce a short presentation analyzing the following: "I regret I had to write you a long letter, I did not have time to write a short one." Describe an elevator pitch, and explain why it is extremely important. Why is it so difficult to accomplish?

INTERACTIVE LEARNING ON THE WEB

Test your knowledge of the chapter using the book's interactive web site.

ENDNOTES

1. For an instructional guide on how to put an investors' presentation together, visit the "Learning Center" at http://ideapitch.smeal.psu .edu. This guide is used successfully in many courses at different universities and is also the basis of a virtual business plan competition.

2. Craig Bandes, interview, July 2008.

3. Stanley E. Pratt, *Pratt's Guide to Venture Capital Sources* (Wellesley, MA: Venture Economics, published annually). For a list of libraries where you can find this complete guide, see www.worldcat.org.

4. William A. Frezza (partner, Adams Capital Management) interview, May 2004. Frezza can also be seen talking about a number of topics in entrepreneurial companies on the book's web site.

5. The authors thank a team of MBA students at Penn State for this example developed in the Opportunity Development Course in 2003.

6. See www.youtube.com/watch?v=Tq0tan49rmc for a short introduction to the elevator pitch. There are a number of examples on YouTube.

7. We thank Ankit Patel, a member of an MBA class at Penn State in 2004, for his permission to use this material from a business plan competition based on concepts from Resco Inc., in Kingston, Ontario.

11 Exiting the Venture

"Think of yourself as on the threshold of unparalleled success, a whole clear life lies before you. Achieve. Achieve."

Andrew Carnegie, Industrialist and Philanthropist

OBJECTIVES

- Understand the need to have an exit strategy and plan for it.
- Learn how to use alliances to sell an equity stake in the venture.
- Identify the various sources to develop an exit strategy.
- List the exit options available for entrepreneurs.
- Learn ways of valuing later-stage companies.
- Describe the process and sequence of events in selling a business.
- Describe the selling memorandum and its contents.
- Understand ESOP and MBO.
- Learn the process of launching an initial public offering.
- Understand the advantages and disadvantages of going public.

CHAPTER OUTLINE

Introduction

Profile: Alan Trefler: Private to Public Ownership

Why Create an Exit Strategy and Plan

Selling an Equity Stake to a Strategic Partner

Valuing a Later-Stage Company

Implementing the Plan of Action

Selling the Business

Preparing a Selling Memorandum

Merge with Another Business

Introduction

Some entrepreneurs start with the intention of creating an exit for their investors. But, as we have seen, many entrepreneurs, more interested in their lifestyle, never intend to give up control of their companies. However, personal aspirations change over time, and lifestyle entrepreneurs may eventually also decide to find a way to take more than just income out of the company by selling part or all of the enterprise. Alternatively, they may wish to transfer the ownership of the company to members of their family or personally chosen managers (see Chapter 14, "Family Business Management," for more details). This chapter provides the knowledge to identify the best exit plan for the entrepreneur of either group and the venture's shareholders and how to be in the strongest position to manage the process. Not until the shares of the company are purchased by a third party can investors sell their ownership positions and cash out, preferably at a profit. This is called a *liquidity event*.

A number of techniques and strategies can help the entrepreneur develop an exit plan. This chapter highlights the methodology, procedures, and options available for entrepreneurs when considering an exit strategy. There are several ways a company can realize an exit plan from the value it has created. Described in this chapter are the most common methods, namely, to sell an equity stake to a partner, sell the business, merge with another company, implement a leveraged buyout, or sell the company to its employees or to heirs. We also discuss the planning for a public offering that provides an option to sell a portion of the venture. In all cases, researching and carrying out an exit require the communication skills learned in Chapter 10.

Profile: Alan Trefler: Private to Public Ownership

Alan Trefler started playing chess at a young age and became a world-class player.[1] He reasoned that if you could program a computer to play at that level, it should be possible to create software to make complex management decisions. So in 1983, with a loan of $500,000 from family members, he started Pegasystems Inc. The Massachusetts-based business creates software that wades through databases to help corporations capture useful information about their customers. The company grew rapidly, and he managed to pay back the loan in just four years. Back in the late 1970s, Trefler actually offered to create software for his previous employers at Citibank, but they turned him down. Ironically, the bank signed on as one of Pegasytems' first customers. Through the 1980s, Trefler bootstrapped the business completely, never seeking or accepting a dime of

> "Although selling an equity stake of a business is financially attractive, entrepreneurs must consider where they are in regard to their personal plan and at what point they are willing to give up control of their business. For many entrepreneurs, the control issue is as important if not more important than the financial gain."
>
> Liz Elting
> *President and CEO,*
> *TransPerfect*
> *Translations, Inc.*

venture capital. He eventually did something every entrepreneur dreams of but few accomplish: he took his company public in 1996 and retained more than 70 percent of the equity. Because so few people owned stock, he was free to keep a huge chunk of the outstanding shares for himself. Pegasystems has grown to more than $250 million in annual revenues and a market capitalization of around 1.6 billion dollars since then. Despite selling a large proportion of his shares over the last few years to the public, a major benefit of public ownership, Trefler, with around 10 percent of the company, is left with a considerable fortune through his ownership. Trefler, who remains the CEO, believes that his success is largely dependent on the diverse culture that he has built at Pegasystems.[2] On this issue, Trefler quotes William Wrigley Jr., "When two men in business always agree, one of them is unnecessary."

Why Create an Exit Strategy and Plan

Entrepreneurs spend so much time creating a business that many do not plan for a successful exit. The entrepreneur often sees selling the company as selling out and, in most cases, not meeting the expectations of investors or the management team. Realization may occur when new technologies impact the current product revenues or when competitors gain market share and the company loses its market position; then it is too late.

Often the entrepreneur begins to develop reasons for exiting the business, including the stress level of managing the business and not finding enough time for the company because of family commitments. The opposite may also occur: the entrepreneur spends so much time on the venture that her family commitments suffer. Another first sign, which usually occurs in the early stages of growth, is the struggle for the company to stay alive. Therefore, it is important to prepare the exit plan early in the business cycle and at the right time. As discussed in Chapter 8, any entrepreneur seeking equity funding for growth must have plans for an exit prior to accepting external investors. There are several ways a company can realize an exit from the value it has created; the most common follow.

ROADMAP

IN ACTION

Entrepreneurs may want to exit the business by establishing a strategic alliance and selling an equity stake in the business. An effective equity alliance can substantially increase the value of the venture and offer an exit option at a later date.

Selling an Equity Stake To a Strategic Partner

Selling an equity stake in the business to a strategic partner can substantially increase the value of the venture and offer an exit option to the entrepreneur. However, it takes research and due diligence to sell a minority or majority equity interest in the venture to a strategic partner. Just picking up the phone and calling as many big players as possible in the hopes that they will want to buy an interest will generate lots of effort but few results. A well-researched and targeted effort is needed to determine why an alliance partner should purchase a stake and the reasons and justification for the sale. Usually, for the entrepreneur to sell an equity position, the partnership must be beneficial to all parties. In most cases, an exploratory alliance is formed first. After measuring the success of the relationship, an equity position is negotiated[3] to sell out completely or receive a minority stake in the venture. As an example, to initiate the alliance, the entrepreneur can offer the company licenses to patents, copyrights, or trade secrets, and the other company can bring a stronger marketing organization with an eye toward growing the business. When the companies have complementary skills, the alliance can accomplish tasks that neither party could do alone. This positions the relationship for equity participation. The parties can also share customer relationships and costs and reduce their individual exposure to risk. The alliance can be mutually beneficial by obtaining additional revenue from existing products, limiting the amount of capital to invest in needed capacity, and avoiding the need to add personnel. Additional benefits can increase the chances of getting into the market faster or obtaining first-mover advantage and possibly gaining exclusive access or license to a product. Success in any or all of these factors of strategic alliances develops the relationship for the partners to purchase an equity stake in the venture. Revisit the Jason Kong/AutoESL case in Chapter 8 to see how strategic investments may enhance a company.

Valuing a Later-Stage Company

ROADMAP	
IN ACTION	At later stages in the company's growth, the major factor that determines the value of a business is the cash flow and generation of profits in the marketplace. Other valuation factors include the history, characteristics, and industry in which the business operates as well as the strength and weakness of the management team and risks in investing in the business.

Later-Stage Valuations

These are methods used for raising funds at a more mature stage or at an exit. Business valuations should always be considered as a starting point for the buyer and seller.[4] The goal is to determine a working valuation from which one can negotiate a fair price. The key factor in the value of any later-stage business is the focus on the company's cash flow and its ability to generate consistent profits in the marketplace. Other valuation factors include the history, characteristics, and industry in which the business operates; the strengths and weaknesses of the management team; the growth trajectory of the company; and risks in investing in the business. Another financial factor to consider in the analysis is comparing the company to other companies in the industry and the stock price of similar companies in the industry. This can include the price-to-earnings ratio of similar companies and understanding the company's financial condition. The master case and readings provide some real insight into the IPO process and the dynamics of pricing the stock in a volatile public market.

ROADMAP	
IN ACTION	The valuation process involves trial and error; there is no single best method. The best is a combination of valuation methods that may apply to a given situation.

Earnings valuation is more suitable for a company with an established track record and involves valuing the business based on the following:

- Historical Earnings: valuation based on how profitable the business has been in the past

- Future Earnings: the most widely used method of valuing a business, which provides the investor with the best estimate of the probable return on investment

Once the buyer or seller has decided on the time frame (i.e., historical vs. future earnings), the earnings figure must be multiplied by a factor to determine its value. Generally, a price/earnings (P/E) multiple is used. For example, if the company is expected to have earnings of $1.5 million in five years and if similar companies are likely to go public at a price-to-earnings ratio of 10, the company is projected to be worth $15 million five years from now. The appropriate P/E multiple is selected based on the norms of the industry and the investment risk.

To value a private company in a particular industry, research a set of comparable publicly traded companies, or comps, to benchmark the private company.

Asset valuation is based on the worth of the business's assets. This is a useful starting point for negotiations, for it constitutes the *minimum* value of the business. It would not be appropriate to value most companies using an asset-based approach, especially in the case where the company is a typical earnings-based concern with few fixed assets, such as a software company, or its assets are largely intangible, such as a portfolio of patents. Indeed even for the S&P 500, the largest 500 companies in the United States, the average market valuation is approximately three times their asset value. Shareholders place significant value on so-called intangible assets and other factors. The asset approach is most appropriate when used in a liquidation scenario and/or in valuing an asset-based company such as a real estate holding company or investment holding company.

Discounted Cash Flow Valuation

The real value of any ongoing business is its future earnings power.[5] Accordingly, this approach is often used to value a business. The discounted cash flow (DCF) method projects future earnings over a three-to-five-year period and then calculates their present value using a certain discount or present value rate (e.g., 15 percent). The total of each year's projected earnings is the company's value. The basic principle underlying this method is that a dollar earned in the future is worth less than a dollar earned today. Thus, it is not only the amount of projected income (or net cash flow) that a company is expected to generate that determines its value but also the timing of that income. This method can be used for companies at any stage, but for an early-stage company, where greater uncertainty is attributed to future cash flow forecasts, a higher discount rate is used to account for the larger risk and uncertainty.

In a DCF valuation, the value of a company is the present value of the expected cash flows that will be generated by the company's assets. Every asset has an intrinsic value that can be estimated, based on its characteristics in terms of cash flows, growth, and risk that it can generate.

Information that is needed to use DCF valuation includes data on the estimated life of the asset, the cash flow forecasts during the life of the asset, and the discount rate to apply to these cash flows.

The Steps Involved in Discounted Cash Flow

First, estimate the discount rate or rates to use in the valuation. Discount rates can vary across time and are higher when there is a greater uncertainty in future cash flows. Next, estimate the current earnings and cash flows of the company to either equity investors or stakeholders. Estimate the future earnings and cash flows on the asset being valued, generally by estimating an expected growth rate in earnings. Finally, estimate when the firm will reach *stable growth* and what characteristics it will have when it does. Now calculate and value the DCF.

When using this approach in valuing a company, one must decide how to value the cash flows after the forecast period is over. If you were to limit your DCF calculation to just the three or five years in the forecast, you would omit any value that would accrue from Year 6 and beyond. The way this value is typically captured, as discussed earlier, is by using some P/E to indicate what the selling value of the business would be after Year 6, for example.

Let's assume that you will receive $100,000 today and $100,000 a year over the next four years. What is today's value (present value) of the total $500,000 income stream? To determine the value of the transaction, you must use present-value factors. Now let's construct Table 11.1, which will show you how the total $500,000 payments would be valued today and over the next four years. To compute the value, indicate the amounts by year and apply an 18 percent present-value factor to each amount.

As shown in Table 11.1, the total income of $500,000 over five years is worth $369,000 today. This is called the net present value (NPV) of the cash flow. That represents 30 percent less than the $500,000 you thought you were going to receive over the five-year period. This method can be used to value a company when you have a high confidence in future cash flows. Table 11.2 provides a table of present value for different discount rates for between one and twenty years.

Table 11.1 Today's Value of Income

Year	Inflow	18% PV factor	Value today
Today	$100,000	1.000	$100,000
1	100,000	0.847	84,700
2	100,000	0.718	71,800
3	100,000	0.609	60,900
4	100,000	0.516	51,600
	$500,000	3.690	$369,000

Table 11.2 Present Value of 1 Due in n Periods

	6%	7%	8%	9%	10%	11%	12%	13%	14%	15%	16%	20%	30%
1	0.9434	0.9346	0.9259	0.9174	0.9091	0.9009	0.8929	0.8850	0.8772	0.8696	0.8621	0.8333	0.7692
2	0.8900	0.8734	0.8573	0.8417	0.8264	0.8116	0.7972	0.7831	0.7695	0.7561	0.7432	0.6944	0.5917
3	0.8396	0.8163	0.7938	0.7722	0.7513	0.7312	0.7118	0.6931	0.6750	0.6575	0.6407	0.5787	0.4552
4	0.7921	0.7629	0.7350	0.7084	0.6830	0.6587	0.6355	0.6133	0.5921	0.5718	0.5523	0.4823	0.3501
5	0.7473	0.7130	0.6806	0.6499	0.6309	0.5935	0.5674	0.5428	0.5194	0.4972	0.4761	0.4019	0.2693
6	0.7050	0.6663	0.6302	0.5963	0.5645	0.5346	0.5066	0.4803	0.4556	0.4323	0.4104	0.3349	0.2072
7	0.6651	0.6227	0.5835	0.5470	0.5132	0.4817	0.4523	0.4251	0.3996	0.3759	0.3538	0.2791	0.1594
8	0.6274	0.5820	0.5403	0.5019	0.4665	0.4339	0.4039	0.3762	0.3506	0.3269	0.3050	0.2326	0.1226
9	0.5919	0.5439	0.5002	0.4604	0.4241	0.3909	0.3606	0.3329	0.3075	0.2843	0.2630	0.1938	0.0943
10	0.5584	0.5083	0.4632	0.4224	0.3855	0.3522	0.3220	0.2943	0.2697	0.2472	0.2267	0.1615	0.0725
11	0.5268	0.4751	0.4289	0.3875	0.3505	0.3173	0.2875	0.2607	0.2366	0.2149	0.1954	0.1346	0.0558
12	0.4970	0.4440	0.3971	0.3555	0.3186	0.2858	0.2567	0.2307	0.2076	0.1869	0.1685	0.1122	0.0429
13	0.4688	0.415	0.3677	0.3262	0.2897	0.2575	0.2292	0.2042	0.1821	0.1625	0.1452	0.0935	0.0330
14	0.4423	0.3878	0.3405	0.2992	0.2633	0.2320	0.2046	0.1807	0.1597	0.1413	0.1252	0.0779	0.0254
15	0.4173	0.3624	0.3152	0.2745	0.2394	0.2090	0.1827	0.1599	0.1401	0.1229	0.1079	0.0649	0.0195
16	0.3936	0.3387	0.2919	0.2519	0.2176	0.1883	0.1631	0.1415	0.1229	0.1069	0.0930	0.0541	0.0150
17	0.3714	0.3166	0.2311	0.2311	0.1978	0.1696	0.1456	0.1252	0.1078	0.0929	0.0802	0.0451	0.0116
18	0.3503	0.2959	0.2120	0.2120	0.1799	0.1528	0.1300	0.1108	0.0946	0.0808	0.0691	0.0376	0.0089
19	0.3305	0.2765	0.1945	0.1945	0.1635	0.1377	0.1161	0.0981	0.0829	0.0703	0.0596	0.0313	0.0068
20	0.3118	0.2584	0.2145	0.1784	0.1486	0.1240	0.1037	0.0868	0.0728	0.0611	0.0514	0.0261	0.0053

Implementing the Plan of Action

The first principle in positioning the alliance partner to acquire an equity stake is to know what value the partner sees in the business.[6] The most common value for most alliances is increasing the revenue or decreasing the costs of operation. Before any serious negotiation, however, this value needs to be determined, and both sides require an evaluation to quantify the present and potential market opportunities. Also, the entrepreneur needs to identify what the alliance will cost in time and money. For example, a relationship with a partner may limit the chances of selling the venture to the company's competitors. The following actions serve as a guide for establishing an alliance:

- Identify the objective of a proposed alliance. The entrepreneur should determine the time requirements and the expectations of the parties involved in the process.

- Build a target list of possible candidate companies. It is best to go after more than one possible partner, and a mixture of size and scope is important. Although it might be exciting to go after a global brand, in some instances (especially on the support and development side) finding a possible smaller regional partner with existing industry experience, may be a smarter move. The parties will be more interested in partnering and making the relationship work.

- Research the candidates and examine their web sites and press releases. Determine who is in charge of business development—the CEO or the president. Analyze information, including articles that mention them. The key is to find out the company's mission and focus. Build a document on each target, including contact information and phone numbers.

- Present the finding on each target to the key members of the areas that will be impacted by the relationship (e.g., software development, IT, marketing, sales) and gather their input, concerns, and interests.

- Develop a nonconfidential introduction kit and cover letter to send to possible alliance partners. (This could be an e-mail with attached document or PDF. More about creating such a document is covered in Chapter 10.) The letter should be short and to the point, highlighting why the relationship would be of value to the partner. The goal should be an in-person meeting. It is best that the first meeting be on the potential alliance partner's terms and location. In this way, you can make an on-site inspection, and they will be more comfortable and more likely to know that you are showing commitment. A sample meeting agenda should be prepared as follows.

Meeting Agenda

- Introduction with names, titles, and contact information.

- State the goals and desired outcomes of the meetings.

- Prepare an overview of the business and role (have hard copies, including extras).

- Review the specific reason for the meeting and the driving reason for an alliance.

- Prepare a general business overview.

- Conduct a walk-through and tour. No matter how small an office, walk the floor and talk with people; get a sense of the environment and the culture.

- Review the level of interest and get ideas on how the two businesses would work together.

- Agree on the relationship, timing, next steps, action, and who will be the responsible persons on each side.

Making an alliance work requires constant involvement and communication. The companies need to stay connected and be in constant communication. Because of this time commitment and effort, the company should target only a few key alliances. Otherwise the alliances will die off, and the cost of time, legal, and emotional investments will never be recouped.[7]

Starting the Negotiation Process

When the negotiating starts, both companies should use their best efforts to make it work. The parties should establish relationships with the highest officers and decision makers. The entrepreneur should make sure he is kept informed and does not entrust the fate of the partnership to a lower-level person. To determine the price or value as part of the negotiation, the outline of the selling memorandum shown later in this chapter will assist in maximizing efficiencies. When the contract is prepared, keep in mind that the best results for a successful alliance are the responsibility of both parties.

Selling the Business

Selling the business is another option in the entrepreneur's exit plan. As shown in Figure 8.1 in Chapter 8, this is the most common form of exit for entrepreneurs and investors. In order to create the highest value, you should build valuable assets and identify them clearly in the selling process.

The **essential company** is a concept that can help you identify the most appropriate assets. If you plan to sell the company to an existing larger corporation, you should develop a list of potential targets early on in the venture. Analyzing the strengths and weaknesses of your target buyers will guide you to where you should direct your resources in preparation for a sale. For example, a larger company is unlikely to see value in your brand, your office furniture, your fancy web site, or your expensive sales force and distribution network. They already have these. For a technology-based company, intellectual property and evidence of the innovation's practicality will be on top of the list; for a biotech company, positive results from animal and phase I clinical trials; for a medical device company, FDA 510-K approval; for a retail company, long leases on prime locations; for a software company, proof of demand and the ability to create high gross margins; for a service company, long-term contracts with customers, key employees, and suppliers; and so on. Therefore build only the *essential* assets that will be valued by a purchaser. This will help you maximize the value you create from limited resources. Don't waste money on assets that will be largely discounted by a buyer. The obvious fixed assets such as inventory, receivables, equipment, and real estate will be valued at book value at best.[8] Most importantly, if you can demonstrate that your assets can radically affect the competitive forces between a small number of target companies, you may be able to demand a very high value.

Along with negotiating an acceptable price, the entrepreneur should determine the kind of compensation or payment that is acceptable. It is common practice to hold back some of the payment in an escrow account until certain milestones have been reached. Holdbacks of up to one-third are typical. Payment may be in cash only, stock in the purchasing company, or a mixture of both. It is usual for the key employees to work for up to a year for the purchaser, which serves to provide continuity and ensure that the milestones can be attained. These arrangements are termed *earnout agreements*. These employment agreements will have certain restrictions such as non-compete clauses which may extend beyond the employment period. You should be flexible in the negotiations.

EXAMPLE: PEPSICO™ VERSUS COCA-COLA™

Imagine that you have developed a new recipe for a dark brown, bubbly, thirst-quenching soda that has a taste somewhere between these two leading brands. Its ingredients are trade secrets, and you have also filed for a patent on certain aspects of the product. The ingredients are already on the FDA-approved list of food additives. You wish to build a new company based on your product, but understandably you are turned down by every source of funding you approach—you need too much money and your competition is far too entrenched. You then find out in taste tests that when people drink your product, they have an immediate distaste for the two incumbents' products; they just don't like them anymore. With these results, you now have an extremely valuable asset, which, in the hands of either of the leading soda companies, has the potential of drastically shifting market share. You now invite representatives from the two companies to witness the tests and then suggest that they make an offer to buy your assets; you will sell to the highest bidder. Clearly you have no potential to become a direct competitor; yet you have an "essential asset" that could command an enormous value. This is, of course, an extreme illustrative case. However, when you have an asset that could impact the competitive forces in an established oligarchic market sector, you may extract a high value on the sale.[9] This is referred to as a sale to a "strategic" buyer whereby the entrepreneur captures some of the value, real or perceived, already invested by existing competitors.

Preparing a Selling Memorandum

For a company that has established a history of operations, the sale is more likely to be for a *going concern*. In this case, entrepreneurs should use the business plan as a marketing tool to help sell the company. A selling memorandum normally includes information about the company's history, the market in which the company competes, the company's products, its operations, and its strengths. The memorandum should be a comprehensive document because it reflects the quality of the organization. Once the selling memorandum is completed, the company is in a good position to refine the preliminary valuation and begin determining an appropriate range of selling prices.

Outline of a Selling Memorandum

Executive Summary

The executive summary should explain the purpose of the memorandum and describe all the key elements of the memorandum in just a few pages. A well-written summary should convince the prospective buyer to continue reading. The summary has another important use. It can be sent separately to people who may not be serious buyers. If, after reviewing the summary, they are still interested in seeing the whole plan, the entrepreneur can release it to them after they sign a confidentiality agreement to protect the confidential details of the memorandum.

Products and Services

The memorandum should describe the company's products and services. How are they different from others on the market? Are they patented? Are there follow-on products? What R&D is required and what technological risks exist? Include any product literature that is available.

Marketing and Sales

Describe the market for the products and services. Explain the dynamics of the market, market size, market trends, growth potential, user demographics, and so on. What are the company's marketing strategies, pricing strategies, penetration targets, and advertising and promotional plans? Include a competitive analysis, listing direct competitors and their strengths and weaknesses, market share, financial information, and the like.

Manufacturing

How are the products manufactured? How will the resources be used? Describe required raw materials and their sources. Are there second sources for all critical items? Describe production facilities and capacity requirements and constraints. What warranties do the products carry? How is the service provided?

Management

Describe the current organization. List key personnel who will be staying with the company and describe their positions and experience. Do not disclose their compensation, however, since this could provide recruiting information to competitors.

Employees

Describe how the employees are compensated. What major benefits are provided? Does a union represent them? If so, what are the significant terms of the contract? How have relations been with the union?

Historical Financial Statements

Present financial statements for the most recent interim periods, including comparisons with prior years' results and with budgets. Also include statements for the past three fiscal years, including auditors' reports, if any.

Financial Projections

Prepare financial projections for the next three to five years. Some sellers include their projections and the assumptions underlying the projections in the selling memorandum.[10]

When the selling memorandum is complete, a search for potential buyers begins. Who might be interested in purchasing the company? The potential list that is prepared can include individual investors or entrepreneurs, existing management, other employee groups, competitors, customers, vendors, investment groups, and foreign investors. Each of these groups has different motivations to buy, and depending on the company's situation, some groups may be more appropriate than others as potential buyers.

ROADMAP

IN ACTION The most desirable way for the entrepreneur to find the right buyer is to have a file of prospective buyers who have contacted the company. In addition to personal contacts, other sources of potential buyers include trade associations, investment and commercial bankers, and accountants.

It is common in these situations for the company to employ an investment bank to act as agent to help with finalizing the selling memorandum, identifying the target list of buyers, setting up contacts and presentations, and advising during the negotiations.

Several types of professional intermediaries are available to help identify potential buyers:

- The major investment banking firms have mergers and acquisitions departments that specialize in providing a wide range of services for these types of transactions. These firms are probably the most sophisticated and generally focus on transactions where the purchase price is $25 million or more.

- Commercial banks recently have developed affiliates that provide services similar to the services of investment banking firms. As affiliates of banks, they have information about and access to the bank's client companies.

- Finally, smaller independent firms that specialize in these areas can be highly qualified intermediaries. They often specialize in certain market sectors and participate in a range of transactions from small ones to those of about $20 million, with the majority on the smaller side.

Mini-Case: AEC

As an example, in 2010 American Education Corporation (AEC) of Oklahoma City, an educational software firm with under $50 million in total sales, engaged Parchman, Vaughan & Company, LLC, a boutique investment banker based in Baltimore to act as an agent for the sale of the company. Parchman, Vaughan & Company only advises in transactions in the education marketplace. American Education was purchased by K12 Inc., a public company in Virginia, a few months later. The deep knowledge and relationships in the educational marketplace provided by the investment bank enabled this sale to proceed smoothly and to the satisfaction of all parties. Investments banks traditionally announce their role in successful transactions using a "tombstone-like" design. Examples can be found on the web-site of Parchman, Vaughan and Company, LLC, where the AEC/K-12 tombstone can be found, among others.[11]

Lehman Formula Fee Schedule

The intermediary's key role is to identify potential candidates and assist both parties throughout the entire process to consummate the sale. This task is usually undertaken on an exclusive basis. Fees for bringing together the buyers and sellers are generally guaranteed by the seller, who provides an up-front retainer and a substantial amount contingent upon completion of the transaction. The total fee is often based on the "Lehman formula," which calls for fees of 5 percent of the first $1 million of purchase price, 4 percent of the second million, 3 percent of the third, 2 percent of the fourth, and 1 percent of amounts in excess of $4 million. Variations of the Lehman formula usually work well for midsize transactions. However, a different arrangement may be negotiated for very small and very large transactions.

Create the Letter of Intent

After a series of meetings ending up in an agreed set of purchase terms, the buyer will want to know that the seller is interested in continuing the process. A letter of intent is often written to confirm the interests of the two parties and to outline the basic terms that have been agreed on in the initial phase of negotiation. The letter of intent is, in many ways, similar to the term sheet for venture investments discussed in detail in Chapter 8.

The letter of intent is an agreement by the parties to continue to negotiate in good faith. Generally, it contains provisions that the terms are subject to a definitive contract and proclaims the document to be only an expression of intention. The letter of intent will have many escape clauses in it to allow both parties the opportunity to withdraw from the deal at any point. Such clauses may include requirements for approval by the board of directors or by the stockholders.

Certain issues related to the transaction are normally addressed at this stage, and the preliminary resolution of these issues will be contained in the letter of intent[12]:

- *The Purchase Price.* This is either its amount or an agreed-on formula for its computation.

- *What Is Being Purchased?* The general categories of assets, liabilities, and operations that are being transferred to the buyer and those being retained by the seller should be identified.

- *The Structure.* The parties need to agree about whether the sale will be a sale of assets, a sale of stock, a merger, or some other structure.

- *The Payout or Types of Compensation.* Will it be cash, notes, equity, or some combination of these?

- *Escrow for Contingencies.* The buyer may want to establish an escrow account into which a portion of the purchase price will be deposited. This escrow might cover such items as unrecorded liabilities that later surface, or recorded items that are only estimates (e.g., the allowance for uncollectable accounts).

- *Other Significant Terms.* These include contingent payments, covenants not to compete, and employment contracts.

- *Other Required Agreements.* These include renegotiated leases and long-term purchase contracts.

- *The Purchase Agreement.* What is the expected timing for preparing the purchase agreement? Who will draft it? Typically, the buyer's counsel will be the drafter.

- *Due Diligence.* What are the timing and extent? What are the buyer's expectations for documentation? Are management personnel and records available? (See the book web site for Chapter 8 for a complete due diligence checklist for investment and purchase transactions.)

- *Professional Fees.* Who will be responsible for the various related fees, including fees for attorneys, accountants, appraisers, and investment bankers?

- *Exclusivity Agreement.* A buyer will want to negotiate with the seller on an exclusive basis. The seller will usually grant such a right for a defined period, such as ninety or one hundred and twenty days.

- *Bust-up Fees.* It has become fairly common for the buyer to want a provision for bust-up fees if the company is ultimately sold to another bidder. The buyer will argue that, by putting the company in play (i.e., performing a valuation and beginning negotiations so other companies are aware the target company is seriously for sale), the buyer has added value to the target company. If another buyer then outbids the original buyer, the original buyer should receive a portion of the increased price as compensation for this value added. Sellers, of course, will try to avoid such a fee.

Other Conditions

The following conditions for closing will also be included in the letter of intent:

- *Applicable Law.* If the transaction involves parties located in different states, it is common to identify which state laws will govern the agreements.

- *Adjustments of Purchase Price for Interim Results.* A purchase price is usually negotiated based in part on historical financial information. The price may be adjusted for any income or losses that occur through the actual closing date.

Performing Due Diligence

Both the buyer and the seller will have to perform legal due diligence. The seller and advisers will review and prepare the disclosure schedules of information that are requested by the buyer to investigate the affairs of the company. They will also perform a legal audit to render an opinion on legal contingencies and other legal issues as of the closing.[13]

The typical information requested includes all corporate records (articles of incorporation, bylaws, minutes, stock records, etc.), material contracts, loan agreements, pending or threatened litigation, royalty agreements, labor agreements, leases, commitments, employment contracts, and stockholder agreements. An increasingly important area is environmental liability, as current owners of businesses may be held responsible for cleaning up toxic chemicals left by prior owners. Also, the need for regulatory clearance relating to restriction of trade concerns may have to be identified and obtained. The seller's counsel will issue a legal opinion at the closing that generally covers (1) the legality of the transaction (i.e., the company is authorized to do it and has all the requisite approvals), (2) the confirmation of capital stock information, (3) the validity and enforceability of all material contracts, and (4) the knowledge and status of pending or threatened litigation.

Preparing the Purchase Agreement

As the buyer's team begins its detailed evaluation of the company, the attorneys will be preparing the purchase agreements. The drafting of the documents will give rise to rounds of negotiations to resolve some of the obstacles deferred earlier in the process and to renegotiate issues previously agreed on but modified because of information that comes to light in the evaluation process.

The purchaser's attorney usually drafts the purchase agreement. Although the letter of intent will serve as the outline for this agreement, the final document will generally be quite lengthy. New issues often arise as a result of the due diligence process, and much time is spent in drafting the representations and warranties of both the buyer and the seller, as well as in drafting the indemnification provisions.

Closing the Deal

Once all these issues have been resolved and the financing commitments have been received, the deal is in condition to close; all the documents are signed, the stock or assets are transferred, and the consideration exchanges hands.

Often, certain time-consuming procedures such as obtaining a tax ruling, receiving an audited balance sheet, or perfecting the title on assets are a prerequisite to consummating the deal. Rather than wait until everything is done, the parties will agree to a deferred closing. The purchase agreement may be signed, and the consideration may change hands, but the actual passage of title may occur at a later date. *Conditions* are obligations that must be met for the deal to legally close. Typical conditions include fulfillment of key employment agreements; delivery of financial statements; maintenance of minimum net worth requirements; provision of accountants' comfort letters and legal opinions; and if applicable, gaining third-party consent on the transfer of material agreements, licenses, or rights.

Merge with Another Business

A merger is a transaction between two companies and is an alternative to selling the business or selling an equity stake to a strategic partner. A merger between two businesses ranges from survival to value-added services for the growth of the new venture. When a company loses its competitive advantage in the marketplace, a merger may be the only path center to follow.

On creating a merger, the entrepreneur should identify areas of similarity and differences and define the capability that shows the value of each company.

Planning a merger requires calculating the values of both the business and all existing resources. (Use Chapter 8 to determine which valuation methods are best and how to evaluate the other company's management and capabilities.) The benefits of a merger can be the route to instant product diversification and quick completion of product lines. It also can provide technical know-how, greater executive depth, economies of scale, improved access to financing, entry into otherwise closed markets, vertical integration of manufacturing operations, and new marketing strength.

Using an Employee Stock Ownership Plan (ESOP)

Under an employee stock ownership plan (ESOP), companies provide their employees with the opportunity to acquire the company's shares at a reduced price over a period of time. Direct purchase plans allow employees to buy shares in the company, which can be owned by the founder, with their own, usually after-tax, money. In the United States and several foreign countries, however, there are special tax-qualified plans that allow employees to buy stock either at a discount or with matching shares from the company. For instance, in the United States, employees can put aside after-tax pay over some period of time (typically six to twelve months) and then use the accumulated funds to buy shares at up to a 15 percent discount at either the price at the time of purchase or the time when they started putting aside the money, whichever is lower. In this way, the founding entrepreneur can gradually transfer her ownership to the employees who have an incentive to keep the company on a sustainable profitable growth track and retain its unique culture and values. Refer to the Paul Silvis profile in Chapter 10. Paul wished to preserve the culture of Restek as one of its greatest assets. Therefore he sold the company to the employees using an ESOP even though he had higher cash offers from other corporations.

Using a Management Buyout (MBO)

A management buyout (MBO) describes the process whereby the managers and/or executives of a company purchase controlling interest in a company from existing shareholders. These can of course, be the founding team. In most cases, the management will buy out all the outstanding shareholders. If the company is already publicly traded, they will usually then take the company private because they feel that they have the expertise to grow the business better when controlling the ownership. Quite often, the management will team up with a venture capitalist to acquire the business as significant capital may be required. There are several large private equity firms that specialize in MBOs. If the founding entrepreneur wishes to influence how the company will be managed subsequent to being bought out, it is important that she recruit the management team and involve them over several years within the company prior to the buyout. Unfortunately, this is rarely the case, and a buyout is forced upon the founders for some external reason when it is then too late to guide the future of the company.

Consider a Public Offering

Entrepreneurs can realize a harvest from the value they have created by considering a public offering. In deciding whether to go ahead with a public offering, it is important that entrepreneurs remember that the initial public offering (IPO) is neither more nor less important than any of the exit options we have discussed. As mentioned earlier, going public is a relatively rare exit method for entrepreneurs, and it should be reviewed with considerable care. The market for IPOs is booming, and *Alibaba Group Holding* <u>BABA</u> made the largest ever stock market debut. But other highly valued private companies such as Uber, are deciding that rushing to go public isn't worth the trouble. It is usually one that a company may undertake over time. An important consideration for an IPO is the timing of the transaction, as the demand for newly issued stock can be extremely volatile. In deciding whether to do an IPO, it is always advisable to proceed with a backup plan. Even if the company is well prepared and the market is favorable, the economy can change by the date of the IPO.[14] Going public represents a rite of passage for a company and provides both benefits and obligations that should be carefully considered. The IPO process is difficult, the pitfalls are numerous, and the stakes are high. Despite initial positive performance after the offering, many companies discover that the values recede soon after going public, and the company underperforms in both profits and share price.

The following questions need to be addressed in making an IPO decision:

- Are you ready to share the ownership of your company with the public?

- Are you prepared to disclose your company's most closely held secrets?

- Can you live with the continued scrutiny of investors and market analysts? Can you devote the required 100 percent of your time for six to eight months and pay the substantial fees that it takes for a typical IPO?

- Are you prepared to take on the issues, challenges, costs, and responsibilities of going public?

The Benefit of Going Public

The benefits of going public are many and diverse. To determine whether they outweigh the drawbacks, you must evaluate them in the context of personal, shareholder, and corporate objectives. Some of the most attractive benefits include the following[15]:

- *Improved Financial Condition.* Selling shares to the public brings equity money that does not have to be repaid, immediately improving the company's financial condition.

- *Benefits to the Shareholder/Investor.* Going public offers liquidity to existing investors despite the sales restrictions imposed on the major investors, officers, and directors of the company. Underwriters will restrict the founding stockholders and management from selling their sales through lockup agreements for a specific period of time (normally one hundred and eighty days); eventually they can convert their shares into cash. The value of the stock may increase remarkably, starting with the initial offering. Shares that are publicly traded generally command higher prices than those that are not. Investors are usually willing to pay more for public companies because of (1) the marketability of the shares, (2) the maturity/sophistication attributed to public companies, and (3) the availability of more information.

- *Diversification of Shareholder Portfolios.* Going public makes it possible for shareholders to diversify their investment portfolios. IPOs often include a secondary offering (shares owned by existing shareholders) in addition to a primary offering (previously unissued shares). The entrepreneur must ensure that potential investors and shareholders do not perceive the secondary offerings as a bailout for shareholders. Underwriters frequently restrict the number of shares that can be sold by existing shareholders in a secondary offering.

- *Access to Capital.* Accessing the public equity markets enables you to attract better valuations, accept less dilution of ownership, and raise more money. The money from an IPO can repay debt, fund special projects, and be used for acquisitions. For example, the proceeds can be used to acquire other businesses, repay debts, finance research and development projects, and acquire or modernize production facilities. Another plus is that raising equity capital through a public offering often results in a higher valuation for your company through a higher multiple of earnings (or price-to-earnings ratio) as compared with many types of private financing. Thus, it often results in less dilution of ownership than with some other financing alternatives, such as venture capital. Raising capital in this way also avoids the interest costs and cash drain of debt financing.

- *Management and Employee Incentives.* The company can issue stock options to the management and employees. This can be more motivating and rewarding to employees than issuing illiquid stock and will attract and retain the key executives.

  Many companies do need to go public to obtain enough funds to buy other companies. Publicly traded stock also helps reward early employees who can cash in stock options received as an incentive when the company was starting out.

- *Corporate Reputation.* The company's public status and listing on a national exchange can provide a competitive advantage over other companies in the same industry by providing greater visibility and enhanced corporate image. This can lead to increased sales, reduced pricing from vendors, and improved service from suppliers.

- *Improved Opportunities for Future Financing.* By going public, an entrepreneurial venture usually improves its net worth and builds a larger and broader equity base. The improved debt-to-equity ratio will help the company borrow additional funds as needed or reduce the current cost of borrowing. If the stock performs well in the continuing aftermarket, the company is more likely to be able to raise additional equity capital on favorable terms. With an established market for the stock, the entrepreneur will have the flexibility to offer future investors a whole new range of securities with liquidity and an ascertainable market value.

- *A Path to Acquisitions.* Private companies often lack the financial connections and resources to assume an aggressive role in acquisitions. Well-conceived acquisitions can play a big part in corporate survival and success. Going public enhances a company's financing alternatives for acquisitions by adding two vital components to its financial resources: (1) cash derived from the IPO and (2) unissued equity shares that have a ready market. Public companies often issue stock (instead of paying cash) to acquire other businesses. The owners of an acquisition target may be more willing to accept a company's stock if it is publicly traded. The liquidity provided by the public market affords greater flexibility and ease in selling shares using shares as collateral for loans.

The Disadvantages of Going Public

The benefits of going public must be weighed against its drawbacks. Here again, the entrepreneur must view the possible drawbacks in the context of personal, company, and shareholder objectives. In many cases the impact of these drawbacks can be minimized through thoughtful planning backed by the help of outside advisors.[13]While early investors expect—and generally get—a much higher price when a company goes public, some in recent years have seen enthusiasm fizzle at the IPO. Those who bought into <u>Zynga</u> at $14 a share, for example, when the game company was still private, had to deal with an IPO priced at $10. It is now trading at less than $8:

- *Timing is Critical.* The stock market is very volatile, and synchronizing an IPO for a particular company is extremely difficult and uncertain. Often an IPO is withdrawn on the day prior to the event because there is not enough public demand at the price the company finds attractive. The public is fickle and follows fads, as was clear during the dot.com boom. After the bust, it was impossible to take an Internet company public for several years, even if it was potentially a great company.

- *Up-front Expenses.* Going public can be costly and will result in a tremendous commitment of the management's time and energy. The largest single cost in an IPO ordinarily is the underwriter's discount or commission, which generally ranges from 6 to 10 percent of the offering price. In addition, legal and accounting fees, printing costs, the underwriter's out-of-pocket expenses (generally not included in the commission), and filing fees, as well as registrar and transfer agent fees, can typically add another $300,000 to $500,000.

- *Loss of Control.* Depending on the proportion of shares sold to the public, the entrepreneur may be at risk of losing control of the company now or in the future. Retaining at least 51 percent of the shares will ensure control for now, but subsequent offerings and acquisitions may dilute control. However, if the stock is widely distributed, the management usually can retain control even if it holds less than 50 percent of the shares. To retain voting control, it is possible to have a new class of common stock with limited voting rights. However, such stock may have limited appeal to investors and may, therefore, sell for less than ordinary common stock.

- *Sharing the Success.* Investors share the risks and successes of the new venture to which they contribute capital. If the entrepreneur realistically anticipates unusually high earnings in the next two or three years and can obtain bank or other financing, he may wish to temporarily defer a public offering. Then when the company does go public, the shares will, most likely, command a higher price.

- *Loss of Privacy.* Of all the changes that result when a company goes public, perhaps none is more troublesome than the loss of privacy. When a company becomes publicly held, the Securities and Exchange Commission (SEC) requires disclosure of much information about the company—information that private companies don't ordinarily disclose. Some of those disclosures contain highly sensitive information such as compensation paid to key executives and directors, special incentives for the management, and many of the plans and strategies that underlie the company's operations. These disclosures rarely harm the business. For the most part, employee compensation and the prices paid for materials and received for the products are governed by market forces, not by the disclosed financial results.

- *Limits on the Management's Freedom to Act.* By going public, the management surrenders some degree of freedom. While the management of a privately held company generally is free to act by itself, the management of a public company must obtain the approval of the board of directors on certain major matters; on special matters, it must seek the consent of the shareholders. The board of directors, if kept informed on a timely basis, can usually be counted on to understand the management's needs, offer support, and grant much of the desired flexibility.

- *Demands of Periodic Reporting.* The management is required to comply with SEC regulations and reporting requirements. These requirements include quarterly financial reporting (Form 10-Q), annual financial reporting (Form 10-K), and reporting of current material events (Form 8-K). Reporting the requirements of a registrant demands significant time and financial commitments. Security analysts will also demand the management's time. Recently the additional costs and personal burdens imposed by the Sarbanes–Oxley legislation for financial reporting have become a further concern to senior management.

- *New Fiduciary Responsibilities.* As the owner of a private business, the money invested and risked is the owner's. However, as the manager of a public company, the money invested and risked belongs to the shareholders. The entrepreneur is accountable to them, so she must approach potential conflicts of interest with utmost caution. It also will be necessary to work with the board of directors to help them discharge their fiduciary responsibilities when acting on corporate matters.

Managing the IPO Event

Once the board makes the decision to undertake an IPO, it is vital to retain a lead investment bank to manage the process as the IPO event requires many months of careful preparation.[16]

Selecting the Underwriter

The lead underwriter that manages the offering plays a critical role in the success of the IPO, preparing the company's Registration Statement and selling the company's securities. In selecting an underwriter, the following factors are important:

- *Experienced Industry Analyst.* The underwriter should have an analyst experienced in IPOs and the industry you are in.

- *Synergy.* The company should feel comfortable with the individual bankers. The right synergy between the bankers and management is important.

- *Distribution.* The investment bank should have the resources of a retail sales force to sell the stock as well as the ability to syndicate the IPO to other investment banks with which it has a relationship.

- *Post-IPO Support.* The underwriter should have a strong record of the post-IPO price performance of companies it has recently taken public. A solid track record will indicate how well the investment bank priced recent transactions.

The IPO event usually lasts between ninety and one-hundred and twenty days, but some take up to six months.[17] It includes preparing and filing the Registration Statement (and one to three amendments responding to comments from the SEC), going on the road show, and the closing and buying of the company stock by the underwriting syndicate. Other events will include the first periodic reports, proxy solicitation, and dealing with restricted stock.

The Registration Process

The registration process begins when the entrepreneur has reached an understanding with an underwriter on the proposed public offering. From this point on, he becomes subject to SEC regulations on what may or may not be done to promote the company. The center of the process is preparing the Registration Statement (S1), which includes a complete description of the company, its business, the market for its products, and the regulatory environment in which it operates. This entails establishing the appropriate internal accounting policies for the business, systems, and management and preparing the required financial data, including highlights and timing. The financial statements must be audited and should reflect income statements for the preceding three years, balance sheets for the prior two years, and interim financial statements for the applicable periods. The statement also lists the company's officers and directors, biographies, compensation, and stock ownership. Other factors to consider are employment contracts, compensation, and the board of directors. The Registration Statement is usually approved by company counsel and has comments from the underwriter, management, and company accountants. The prospectus, which is a part of the Registration Statement, becomes the marketing document for the IPO.

Filing the Registration Statement

Once outstanding issues have been resolved and the company officers and majority of the board of directors have signed the Registration Statement, it is filed with the SEC (normally electronically) on the SEC's EDGAR system. In addition to filing with the SEC, the statement is also filed with any state in which the securities will be offered and with the National Association of Securities Dealers. At closing, documents are executed and stock certificates are exchanged. Usually company officers, counsel, the transfer agent, and managing underwriters attend the final closing.

Waiting during the Quiet Period

The SEC places restrictions on what a company can do while *in registration*. These restrictions apply during the *quiet period*. This is defined as the time and date the company agrees with the investment firm to offer the securities to the public until twenty-five days after the securities become available to the public. During the quiet period, any publicity release can raise questions or concerns about whether the publicity is part of the selling efforts—even if the publicity does not specifically mention the public offering. However, this does not preclude the normal ongoing disclosure of the factual information about the company. The SEC encourages companies to continue product advertising campaigns, periodic reporting to shareholders, and press announcements on factual business and financial developments, such as new contracts, plant openings, and issuance of patents.

The company, however, can publish a limited notice of the offering, including the amount of the offering, the name of the company, a description of the security, the offering price, and the names of the underwriters. Known as *tombstone ads* because of their stark appearance, these notices are typically published in newspapers shortly after the initial filing of the Registration Statement and are not considered sales literature.

The Road Show

After the Registration Statement has been filed, the underwriters generally will take representatives of the company on a traveling road show, also referred to as a dog and pony show. These meetings give prospective members of the underwriting syndicate, institutional investors, and industry analysts an opportunity to meet the company's management team and ask questions about the offering and the company. The participants probably will be the company's chief executive officer and chief financial officer, whose major task will be to generate interest among the investors and investment bankers, who will manage the tour and monitor the book or computerized log of orders. Typically, the road show consists of five to seven back-to-back meetings every day for two weeks. The presentations are not dissimilar to those described in the previous chapter targeting private investors.

ROADMAP

IN ACTION

The road show presents the opportunity to tell the company's story to the people who will help sell the securities and influence potential investors. It will also allow the CEO to meet many of the people who will follow the company after the public offering. The show is so challenging that no one can ever be completely prepared. The plan is to present a balanced view of the business, market, and competition and why the company will be a huge success.

The Expenses of Going Public

Underwriters' Compensation

The underwriters will receive a discount (spread) between the price at which they buy stock and the price at which they sell the same stock to the public. The amount of the spread is negotiated based on the size and risk of the offering. A typical firm commitment offering discount is approximately 7 percent of the public offering price of the stock.

Underwriters may also be granted warrants as partial compensation for an offering. Other compensations may include reimbursement of expenses and rights of first refusal on future underwriting, directorships, and consulting arrangements.

Accounting and Legal Fees

The lawyers' and accountants' fees depend on the amount of work involved in preparing the Registration Statement and reviewing the financial statements and other financial data. The company should endeavor to do as much of the work of preparing the Registration Statement as possible to cut costs.

Directors' and Officers' Insurance

Before going public, a company needs to take out a personal liability insurance policy that will protect the officers and directors from being held personally liable if a shareholder suit is brought based on incorrect information in the Registration Statement.

Post-IPO Actions

When the IPO is completed and finalized, the entrepreneur and the management team must begin meeting the shareholders and board of directors. Investors and shareholders are very well informed, and if the company misses earnings projections by even a small amount, the stock price can drop 10 percent or more the next day. It can take six quarters of on-target performance to win the market back. The challenge after the IPO is to deliver the value that the company promised in the business plan and offering memorandum. Delivering the value is a balancing act that involves meeting and exceeding the expectations of the market and all the stakeholders while the company implements the strategic initiatives on time and on budget.

For the entrepreneur/CEO of a public company, credibility is important. Yet many elements cannot be controlled, such as the fluctuations of the industry, the stock market, and the national and world economics. Nevertheless, the entrepreneur should continue to provide strong leadership by delivering the growth that is promised and by communicating to the stakeholders. The pressure most public companies face is to maintain short-term earnings growth. The financial markets generally react adversely to reports of lower earnings, even if the long-term strategic decisions from which they result are sound. Consequently, companies are often tempted to maintain share prices by sacrificing long-term profitability and growth for short-term earnings. The entrepreneur must plan and implement a business strategy that balances short-term and long-term needs and communicate the plan to shareholders and the financial community.

SUMMARY

It is important to prepare an exit plan for the business to be executed at the right time. A company can realize the value it has created in several ways. The most common are selling an equity stake to a strategic partner, selling the business, merging with another business, and employing a public offering. Selling an equity stake to a strategic partner can attract needed capital from a source interested in the technology and can lead to completely selling the business at a later time. Selling the business is another option but might be risky in a weak economy. Entrepreneurs might have to agree to long-term payment plans that include a stock-for-stock exchange that may result in stock price declines. Merging with another company involves a transaction between two companies and is an alternative to growing a business. When a company loses its competitive advantage in the marketplace, this alternative can be a viable option. The founders can also sell the company, usually over time, to the management team (an MBO), to a broader group of employees through an ESOP,[18] or pass the company on to family members (see "Family Business

Management," Chapter 14). In these three cases, it is important that considerable time be devoted to getting the management succession plan in place to ensure a smooth handover and long-term stability of the company. When an exit via a handover to family members is contemplated, significantly greater risk of failure is encountered. The entrepreneur can also arrange an exit by going public. This option can be the most profitable strategy for the entrepreneur, but it has the disadvantages of costing a great deal of time and money and demanding significant financial commitments. Security analysts will also demand the management's time. The proceeds from an IPO can repay debt, fund special projects, and be used for acquisitions.

STUDY QUESTIONS

Q.1 What are the various options for establishing an exit strategy?

Q.2 Briefly describe the procedures in selling a business.

Q.3 List the major pitfalls in creating an alliance.

Q.4 Describe the methods that make alliances successful.

Q.5 What are the similarities and differences between an ESOP, MBO, and Family Transition Exits?

Q.6 Give three reasons why family businesses have a high failure rate when founders hand over to the next generation. Compare this situation with a case in which the handover is to a new nonfamily management team.

Q.7 What five steps must be taken to prepare a company for a successful MBO or family succession?

EXERCISES

Develop an Exit Strategy

11.1 Prepare and list an entrepreneur's reasons for developing an exit strategy:

11.2 When does an alliance start and end in selling an equity stake?

11.3 Describe a scenario in which an equity alliance will succeed.

Reason for an Exit Strategy	Importance (1–10)	Company/Strengths/Weaknesses		
		Low	Average	High
1.				
2.				
3.				
4.				
5.				

Alliance Analysis

11.4 List the types of alliances and complete the table with descriptions and figures:

Name	Approx. Sales	Target Market	Type of Alliance
1.			
2.			
3.			
4.			
5.			

Selling a Company

11.5 Complete the following table by describing the company's exposure to the risks listed on the left and the company's planned response to an exit strategy:

Area of Potential Risk	Company Exposure	Exit Strategy
Industry growth		
Product technology or liability		
Financial		
Management changes		

11.6 Refer to the DBI case in Chapter 3 and the content in Chapter 14 and view the video interviews with Neal DeAngelo on the book web site. DBI is still owned by the DeAngelo family members. Is the company a lifestyle company? What specific issues does this private, family-owned structure raise with regard to financing growth, management succession, and eventual cashing out of the value that has been built?

11.7 Value a stock in a company of your choice using a discounted cash flow model. List the key drivers of value for the company. (Identify the key assumption or variable that you would focus on in doing a discounted cash flow valuation. Examples would include the growth rate assumption, the growth period assumption, and the net capital expenditure assumption.)

11.8 Prepare a list of comparable companies, using criteria you think are appropriate. Choose a multiple that you will use in comparing firms across the group. (You may have to try out a number of multiples before making this choice.) Evaluate the company against the comparable firms using the multiple that you have chosen for your valuation. Determine if the company is under- or overvalued.

11.9 Consider Uber in the context of why and when a venture should consider an IPO. Mutual-fund managers Fidelity Investments, Wellington Management, and BlackRock Inc. (BLK) led a $1.2 billion round of financing for Uber Technologies Inc. in June 2014. The investment valued the car-hailing company at $18.2 billion. As an investor who puts money into highly valued private companies, such a large valuation raises the bar for the price that they would need to get later to cash out at a substantial profit. At these levels, the most likely way to get an attractive exit would be to go public. Discuss the pros and cons of both the private equity round of Uber and a later public offering for the investors.

INTERACTIVE LEARNING ON THE WEB

Test your knowledge of the chapter using the book's interactive web site.

ADDITIONAL RESOURCES

- **AllianceStrategy.com**, http://www.strategic-alliances.org/
- **Association of Strategic Alliance Professionals**, www.strategic-alliances.org
- **Booz Allen Hamilton**, www.boozallen.com

ENDNOTES

1. This profile was garnered from a personal interview in October 2000 with Trefler as well as the article in reference 2.

2. See Adam Bryant, "Your Opinions Are Respected (and Required)," *New York Times*, August 7, 2011, http://www.nytimes.com/2011/08/07/business/alan-trefler-of-pegasystems-on-valuing-employees-opinions.html?_r=0.

3. Refer to the AutoESL case in Chapter 8.

4. See Tom Copeland, Tim Koller, and Jack Murrin, *Valuation: Measuring and Managing the Value of Companies* (New York: John Wiley & Sons, 2000).

5. See Shannon P. Pratt, Robert F. Reilly, and Robert P. Schweihs, *Valuing a Business: The Analysis and Appraisal of Closely Held Companies*, 3rd ed. (Irwin Press, New York, NY 1996), 45–47.

6. David Carrithers (consultant and author of articles on employee culture and performance) interview. He can be found at www.businesshive.com.

7. Laurence Charney (partner, Ernst & Young), interview, New York, May 2001.

8. For a discussion on creating early exits from "essential" companies, see Basil Peters, *Early Exits* (Vancouver: Meteor Bytes Press, 2009).

9. Refer again to the Coretek case in Chapter 8. The high value paid before any commercial product was sold is derived from the perception that Coretek's technology would have a major impact on the market share in the telecommunications sector. Several large companies were in the bidding.

10. Michael Bucheit (partner, Advanced Infrastructure Ventures) interview, New York, June 2002.

11. For an example of a specialist or "boutique" investment banker, see www.parchmanvaughan.com/. This company advised American Education Corporation using its extensive knowledge and contacts in the education market sector.

12. See Stephen C. Blowers et.al., *The Ernst & Young Guide to the IPO Value Journey* (New York: John Wiley & Sons, 1999), 97–99.

13. See Jack M. Kaplan, *Getting Started in Entrepreneurship*, 2nd ed. (New York: John Wiley & Sons, 2001), 173.

14. See Stephen C. Blowers et.al., *The Ernst & Young Guide to the IPO Value Journey* (New York: John Wiley & Sons, 1999), 97–99.

15. Ibid., 32–35.

16. See Ira A. Greenstein, *Going Public Source Book* (New York: R. R. Donnelley Financial, 1999), 5–7.

17. Laurence Charney interview, May 2001.

18. *See Dwight B. Crane* and Indra Rein berg, "Employee Stock Ownership Plans (ESOPs) and Phantom Stock Plans," *Harvard Business Review* (November, 2000): 5–6.

GLOSSARY OF TERMS

accredited investors Individual or institutional investors who meet the qualifying SEC criteria with respect to financial sophistication or financial assets.

adoption cycle Usually applied to new technologies, the phases of use that follow a distinct and predictable pattern. See **early adopters**.

advisory board A group of individuals willing to serve in an advisory capacity in exchange for stock or other benefits.

angel A private investor who often has nonmonetary motives for investing as well as the usual financial ones.

B2B A business that sells directly to other companies.

B2C A business that sells directly to consumers.

balance sheet This is also called the statement of financial position and provides a picture of the business's financial position at a particular point in time. It encompasses everything the company owns (assets) or owes (liabilities), as well as the investments into the company by its owners and the accumulated earnings or losses of the company (equity).

Berkus valuation method A simple technique for estimating the value of an early-stage company based on milestone achievements.

board of directors Individuals elected by stockholders of a corporation and who are responsible to that group for overseeing the overall direction and policy of the firm.

board visitation rights The right to be present at board meetings as an observer but with no voting rights.

book value The difference between the *tangible* assets of a company and its liabilities. For an early-stage company, the book value is often negative. As the company grows and matures, the value may be many times the book value.

bootstrapping Accessing cash and noncash resources to build a company, avoiding the sale of stock.

brainstorming A management technique used to foster ideas, solve problems, set goals, establish priorities, and determine who on the team will be responsible for following through with the various tasks needed to accomplish the goals and priorities established.

breakeven analysis A means of determining the quantity that has to be sold at a given price so that revenues will equal cost.

bridge financing Financing obtained by a company expecting to secure permanent financing (such as through an initial public offering) within a short time, such as two years.

burn rate The cash needed on a month-to-month basis to sustain a company's operations (see **runway**).

business model The way that a company combines all of its functions and relationships to create a way of doing business.

business model canvas A useful tool developed by Alexander Osterwalder for developing business models.

buy–sell agreement Contract among associates that sets the terms and conditions by which one or more of the associates can buy out one or more of the other associates.

by-laws Rules under which a corporation is governed. These rules can be amended as provided by state law and by the by-laws themselves. Rules and regulations under which a board of directors operates a corporation.

C-corporation The most common form of business ownership and the one preferred by investors. As a separate legal entity apart from its owners, it may engage in business, issue contracts, sue and be sued, and pay taxes directly.

crowdfunding The practice of funding a project or venture by raising monetary contributions from a large number of people, typically via the Internet.

crowdsourcing The process of obtaining needed services, ideas, or content by soliciting contributions from a large group of people, especially from an online community rather than from traditional employees or suppliers.

cap table Also known as the capitalization table. A list of all the owners of a company with the percentage ownership, class of securities including warrants, and options to purchase shares.

cash flow statement This is also called the source and use of funds and shows the amount of cash that the company has at the end of each accounting period, usually monthly. It is related to a cash flow forecast, which aids in planning to avoid an inability to meet **payables** on time.

cash-out (1) The time interval before a company no longer has any cash for operations, also known as **runway**; (2) investors are said to cash out of a company at a **liquidity event**.

chief financial officer (CFO) A member of a company's upper management who oversees all the financial aspects of the business.

closed innovation The opposite to **open innovation**.

closing (1) In accounting, when the books are summarized in financial statements for a specific time frame and no further entries are allowed for this period; (2) in real estate, when the buyer and seller (or their agents) meet to finalize the transaction. Sometimes called the settlement, this is the point at which the transfer of property and funds takes place. The term also applies generally to business transactions such as an investment, loan, or company sales event.

cocreation A management initiative that brings different parties together, for instance, a company and a group of customers, in order to jointly produce a mutually valued outcome.

collaborative filtering A method by which data from a number of sources are analyzed to find ways of creating additional value to customers, suppliers, and so on beyond what can be found by just looking at the data from an individual.

comfort letter A letter provided by a company's independent auditors detailing procedures performed at the request of the underwriters. The letter supplements the underwriter's due diligence review.

commercial bank State or nationally chartered bank that accepts demand deposits, grants business loans, and provides a variety of other financial services. Typically used by the entrepreneur as an asset lender.

common and preferred stock Shares that represent the ownership interest in a corporation. Both common and preferred stocks have ownership rights, but preferred stock normally has a prior claim on dividends and assets (in the event of liquidation). Both common and preferred stockholders' claims are junior to claims of bondholders or other creditors of the company. Common stockholders assume the greater risk but have the voting power. They generally exercise the greater control but may gain the greater reward in the form of dividends and capital appreciation. The terms *common stock* and *capital stock* are often used interchangeably when the company has no preferred stock. Preferred stock may usually be converted into common stock upon a liquidity event.

confidentiality agreement A contract between two or more parties signed to protect information which one or more entities deem confidential. Also referred to as a **nondisclosure agreement**.

consulting agreement A contract between a company and another entity such as a consulting firm or an individual consultant. This document spells out clearly who owns the results of the consultant's work. The agreement usually stipulates a **work-for-hire** arrangement.

contingent litigation A process in which an attorney will receive a percentage, typically 50 percent, from the proceeds of a successful lawsuit in exchange for not charging a fee for work done. Small companies sometimes use this process for patent litigation against larger companies.

convertible debentures A form of investment whereby the investor loans the company funds carrying a "coupon," or interest, which usually accrues. Within a defined period, the investor may convert the loan and the accrued interest into stock at an agreed-on price. This arrangement gives an investor greater flexibility in managing the investment.

cooperative A business model whereby a group with similar missions combine their efforts often but not necessarily to fulfill a social mission.

copyright An exclusive right granted by the federal government to the creator to publish and sell literary, musical, or other artistic materials. A copyright is honored for fifty years after the death of the author.

covenants Restrictive terms in a loan or stock sale agreement that protect the lender or investor.

debt capital Funds or assets acquired by borrowing.

dilution The reduction of a stockholder's percentage of ownership in an enterprise, usually arising from selling more common stock to other parties, sometimes called *watering the stock*. Investors may require *antidilution* protection so that their ownership position is protected in preference to the founders should certain milestones not be attained.

disbursement The act of paying out funds to satisfy a financial obligation.

dual mission model A business model whereby both social and wealth-creation missions coexist.

D&O insurance An insurance policy that protects directors and officers of a company from lawsuits, particularly from shareholders. The cost of such insurance has escalated since the recent number of corporate fraud cases.

due diligence The responsibility of those preparing and signing the registration statement to conduct an investigation in order to provide a reasonable basis for their belief that statements made in the registration statement are true and do not omit any material facts. Proper due diligence can help protect these parties from liability in the event that they are sued for a faulty offering. The company, on the other hand, has strict liability for errors or omissions in the regulation statement. Due diligence is also undertaken by private investors and banks before reaching a final agreement on terms and releasing funds.

early adopters A group of customers that wish to be the first in owning the "newest and best" new product irrespective of cost. This sector is often targeted by high-technology product companies upon launch of a new product.

earnings report A statement issued by a company reflecting its financial situation over a given period of time. This report lists revenue, expenses, and the net result.

EBIT The company's earnings before interest and taxes.

EBITDA The company's earnings before interest, taxes, depreciation, and amortization of long-term assets. It therefore reflects the inherent quality of the day-to-day operations of the firm.

elevator pitch A slang term referring to the twenty to sixty seconds an entrepreneur has to interest a venture capitalist in his or her business idea.

employment agreement A contract between an employee and a company, usually signed upon hiring.

entrepreneur Derived from the French word *entreprendre*, meaning to undertake. Someone who is willing and eager to create a new venture to present a concept to the marketplace.

equity (1) Total assets minus total liabilities equals equity, or net worth; (2) money invested in a company that is not intended to be repaid but represents an ownership interest.

escrow Placing money in a special and separate account under the control of another party, usually a financial institution, to be held until the completion of conditions set forth in an agreement.

ESOP Employees' stock ownership plan by which the employees can acquire ownership of a company over time. This transfer of ownership carries certain tax advantages and is one way in which founders and investors can create an exit strategy for themselves. This route is not favored by venture capitalists, since the time frames are extended and the valuations usually low.

essential company A company designed and built solely for the sale of its assets to an existing larger company.

exit strategy (1) The way an entrepreneur gets his or her money out of the venture; (2) the vehicle for selling the enterprise; (3) what venture capitalists look for when funding new ventures—their way to realize the dollar profits from the investment. See **liquidity event**.

factor Financial institution that buys accounts receivable from a firm and bills customers directly, as opposed to a bank that lends only on accounts receivable. Factors can move quickly to get funds to a business but are usually the most expensive way to finance accounts receivable.

family business A commercial organization in which decision-making is influenced by multiple generations of a family—related by blood or marriage—who are closely identified with the firm through leadership or ownership.

financial institution Any firm that deals with money and/or securities. Banks, savings and loans, insurance companies, hard-asset lenders, credit unions, stockbrokers, consumer financial companies, and investment bankers, as well as a host of other highly specialized organizations, are examples of the institutions that operate in the huge and highly complex world of finance.

financial ratios Measurements used to establish common standard figures that can be compared from year to year, company to company, or company to industry.

financial statement Periodic accounting reports of a company's activities, which usually include a balance sheet, an income statement, and a cash flow statement.

finder's fee Commission paid to a person for furnishing to the payer a buyer or a property or for arranging an introduction that leads to a deal.

first-mover advantage The competitive lead that a company can build by being first into a new market and capturing market share before competitors emerge.

five-component model A useful tool for designing business models.

forms 10-K and 10-Q The annual and quarterly report public companies file with the SEC. The reports are prepared by the independent accountants of the company.

franchise A right conferred by a franchisor to a franchisee to operate a business using a defined brand, image, and stipulated business processes in exchange for a fee usually based on a percentage of sales.

freemium A pricing strategy by which a product or service (typically a digital offering or application such as software, media, games, or web services) is provided free of charge, but money (premium) is charged for proprietary features, functionality, or virtual goods.

full disclosure The ethical obligation to tell the full truth about any matter that the other party should know to make a valid decision. There is a legal requirement in many cases, such as when seeking investors or lenders. The concept also applies when analyzing conflict-of-interest issues and ethical dilemmas where all stakeholders should receive full disclosure of all the relevant facts.

gazelle A company that is growing its revenues by at least 20 percent per annum for four years in succession.

going public The process by which a corporation offers its securities to the public.

goodwill The difference between the market value of a firm and the market value of its net tangible assets.

greentech A technology that reduces the use of the Earth's resources and protects the environment, often related to sustainable technologies.

harvest Liquidating the accumulated assets and equity of a venture; converting profitable investment into cash to realize a profit.

hybrid business model A combination of for-profit and nonprofit entities often used by social entrepreneurs.

hype cycle In the early stages of development, a new technology is often oversold and overpromoted, with a subsequent fall in reputation as the difficulties in commercialization become more apparent.

incentive stock option plan Provision of **stock options** to employees as a component of compensation. Plans may be qualified or nonqualified, depending on the tax treatment sought.

income statement A financial statement that shows the amount of income earned by a business over a specific accounting period. All costs (expenses) are subtracted from the gross revenues (sales) to determine net income, which outlines the profit-and-loss financial statement (P&L).

incubator Accommodation for early-stage companies providing low rent and shared services.

information rights The rights of a lender or investor to receive certain defined information concerning the progress of the company on a periodic basis. This right is commonly sought by lenders who seek an early warning if the company is not meeting its projections.

initial public offering (IPO) A privately held company that elects to sell a portion of its common shares of stock to the public, often used when a small company seeks outside equity financing for expansion.

intrapreneur A term coined by Gifford Pinchot III to identify an entrepreneur working within the confines of a corporation while retaining some degree of independence. Often the term *corporate venturing* is used.

inverse commons A method by which the greater the number of persons that contribute to an initiative, the larger the value created for the total community; often used with **open innovation**.

investment bank A company regulated by the Securities and Exchange Commission that acts as an agent for a company to sell stock to the public, private investors, or to another company. In the first case, they are said to act as an underwriter.

joint venture Usually refers to a short-lived partnership with each partner sharing in costs and rewards of the project; common in research, investment banking, and the health care industry.

key-man insurance An insurance policy that protects investors or lenders from the death or disability of key employees on which an early-stage company may depend.

lean start-up A company that is built with minimum resources. See also **bootstrapping** and **virtual company**.

Lehman formula A schedule of fees paid to an investment bank for services.

letter of intent A preliminary, nonbinding agreement between the company and the venture capital firm and/or investors specifying the terms of raising capital and the financial equity investment that will be contained in a formal agreement.

leveraged buyout A method by which a firm is purchased by a private investment company and a significant part of the financing is accomplished using debt. These transactions require that the company have a dependable and sufficient cash flow to service the debt. The LBO firm may install its own management team or retain the existing management structure.

license A right conferred on a licensee by a licensor to use intellectual property owned by the licensor under defined conditions in return for a license fee, usually in the form of a recurring royalty payment.

lifestyle entrepreneur An entrepreneur that starts and manages a company to fit his or her individual lifestyle rather than as a way of creating value for investors.

limited liability corporation Also known as an LLC, a separate legal entity that allows a corporation to have "members" rather than stockholders. It is not subject to corporate tax, and therefore, tax liabilities or credits "flow through" to the members as in an **S-corporation**.

limited partnership A form of partnership composed of both a general partner(s) and a limited partner(s). The limited partners have no control in the management of the company and are usually financially liable only to the extent of their investment in the partnership. The majority of VC firms are formed as a limited partnership.

line of credit Short-term financing usually granted by a bank up to a predetermined limit; debtor borrows as needed up to the limit of credit without needing to renegotiate the loan.

liquidation The requirement by order of a bankruptcy court, sometimes called compulsory liquidation, that a business dissolve operations and sell off or dispose of assets by converting assets into cash.

liquidity event An event that occurs when the stock of a private company has a market for sale usually either through an IPO or through a sale to another company. The venture capitalists' objective is to reach a liquidity event when they can cash out their shares and receive a return on investment.

lock-in Development of a two-way valuable relationship between a customer and a company so that moving to another relationship has a high barrier. The barrier is often referred to as the **switching cost**.

long-tail The part of a product range that consists of a multitude of different products, each of which has a small demand but taken as a whole may have a significant market value.

M&A transaction A merger or acquisition of one company with or by another. This term is commonly used to describe the liquidity event in which an entrepreneur's company is sold to another.

margin The amount the entrepreneur adds to a product's cost to obtain its selling price. This is also called markup.

marketing plan A written formulation for achieving the marketing goals and strategies of the venture, usually on an annual basis. Business plans always contain a marketing plan section.

management buyout The purchase of a company by the management, often financed by a private equity firm; also called an MBO.

mezzanine financing Transitional money that helps entrepreneurial companies build to a level of growth that permits a public stock offering or a sale to another company, providing an exit strategy for investors.

microequity funds Small amounts of financing provided by a localized network of angels targeted at very early-stage (preseed) rounds of investment. They are often coupled with a strong mentoring network for entrepreneurs. Examples include DreamIt Ventures and Y Combinator.

microloans Very small loans made to entrepreneurs often without any security. These loans may be from special banks such as Grameen, formed to help people in developing countries, or between individuals via social networks such as Kiva.

minimum viable product That version of a new product which can collect the maximum amount of validated learning about customers with the least effort. Often used in **lean start-up** or **virtual company**.

multiple A firm's price-to-earnings ratio that is used for quick valuations of a firm. (For example, a firm that earns $5 million a year in an industry that generally values stock at ten times earnings would be valued at $50,000,000.)

net present value (NPV) The current value of a future cash flow stream, discounted back at a defined discount or interest rate.

network effect The way that the value of a product grows nonlinearly by how many have been sold.

new venture A new business providing products/services to a particular market.

niche market A market in which a limited and clearly defined range of products is sold to a specific group of customers, often not supplied by an existing major company and hence suitable for a smaller company to serve.

noncompete/nondisclosure agreement Legal agreement(s) that stipulates that the signees must not disclose confidential information about the company and/or product. It also prevents the signee from joining or starting a similar venture.

nondisclosure agreement See **confidentiality agreement**.

offering The financial "package" presented by a new venture.

open innovation A paradigm that assumes that firms can and should use external ideas as well as internal ideas, and internal and external paths to market, as the firms look to advance their technology. See **inverse commons**.

operating budget A financial plan outlining how a company will use its resources over a specified period of time.

partnership Business association of two or more people. There are two types of partnerships: general and limited.

patent Federal governmental grant to an inventor giving exclusive rights to an invention or process for twenty years from date of filing. A U.S. patent does not always grant rights in foreign countries.

path dependency The concept that every way forward is somehow constrained by what happened in the past.

payables The outstanding bills that the company must pay within a short term.

post-money valuation The value accorded to a company after investment by venture capitalists or angels.

pre-money valuation The value accorded to a company prior to investment from venture capitalists or angels.

private equity An umbrella term for investments that include venture capital and buyout funds. Sometimes used (especially in Europe) as a synonym for venture capital.

private placement A transaction involving the sale of stocks or bonds to wealthy individuals, pension funds, insurance companies, or other investors. It is done without a public offering or any oversight from the SEC. The document defining the transaction is called a private placement memorandum or PPM.

professionalization The process to make an activity into a job that requires special education, training, or skill. In a **family business** context, to change from a casual management style to a professionally run organization.

proprietary That which is owned, such as a patent, formula, brand name, or trademark associated with the product/service.

provisional patent A low-cost patent application filed with the U.S. Patent and Trademark Office, which establishes the date of an invention. This application is not published or reviewed by patent examiners and may be abandoned later, or it may be used as the basis of a full patent application.

public offering The sale of a company's shares of stock to the public by the company or its major stockholders.

quiet period The period starting when an issuer hires an underwriter and ending twenty-five days after the security begins trading, during which the issuer cannot comment publicly on the offering due to SEC rules.

receivables The short-term payments due to the company.

registered stock Stock that has been registered with the SEC and, thus, can be sold publicly.

registration rights The right that a shareholder has to register his or her stock along with the founders at the time of an IPO.

regulations Conditions imposed by government agencies that must be met before a product or service can be sold to the public.

reputational capital The sum of the value of all corporate intangible assets, which include business processes, patents, and trademarks; reputations for ethics and integrity; and quality, safety, sustainability, security, and resilience. In the context of a **family business**, this includes the additional assets of family values, legacy, name, and so on.

restricted stock Issued stock that cannot be traded until the restriction deadline has passed. Founders' stock is usually restricted for up to one year after a company has gone public, as the new investors do not want to see the insiders selling too early and, thereby, devaluing the share price.

return on equity (ROE) Measures the return on the owner's investment in the company and is perhaps the most important measure of a business's financial viability. The higher the ratio, the higher the rate of return on the owner's investment.

revolvers Another term for a bank line of credit, which enables companies to borrow and use funds as necessary, usually with a one-to-two-year payback requirement.

risk capital Another term for equity investing, sometimes also referred to as investment capital or venture capital.

road show The process during a public offering in which the management of an issuing company and the underwriters meet with groups of prospective investors.

rounds of investment Investments made at different stages of a company's growth. These are referred to as *preseed* when the idea is embryonic and *seed* when the company builds a prototype before it has any sales. Those are followed by a series of development rounds called A, B, C, and so on.

runway The time until a company no longer has any cash on hand to continue its operations; also referred to as **cash-out**.

sales channel A way of bringing products or services to market so that they can be purchased by customers. A sales channel can be direct to its customers, or it can be indirect if an intermediary such as a retailer or dealer is involved in selling the product to customers. The Internet has become an important sales channel.

sales per employee An important measure of a firm's overall productivity, its ability to manage the overhead associated with its workforce, and its long-term financial health. The higher the sales per employee, the more productive the employees.

Sarbanes–Oxley Act (SOX) An act passed by Congress in 2002 to protect investors from the possibility of fraudulent accounting activities by corporations.

SBA loan A variety of loan programs that assist owners in obtaining financing (SBA does not provide direct loans to businesses). The most common source of SBA financing is the 7(a) loan guaranty, which is obtained through a lender who receives a guarantee of repayment from the SBA (the collateral holder).

SBIR program The Small Business Innovation Research grant program of the U.S. government.

S-corporation (subchapter S-corporation) A firm that has elected to be taxed as a partnership under the subchapter provision of the Internal Revenue Code.

scale-free network A network that grows not through contacts between local neighbors, but through nodes that provide immediate benefit to visitors. One example is the hub-and-spoke structure of most airlines. Such networks have become more prevalent through the Internet. (See **social network**.)

separation agreement A contract between an employee and a company signed when the employee leaves the company, whether via a resignation or termination.

serial entrepreneur An entrepreneur who starts and exits several companies one after the other.

smoke-screen market research The use of Web 2.0 tools, such as social networks, Google AdWords, etc., to undertake market research for a new product or service at the conception stage at low cost. Usually it requires setting up a "dummy" website.

social entrepreneur An entrepreneur focusing on a mission to solve society's problems using innovative solutions.

social network A network of individuals who have a common interest. Recently such networks have been created using the Internet as the meeting venue. Examples include Facebook, MySpace, LinkedIn, and others.

sole proprietorship A business firm owned by only one person and operated for his or her profit.

spiderweb model A visual representation of an early-stage company indicating its fragility and that it can be severely damaged suddenly by events coming unexpectedly from many directions.

stakeholder A person or entity that has an interest, financial and/or otherwise, in the outcome of an action. In a start-up situation, the list includes owners, investors, lenders, employees, customers, suppliers, landlords, and others.

standards A set of conditions imposed by members of an interested group of companies, or government agencies, which define the performance criteria, interchangeability, and so on. that should be met by products and services being offered for sale. The motivation for standards is to help all companies benefit from a growing market. Often there are standard wars, where two or more groups of corporations compete to establish their preferred standards as the norm. This usually results in all parties losing as the market is repressed.

standstill agreement An agreement between two parties that they will not enter into another agreement for a defined time. This allows parties to invest in due diligence processes without the concern that their efforts will be pre-empted.

start-up capital Money needed to launch a new venture before and during the initial period of operation.

start-up stage A stage of development a company may experience, characterized by a need for planning, people, and financial resources.

statement of cash flows A financial statement that reflects the increases and decreases in cash for a certain time period.

stock certificate A document issued to a stockholder by a corporation indicating the number of shares of stock owned by the stockholder.

stock dividend A proportional distribution of securities to the company's stockholders.

stock options A right to buy a stated number of shares in a company at a defined price (the strike price) within a defined time period. Stock options are often used as part of the compensation for key persons in a company. The owner of the options can "exercise" them within the defined period, and if the stock price has appreciated, they will have a capital gain. If the share price has declined below the strike price, the options are "under water" and have little or no value.

stockholder's equity The portion of a business owned by the stockholders.

STTR program The Small Business Technology Transfer Research grant program to assist the formation of companies based on research carried out in universities and government laboratories in the United States.

succession planning The process for identifying and developing internal people with the potential to fill key business leadership positions in the company. This is particularly important within a **family business**.

super-angels Private investors that fund early-stage companies at a higher level than most angel investors. Super-angels invest their personal wealth and may compete with institutional venture capital partnerships.

supply chain The logistics network in which a company is embedded. It may include suppliers, customers, partners, distributors, and so on.

switching cost See **lock-in**.

syndication A means by which investors or bankers spread their risk by bringing in partners to share the transaction.

teaser A slang term for a one-or-two-page document that provides just sufficient information to grab the attention of an investor or lender without disclosing too much; a written version of an elevator pitch, which is similar to an executive summary.

technology entrepreneur An entrepreneur who starts a venture based on a highly technical, scientific, or engineering innovation.

technology roadmap The pathways that define how one technology relates to developments in similar fields as well as those that may be more loosely relevant in some way, depending on different market applications.

term loan A loan that must be fully paid back by an agreed date. If a lender does not meet the terms of the covenants of the loan, the lender may have the right to "call the loan" by shortening the term.

term sheet A summary of the principal conditions for a proposed investment by a venture capital firm or lender.

tipping point In the growth of use of a product or service, the stage at which the acceptance becomes self-generating; often associated with **viral effect**.

total available market (TAM) The total annual sales that a company would derive if it were able to capture 100 percent of its targeted market.

trademark A brand or part of a brand that is given legal protection because it is capable of exclusive appropriation.

underwriter An intermediary between an issuer of a security and the investing public, usually an investment bank.

upsell The process by which an existing customer purchases additional services, products, or benefits after using either a free offering or a lower cost option. See **freemium**.

value proposition A promise of **value** to be delivered and acknowledged and a belief from the customer that **value** will be delivered and experienced.

venture capital Money from investment pools or firms that specialize in financing young companies' growth, usually in return for stock.

venture capital valuation method A method used by venture capitalists to value a young company based on a discounted value of an anticipated exit using either an IPO or, more likely, a sale to a large company.

venture capitalist An investor who provides early financing to new ventures—often technology based—with an innovative product and the prospect of rapid and profitable growth.

vesting period The time between the issuance of a benefit or right and the time it can be accessed. This often applies to stock options, which may not be exercised until the recipient has been with the company for a defined time.

viral effect See **tipping point**.

viral marketing A means by which customers are acquired through recommendations from existing customers and users. The Internet often supports such marketing methods.

virtual company A company built through networks without any fixed assets or location. Persons with appropriate skills contribute from time to time, often on a contract basis rather than as employees. Such companies are made possible by the Internet and social networks. See also **lean start-up**.

warrant An option to buy for a stipulated price a certain amount of stock that is transferable and can be traded.

Web 2.0 A broad term to describe applications of the Internet that are interactive rather than just one-way.

working capital The amount of funds available to pay short-term expenses, such as unexpected or out-of-the-ordinary, one-time-only expenses. Working capital is determined by subtracting current liabilities from current assets.

work-for-hire agreement See **consulting agreement**.

INDEX

CPSIA information can be obtained
at www.ICGtesting.com
Printed in the USA
BVOW09s0116150218
508191BV00002B/2/P